Feminism and Psychoanalysis

FEMINISM AND PSYCHOANALYSIS

EDITED BY

RICHARD FELDSTEIN

AND

JUDITH ROOF

CORNELL UNIVERSITY PRESS

ITHACA AND LONDON

First published 1989 by Cornell University Press.

International Standard Book Number 0-8014-2298-1 (cloth)
International Standard Book Number 0-8014-9558-X (paper)
Library of Congress Catalog Card Number 88-43235
Printed in the United States of America

The editors thank the publishers and agents for permission to quote passages from the following:
From *The Greengage Summer* by Rumer Godden, copyright © 1957, 1958, renewed © 1985, 1986 by Rumer Godden. All rights reserved. Reprinted by permission of Viking Penguin Inc., and Curtis Brown Ltd., London.
From *During the Reign of the Queen of Persia* by Joan Chase, copyright © 1983 by Joan L. S. Chase. Published by Virago Press Ltd., 1984. Reprinted by permission of Harper & Row and Virago Press.
From *Housekeeping* by Marilynne Robinson, copyright © 1980 by Marilynne Robinson. Reprinted by permission of Farrar, Straus and Giroux, Inc., and Curtis Brown Ltd., London.
From *Annie John* by Jamaica Kincaid, copyright © 1983, 1984, 1985 by Jamaica Kincaid. Originally appeared in *The New Yorker*. Reprinted by permission of Farrar, Straus and Giroux, Inc.

Librarians: Library of Congress cataloging information
appears on the last page of the book.

The paper in this book is acid-free and meets the guidelines for permanence
and durability of the Committee on Production Guidelines for Book Longevity
of the Council on Library Resources.

For our teachers

Contents

vii

Contents

Preface

This collection of essays represents a new phase of the complex negotiation between feminist theory and psychoanalysis. It has its origins in papers delivered at the Conference on Feminism and Psychoanalysis held at Normal, Illinois, in May 1986, which was inspired in large measure by the interdisciplinary questions posed by feminist psychoanalytic critics in the early part of this decade. These essays further the debate produced at those points of critical impasse where psychoanalysis is applied to feminist theory, critique, and practice.

Because the conference and the book share a common genesis, we thank those faculty and students at Illinois State University who contributed to the work of the former: James Baran, Eric R. A. Constantineau, Susan Day, Dana Deal, Ronald Fortune, Sharon Groves, Charles B. Harris, Victoria Harris, Karen Johnston, William Morgan, and William Woodson. We especially thank Kate Mele and Kristina Straub, our coordinators for the conference.

We are also grateful for the editorial assistance of those who helped in the preparation of this manuscript, particularly Kathryn Zeidenstein, Tipa Thep-Ackpong, Dorothy Howarth, and Priscilla L. Young. Finally, we thank Ellie Ragland-Sullivan, Carol T. Neely, Robyn Wiegman, and Mark D. Johnston for their excellent advice and support and Celeste Schenck, Shari Benstock, and Bernhard Kendler for their good counsel and perceptive readings.

Steve Fagin and Laura Kipnis kindly granted permission to use stills from their video productions. We also thank the University of Chicago Press for permission to reprint a chapter of *Uneven Developments: The Ideological Work of Gender in Mid-Victorian England* by Mary Poovey. Copyright © 1988 by The University of Chicago. All rights reserved.

R. F. and J. R.

Feminism and Psychoanalysis

Introduction

Richard Feldstein and Judith Roof

In recent years, feminist critics have characterized the exchanges between feminism and psychoanalysis as a two-party, one-on-one affair. Historically, many feminists viewed psychoanalysis with hostility. In famous critiques, Kate Millett and Simone de Beauvoir, for instance, described an antagonistic confrontation between feminist theory and the "masterful phallocratic" theories of psychoanalysis. More recently, many feminist critics who read psychoanalytic and literary texts have presented romantic and familial scenarios that range from such harlequin comparisons as "pair," "couple," "dating," "courtship," "affair," "ménage," "charmed union," and "marriage" to variations of the family romance implied in such now-familiar formulas as "the daughter's seduction," "the rebellious daughter," "the hysteric," and "the (m)other tongue." Though not the only set of metaphors used to portray this difficult dialogue, the familial paradigm has become the most visible and emblematic. As suitable parables for what is perceived to be a problematic and evasive drama of love, hate, and incompatibility, metaphors of romantic ambivalence reflect the wary absorption of feminism and psychoanalysis with one another.

This use of the family romance as a predominant metaphor is not merely a random or convenient choice. For example, we could have continued the early adversarial characterization of a perceived masculinist bias in psychoanalysis by echoing Betty Friedan, Germaine Greer, Kate Millett, and Simone de Beauvoir, plaintiff feminists who sue Freud et al. on grounds of libel, slander, and fraud for defining women as lesser and for perpetuating that myth. And such initial suits (instead of suitors) and appeals through court (instead of courtship) have resulted in review by "higher" courts such as Jane Gallop's *the Daughter's Seduc-*

tion and the recent feminist reconsiderations of the Dora case. The point is not that legal metaphors are more appropriate than familial tropes but that we have somehow chosen to depict the feminist-psychoanalytic endeavor in such a way as to avoid the overt appeal to third terms such as the law (or the "law of the father"), which we already suspect of being sexually biased. While feminist psychoanalytic criticism has always sustained a kind of assertiveness, its need to attend to the third term has been modestly declaimed or mediated by the insistence of the romantic family metaphor and the concomitant need to work out "personal" affairs by insulating analysis within a cultural realm regarded as safe.

However useful, this romanticized set of interpersonal analogies demonstrates a kind of metaphorical dependency, invoking the invisible tolerance of an authorizing society and replicating, if only in jest, the sets of binary oppositions insistently aligned with sexual difference. Suggesting a reversion to gender categories in which feminism is conceived as feminine and psychoanalysis as masculine, the family romance model has proved attractive because it both mirrors and embodies the indescribable and oppressive relation between feminine and masculine that feminist psychoanalytic critics seek to understand and employ. Situating feminism and psychoanalysis in the comfortable, suspicious, but conveniently indeterminate norms of human relations, however, results neither in subversion nor in critique of that set of relationships nor even in any particularly precise characterization of the relationship between feminism and psychoanalysis; rather, it functions to reaffirm the family's binary ties as expressed in the terminology of a habitual and normative discourse. As a product of a domesticated discourse, the association between feminism and psychoanalysis becomes a family affair, relegated to the private relations between individuals—to a stereotypically female space. If we logically follow the sets of gender-stereotyped oppositions linked to feminism and psychoanalysis, the entire dialogue between this on-again-off-again flirtation of lovers takes place in the sexualized, emotionalized, personalized, privatized, erratic sphere of the home and bedchamber rather than in the structured, impersonal, public realm.

And of course that is misleading. If the feminist-psychoanalytic defiance/alliance has taught us anything, it is to read representations as symptoms, as systemic codes that reveal in their gaps and gaffes the unspoken and the invisible. While our reliance upon the familial model might superficially indicate an insecurity about symbolic structure and our uncertainty in relation to it, fixing our focus on the couple reveals a wider cultural gap, a missing term that shifts from a familial (micro) to a societal (macro) cultural analysis, linking the family structure to the patriarchal grid within which it fits. Though the family is often seen as a three-term, oedipal configuration, the prevalence of metaphors patterned on the problematic bond between two of the parties—the father-daughter or mother-daughter couple—draws attention away from the missing third family member, ignoring rather than denying her or him. In a similar way, the apparent binary balance of the heterosexual romantic couple masks the brooding omnipresence of multiple "other" terms, such as the state or religion, which create, sanctify, and otherwise control the couple's existence. In either case, the omission of any third term is somewhat suspicious since what is omitted or repressed signifies through its absence the need for analysis.

In a figurative sense, this missing term is broadly analogous to Jacques Lacan's notion of the "third term" as that which destroys the symmetry of binary oppositions postulated in both early feminist and early psychoanalytic theory. In the practice of feminist psychoanalytic criticism this third term, itself irreducible to the violence of the binary, thus becomes that "other" alien force, that which founds, mediates, or affects discourses, ideologies, categories, or even agents (language, the state, violence, historical effect) recognized as distinct from either feminism or psychoanalysis, but which affects feminism and psychoanalysis and can be analyzed and critiqued by them. Furthermore, one thing we have learned from psycho-feminist criticism is the extent to which texts, like families, implicate themselves in an opposition that expresses itself symptomatically as a radical and irreducible otherness. Because they serve so well as symptoms, literary, cinematic, and psychoanalytic texts have provided a primary setting for the feminist psychoanalytic efforts to understand the construction of a gendered subject, to trace the operations of a system of representation which tends to return all to an opposition of presence and lack, to define questions of sexual difference and sexuality, and to negotiate the conflicts between feminism and psychoanalysis themselves. In recent years, feminist psychoanalytic critiques have passed beyond issues that initially concerned this community of scholars to come to grips with terms like theory, philosophy, history, language, and law. Emerging from the household, shifting from the illusion of privatized and public spheres, from the family to the acknowledgment of and open confrontation with the interlocutory terms of cultural mediation, feminist critics have shirked the dependency of the familial relation with an urgency increased by problems of rupture, violence, and exclusion, which have coexisted all along and thus have been intrinsic to feminist critiques of patriarchal culture. Such critiques become central to this volume. Divided into two sections, "Theoretical Texts" and "Literary Texts," the essays offer a reconsideration of the domestic paradigm as well as an investigation of texts in relation to third terms and the possibilities such exchanges might have for feminist praxis.

Jane Gallop's essay, "The Monster in the Mirror: The Feminist Critic's Psychoanalysis," introduces the first section of the collection, "Theoretical Texts." Reading *Yale French Studies* 62, edited by seven women—the "seven-headed monster"—from Dartmouth, Gallop dissects the "monster" to reveal the interconnected set of dichotomies—collectivity/individual, mother/daughter, mother-text/daughter-reader—which form the binary background that Gallop exposes as she advances alternative points of view. Luring us into answering oppositionally whether the mother or the "self" is the monster of ill proportion, Gallop explains that "the monster *is* that difficulty" we encounter in trying to decide, the difficulty of entrapment in an economy of dualities. Posing monstrosity, then, as a function of the limits of binary oppositions, Gallop suggests that the identity of third term, what is truly other, is both the fear the monster displaces and the question that needs to be addressed.

Gallop's exhortation to examine the third term introduces the other essays in the section, which treat questions of violence, language, and philosophy in relation to the discourses of cinema, video, history, psychology, and popular culture. Moving beyond a well-rehearsed, divide-and-conquer strategy, Jacqueline Rose questions how analyses that avoid dichotomous thinking help to expose the violence evoked by a rigid perception of sexual difference. Rose begins with Wilhelm Reich's question "Where does the misery come from?" which is another way of asking whether grief originates within the individual or is imposed from outside. Rose points out that Reich's need for such dichotomies placed him in stark contrast to Freud, whose theories often presented paradoxical points of insight. She then links Reich to Jeffrey Masson, whom she accuses of stepping up "the aggression of the outside world" and sexually differentiating it, conceiving it "in terms of seduction, mutilation, and rape." Rose notes that Reich and Masson share one quality, an "unquestioned image of sexual difference," which is "the real violence." In Freud's work, however, she finds theories that confound such dualities as "inside/outside, victim/aggressor, real event/fantasy," dualities that "follow any rigid externalization of political space" and whose expression is an indication of the impulse toward mastery by which violence is enacted.

Ellie Ragland-Sullivan also sees the third term, in this case the Lacanian notion of the materiality of language, as a way of breaking gender-oppressive dualisms. Ragland-Sullivan contrasts the third term from a number in a count sequence (one, two, three . . .) by distinguishing it as an aspect of the unconscious which belies dichotomous distinctions, including any rigid differentiation of sexual difference. Her analysis of language becomes indispensable in the attempt to define two current approaches to Lacanian theory. One, heavily informed by Derridean deconstruction, locates binary oppositions in linguistic play, recreating rather than defying gender differences by equating femininity with passivity and masculinity with writing in a binary opposition that relegates the image of woman to "nothing-ness." For feminist praxis, Ragland-Sullivan suggests that this Derridean Lacan be replaced with "the psychoanalytic Lacan who cared about *jouissance* and who elevated desire over reason and logos." She argues that a recognition of the third term is a way to overcome the "binary politics" that result from a repression that reduces metaphorical thought "to the infinitization of substitutions."

Both Cynthia Chase and Paul Smith introduce the work of Julia Kristeva into their considerations of the possibility for situating the subject outside the binary oppression of sexual difference. Chase begins by challenging Lacan's version of psychoanalytic structuralism in her examination of how the process of identification functions in relation to desire in Lacan's account of *la belle bouchère*, before she determines that an identification with the phallus could prove helpful to "a *feminist* understanding of desire and meaning" distinct from "the structuralist conception of signification as ultimately *determined*." As an alternative to this Lacanian trajectory of desire, Chase suggests that Julia Kristeva's theory of the abject, while "disquieting" in some of its claims, provides an alternative to grounding the sign in the truth of "mutual determination." Proposing a Kristevan rereading of the account of *la belle bouchère*, Chase reinterprets the identification of the butcher's wife with her husband's desire as an indicator of a pre-mirror-stage identification between child and mother, a precarious identification problematized by the Kristevan notion of the abject, according to which a child identifies with an imaginary father while dismissing as abject what is incomprehensible and chaotic. This abject, Chase argues, reintroduces "the indeterminable significative status of the sign" that refuses to guarantee the signification of the phallus.

In contrast to Chase's perception of the radical usefulness of Kristeva's theory, Paul Smith suggests that the theory of the abject threatens to recuperate an even more rigid binary fixity that undermines the cohesiveness of "the subject in process." According to Smith, Kristeva's abject is a transhistorical concept that stands outside of a dialectic between the imaginary and the symbolic, representing an impossibility conceived to oppose "the fixed object (and the urge toward objectification) in the history of the West." Smith says that the Kristevan abject depoliticizes discourse by leapfrogging the social network of signification to emerge at the transcendental realm of the archetype, where an identification with the imaginary father of prehistory and the consequent abjection of the primordial mother are essentialist conceptions. These, intermixed with political questions of conscience, cast Kristeva in the reactionary posture of depicting America as "David facing up to the growing Goliath of the Third World."

Continuing the investigation of philosophical third terms, Mary Ann Doane traces how psychoanalytic and philosophical discourses parallel the cinematic convention of the veiled woman as representative of "either truth or its fading." Challenging the theoretical employment of woman as a substitute for truth, Doane believes not only Lacan but also Nietzsche, Derrida, and the antimetaphysical school itself have condemned women to "carry the burden of the philosophical demonstration . . . [to] be the one to figure truth, dissimulation, *jouissance*, untruth, the abyss . . . [to be] the support of these tropological systems." She observes that in Nietzsche's system woman represents "the pretense of essence," a veiled, nonexistent truth that nevertheless dissimulates a conjured, fantasized presence through its absence, while in Derrida's topology woman is but one name for the "untruth of truth, [which] diverges from itself, [and] is not reducible to the evidence of self-presence." In Lacan's work she sees a tendency to situate woman as excess, as existing in the field of the Other, which the phallus wishes to know but about which it is refused finite knowledge. Doane compares these philosophical images of woman to the function of the veiled woman in cinema and parallels Lacan's phallocentric and Derrida's phallogocentric metaphors of woman as "the limit of what is theorizable" to cinematic embodiments of the veiled woman as the limit of what is seeable.

Also critiquing the function of woman in spectacle, Andrew Ross demonstrates how video art participates in a political practice that interrogates our notions of history and representation. Analyzing the relations among the myth of instantaneity in video, history, and the quandary of the viewing subject facing the paradoxically instantaneous reproduction of history, Ross shows how video can critique the commodification of history. He compares the myth of "instantaneous access" and the myth of woman as dissimulator as explored by Steve Fagin's video *Virtual Play*, a new-historical-realist treatment of Lou Andreas-Salomé, Nietzsche's mistress and a friend and student of

Freud's. Ross suggests that Fagin's video offers a "displaced scene of instruction" complicated by "simultaneous narrative accounts," which raise rather than answer questions too long personified by the figure of woman. Laura Kipnis's video *Ecstasy Unlimited: The Interpenetration of Sex and Capital* offers Ross another parallel by relating instantaneity to women and sex as material commodities and by playing on the myth of "instantaneous access" promised to women by the birth control pill and proponents of the sexual revolution, now refashioned as one of the "powerful commodity myths today."

Exploring the psychoanalytic tendency to endorse a rigidly binary heterosexuality, Shirley Nelson Garner observes how easily theories of sexuality adhere to a heterosexual norm, even when that norm is questioned. Beginning with the works of Freud, Karen Horney, Erik Erikson, and Nancy Chodorow and continuing her exploration through more recent feminist psychological theory, Garner finds a crucial rebellion in Luce Irigaray's observations on feminine sexuality but believes that she, like Horney and Chodorow, is locked in a dialogue with the founding father, Sigmund Freud. Remarking that much feminist work on lesbianism does not take psychoanalysis into account, Garner says that only a feminist psychoanalytic approach provides a theory of sexuality that can be a successful alternative to the oppositions by which heterosexuality is typically constructed as the only sexuality.

Beginning the section "Literary Texts," Jerry Aline Flieger's essay "Entertaining the Ménage à Trois: Psychoanalysis, Feminism, and Literature" returns to the domestic paradigm to urge that feminist psychoanalytic criticism place itself outside the figural home when questioning the oedipal master plot. Flieger maintains that feminist narratives must find alternatives to the oedipal pattern by imagining it from the mother's viewpoint; this stance, she believes, does not recreate the domestic scenario, nor does it simply reproduce more of the same or necessarily advocate the use of object-relations theory, which she rejects, "arguing against a tendency in feminist theory toward overemphasis on the maternal function of essentialization of femininity itself." Instead, Flieger recommends the use of a poststructuralist psychoanalysis suspicious of its own phallocentric tendencies, to give voice to a "feminist practice that seeks to grant full subjectivity to the other."

Carol Neely and Mary Poovey use history as a mediating term of reference in considering ways of understanding the difficulties of the literary representation of female sexuality. In "Constructing Female Sexuality in the Renaissance: Stratford, London, Windsor, Vienna," Neely proposes "a feminist criticism that is psychoanalytic and materialist, that takes into account subjectivity and class and sexuality" to show how "women's power and sexuality may be made possible when this power operates within and upholds the family and the community and when the ruler's power . . . is assumed rather than contested." Her readings of *The Merry Wives of Windsor* and *Measure for Measure* explore how the "anomalousness" of the plays "is connected with their constructions of female sexuality, their representations of gender relations, and their cultural contexts." Mary Poovey also takes a psycho-historical approach to literary criticism, studying the line of demarcation between family and community which is blurred, she says, by the figure of the governess, "who had to be paid for doing what the mother should want to do for free." Examining contemporary perceptions of the governess, Poovey illustrates her difficult and paradoxical position as representative both of middle-class familial and sexual propriety and of potential sexual impropriety and instability. She connects the difficult position of the governess to Charlotte Brontë's narrative treatment of Jane Eyre, who was sharply criticized by contemporary reviewers for being out of her allotted societal place. While Poovey uses psychoanalytic concepts such as doubling, displacement, and hysteria to construct her argument, her aim is to show that any claim for universality of psychoanalytic concepts must be rejected, any inclusion of "universal paradigms of meaning" politicized, any application of psychoanalysis to feminism historicized. Feminist psychoanalytic criticism must view theory as an ideological construct that is temporally specific and thereby useful to a cultural critique of the unconscious.

Both Barbara Johnson and Richard Feldstein use Charlotte Perkins Gilman's story "The Yellow Wallpaper" to comment on the biases of psychoanalysis and to show how the story itself forces critical consideration of third terms. In her essay Johnson turns to Douglas Hofstadter's figure/ground analysis, which differentiates between "a cursively drawable figure . . . whose ground is merely an accidental by-product of the drawing act" and "a recursive figure . . . whose ground can be seen as a figure in its own right." On the basis of this model, Johnson asserts that the dream of psychoanalysis has been to represent sexual difference as a "figure in which both figure and ground, male and female, are recognizable complementary forms." Applying this metaphor to Hawthorne's story "The Birthmark" (where woman is accentuated as figure) and to "The Yellow Wallpaper" (where the nameless protagonist identifies herself with a pictorial ground), Johnson observes that the woman fades from view, leading to the suspicion that these stories are readable as allegories representing the willingness of psychoanalysis to erase difference by reducing "woman to 'toute,' to ground, to blankness." The disappearance of woman, however, brings into question the symmetrical operation of gender-based oppositions. Feldstein questions the gender-based equilibrium of madness/sanity, entering the current debate over whether the protagonist of "The Yellow Wallpaper" has triumphed or failed. Offering an ironic reading of the story, Feldstein suggests an alternative to the opposition of sanity and madness, that "the narrator's madness becomes questionable and the question of madness itself an issue" in a reading of this text. Mediating among interpretations of tragic madness or triumphant sanity, Feldstein situates the story as an example of modernist sensibilities in a premodernist time, "a means of reading that allows for a play of difference."

The last three essays, like Flieger's, question the necessity for the dominance of Freudian narrative formulas such as the oedipal master plot and the hysterical structure as typified by the Dora case. In her essay on Henry James's *the Bostonians,* Claire Kahane maintains that its experimental stylistics and fragmented, decentered characters present us with "symptomatic narratives" that parallel the fragmentary and discursive nature of hysterical discourse. Kahane differentiates, however, between the compromise formation of "silent" hysterical discourse and an ever more articulate feminist rhetoric that appeared simultaneously at the turn of the century. Kahane calls *the Bostonians* "a novel about the feminist subversion of difference through the figure of the speaking woman," and she sees that figure as a metaphorical third term who disrupts the binary oppositions aligned with sexual difference.

Madelon Sprengnether traces contemporary feminist revisions of the biblical story of the Fall which reconfigure the myth to emphasize the daughter's separation from the (m)other, a painful process tied to the acceptance of mortality. Echoing Gallop's analysis of *Yale French Studies* 62, Sprengnether describes how difficult it is for the daughter to accept the inevitable fact of her mother's otherness, suggesting that we keep this mythical mother alive because the thought of her death marks us in a cycle of generation in a world of gender difference and of intersubjective splits born in the Edenic second between the impulse to bite the apple and the ingestion that attends the bifurcated knowledge of good and evil. In emphasizing the mother-daughter tie, these contemporary myths shift from the oedipal master plot to a female-centered pattern that subverts the dominance of the law of the father.

In the final essay, Judith Roof analyzes the subversive theatrical strategies of Marguerite Duras's drama *Véra Baxter,* which offers a model for a feminist theater that both plays on and dismantles the position of woman as theatrical commodity. Comparing the character

Véra to Freud's Dora, Roof suggests that, like Dora, Véra exposes the desire of the audience/analyst by terminating the dialogue in the middle of the analyst/audience's countertransference. As a result of this termination Véra is freed from her objectification as a stage spectacle and source of desire. Duras's play offers a theatrical paradigm of resistance which undermines the closure of both an oedipal plot and the spectacle of woman by means of refused identifications and a subversive subcurrent of "outside turbulence," a kind of third-term scenario that gains significance only at the end of the play.

This enunciation of the examples by our contributors indicates that, while feminism and psychoanalysis have hardly called a truce, they have for the present embarked upon a joint effort to understand the cultural construction of sexual difference, to locate the sources of sexual violence and oppression, and to deconstruct the ways in which the "fall" into representation implicates us all. As the essays in this collection suggest, however, the investigation of the indeterminate line of demarcation drawn against an inaccessible Other continues to evoke provocative questions.

THEORETICAL
TEXTS

The Monster in the Mirror:
The Feminist Critic's Psychoanalysis

Jane Gallop

In 1981 *Yale French Studies* finally published a feminist issue, number 62, *Feminist Readings: French Text/American Contexts.* The volume is an interesting collection of work which successfully combines engaged feminist analysis with sophisticated literary and psychoanalytic theory. But the beginning, the first sentence, disturbs me. *YFS* 62 (as I will henceforth refer to it) opens thus: "This is a very unusual issue of *Yale French Studies,* in that its guest editor is a seven-headed monster from Dartmouth."

A striking, somewhat troubling image. Of course the notion of a monster from Dartmouth is quite funny. As swiftly as it appears, the monster is domesticated. Unhuman it might be, but at least it is Ivy League.

The seven-headed monster literally refers to the seven Dartmouth faculty women who edit *YFS* 62. The monster is a figure for the seven individuals working together as one body. The next two pages give a glowingly positive description of this collaboration, of collectivity as method. Since the image appears in the introduction signed by the editors, it constitutes a self-portrait—an ironic one. The editors are saying: Look, we are horrifying, we are monstrous, we are inhumanly ugly. This turns out to be an ironic way of saying: Look, we are "very unusual," we are beautiful, we are extraordinary.

Once the ironic reversal is decoded, the self-portrait is revealed as immodest boasting. The image of the monster thinly disguises a monstrous narcissism. This reader, for one, recoils from such an unseemly proclamation of one's own rare beauty. The irony of this irony is that when the editors say they are ugly to mean they are beautiful, they become ugly.

Jane Gallop

But let us consider this vivid image as something more interesting than an infelicity of taste, as something more interesting than even a witty example of a rhetorical stampede unseating and trampling the speaking subject. We will read this as a symptom, in the psychoanalytic sense, by assuming, as Freud does in *The Psychopathology of Everyday Life*, that in every infelicity of language something is quite successfully getting said. In other words, I would like here to check my impulse to recoil and rather try to understand this monster, perhaps at the risk of my own terror, my own horror.

The monster represents the collectivity. It is a way of indicating this new kind of being in which seven individuals are neither totally merged (they would then presumably have only one head) nor totally separate. The first section of the introduction describes how, belying the "skepticism" and "amazement" of their "male colleagues," collaboration was a totally positive experience—"productive," "rigorous," "audacious." Others, presumably male others, warned them of inefficiency or reductive thinking, but all fears proved groundless. Yet if we take seriously the ironic return of the monster's monstrosity, then it may well signal something unnatural about this pure positivity, something terrifying about an unambivalent giving up of individuality.

The enumeration of the glories of collectivity ends thus: "We have not, of course, abandoned our 'individual' research; but we have found it enriched by the reverberations between the two styles of work" (3). The word *individual* in this sentence, is placed in quotation marks. "Individual" research does not quite exist as such. The we who speaks for the collectivity recognizes the illusoriness of individuality and, what is more, has a stake in proclaiming the truth that all research stems from dialogue, is in interlocution with other research; so the boundaries that separate one individual's contribution from another's are never absolutely clear. The anguish a scholar feels about those writing on the same topic, what Harold Bloom calls the "anxiety of influence," for example, is an apperception of the irremediable uncertainty of the individuality of one's work. This monster knows that.

But what we call "individual work," if illusory, nonetheless exists. And the purport of the sentence is not just to call individuality into question through the quotation marks but to alert us to the deeper connections, the "reverberations" between individual and collective work.

Only one of the seven members of the collective, Marianne Hirsch, published an article in YFS 62. And in Hirsch's article, the word *monstrous* appears: "To study the relationship between mother and daughter is not to study the relationship between two separate differentiated individuals, but to plunge into a network of complex ties, to attempt to untangle the strands of a double self, a continuous multiple being of *monstrous* proportions stretched across generations, parts of which try desperately to separate and delineate their own boundaries" (73, emphasis mine).

The word *monstrous* here refers to a "continuous multiple being," which is to say that *this* monster *too* represents a being whose multiple parts are neither totally merged nor totally separate. There are many possible ways of being monstrous, but the same type of abnormality that figures in editors' introduction also figures in Hirsch's text—the monstrosity of a being whose boundaries are inadequately differentiated, thus calling into question the fundamental opposition of self and other. Such a being is terrifying because of the stake any self as self has in its own autonomy, in its individuation, in its integrity.

Whereas in the introduction the monster image is the sole hint of something frightening, in Hirsch's essay the negative impression produced by the word *monstrous* is amplified by the melodramatic phrase: "parts of which try desperately to separate and delineate their own boundaries." The individual's text can speak the desperate need for individuation which the collective we suppresses in order to pronounce itself.

The monstrous in Hirsch's article specifically refers to the mother and daughter, who are not "two separate individuals" but a "double self." Hirsch derives this notion of the lack of separation between mother and daughter from feminist psychoanalytic theory. Particularly important is the work of Nancy Chodorow, who—drawing on the English school of psychoanalysis called object-relations theory—has posited that the female self is less individuated than the male self since both are formed in relation to the mother, but the male self has the fact of sexual difference to institute and ensure differentiation.[1]

The section of Hirsch's article which presents this psychoanalytic theory and which concludes with the appearance of the word *monstrous*, begins with a quotation from the French feminist psychoanalyst Luce Irigaray, taken from a little book titled *Et l'une ne bouge pas sans l'autre* ("And the One Doesn't Move without the Other").[2] Immediately following the quotation, Hirsch writes: "In *Et l'une ne bouge pas sans l'autre*, a lyrical and personal address to her mother, . . . Irigaray pleads for distance and separation, laments the paralysis she

[1]Nancy Chodorow, *The Reproduction of Mothering: Psychoanalysis and the Sociology of Gender* (Berkeley: University of California Press, 1978).

[2]Luce Irigaray, *Et l'une ne bouge pas sans l'autre* (Paris: Minuit, 1979), translated as "And the One Doesn't Stir without the Other," by Hélène Vivienne Wenzel, *Signs: Journal of Women in Society and Culture* 7.1 (1981), 60–67.

feels as a result of the interpenetration between mother and daughter, calls *desperately* for a new kind of closeness possible only between two separate individuals" (69, emphasis mine). Notice the adverb *desperately*. Irigaray, in the role of daughter, "calls desperately for" the possibility of "two separate individuals." The adverb returns at the conclusion of this section of the article when the "parts" of the "monstrous being" "try *desperately* to separate and delineate their own boundaries." Although Chodorow, an American, has made the most extensive and explicit contribution to the study of the mother-daughter bond, Irigaray's little lyrical text most effectively conveys the desperation of the daughter's situation. The title of Irigaray's book could also represent the plight of the seven-headed monster. Because the heads all share the same body, the same limbs, one cannot move without the other(s).

Having been alerted by the introduction to look for "reverberations," I read Hirsch's article not merely as a separate contribution but also as a continuation of the collaborative text of the introduction. Her elaboration of the daughter's bind also voices the dilemma of the individual member of the collective.

This is, I believe, more than a clever analogy. The psychological condition of possibility for the feminist collective is the daughter's ongoing infantile connection to the mother.[3] According to Hirsch and Chodorow, any daughter, that is, any woman, has a self that is not completely individuated but rather is constitutively connected to another woman. Thus the formation of groups of women draws upon the permeability of female self-boundaries. The collectivity reactivates, reenacts the mother-daughter bond. One monster cannot be separated from the other.

In 1982 *Diacritics* published a feminist issue whose first article is titled "My Monster/My Self."[4] Although that feminist issue has no introduction, in a way it too opens with a suggestive self-portrait as monster. In that article Barbara Johnson discovers that Frankenstein's monster is a figure for the self-portrait as such. In alluding to Nancy Friday's popular *My Mother/My Self*,[5] Johnson's title implies both that my monster is my self and that my monster is my mother. Who is the monster? The mother or the self? The inability to answer that urgent question is certainly tied to the difficulty in separating mother from self. As we have seen, the monster *is* that difficulty.

---

[3]See Jane Flax, "The Conflict between Nurturance and Autonomy in Mother-Daughter Relationships and within Feminism," *Feminist Studies* 4.1 (1978), 171–89.

[4]Barbara Johnson, "My Monster/My Self," *Diacritics* 12.2 (1982), 2–10.

[5]Nancy Friday, *My Mother/My Self* (New York: Dell, 1977).

Hirsch writes, in the sentences already quoted, "To study the relationship between mother and daughter is not to study the relationship between two separate differentiated individuals, but to *plunge* into a network of complex ties." Note the verb *plunge*. Although the sentence appears to be saying that in studying the mother-daughter relationship the object of study is different from what one would suppose, the sentence also says: "To study the relationship between mother and daughter is not to study . . . but to plunge." The scholar is immersed in her object of study. Distance and the sense of proportion are lost. The being of "monstrous proportions" threatens to envelop whatever would stand outside and observe.

The sentence then supplies one last verb phrase to describe the activity of the student of mother-daughter relationships: "To study the relationship between mother and daughter is not to study . . . but to plunge . . ., *to attempt to untangle* the strands of a double self, a continuous multiple being . . . parts of which try desperately to separate and delineate their boundaries." The scholar "attempts to untangle." In so doing, she comes to resemble the "parts" of the being which "try to separate and delineate." The only difference, and an important one it is, is the adverb *desperately*. The researcher here has come to resemble her object of study. What she contemplates could be said to mirror her. And although not yet desperate herself, there is something threatening in the mirror.

Two sentences later, this theoretical section of the article concludes with the following sentence: "This basic and continued relatedness and multiplicity, this mirroring which seems to be unique to women have to be factors in any study of female development in fiction." In this sentence a second image appears in apposition, another way of describing the mother-daughter bond: "this basic and continued relatedness and multiplicity," in other words, "this mirroring." If the relationship being studied is itself a mirroring, then when the scholar who "attempts to untangle" finds herself reflected in the parts which "try to separate and delineate," she is both observing a mirroring and acting it out. Thus, uncannily, when Hirsch writes that "this mirroring which seems to be unique to women ha[s] to be [a] factor in any study of female development in fiction," we might take her statement to mean not only that it has to be discussed but that it has to be a "factor in any study," something that takes place, something that happens to the scholar.

That "this mirroring . . . seems to be unique to women" then could lead us to pose some questions as to whether women's studies, studies by women, differ from those performed by male scholars in that the woman, perhaps because of her more permeable self-boundaries, tends to get entangled in a mirroring with the object of study. And, whether or not this entanglement is "unique to women," we might also go on to ponder the more epistemologically radical question of whether it is a good or a bad thing, which is another way to ask whether the monster in *our* self-portrait is ugly or beautiful.

The term *mirroring* gets much wider use in the next article in *YFS* 62, a piece by Ronnie Scharfman, equally devoted to the mother-daughter relationship, whose title couples the two gerunds "Mirroring and Mothering." The term *mirroring* derives from the work of D. W. Winnicott, an object-relations theorist. "Winnicott asks what a baby sees upon looking at the mother's face . . . 'ordinarily, what the baby sees is himself or herself'" (91).[6] Again drawing on Winnicott, Scharfman describes an "unsuccessful mirroring bond": "When a mother reflects her own mood or the 'rigidity of her own defenses' rather than her child's, what the baby sees is the mother's face, and the 'mother's face is not a mirror.' The consequences are tragic" (99). Thus, tragedy lies in looking at the other and seeing her as other, rather than seeing yourself.

The first article in *YFS* 62 is also concerned with mirroring. Shoshana Felman there discusses the recognition scene in the denouement of Balzac's *La fille aux yeux d'or:* "Henri beholds in his enemy the exact reflection of his own desire and of his own murderous jealousy; the enemy has his own voice, his own face; the enemy, in other words, *is himself*" (33).

This recognition scene immediately follows a murder. In Felman's text, the consequence of tragedy is looking at the other and seeing her as same. In Scharfman's article, tragedy is the consequence of looking at the other and seeing her as other. Which is the tragedy?

As early as the second sentence of "Mirroring and Mothering," Scharfman asks: "Is the kind of mirroring which this bond implies *reflected* in the writing itself, and, perhaps in reading as well?" (88, emphasis mine). Is mirroring *reflected?* Her answer is yes. The upshot of reading as mirroring turns out to be the final point of Scharfman's article: "A feminist aesthetic can . . . dramatiz[e] . . . the possible bonds between the text as mother, and the daughter-reader it produces" (106).

The text will be mother. As we have seen, Scharfman considers that good mothering is mirroring and that if the mother does not mirror the

---

[6]Scharfman is quoting from D. W. Winnicott, "Mirror-Role of Mother and Family in Child Development," in *Playing and Reality* (New York: Basic Books, 1971), 111–18.

daughter, "the consequences are tragic." The question of mirroring finally reveals itself as a question about reading. In Scharfman's model, a good text, like a good mother, reflects the reader: in a happy reading, the text provides the reader's self-portrait. If the reader does not see herself but perceives something other, that will be tragic. A good, healthy feminist reading will consist precisely in what has traditionally been condemned as projection. And so I recoil from this daughter-reader as if she too were a seven-headed monster. Her monstrosity, like the one disclosed through the workings of irony, seems to be yet another case of unseemly narcissism.

Narcissism is, in fact, explicitly considered in Scharfman's study, which is a reading of two Antillean novels: one by Simone Schwarz-Bart, the other by Jean Rhys.[7] Of the mother figure (actually the grandmother) in Schwarz-Bart's novel, Scharfman writes, "Grandmother is not other, but rather same. She encourages the narcissism which psychoanalytic theory assures us is fundamental to the healthy constitution of an autonomous self" (91). Psychoanalytic theory *assures us* that narcissism is healthy.

The monolithic, undifferentiated "psychoanalytic theory" here referred to is particularly troubling in that, but a page earlier, it becomes apparent that Scharfman is writing in polemical opposition to Jacques Lacan's psychoanalytic theory in which mirroring is considered alienating and unhealthy. At least one stage of Lacan's work is a direct attack on the assurance of the then-reigning psychoanalytic theory that narcissism is healthy.[8] It seems that there are at least two different psychoanalytic theories: one that "assures us" and another that Scharfman writes against. But this differentiation may actually screen a more complicated relationship, one that combines difference and connection in what, for us, is becoming a familiar mode. As Hirsch informs us, "Winnicott's specular relationship between mother and infant [is itself] based on Lacan's 'mirror stage'" (71). I am not prepared here to go into the relationship between Winnicott's and Lacan's theories. Suffice it to say that this connection-in-difference is not only at play in Scharfman's article, not only at large in YFS 62, but "has to be a factor in any study"

---

[7]Simone Schwarz-Bart, *Pluie et vent sur Télumée Miracle* (Paris: Seuil, 1972); Jean Rhys, *Wide Sargasso Sea* (New York: Popular Library, 1966).

[8]Jacques Lacan, *Ecrits* (Paris: Seuil, 1966). See especially "Le stade du miroir comme formateur de la fonction du je," 93–100, and "La chose freudienne," 401–36; translated by Alan Sheridan in Jacques Lacan, *Ecrits: A Selection* (New York: Norton, 1977), as "The Mirror Stage as Formative of the Function of the I," 1–7, and "The Freudian Thing," 114–45.

of the connection-in-difference between French and American feminism. For our purposes here, let us return to the narrower point that, having oppositionally differentiated her position from Lacan's, Scharfman goes on to constitute a unified and sympathetic "psychoanalytic theory," which, like a good parent, can reassure her that "narcissism is fundamental to the healthy constitution of an autonomous self."

Yet, even in this essay narcissism is not always a good thing. I quote from Scharfman's account of Rhys's novel: "Self-absorbed, [the mother] is imprisoned in a destructive narcissism. [The daughter] . . . watches her look at herself in the mirror. . . . But she never sees herself reflected there. [The] mother's concern for [the daughter] is mainly as a disappointing narcissistic extension of herself" (100). There apparently are two kinds of narcissism: a daughter's narcissism is good; a mother's is bad.

Through the final identification of reader with daughter, it becomes evident that Scharfman writes from the daughter's perspective. This daughter's voice is exemplified in complaints such as "We as readers are left unrooted, disoriented, disturbed and unsatisfied. . . . [The text] keeps us at a distance, rejects our efforts to be present in it" (106). Yet the case is more complex, for although the article's narrator is a reader, the article itself is a text. In other words, the daughter is a persona through which the mother speaks.

Once a reader speaks her reading, the reading is itself a text. The daughter cannot be separated from the mother. This is the specific dilemma of the literary critic, for the critic produces a text that is at once a reading and a text. Literary criticism is always double, both text and reader, mother and daughter. The plight of the critic, of whatever sex, is that of Chodorow's female self. The literary critic is that kind of monster.

Now, if we follow Harold Bloom, we understand that any text is a reading.[9] That is perhaps why, despite his male orientation, Bloom is so frequently cited by feminist critics. Every text is implicitly a monstrous, female double self. But in the critical text, this duplicity is explicit—unless, of course, it is covered over by an identification with the daughter or by the critical text's *méconnaissance*, constitutive lack of recognition of itself as text, by the refusal to recognize oneself as mother.

Yet what is a mother? In the feminist collective, the collective as a whole functions as nurturing and stifling mother, as body of monstrous proportions, whereas any individual, whatever her reproductive his-

[9]Harold Bloom, *The Anxiety of Influence: A Theory of Poetry* (New York: Oxford University Press, 1973).

tory, plays the role of daughter. Actually, just as any text is also a reading, any mother is also a daughter, also an individual struggling for autonomy, trying to untangle herself from the mothering web. Although Hirsch's article focuses on the daughter's dilemma, in the theoretical section when she writes about the "parts" that "try desperately to delineate their own boundaries," the plural word *parts* implies that both daughter and mother are desperate for autonomy. The problem is that the term *mother* is already confusedly double. The apparently singular term means both one of the parts *and* the whole monster.

According to Chodorow, "male theorists ignore the mother's involvements outside of her relationship to her infant and her possible interest in mitigating its intensity. Instead, they contrast the infant's moves toward differentiation and separation to the mother's attempts to retain symbiosis."[10] The theorist who attempts to untangle the double being mother-daughter assigns to the daughter term the desire for autonomy—an attribute of both individuals insofar as they are individuals—and to the mother term the desire for symbiosis—which both parts share insofar as they are connected. Not just male theorists, I would add, but any theorist who writes from a position of identification with the child (son or daughter) rather than the mother.

Perhaps the only way to maintain the distance appropriate to theory, is through identification with the term that desires individuation. Since the student of the mother-daughter relationship, as we have seen, comes to reenact that bond in her relationship to her object, then she must desire the proper distance in order to theorize, in order not to become inextricably entangled. That may be why theory is sometimes characterized as male. Since theory is supposed to be abstracted from any specific object of study, it demands reliable separation. And at least in our current child-raising arrangements, maleness represents separation from the mother.[11] Female theory, theory that is inadequately distanced from its object, or feminist theory, theory grounded in allegiance to the collective body of women, is then monstrous.

In her contribution to *YFS* 62, Naomi Schor, following Freud's lead, links theory to paranoia. Her rereading of Freud's only case history of a female paranoiac,[12] reminds us that this individual fears another woman who "resembles her mother." In the context, Schor also makes

[10]Chodorow, 87.

[11]See Dorothy Dinnerstein, *The Mermaid and the Minotaur* (New York: Harper Colophon, 1976).

[12]Sigmund Freud, "A Case of Paranoia Running Counter to the Psychoanalytic Theory of the Disease," in *The Standard Edition of the Complete Psychological Works,* ed. and trans. James Strachey (London: Hogarth, 1953–74), 14.263–72.

Jane Gallop

reference to "the daughter's homosexual bond with her mother." The daughter's feeling of persecution is the other side of this close erotic bond. Female paranoia and female theory, which is its more socially acceptable form, thus bespeak a daughter's terror of the ubiquitous mother who is always there to witness because she is integrally linked to the daughter's self, a particularly desperate form of this terror.

Schor's essay suggests that there is something deviant, something abnormal or criminal about theory. Not only is it guilty by association with paranoia, but it produces phrases like "my progress is not innocent," "basing myself on a . . . literally perverse reading." Schor then goes on brazenly to found the clitoral school of theory. Gayatri Spivak, in her essay in *YFS* 62, reminds us that there is something deviant about the clitoris. At the close of the article she speaks of the "liberated heterosexual woman" who "confronts, at worst, the 'shame' of admitting to the 'abnormality' of her orgasm: at best, the acceptance of such a 'special' need" (184). The words *shame, abnormality,* and *special* are in quotation marks to be sure, but the image is nonetheless vivid and touching.

Schor's text passes quickly from the motherlike persecutor to the throbbing clitoris. I wonder about the relation between the clitoris and the mother. According to Chodorow, both the man and the woman experience coitus as a return to fusion with the body of the mother. Anatomically, the clitoris stands outside coitus, outside that merger. Although excited by it, it is not lost in it. Like a synecdoche for the fragile female self, the clitoris is both separate from and attached to this merger with the continuous multiple maternal body. Spivak writes that "an at least symbolic clitoridectomy has always been . . . the unacknowledged name of motherhood" (181). The institution of motherhood deprives the daughter, the mother, of the clitoris. To give in to the entangling web of mothering, to lose one's individual self to the collective being of monstrous proportions, is to lose one's clitoris, to lose one's theory.

The clitoral phase of female sexuality, what Freud used to call the phallic phrase,[13] is characterized by autoerotic manipulation of the clitoris with accompanying images, fantasies, representations of the mother. These fantasies bespeak a certain separation from the mother, precisely in that they constitute her as separate object to be reappropriated. At the same time that they posit the mother as object of desire (and thus avoid the more guilty rejection of the mother), they structurally institute the mother as separate and thus implicitly fulfill an-

[13]Freud, "The Infantile Genital Organization," in *Standard Edition*, 19:41–48.

other wish, the wish for separation. That this compromise formation (explicit wish for union, implicit wish for separation) characterizes the reign of the clitoris is noteworthy. To lose one's clitoris is then, perhaps, to lose this fragile compromise and fall into the unbearable choice: either total merger with the mother or total loss of her.

In her institution of clitoral critical theory, Schor connects the clitoris with the detail. To be able as reader to manipulate the detail is then perhaps to be able to maintain that fragile balance where neither object nor subject is totally lost, where the critic can indulge her desire for the text without losing her separate place as reader.

But the danger in this model is that the text-mother will become merely the reader's fantasy, a pleasing fantasy to accompany her autoeroticism. Freud assimilates clitoris to phallus; Schor would separate them. The phallus assumes that its other is a negative space to be filled with its products, projections, ejaculations, whereas the clitoris could presumably coexist with another clitoris (even if that other clitoris were a penis). We must come to recognize the mother's clitoris. The mother must be untangled from the web of the daughter's phantasmal projections. The mother too needs separation as well as merger. The detail we must hold onto is not ours but the text's. The reader must look for the text's clitoris, the little detail that easily escapes notice and yet if attended to can cause the text to open up.

It is not only, as Spivak suggests, that the clitoris is the focal point of the female self's "abnormality," but perhaps more interesting, in *Feminist Readings* the monster is the text's clitoris. I have tried here to manipulate that detail as a mode of intercourse with this collective body. Not that such a multiple text can be synechdochically reduced to this one point, but to recognize the monster may be a way to undo the symbolic clitoridectomy that makes a projective mother of the collective and the text.

I would just add that there are other quite sympathetic monsters in *YFS* 62. Domna Stanton and Elissa Gelfand demonstrate that, historically, masculinist scholars, literary and sociological, have condemned powerful women as monsters. The Contributors Notes list Gelfand as the author of a book titled *Literary Teratology* (teratology is the study of monsters).[14] Feminism is precisely the defense and valorization of such "monsters," the celebration of their beauty. Feminism has saved such

---

[14]Although this was the title of the manuscript, the book was published as *Imagination in Confinement: Women's Writings from French Prisons* (Ithaca: Cornell University Press, 1983).

monsters from the loneliness of their singularity and recognized them as members of the collective body of women.

The psychoanalytic and textual emphasis of my essay risks avoiding the political. In *YFS* 62, Spivak's troubling text represents the strongest reminder of the necessity of thinking that dimension. I am not here, not yet, prepared to go that route, but I see a connection between the problem I am pursuing and Spivak's critique of Western feminist theory. She argues that Western elite feminism can only project onto Third World women. As an antidote to such narcissistic projection, she advocates a new question for feminism to ask. That antidotal question seems equally appropriate to the dilemma I have traced here, seems a gesture toward recognizing the mother's clitoris, a way of breaking up our fascination with the monster in the mirror; so I will close with Spivak's words: "However unfeasible and inefficient it may sound, I see no way to avoid insisting that there has to be a simultaneous other focus: not merely who am I? but who is the other woman?" (179).

2

Where Does the Misery Come From?
Psychoanalysis, Feminism, and the Event

Jacqueline Rose

A classical political dichotomy, not without relevance for feminism, is captured by the question Wilhelm Reich placed at the heart of his dispute with Freud in a conversation with Kurt Eissler in 1952: "From now onward, the great question arises: *Where does that misery come from?* And here the trouble began. While Freud developed his death-instinct theory which said 'The misery comes from inside,' I went out, out where the people were."[1] We can immediately recognize the opposition that is central to Reich's complaint: between a misery that belongs to the individual in her or his relation to her- or himself, which is also, in Freud's theory of the death instinct, a species relationship, and a misery that impinges on the subject from the external world and that therefore refers to a social relationship. Here, the dynamic is not internal to the subject but passes between the subject and the outside, an outside that has direct effects upon psychic processes but is seen as free of any such processes itself. And we can see too the easy slide from that opposition to another that so often appears alongside it in political debate: the opposition between misery conceived as a privatized, internalized angst (the product of a theory that, like the psyche it describes, is *turned in on itself*) and the people, "out where the people were," that is, where it is really happening, with the poeple. These people who are outside, the place from which Reich claims to speak, have, therefore, two different meanings. They are outside of psychoanalysis seen as a socially delimiting and self-blinding

---

[1] Wilhelm Reich, *Reich Speaks of Freud. Conversations with Kurt Eissler*, ed. Mary Higgins and C. M. Raphael (New York: Farrar, Straus, and Giroux, 1967), 42–43, hereafter cited in the text.

institution but also—and this second meaning follows from the first—
they themselves only *have* an outside, since whatever they are and
suffer is a direct effect of a purely external causality and constraint.
Reich's question to Freud, with its dichotomy between inside and outside, thus contains within it two more familiar versions of the opposition by means of which politics is pitted against psychoanalysis: the opposition between public and private (the people versus analytic space)
and between social and the psychic (social oppression versus the drive
to death).[2]

In Reich's case, as we know, these views resulted in the gradual
repudiation of any concept of psychic dynamic and the unconscious in
favor of the notion of a genital libido, dammed up or blocked off by a
repressive social world, a natural stream that "you must get back into
its normal bed and let it flow naturally again" (44). This essentially pre-
Freudian and normative concept of sexuality reveals the most disturbing of its own social consequences in Reich's attacks on perversion,
homosexuality, Judaism, and women, together with the inflation of his
own sexual prowess which accompanied them: "It is quite clear that
the man who discovered the genitality function in neurosis and elaborated the orgastic potency question could not himself live in a sick
way" (104). This moment lays down the terms of the most fundamental
political disagreement with psychoanalysis, which then finds one of its
sharpest representations in a much more recent and more obviously
feminist political debate in relation to Freud, whose underlying issue
perhaps becomes clear only through a comparison between the two
moments. Kurt Eissler has the distinction (dubious, fortunate, or unfortunate, depending on which way you look at it) not only of having
conducted that interview with Reich in 1952 but also of later becoming
the key figure within the analytic institution in what has come to be
known as the Jeffrey Masson dispute, personally giving Masson access
to the archives through which he mounted his critique of Freud. Masson's critique—in which he challenges Freud on the relinquishment of
the seduction theory of neurosis in favor of fantasy and the vicissitudes
of psychic life—is expressed quite unequivocally in terms of the same
dichotomy between inside and outside: "By shifting the emphasis from
an actual world of sadness, misery, and cruelty to an internal stage on
which actors performed invented dramas for an invisible audience of
their own creation, Freud began a trend away from the real world that, it
seems to me, is at the root of the present-day sterility of psychoanalysis

---

[2]The key text in which Freud introduced the concept of the death drive is *Beyond the
Pleasure Principle* (1920).

and psychiatry throughout the world."[3] If the dichotomy appears this time as a feminist issue, it is because the aggression of the outside world has been stepped up and sexually differentiated and is now conceived of in terms of seduction, mutilation, and rape.

The similarities between these two moments are, I think, striking. We can point to the inflated view of sexual prowess, which in relation to Masson—the famous and now legally contested reference to his thousand and one nights[4]—merely mirrors in reverse the grotesque image of masculinity which runs through the whole book. What the two have in common is the utterly unquestioned image of sexual difference whose rigidity is, I would argue, the real violence and, in Masson's case—with a logic to which he is of course totally blind—leads directly to it. Reich also had his image of sexual violence, only the other way round: the misogyny-cum-vampirism worthy of Henry James's *The Sacred Fount* which can be detected in his observation that he has frequently observed couples in which the man is "alive," the woman "somehow out," inhibiting then drawing off, by implication, his vitality and power (117). But most important is that we can detect behind these two moments (the Reich and Masson disputes) this question of violence, which presents itself today as an explicitly feminist political issue but which was already there in the dispute over the death drive at the centre of the earlier political repudiation of Freud.

It is this issue of violence, and with it that of the death drive, which has become a key issue for any consideration of psychoanalysis in relation to feminism today. Clearly, the question of sexual violence is crucial to feminism in the 1980s (violence is, of course, also a political issue in a much more global sense). It is central to the discussion of pornography, to take just one instance. Reich himself spoke of the pornographic drives, although for him they were not a part of genital sexuality but the effect of a deviation from it. But Masson's book can, I think, be read as a key pornographic text of the 1980s as well as a text on pornography, much in the same way as we can, or have to, read Andrea Dworkin's writing on pornography, a form of feminism to which Masson now explicitly claims allegiance.[5]

[3]Jeffrey Masson, *The Assault on Truth, Freud's Suppression of the Seduction Theory* (New York: Farrar, Straus, and Giroux, 1984), 144.

[4]In 1983 Janet Malcolm interviewed Jeffrey Masson and used the material as the basis for two articles published first in the *New Yorker* and then as a book, *In the Freud Archives* (New York: Knopf, 1984). Masson subsequently sued Malcolm. The reference here is to his statement that he had slept with a thousand women.

[5]Chris Reed, "How Freud Changed His Mind and Became a Chauvinist," Guardian Woman, *Guardian*, 20 February 1985. Masson had also published a long article in the radical feminist journal *Mother Jones*.

Jacqueline Rose

For isn't the argument finally that psychoanalytic theory, by ignoring the pressing reality of sexual violence, becomes complicit with that violence and hands women over to it? Isn't the argument therefore that theory itself can cause death? And isn't that merely one step on from Reich's insistent relegation of all death to the outside, which then, in a classic inversion, leads directly to this persecutory return, for which psychoanalysis is held accountable? Reich himself was clearly operating in some such terms as this: "[Freud] sensed something in the human organism which was deadly. But he thought in terms of instinct. So he hit upon the term 'death instinct.' That was wrong. 'Death' was right. 'Instinct' was wrong. Because it's not something the organism wants. It's something that happens to the organism" (89).

Where to locate violence? This was the question sensed in all its difficulty in that earlier political debate. It is worth looking back at that moment to see how it was played out. What then emerges is that violence is not something that can be located on the inside or outside, in the psychic or the social (the second opposition, which follows so rapidly from the first), but rather something that appears as the effect of the dichotomy itself. I want to suggest that feminism, precisely through its vexed and complex relationship with psychoanalysis, may be in a privileged position to recast this problem, refusing the rigid polarity of inside and outside together with the absolute and fixed image of sexual difference which comes with it and on which it so often seems to rely. But I also want to suggest why the feminist undoing of this polarity needs to be different from other deconstructions that might be and have been proposed, especially because of the form of feminism's still-for-me-necessary relationship to psychoanalysis itself.

So where does violence go to if you locate it on the outside? In Reich's case, in a structure reminiscent of foreclosure, it returns in a hallucinatory guise. His insistence on the utter health of the subject brings murder in its train:

In order to get to the core where the natural, the normal, the healthy is, you have to get through the middle layer. And in that middle layer there is terror. There is severe terror. Not only that, there is murder there. All that Freud tried to subsume under the death instinct is in that middle layer. He thought it was biological. It wasn't. It's an artefact of culture. It is a structural malignancy of the human animal. Therefore before you can get through to what Freud called Eros or what I call orgonotic streaming or plasmatic excitation, you have to go through hell. . . . All these wars, all the chaos now—do you know what that is to my mind? *Humanity is trying to get at its core, at its living, healthy core. But before it can be reached, humanity has to pass through this phase of murder, killing and destruction.* (109)

28

This is apocalyptic—a kind of hideous born-again anticipation of that vision of a necessary hell put forward by some of the most extreme proponents of the New Right. It expels terror into the outer zone and then brings it back as a phase of human development, a catharsis whose purgatorial nature is not concealed by the concept of cultural artefact through which Reich tries to bring it to ground. Horror in Reich's argument operates at two levels. It is the product of culture (something that happens to the organism) and it is part of a vision (something his own language so clearly desires). But that link between two absolute outsides—one relegated to something called culture and the other to the nether depths of all humanity and all history—is not, I suspect, unique to Reich.

Against these rigid extremes, what Reich could not countenance was contradiction—the contradiction of subjectivity in analytic theory and the contradiction that, if it has any meaning, is the only meaning of the death drive itself. For a theory that pits inside and outside against each other in such deadly combat wipes out any difference or contradiction on either side: the subject suffers, the social oppresses, and what is produced, by implication, is utter stasis in each. At one level Freud's concept of the death drive was also about stasis—the famous return to the inorganic which indeed hands the concept over to biology and determinism alike. But if we follow the theorization through, deliberately avoiding the *fort-da* game through which it is most often rehearsed, it is the oscillation of position, the displacement of psychic levels and energies, which the concept of the death drive forces on the theory, the problem it poses in relation to any notion of what might be primary or secondary, which is striking. Challenging Freud on the concept of masochism, Reich commented: "When I asked him whether masochism was primary or secondary, whether it is turned-back sadism or aggression or a disturbance of aggression outward, or whether it's a primary death instinct thing, Freud, peculiarly, maintained both" (89). The ambiguity of the concept is the concept itself. In the chapter "The Classes of Instinct" in *The Ego and the Id*, Freud addressed the question of whether ambivalence—the transposition of love into hate and its reverse—throws his new dualism of the life and death instincts into crisis. Doesn't the shifting of one form of affect into another suggest a form of energy characterized by nothing other than the form of its displacements? And doesn't that in turn throw into question our understanding of the instinct as such: "The problem of the quality of instinctual impulses and of its persistence throughout their various vicissitudes is still very obscure."[6]

[6]Sigmund Freud, *The Ego and the Id*, in *The Standard Edition of the Complete Psychological Works*, ed. and trans. James Strachey (London: Hogarth, 1953–74), 19:40–47, p. 44.

Jacqueline Rose

What Reich therefore misses in his biology/culture opposition is that the theorization of the death instinct shows the instinct itself at its most problematic. For it gives us Freud articulating most clearly the concept of the *drive*, that is, a drive that is only a drive, because of its utter indifference to any path it might take. Freud uses the erotic cathexis and its indifference to the object as the model for this dynamic, but in a twist that mimics the very process he describes, the reference to Eros leads him straight into the arms of death:

> [This trait] is found in erotic cathexes, where a peculiar indifference in regard to the object displays itself. . . . Not long ago, Rank published some good examples of the way in which neurotic acts of revenge can be directed against the wrong people. Such behaviour on the part of the unconscious reminds one of the comic story of the three village tailors, one of whom had to be hanged because the only village blacksmith had committed a capital offense. Punishment must be exacted even if it doesn't fall upon the guilty.[7]

This utterly random *drive to* punishment links up with the concept of a *need for* punishment, the very concept Reich so criticized because it contradicted the earlier libidinal theory, which had stated that sexual desire does not seek punishment but fears it (the theory of repression). It was this concept of a need for punishment which upset Reich's conception of a purely extraneous causality (suffering as an external event). Freud summed it up in his observation in "The Economic Problem of Masochism," written immediately after *The Ego and the Id*: "It is instructive, too, to find, contrary to all theory and expectation, that a neurosis which has defied every therapeutic effort may vanish if the subject becomes involved in the misery of an unhappy marriage, or loses all his money, or develops a dangerous organic disease."[8] Of course, if it weren't all so deadly serious, what is most noteworthy about this, as with the story of the village tailors, is the utter comedy of it all.

In following these arguments, I should make it clear that I am not suggesting simply that the psychic dimension should be prioritized over the cultural and biological determinism of Reich (which turn out finally to be the same thing within Reich's own theory, since the concept of cultural repression depends on that of a preordained genital drive). For to argue in these terms leads almost inevitably to the reverse dualism of Janine Chasseguet-Smirgel and Bela Grunberger's book on

[7]Ibid., 45.
[8]Sigmund Freud, "The Economic Problem of Masochism," *Standard Edition*, 19:166.

Reich, which opposes to Reich's refusal of internal factors, psychic processes that they directly and with unapologetic reductionism make the determinant of social life. Also, although they insist on the difficulty of the internal factors and on that basis criticize Reich's glorification of the id, they do so in terms of a reality-differentiating ego, which has to succumb to the constraints on instinct offered by the real world, and thereby hand the concept of psychic conflict over to that of adaptation to reality—which might explain the defense of maturation, Oedipus, and sexual difference, not to mention the dismissal of all politics as reality-denying, which seems to follow.[9] The book ends with two quotations "Wo es war soll ich werden" ("Where id was, there ego shall be": Freud) and "Wo ich war soll es werden" ("Where ego was, there id shall be": roughly Reich), the first much-contested, much-interpreted statement presented unproblematically as the "goal of the analytic process" (237). The statement "Wo es war soll ich werden" was of course the phrase retranslated by Lacan from Strachey precisely because of the normative ethics of ego and adaptation it implied.[10] The implication is that Reich wanted to replace ego with id, whereas the objective of analysis should be the reverse. Faced with this, one might concede that Reich had an important point.

But what emerges instead in looking at Freud's theory of the death drive is precisely the impasse it produces in Freud's own thought around this very issue of location and dualism, to which I would want to assign both more and less than Derrida who makes of it in *La carte postale* the exemplary demonstration of the impasse of theorization itself (of metalanguage, knowledge, and mastery),[11] thereby evacuating the specific dynamic—of masochism, punishment, and the drive to death—which has historically been, and still is I would argue, the point of the political clash. For the failure to locate death as an object, the outrageous oscillation this failure introduces into causality and the event, signals for me something that has a particular resonance for a feminism wishing to bring the question of sexuality onto the political field: and that is that a rigid determinism by either biology or culture, by inside or outside—an outside that then turns into man posed in his

[9]Janine Chasseguet-Smirgel and Bela Grunberger, *Freud or Reich? Psychoanalysis and Illusion*, trans. Claire Pajaczkowska (London: Free Association Books, 1985), see esp. 10.

[10]Sigmund Freud, "The Dissection of the Psychical Personality," *New Introductory Lectures*, in *Standard Edition*, 22:80; Jacques Lacan, "L'instance de la lettre dans l'inconscient; ou, La raison depuis Freud," *Ecrits* (Paris: Seuil, 1957), 493–528, p. 524; "The Agency of the Letter in the Unconscious; or, Reason since Freud," trans. Alan Sheridan in *Ecrits: A Selection* (New York: Norton, 1977), 146–78, p. 171.

[11]Jacques Derrida, *La carte postale: De Socrate à Freud et au-delà* (Paris: Flammarion, 1980).

immutable and ahistorical essence as man—simply will not do. Wasn't it precisely to bypass both of these causalities (of culture or of biology) that Juliet Mitchell turned to psychoanalysis in the first place?[12] Then the question was posed in terms of how to understand the origins of femininity and sexual difference (where does sexual difference come from?). To which I would merely add that the question of determinism reveals itself today as the issue of violence and its location (determinism precisely as a violence).

Like Reich before him, Masson insists on the externality of the event, only this time he calls it man. He is perhaps useful only to the extent that he anthropomorphizes the inside/outside dichotomy, turning it unmistakably into an issue of whether it is our (women's) or their (men's) fault. It seems to be the inevitable development of the basic dichotomy, since a reality split off into a realm of antagonism cannot finally be conceptualized as anything other than violence, or perhaps even rape. But to ask for a language that goes over to neither side of this historical antagonism, and to suggest that we might find the rudiments of such a language in the very issue of the death drive, is merely to point to something that is in a way obvious for feminism—the glaring inadequacy of any formulation that makes us as women either pure victim or sole agent of our distress. The realm of sexuality messes up what can be thought of in any straightforward sense as causality. Precisely, then, through its foregrounding of sexuality, feminism may be in a privileged position to challenge or rethink the dualities (inside/outside, victim/aggressor, real event/fantasy) which seem to follow any rigid externalization of political space.

There is, however, another discourse, with its own relation to feminism and to psychoanalysis, which has quite explicitly addressed this polarity of inside and outside, aiming to undo these polarities in which it also locates a violence. This is a violence not against women but against something that can be called the rhetoricity of language, insofar as the binary is always the point at which—under the impact of an impulse to mastery and control—the oscillation and randomness of language is closed off. Not only in Derrida's writing, but also in Shoshana Felman's book on madness and the literary thing, Barbara Johnson's essay on Poe, Lacan, and Derrida, and Samuel Weber's reading of Freud, the specific polarity of inside and outside appears as the stake of their discourse. One quotation from each of them can serve as illustration:

[12]Juliet Mitchell, *Psychoanalysis and Feminism* (New York: Random House, 1974).

To state that madness has well and truly become a commonplace is to say that madness stands in our contemporary world for the radical ambiguity on the inside and the outside, an ambiguity which escapes speaking subjects who speak only by misrecognising it. . . . A discourse that speaks of madness can henceforth no longer know whether it is inside or outside, internal or external, to the madness of which it speaks.[13]

The total inclusion of the "frame" is both mandatory and impossible. The "frame" thus becomes not the borderline between the inside and the outside, but precisely what subverts the applicability of the inside/outside polarity to the act of interpretation.[14]

The specific problem posed by anxiety is that of *the relation of the psychic to the nonpsychic, or in other words, the delimitation of the psychic as such.* But if anxiety poses this problem, its examination and solution are complicated by the fact that anxiety itself both simulates and dissimulates the relation of psychic to nonpsychic, of "internal" to "external." . . . [Freud's attempt] is intended to put anxiety in its proper place. But his own discussion demonstrates that *anxiety has no proper place.* . . . The psychoanalytic conception of the psychic can neither be *opposed* to the nonpsychic nor *derived* from it; it cannot be expressed in terms of cause and effect, outer and inner, reality and unreality, or any other of the opposing pairs to which Freud inevitably recurs.[15]

And at the Conference on Feminism and Psychoanalysis held at Normal, Illinois, in May 1986 Barbara Johnson said in discussion: "For pedagogy, aesthetics, therapy, you have to have a frame, and if you have a frame, what you get is pedagogy, aesthetics, therapy (which doesn't mean that you can do without one)." Now there are obvious differences among these statements and of course among the individual writers, but nonetheless a number of important links—both among them and in relation to what I have been describing—can be made. First, the problem of externality, delimitation, as a problem that encompasses the object—whether madness, literary enunciation, or anxiety—also includes the very theorization through which that object can be thought. The impossibility of delimiting the object becomes, therefore, the impossibility for theory itself of controlling its object, that is, of knowing

[13]Shoshana Felman, *Writing and Madness,* trans. Martha Noel Evans and the author (Ithaca: Cornell University Press, 1985), 12–13, originally published as *La folie et la chose littéraire* (Paris: Seuil, 1978), hereafter cited in the text.

[14]Barbara Johnson, "The Frame of Reference: Poe, Lacan, Derrida," *Yale French Studies* 55/56 (1977), 481, hereafter cited in the text.

[15]Samuel Weber, *The Legend of Freud* (Minneapolis: University of Minnesota Press, 1982), 50, 58–59, hereafter cited in the text.

it. Felman asks, "How can we construct the theory of the essential misprision of the subject of theory?" (221). Barbara Johnson: "If we could be sure of the difference between the determinable and the under-terminable, the undeterminable would be comprehended within the determinable. What is undecidable is precisely whether a thing is decidable or not" (488). And Weber: "Such a *reality* [the 'real essence of danger'] can never be fully grasped by theoretical 'insight,' since it can never be seen, named or recognised as such" (59).

Second, and as an effect of this, the characterization of the object shifts into the field of its conceptualization, or the impossibility of its conceptualization, so that, in Felman's case, for example, madness becomes precisely *la chose littéraire*, the very *thing* of literature (not *a* literary thing), because literature is the privileged place in which that tension between speaking madness and speaking of madness, between speaking madness and designating or repressing it, which is also the distinction between rhetoric and grammar, is played out. The object becomes the very structure of representation through which it fails to be thought, the impasse of conceptual thinking itself. The classic and dazzling instance of this theorization has to be the moment when Barbara Johnson reads Oedipus as a repetition of the letter purloined from the abyssal and interminable interior of Poe's story, instead of seeing the letter as a repetition of an oedipal fantasy it necessarily and always reproduces (the basis of Derrida's critique of Lacan, in whose reading of the Poe story he locates a classic psychoanalytic reduction) (488).

Third, the shifting of the object into the very form and movement of representation brings with it—cannot, finally, avoid—its own meta-psychology. This appears in the category of grammar Felman sets against rhetoric: the misrecognizing subject that thinks—has to think in order to speak—that it knows itself, has to ignore, as she puts it, that radical ambiguity between inside and outside that madness gives us today. But it is in the theorization of the death drive, the vanishing point of the theory, that the metapsychology of this reading of psycho-analysis becomes most clear. In Weber's reading of Freud's key text on the death drive, *Beyond the Pleasure Principle* (1920), what turns out to be driving the very impulse to death is narcissism, the binding and mastery that Weber identifies not only in the concept of the death drive but also in the very process through which Freud tried to formulate it, "the narcissistic striving to rediscover the same: an aspect of specula-tion Freud was ready to criticize in others, but which he sought to justify in his own work" (129). It is this emphasis on narcissism which saves the death drive from that intangible, generalized, and ultimately transcendent realm of the unfathomable to which the insistence on the failure of conceptualization could so easily assign it. Against this possible reading, which he attributes to Gilles Deleuze, Weber sees in the death drive "just another form of the narcissistic language of the ego" (129). It is a kind of self-accusatory ego psychology, one that laments and undoes its own categories and status even as it gives them final arbitration over psychic life.

Something similar goes on in Derrida's own reading of this same text by Freud (Derrida and Weber refer to each other)[16] through the concept of the "pulsion d'emprise," "pulsion de puissance." At a key moment in Derrida's speculation on this most speculative of Freud's writings, this drive emerges as the very motive of the drive itself: "The holding, appropriating, drive must also be the *relation to itself* of the drive: no drive not driven to bind itself to itself and to ensure its self mastery as drive. Hence the transcendental tautology of the appropriating drive: the drive as drive, the drive of drive, the pulsionality of the drive."[17] The concept appears in a term Freud offers almost as an aside in his discussion of the *fort-da* game: *Bemachtingungstrieb.* Freud's "transcendental predicate" for describing the death drive, it is for Derrida, as for Weber, the term through which Freud's own metaconceptual impulse is best thought.[18]

The concept of the death drive has of course been central to Derrida's reading of Freud since "Freud and the Scene of Writing," when it hollowed out Freud's theory at its weak points of binarism through its *umheimlich* presence (as binding and repetition) inside the very process of life. We could in fact say that it is through the theorization of the death drive that Derrida ultimately thinks the relationship between the proper and that *différance* which subverts any causality, any dichotomy of inside and outside, all forms of language mastery in which he locates the violence (his word) of the metaphysical act.[19] Barbara Johnson, too, draws "The Frame of Reference" to a close through the categories of

[16]Derrida, *La carte postale,* 400n; Weber, 172n.

[17]Derrida, *La carte postale,* 430 (my translation).

[18]Derrida, *La carte postale,* 430–32. Although very close, there does seem to be a difference between Weber's and Derrida's theorization here. For Weber the death drive becomes a manifestation of the drive to mastery; for Derrida the "pulsion d'emprise" is the category through which the death drive is thought by Freud, but it is always exceeded by the death drive, "at once the reason and the failure, the origin and the limit of power." Hence in Derrida's commentary, the last word, so to speak, is given to rhythm: "Beyond opposition, the rhythm." (432, 435).

[19]Derrida, "Freud et la scène de l'écriture," *L'écriture et la différence* (Paris: Seuil, 1967), 293–340; *Writing and Difference,* trans. Alan Bass (Chicago: University of Chicago Press, 1978), 196–231.

Jacqueline Rose

narcissism and death (the inverted message that forces the subject—
and reader—up against an irreducible otherness) (503). Let's call deconstruction, for the moment at least, another way of dealing, another
"savoir faire," with the death drive itself (using and reformulating
Catherine Millot's description of psychoanalysis as a savoir faire with
the paternal metaphor) that manages over and again to assert itself at
the heart of theoretical and political debate.[20]

Let's note too, for all the distance between them, how the two very
different articulations in relation to the death drive I have been describing come uncannily close, how Derrida seems to pick up, or rather
produce from within his own theorization, something of the terms
present in Reich and later Masson: narcissism as phallogocentrism and
the hymen as counterimage, with the relation between them formulated as rupture. Couldn't this also be seen as a grotesque recasting of
the world (now Western metaphysics) under the sign of a massive
violation, if not rape? "Perpetual, the rape has always already taken
place and will nevertheless never have been perpetrated. For it will
always have been caught in the foldings of some veil, where any or all
truth comes undone."[21] No rape because the hymen is the point where
all truth is undone; but always already rape, because always truth,
logos, presence, the violence of the metaphysical act.

The act is metaphor or figuration for Derrida; for Masson figuration,
or fantasy, is the act (figuration is a denial of the reality of the act). The
difference can be seen in the opposite political effects: deconstruction
of a sexual binary in language, which then seems, in Derrida's discourse
at least, condemned to repeat it, or refusal of language itself in favor of
the event. For what is at stake in Masson's rejection of fantasy if not
representation as such, the idea of a discourse at odds with itself with
no easy relation to the real? And isn't that also the key to the radical
feminist critique of pornography, which sees the image as directly
responsible for the act? But by setting figuration against the act in my
own discourse, I am only too aware of the risk of reintroducing that
inside/outside dichotomy which is so often the guarantor of political
space. It is a question that has of course been put many times, not least
by feminists, to deconstruction itself:

This raises an important question which should not be overlooked although we haven't the space to develop it to any extent here: the compli-

[20]Catherine Millot, "The Feminine Super-ego," *m/f* 10 (1985): 21–38.
[21]Derrida is commenting on Mallarmé. Jacques Derrida, "La double séance," *La dis-
sémination* (Paris: Seuil, 1972), 199–318, p. 260; "The Double Session," *Dissemination*,
trans. Barbara Johnson (Chicago: University of Chicago Press, 1981), p. 292.

cated relationship of a practical politics to the kind of analysis we have been considering (specifically the "deconstructive" analysis implicit in your discussion). . . . Just how one is to deal with the inter-relationship of these forces and necessities in the context of feminine [sic—I think this should be "feminist"] struggle should be more fully explored on some other occasion. But let's go on to Heidegger's ontology.[22]

The slip—feminine for feminist—is beautifully expressive of the problem being raised: the absorption of the political (feminist) into the space of representation (feminine). Or as Derrida would insist—as indeed he goes on to insist in the same interview—with reference to a concept like "hymen" or "double chiasmatic invagination of the borders," these terms are present in his own writing as a trope not reducible to the body of the woman as such, at once anchored in and taking off from the recognizable historical reference they inevitably invoke (75).

Crucially however, in both these positions, the problem of how to locate violence and the act brings with it—is inseparable from—the question of how to locate sexual difference. It needed feminism, of course, to make the point.

In three stages, therefore, feminism has returned to and recast the controversies at the heart of the 1920s and 1930s political debate with Freud:[23] first, the issue of phallocentrism, which came originally from within the analytic institution and, in its largely clinical formulation, was at that time marked by the total absence of any political consciousness or critique (it was this criticism that was remade for radical feminism by Shulamith Firestone and Kate Millett in the late 1960s); second, the attempt to use psychoanalysis as a theory of ideology, which had characterized the political Freudians of Berlin.[24] The key figure here is Otto Fenichel, who tried to use psychoanalysis in relation to Marxism without losing, like Reich and the culturalists, the unconscious and sexuality, without sacrificing, like the Vienna and British orthodox analysts, the political challenge to social and sexual norms (Juliet Mitchell's intervention in 1974 is almost an exact retranscription for feminism of this aim.) And finally now, the issue of the death drive, of a violence whose outrageous character belongs so resolutely with its refusal to be located, to be simply identified and then, by

[22]Jacques Derrida and Christie V. McDonald, "Choreographies," *Diacritics* 12 (Summer 1982), 66–76.

[23]For a fuller discussion of this history, see Jacqueline Rose, "Introduction—Feminism and the Psychic," *Sexuality in the Field of Vision* (London: Verso, 1986).

[24]See Russell Jacoby, *The Repression of Psychoanalysis: Otto Fenichel and the Political Freudians* (New York: Basic, 1983).

implication, removed (possibly the only meaning of the persistence, or immutability, of the death drive of which it has so often been politically accused). Perhaps one reason why this issue is now so pressing is that, faced with the hideous phenomenon of right-wing apocalyptic and sexual fantasy, the language of interpellation through which we thought to understand something about collective identification is no longer adequate. At the point where fantasy generalizes itself in the form of the horrific, that implied ease of self-recognition gives way to something that belongs in the order of impossibility or shock.

That this is now a key issue for feminism can be read across the very titles of two texts of contemporary feminism: Andrea Dworkin's *Pornography: Men Possessing Women*, with all that it implies by way of a one-sided (which means outside of us as women) oppression, violence, and control, and the Barnard papers on sexuality, *Pleasure and Danger*, whose ambiguity allows us at least to ask whether the relation between the two terms is one of antagonism or implication, whether there might be a pleasure *in* danger—a dangerous question in itself.[25] In her opening essay, the editor, Carole Vance, puts the question like this: "The subtle connection between how patriarchy interferes with female desire and how women experience their own passions as dangerous is emerging as a critical issue to be explored" (4). In this formulation, although danger is still something that comes from outside—patriarchy makes female desire dangerous to itself—the terms of femininity, passion, and danger have at least started to move.[26] If the deconstructive way of undoing the sort of dichotomy I have outlined leaves me unsatisfied, therefore, it is not just because of the return of the basic scenario of difference but because I cannot see how it can link back to this equally pressing question for feminists—which is how we can begin to think the question of violence and fantasy as something that implicates us as women, how indeed we can begin to dare to think it at all.

It is the problem increasingly at the heart of Kristeva's more recent work, the concept of abjection (already posed as horror and power), which has led inexorably to the question of feminism and violence, "to extol a centripetal, softened and becalmed feminine sexuality, only to exhume most recently, under the cover of idylls amongst women, the sado-masochistic ravages beneath."[27] In Kristeva's case, this difficulty

---

[25] Andrea Dworkin, *Pornography: Men Possessing Women* (New York: Perigree, 1981); Carole S. Vance, *Pleasure and Danger: Exploring Female Sexuality* (Boston: Routledge and Kegan Paul, 1984).

[26] At a two-day all-women event—"Women Alive"—organized in London on 5–6 July 1986 by the Communist party journal *Marxism Today*, these issues were discussed in session under the title "Is There a Feminist Morality?" and "Guilty Pleasure."

[27] Julia Kristeva, *Histoires d'amour* (Paris: Denoel, 1983), 349.

has produced in turn the no less problematic flight into a paternally grounded identification and love.[28]

The question then becomes: what could be an understanding of violence which, while fully recognizing the historical forms in which it has repeatedly been directed toward women, nonetheless does not send it wholesale out into the real from which it can only return as an inevitable and hallucinatory event? How can we speak the fact that violence moves across boundaries, including that of sexual difference, and not only in fantasy. For only by recognizing that boundaries already shift (not *can* be shifted—the flight into pure voluntarism) can we avoid the pitfalls of a Masson (women as utter victim to the event). And only by seeing this as a problem for subjects who recognize, and in so doing misrecognize, themselves and each other as sexual beings, can we seize this problem at the level of what is still for feminism an encounter between the sexes. For psychoanalysis, this difficulty is precisely the difficulty of sexuality itself, or of the death drive, which might be a way of saying the same thing. It certainly seems to be one of the points of greatest theoretical and political difficulty today.

[28]I discuss these shifts in Kristeva's work more fully in "Julia Kristeva—Take Two," *Sexuality in the Field of Vision* (London: Verso, 1986).

3

Seeking the Third Term: Desire, the
Phallus, and the Materiality of Language

Ellie Ragland-Sullivan

Generally speaking, sociological feminists and Marxist feminists locate the source of violence in cultural inequities and political failures. Throughout the teaching of the psychoanalyst Jacques Lacan, one finds a set of answers to the question of where human violence comes from different from those that point to economic first causes. Lacan elaborates a picture of the human ego in which narcissism and aggressiveness are but opposite faces of the same coin. In his view, the ego evolves as a gradually built-up imaginary order system of myths and fictions that function to "suture," or close off, any knowledge of unconscious effects. Put another way, there is a subject of unconscious desire "beyond the ego" which can be studied precisely because the ego has organization. The lineaments of Janus-like narcissism and aggressiveness can be discerned in the all-pervasive human desire for recognition in its correlation to the signifier of the father's name.

The idea that violence typically arises on the side of the masculine is far from new. The theoretical twist Lacan adds lies in his insistence that all cultural (and familial) interpretation of the difference between the sexes makes a difference, a major one. Lacan rereads Freud's *Totem and Taboo* as an allegory of real effect. Freud's mythic father becomes Lacan's real father: the father as unconsciously desiring. But the real, unlike desire, operates on the side of lawlessness and chaos and is, by definition, an order that infers confusion into symbolic codes and imaginary identifications. The problem for males, in Lacan's view, is that they are asked to identify away from the mother in the name of a father who is supposed to be an ideal (in the imaginary and symbolic), but is, in actuality, the source of prohibition. This double bind places the son in a confused position in terms of both ego and desire. He cannot be the mother. He cannot be the father. He can only await from a posture of aggressive frustration the position of power tacitly promised. Feminine structure undergoes no such prohibition. The daughter can be "a little mother" from the start, her identification with her mother, approved by mother and father alike. These are "normative," almost caricatured paradigms, but Lacan taught that they lay behind the structuration of the subject and create a dialectical battle between the sexes which is prior to any class dialectic.

In the 1950s Lacan defined "structure" as those specific transformations that follow certain laws.[1] Yet the idea of structuring laws goes against most twentieth-century thought, which argues that there is no reality of universals except as the logical form of natural laws. Indeed, the idea of any structuration of individual subjects whose laws might be generalizable from culture to culture and throughout history is immediately suspect. The interesting aspect of Lacan's teaching is his proposal for linking a minimal universal to the detail of individual particularities. By making a distinction between substance or essence and structure or order(ing), Lacan evolved a complex set of theories that link epistemology to ontology to aesthetics and "beyond." Moreover, he placed both the individual and the cultural very clearly in his concept of structured orders. To the horror and surprise of those who work with his thought, he postulated one structural universal: the symbol or signifier for sexual difference. He named the structuring mediums of that difference the local symbolic (linguistic), the imaginary (identificatory) and the real orders.

By arguing that Lacan's theory of a structural first cause can best be understood in relation to his conceptions of narcissism and aggressiveness, desire, and the materiality of language, my essay constitutes a polemic against modern epistemologies, as well as a defense of Freud's own idea of what psychoanalysis could be. Psychoanalysis, in the words of Janine Chasseguet-Smirgel and Béla Grunberger, "claims to be not only a key to understanding humanity, but *the* key which unlocks the doors to knowledge of the species, in all aspects of our behaviour and activities. It should be remembered that this was the view of the founder of psychoanalysis, however much one may disagree."[2] Agreeing with Freud, Lacan nonetheless submits Freud's texts to a scrutiny that

[1]Jacques Lacan, "Of Structure as an Inmixing of an Otherness Prerequisite to Any Subject Whatever," in *The Structuralist Controversy: The Languages of Criticism and the Sciences of Man*, ed. Richard Macksey and Eugenio Donato (Baltimore: Johns Hopkins University Press, 1975), 187–88.

[2]Janine Chasseguet-Smirgel and Béla Grunberger, *Freud or Reich? Psychoanalysis and Illusion*, trans. Claire Pajaczkowska (New Haven: Yale University Press, 1986), 30.

evolves new answers as to what psychoanalysis is. Despite the difficulties implicit in reading Lacan's prose, where questions and answers play cat-and-mouse for decades, paradox following paradox, contradiction piled upon contradiction, the syntax of sentences skewed, there are consistent threads of argument developed throughout this fluid, ever-changing teaching. Three interlinked concepts are the imaginary, desire, and the phallus. The ego "writes its own story" of narcissism and aggressiveness in reference to the fictions arising from the mother's desire and its correlate, the father's name. The phallus is the name Lacan gives to the mark of lack that covers over the originary writing out of a subject's oedipal drama or primal scene. The phallus, coextensive with the ego, uses language (or language uses the ego) to "suture" any knowledge of an Other (alien) desire within its walls. The ideological "self-core" of any subject functions, then, to veil or misrecognize the real causes of which subjects are effects.

Lacan postulated that both cultural and subject(ive) "knowledge" organize themselves around four principles: a fundamental taboo against incest between child and mother; a real void at the center of being caused by the fact that loss lies at the heart of consciousness; "objects" of desire that compensate for a primordial and incomprehensible sense of loss; and later efforts to attenuate the experience of loss by clinging to the language and identity myths that constitute subjecthood. Indeed, structuration of the ego and desire demarcates the individual as well as the social and derives from a splitting of the subject into conscious and unconscious parts by means of identification and language. In "La science et la vérité" Lacan calls the phallus nothing other than the point of lack it indicates in the subject.[3] Paradoxically, insofar as the phallus marks lack, it also signifies desire. Slavoj Žižek has called this paradoxical element of the "at least one"—a countable imaginary symbol of difference between the male and female—that which sustains the radical dimension of a gap "in"-consciousness and makes it possible for representation to occur at all as a function of desire.[4]

Clearly, Lacan does not accept Freud's theory that literal castration anxiety is the limit marking sexual difference. Rather, the anatomical difference creates the imaginary confusion or real barrier that places interpretation of this difference at the heart of cultural practices and makes it the cornerstone of individual desire. Neither femininity nor masculinity is natural. Thus both play themselves out as a masquerade around reified myths and inexplicable desires. If the phallic signifier is,

[3]Jacques Lacan, "La science et la vérité," *Ecrits* (Paris: Seuil, 1966), 877.
[4]Slavoj Žižek, "Why Lacan Is Not a Post-structuralist," *Newsletter of the Freudian Field* 1.2 (1987): 31–39.

indeed, the agent denoting a symbolic division of each subject into speaking and repressed (*aphanisis*) parts, taking *its* privilege on the side of law and language, this is because—and merely because—it interprets the one observable image for an identificatory distinction between the sexes; the single thing in nature of which there are only two, privileging the function of difference itself. If this symbol demarcates lack/desire, this is because it is imaginarily (perceptually) detachable, because girls do not have it. If she does not have "it," but he does, the implication is that "it" might come off. But for Lacan none of this has to do with masturbation (castration) fears or with penis envy. It has to do with how meaning is made, first by opposition and then by referential substitutions. One begins to understand why so many three-year old girls refer to their baby brother's penis as something *babies*—of either sex—have and lose. Later this attitude becomes uninterested dismissal on the part of the girl. Boys, on the contrary, may perplexedly attribute this organ to girls. If, indeed, masculinity gives rise to myths grounded on this representational difference, one begins to grasp that the masculine ego might well be fragile. It is *he* who risks loss, not she. Moreover, in the name of this difference—away from nature toward the social—he is supposed to be a cultural symbol of power, prestige, and knowledge.

But the one who identifies with the phallus in an unconscious signifying chain (the at least one countable distinction in the imaginary) must always confront the fact that any privilege based on this difference is a "wizard of Oz" shibboleth. Masculine aggression becomes a matter of trying to align unconscious identity position with imaginary figures (superegos and ideals) in the world and with symbolic conventions. One can conclude that the masculine has always been in a strange and skewed proximity to the death drive, which Lacan names the real. Is the masculine the *Unheimlich* in pursuit of the feminine who is fantasized as *Heim*?

And why does Lacan link the masculine to the word? Is it because the triumph of culture over nature—father's name over mother's body—only occurs at all through, and because of, the substitutive (metaphorical) properties of language? From the moment an infant uses words in an effort to position itself by naming itself—and taming things by naming them as well—language becomes the tool by which any ego can re-present itself to others. Naming opens the way to transference as exchange of differences wherein people try to anchor the imaginary sliding of identificatory perceptions. But by setting boundaries language also alienates and rigidifies egos (superegos) and desires into fictional oppositions. Lacan's insistence on the imaginary and real dimensions that flesh out the symbolic order, requires that one envision a link between an acquired identity position and an oedipal struggle that joins

Ellie Ragland-Sullivan

sexuality to identity, body, and knowledge. The oedipal desiring struggle produces the place of the phallus—mark of lack—which later maintains the conscious subject because an absolute object of desire lacks— for both sexes.[5] Language fills in the gap created by a prohibition against total identificatory fusion (incest taboo) with the mother, and "returns" in a strangeness of functions that goes far beyond information giving and getting.

Freud thought that some thing in being is repressed. Lacan named this thing the "letter." Freud first thought the thing was a lost object, perhaps the idealized breast, which the child wished to monopolize by eradicating the father in order to possess the mother for his total pleasure. The end point of such desire was an oedipal (male) wish to possess the mother. The object was to (re)experience a lost primary pleasure. In Lacan's rethinking of the problems left behind by Freud, the lost object has become loss itself, while the leftover residue of unconscious effects is the *objet a*. But one must be careful. With Lacan the *objet a* is not an object relation or even a relation to a unified whole (such as synecdoche to metaphor). Rather, loss is the fragment of a reference to the function that produced the reference in the first place: the need for food or the desire for recognition. In Jacques-Alain Miller's formulation one can represent Lacan's relationship to object-relations theory thus:[6] What is lost is any chance for a totalizing experience of Oneness with the maternal body or gaze. This taboo sets the limit of human freedom in a refusal to infant and mother to be *all* for one another, a limit that prohibits a potential psychosis when it is foreclosed.

But human subjects do not forget the early yearning for Oneness, the space where demand gave rise to desire. Lacan offered the *objet a* to denote both the cause and the leftover sign of the effects of a mirror-stage structural (logically inferred) moment. By the *objet a* Lacan understands repression as an incomplete mode of shutting out unconscious symbolizations and thus a kind of un-conscious rememoration that dwells on the side of suspended re-presentations. Lacan considered denial (*Verneinung, dénégation*), as itself proof that something dwelt beyond ego fixations/fictions. Repression, thus, becomes an active dynamic in mental functioning, one that points to enigmas, not just to absences. By depicting *dénégation* as the negation of negation rather than the splitting of mind and affect or the distinction of pleasure from

[5]Jean-Guy Godin, "Du symptôme à son épure: Le sinthome," in *Joyce avec Lacan*, ed. Jacques Aubert (Paris: Navarin, 1987), 162.

[6]Jacques-Alain Miller, "A and a in Clinical Structures," *Acts of the Paris–New York Psychoanalytic Workshop, July 1986* (New York: Schneiderman Press, 1987), 14–29.

displeasure, as Freud argued at different times, Lacan joined desire to repression through the medium of representing representations.[7] Desire is not only an erotic (or positive) function, then, but also a signifying (negative) function when representations are linked to repression. Desire, therefore, always exceeds the lack it denotes, marking a place of incompletion or aphanisis in language and unconscious representations, thus pointing to a hole in being that must continually fill itself up, oscillating between being and nothingness. Repressed memories, bobbing just beyond grasp, insinuate the sense of lack into language and being, such that no final resolution for human problems will be found by repairing defective egos, achieving correct political practices, or in perfect analyses either.

If unconscious desire functions as an inherent "lack-in-being" that drives humans to seek resolutions and answers (whether in form or content) because all subjects are incomplete, those who close out any idea of an Otherness "in" consciousness must create endless ruses to convince themselves that they control their own destinies, will their own choices. Indeed, the imaginary push for a sense of Oneness is so strong that the desire not to know works in tandem with ego mortification such that belief systems, relationships with others, fantasies, language as a system (either constructed or deconstructed), material goods, children, sexual proclivities—all become grist to the *dénégation* mill.

Lacan does not simply give us a fancy new picture of Freudian castration anxiety. He confronts us with a real whose power is this. It "writes" into the Other of every subject the impasses and knots created by the effects of subject structuration: unsymbolized and unassimilated lumps punctuating an unconscious set of signifying chains as the *objet a*. On the one hand, we have the phallic signifier denoting a split in the subject. On the other hand, we have a real hole in the Other which produces *jouissance* effects. While the phallic signifier is on the side of language, *jouis-sens* points "beyond." But the phallic signifier is a function (Latin, *functio:* "performance") that is, nonetheless, linked to *jouissance* through desire and the real. It is also that (both language and the phallus) which performs *for someone.* In this sense, the phallus signifies the place of desire in the Other as it floats into the world of others. Lacan says that the phallus plays its role veiled. That is, both language and the ego occult the phallic function by their capacities to substitute one thing for another. For Lacan, language and the ego point beyond the metaphorical to the metonymy of desire. Put another way,

---

[7]Jean Hyppolite, "Commentaire parlé sur la *Verneinung* de Freud," Appendix I, *Ecrits* (Paris: Seuil, 1966), 117–25.

memory and consciousness cancel each other out by making it seem that only the visible or speakable is valorizable, that substitutions and oppositions are infinite, and by supposing that they can account for all subject effects (language, truth, and so on).

Lacan subverts all philosophies of consciousness by adding a third term to binary thinking: a lack in being and an ab-*sens* that is occulted. Moreover, the hole is not a no-thing but a density. Since, however, one cannot think loss directly, binary oppositions of all sorts, imaginary essentializing fantasies, endless dualisms, create conscious life as a prison house of restrictive couples. What is new and striking in Lacan's teaching is the theory that the conscious ability to distinguish and discriminate one thing from another is a trap. The subject makes the imaginary error of believing that different terms are simply interchangeable, generalizable, or infinitely displaceable. But the fiction of interchangeability does not grapple with the reality of the unconscious: that is, in order to substitute any term or letter for another, the "term" must already exist somewhere in our own memory systems of reference. But does this notion merely take us back to Freud's idea of repressed fantasies or Derrida's idea of sounding an unconscious made up only of language effects?

Lacan's phallic signifier points to a *jouissance* beyond desire that links human subjects to unconscious masochism and to a death drive. If, as Lacan claimed, all subjects who are not psychotic possess an unconscious set of identifications with a signifier for the name of the father, then a given subject's unconscious position toward the phallic signifier may well occasion intense narcissistic or aggressive responses at the ego level (correlated to a father's prestige and a mother's desire). Moreover, one would assess this idea by separating the categories imaginary, symbolic, and real in terms of a function of the father's name in each.[8] For example, in the symbolic order this name will signify law or privilege, and in the imaginary, fantasy. In the real it will coalesce with desire and *jouissance*. The phallic signifier that denotes difference in the first place quickly allies itself to a name. More specifically, a father's name takes on meaning in reference to the assumption of a subject position within a signifying network (some minimal family structure). Put in other terms, the phallus orders desire (the mother's) in reference to the father's name on several planes that may be mutually contradictory. But whatever the contradictions between the imaginary and symbolic, the real holds the ace of trumps in this game of life and

[8]Russell Grigg, "The Function of the Father in Psychoanalysis," *Australian Journal of Psychotherapy* 5.2 (1986), 117–25.

death that we call "life." If the signifier for a father's name creates the minimal distance (division) necessary for difference to be perceived at all, oedipal effects and desired objects underlie all subject constitution, making of subjects "inside out" memory banks of the meaning ensembles that constitute them as *material* subjects.

Still, most people would not agree that they live from unconscious data. For most, any myth or idealization is preferable to thinking that identity is constituted by alien effects, only an object of familial and cultural positioning and desire. But if one can consider Lacan's hypothesized orders (his structural topology), one has tools with which to analyze the binary impasses in which conscious thought and methodologies dead-end. In this context Lacan's theories are useful to any ongoing elaboration of feminist, psychoanalytic, or political issues. Theories that dismiss the crux of childhood amnesia in subject structure are doomed to remain descriptive, aesthetic, and formalist. Finally, neither word games nor genetic packets are the *Stoff* that life is made of. Theories that give up on first-cause enigmas end up lacking the tools to do the work of change or to address stubborn problematics behind age-old human mysteries.

Two of the most important thinkers on the contemporary scene have chosen divergent paths regarding first-cause issues. Jacques Derrida, long preoccupied with the history of philosophy, has argued that the unconscious is a fiction whose primary effects are either no-thing or reducible to noise(s). Older by thirty years, the psychoanalyst Jacques Lacan argued long ago that fictions, nonetheless, have the structure of truth. In this context Lacan defined "truth" as "the name of the ideal movement which discourse introduces into reality."[9] In other words, "truth" is to be sought in a particular subject's efforts to say the unsayable: that is the real of desire and *jouissance*. In such a context it makes logical sense that the phallic signifier—as the first pure signifier of difference—will not be represented as a figure but will be experienced as an effect whose referent is the name of the father. Throughout life human beings are plagued by intimations of similar versus the same. As one grasps the degree to which language-perception-identity are in-mixed, it makes sense that Lacan positions the phallus as the repressed third term in human relations around which frames of all kinds are built.

Insofar as repressions continually spurt out as spontaneous and pri-

[9]Jacques Lacan, "Intervention on Transference" (1952), in *Feminine Sexuality: Jacques Lacan and the Ecole Freudienne*, ed. Juliet Mitchell and Jacqueline Rose, trans. Jacqueline Rose (New York: Norton, 1985), 63.

mordial identifications (*Wahrnehmung*) and in the form of conceptual memories (*Bewusstsein*) as well, repression, seen as the desire not to know, is the means by which representations mark synchronic memories with diachronic traces (*Vorbewusstsein*). In this purview, repression cannot be separated from any question of meaning or being—biological, philosophical, or sexual.[10] Lacan's notion of the real, which poststructuralists reject, starts from the idea that conscious knowledge is linked to a preconscious (Freud's *Vorbewusstsein*). That is, each person's memory is structured by groups of related elements forming covariant ensembles that enter into associative (imaginary, symbolic, real) sets. These function by relations that can be valued logically but not by literalist linguistic moves, literal sex acts, or any biological first cause, developmental or otherwise. Nor can these sets be valued by any theory that separates language from desire, human suffering, and sexual difference. While we are all familiar with Lacan's transformation of the still classical biological Freud into a Freud whose unconscious is structured as or like a language (although this formula is generally misunderstood), many are not so familiar with Lacan's idea that language and desire are intimately intricated from the start of life. By adding the voice, the gaze, the phoneme, the "nothing," and the (imaginary) phallus to Freud's primordial objects—the breast and feces—Lacan derived an answer to how perception could reside in an unconscious system in the first place. Seeing and hearing are incorporated as desired/desiring objects: the voice and the gaze. Lacan answered Jean Piaget and other genetic materialists who seek a primary organizing principle in biology. If sensory organs are linked to objects of desire, separable from their organic function, they connect identity and mentality to the effects of language and desire *from outside the biological organism.*

If Lacan is correct in teaching that memory dwells on a plurality of registers, functioning differently on different planes, it makes sense that unconscious memories would determine what we call conscious life. If this maneuver were transparent to us, we would not have spent centuries searching for certain answers. Instead, we would long since have accepted what was for Lacan obvious: that we think by substitutions and displacements, and referentiality is on the side of *aphanisis.* With our own memory bases hidden from us, how can we consider that unconscious assumptions stand behind conscious ones, positioned a bit askew? One sees why consciousness-bound theories must reflect the idea of a logic to language based on its communicative, aesthetic, or

[10]Jacques Lacan, *Le séminaire,* book 3: *Les psychoses* (1955–56), text established by Jacques-Alain Miller (Paris: Seuil, 1981), 202–4.

deconstructable potential. By cross-referencing within a closed book, such theories refuse to consider that nonlinear memory associations have a powerful logic of their own. Yet any theory that discounts the possibility of a "material" unconscious will have to seek a way out of the Saussurean impasse—where the signified inexplicably precedes the signifier—but only by dismissing any formative role played by language, desire, cultural myth, the power of names and naming within histories of ideals and by ignoring the enigmas posed by poetic speech, dreams, schizophrenic language, art, to name a few.

Lacan argued that Freud's genius was to track the source of language back to dreams, fantasies, and psychotic hallucinations.[11] Here, one sees the transformative effects produced by language—where *mot* has become *parole*, "speech, an act"—incorporated into being such that language gives the concrete specificity to desire that will determine any person's fate and will subjectivize all perception. Language, is, in this sense, material because words are desiring acts that both produce and arise from effects caused by the world outside the biological body. *The American Heritage Dictionary* (1976) derives *material* from Middle English *matere* and Old French and Latin *materia*. It means substance that occupies space and has weight, that constitutes the observable universe, and that together with energy forms the basis of objective phenomena. Lacan redefined the word *écrit* to mean that language has weight and motion, that there is an energy in language which cannot be directly read in words or sounds. That some*thing*—the real or *jouissance*—would not be seen as an apolitical concept.

In Lacan's rereading of Freud, an imaginary (identificatory) order of perception suffuses the symbolic (cultural) order, thus protecting men and women alike from direct knowledge of the real. Such a theory suggests that feminism, psychoanalysis, and politics may not be intrinsically at odds. One might well view history as arising out of collectivities of unconscious desires as they write the life stories of individual wills to power. The raison d'être of cultural history would resemble the enigmatic veil any analyst first confronts, an analysand's confusions about his or her life. The repetitive inertia of suffering Lacan called real *jouissance* commands a person's life, although one cannot voice the cause. In analysis the detritus of archaic memories, myths, identifications, fantasies, traumatic experiences, and so on is chopped away piece by piece from the ego's illusion of being a solid, unified identity. Here, the analyst's desire acts as a phallic third term whose analytic function is to dismantle imaginary assumptions.

[11]Jacques Lacan, "Propos sur la causalité psychique," *Ecrits*, 151–92.

Ellie Ragland-Sullivan

In any analysis of a subject or critique of ideology, Lacan's teaching would point to key signifiers that totalize a field and look for founding myths. The *Ur*-myth is the oedipal one, and its generic name is the phallus. But Lacan turned this Freudian notion into an understanding of how dyads are imaginarily ordered and why triads cause instability in dyadic relations. By removing this drama from the realm of biological first cause (a genital drive constituting the need for an incest taboo, and a fear of literal castration), Lacan takes Freud's use of this myth onto other grounds. There is no totalized genital drive, no literal castration anxiety. Instead, subjects respond to voices, gazes, the fear of a void. The haunting other or the *Unheimlich* tell stories of narcissistic joy threatened by the loss of attention that places anxiety in ego responses. "Powerful" egos tell stories of aggressive retaliation in response to the loss of a fantasized perfection. Those who assume positions of moral rectitude can snarl when questioned. In Lacanian terms such oedipal effects are not generally recognized for what they are. The imaginary order ensures that misrecognition and idealization be mutual correlatives. I would go farther and argue that the Lacanian imaginary is analogous to what Marxists call "false consciousness." But the Lacanian concept reverses the sense of falseness—much as it questions Winnicott's idea of a true or false self—by viewing it as *méconnaissance.* Slavoj Žižek has rephrased the Lacanian version of "false consciousness" to read: "They [citizens] know very well what they are doing and, nonetheless, they are doing it anyway."[12]

Žižek's formulation poses the question of why people rationalize their actions when they know at some level just what they are doing. Are "they"—ordinary women and men, political leftists and rightists, homosexuals and heterosexuals, poor people and rich superstars, and all the shadings along the binary spectrum—evil, naïve, stupid, petrified matter? Perhaps Lacan is right about ego, that its structure is that of exclusion. The structure of ego demand would then always be a demand for love—a "mirror, mirror on the wall" constellation. If indeed each subject works from a posture of would-be-totalizing narcissism, then it is logical to point to the imaginary closure through which subjects idealize themselves by building illusions of progress—personal, social, political, intellectual—despite the realities of repetitive failures, vain pretenses, and tarnished dreams that not only characterize individuals but also point to a malaise in civilization which links things as far apart as the history of holocausts and the preverbal infant Saint Augustine

[12]Slavoj Žižek, "Sur le pouvoir politique et les mécanismes idéologiques," *Ornicar?* (Fall 1985), 41. Unless otherwise noted, all translations in this essay are mine.

described, who had murder in his eyes when a newborn sibling usurped their mother's breast. Put another way, a structural lack inherent in conscious life pushes individual subjects to justify their existence by choosing a position of superiority. Even the most debased position can be rationalized as correct, superior, moral. If one can believe that both personal and social ideals function to screen out the knowledge of human fragility and to deny human desire and narcissism and that these are fundamental motivating forces in being, it becomes easier to explain the persistence of human aggression in physical or verbal acts. More particularly, masculinist violence and blind grandiosity lie behind wars and ideological crusades as well as at the heart of "the battle between the sexes." If, indeed, masculine identity derives from a double-bind or paradoxical dilemma that places his *jouissance* in the plight of mastering its own prohibitions, then it is not so strange to think that all relations (positioned toward the phallus) are power relations. But a dialectical antagonism marks the masculine position long before any such conflicts are projected onto others and acted out within interpersonal or sociocultural arenas.

Lacan called the Other an ideal worker. It toils twenty-four hours a day and never takes a rest. In this view there is a tireless unconscious foundation behind all human efforts. It is not surprising that Lacan would describe ego closure, quests for meaning, the search for final solutions as necessary attempts to close out the Other, whose interference in conscious life is felt in a range of affects, including anxiety, confusion, frustration. That subjects would combat this "enemy within" by denying its existence through acts of religious faith or by undermining meaning itself through skeptical theories or pluralistic panoplies of varied sorts is not surprising. Whether motivated at the individual or group level, the goal of imaginary perception is to reject Otherness, thus affirming by denial. Moreover, to eradicate the uncertainty and instability introduced by others, the signifier *tu*, human subjects tend to avoid, ignore, or, at the limit, annihilate said others. Such totalizing propensities obtain as much for kindergarten cliques as for the Hitler Youth, the Mao-inspired Red Guard, or any system of thought or action which espouses a final solution to human problems through imposition of one ideology on another.

One could say that the subject of the imaginary order—the ego—is innocent in its drive toward wholeness. But the cost is the death of thought. For if being right is more important than carrying on the debate, then mental ossification takes over. Yet it is not astounding that people defend their egos at all cost. Fixed at an early age, objectlike, unified by a few repetitious themes, the ego plays a death-giving role in the human arena of exchange because its very structure requires that it resist challenges to its "essence." An internal battle between one's own narcissism and the Other's desire is already dialectical. But this tension finds myriad oases in transference relations where certain others reflect desirable ego ideals and hark (back)forward to acceptable ideal signifiers. When disagreements arise, one sees that denial, blame, love, lies, idealizations constitute human beings as subjects who seek to avoid knowing the structural ordering of desire behind their passions.

To answer Slavoj Žižek's question—If they know what they are doing, why do they do it anyway?—one might suggest that the Other (perforated by *das Ding*) causes them to do it anyway. Repression keeps people from being psychotic, from being swallowed by their Other discourse, and allows an economy of psychic drive based on not knowing. But repression also exacts a price. The ego is a repressive formation whose structure places a paradox at the heart of desire. Narcissistic smugness or aggressive retaliation are so basic to human mentality that no moral or political solution can finally prevent all violence, aggression, or injustice. The power of *méconnaissance*, whose goal is to close out knowledge of lack, cannot but cause humans to function in terms of the three passions Lacan attributes to this structure: love (idealization), hate (denigration), and ignorance (believing that what one knows is what there is to know). For if the battleground of life *is us* as Lacan (after Freud) argued, then no Marxist idealized humanitarian state, no Derridean deconstructive exploding of logocentrism, no semiotic mapping of sign systems has the theoretical or methodological tools to stop a subject from being used by language and, subsequently, lived by "letters" that are only apparently dead or forgotten.

Although the current fetishization of binarism has elevated literary and philosophical problems to a certain level of obvious impasse— because first principles are not directly ascertainable in writing or within systems, nor are they empirically provable—such realizations are not in and of themselves able to cause change. In Lacan's view, words constitute idea packets to which people cling with the life or death fervor that he attributed to imaginary identifications, unconscious desire (positioned toward phallic signification) and real effects *cum* blockages as they circumscribe being and knowing. No feminist or political theoretician will succeed, then, in dismantling the real power implicit in the impasses, singular desires, or ego fictions that emanate from the unconscious merely by using tactics of oscillating ambiguity aimed at smashing the binary. Although both Marx and Derrida gave great consideration to the issue of how meaning is made, neither sought to understand why the binary or the dialectic has such power in the first place. Certainly, neither spoke of an agent of dividing (a phallic third term) or of an unconscious subject of desire.

The Lacanian first cause—the *objet a* or the *points de capiton* of the real—shows up as a linkage of *jouissance* to a signifier of a father's name which knots the imaginary, symbolic, and real to each other. Any subject's desire emanates from this topological structure from which various kinds of discourse issue. Thus, although Derrida critiqued binarism, he remains imprisoned within writing because he considers nothing beyond a certain concept of the text or narrative. Those Marxists who leave the personal (the imaginary) out of their theories fail to go beyond economic injustices in their explanations of where violence comes from. Lacan's addition of the imaginary and real to other cultural (symbolic) systems (linguistic, economic, etc.) gives us the tools to go farther than we already have in our understanding of the causes of violence. If, as Lacan argued, a topological structure gives rise to problems of encounters and impasses concerning difference for any subject and if these differences are structured asymmetrically between the feminine and the masculine, it follows that no simple method or historical rendering will account for a subject who is centered in different orders simultaneously but contradictorily. Lacan had no need to reduce the unconscious to style or to flatten perception out into generic language forms or rhetorical strategies. Instead, unconscious desire infuses any subject who, in turn, signifies various messages, depending on whether the imaginary, symbolic, or real is in command.

The primary signifying chain of unconscious knowledge which Lacan placed behind all the orders places specific effects in the human body and in being and discourse. This chain works both cumulatively and retroactively as a place from which to "read" a subject's desire. But it is not to be confused with grammar, which obscures its own roots in this imagistic/verbal chain of meaning ensembles which puts words to work. Moreover, Lacan's unconscious signifying chain is not linear but made up of the three orders (the Borromean knot) as they chain around a palpable void. Such theories do not easily enter an academic arena. Based on the analytic clinic, Lacan's ideas find their best proof within the clinic, where symptoms, transference, separation of fantasy from symptom, and so on show that ego closure can be detonated and can give way to the naming and creation of desire. Indeed, the goal of this clinic is not so different from that of politically concerned academics: to place a question where an answer had previously stopped up any knowledge of lack (anxiety).

Although one cannot readily invoke clinical data in a university discourse, one can argue that language functions to reconstitute an imaginary ego (and body) with the goal of negotiating desire, evoking responses in others, and restating our own unanswered questions regarding our worth. Such use of language will always exceed the pragmatic and utilitarian and will always already be material (its body residing in the primary representations Lacan called *objet a*). If language (Descartes's *intuitus*) is the medium of human exchange through which illusion, *méconnaissance,* and desiring intentionality all thread their way, placing the unconscious (Descartes's *res extensa*) in conscious life and everyday use of language, then a certain materiality of the "letter" resides in every extended use of language. Unconscious desire emanates not from a concatenation of sounds but from an absent discourse. In Lacanian terms, *we are spoken.* In his homage to Marguerite Duras, Lacan wrote that in her fiction "the practice of the letter converges with the usage of the unconscious." That is, an intrication of Lacan's orders reveals language as neither static, linear, simply narrative nor easily centered. Indeed, in the same essay Lacan described the center as "what is not the same on all the surfaces."[13]

One of Lacan's original contributions to any theory of meaning is the idea that the ego is primordially stitched together to close out knowledge of unconscious desire. If he is right, any theory of social justice must start its reforms at the very beginning of infant life and before. But even radical restructuration of social myths and familial use of language—if these were possible—would still not touch the fact that alien desire lives us—actively—with no regard for our humanity or will. It is hard to know which of these ideas is more threatening: that we are spoken by an unconscious or that we should tamper with family myths, gender fictions, political ideologies, and so on. Both ideas call forth cries of determinism, individual rights, ethical freedom, if not outright disbelief. Human subjects do not like to imagine that they are (or can be) "programmed," that their desire or intentionality may not be theirs to start with.

Lacan's theory of what lies beyond the ego takes into account a third term—a phallic effect—that gives rise to a fourth party (the Other). This fourth party skews the binary oppositions (male/female, Eros/Thanatos, homosexual/heterosexual, etc.) that one takes at face value, without asking why these should be oppositional in the first place. Certainly we do not ask ourselves if narcissism and desire hook up with each other to make each of us a power structure unto itself, a mini-nation-state that functions in response to commands that seem "out

---

[13]Jacques Lacan, "Hommage fait à Marguerite Duras, du ravissement de Lol V. Stein," *Ornicar?* (Fall 1985), 9 (my translation).

there" but are really "in here." If, indeed, an invisible real—in the order of an object or obstacle—operates mentality and identity, how can any comprehensive feminism not take this possibility into account? For if Freud's discovery of an unconscious continent behind conscious awareness accounts for dreams, literary masterpieces, infantile sexuality, neurotic symptoms, not to mention the other enigmas Lacan linked to an unconscious discourse, then such a discovery is truly a cut in the knowledge of Western civilization.[14]

Lacan attributed the creation of an unconscious source of knowledge to what he called castration: the eclipse of the subject by the signifier when the subject encounters language. We remember that he named the agent of this castration the phallic signifier. "The phallus is the conjunction of this parasite, the little piece of tail in question, with the function of the word."[15] But there are also prephallic agents of separation, the *objets a* of desire. These agents of disjunction all have the character of being perceptually detachable, thereby introducing loss into infant perception by the *fort-da* nature of their appearance. The *objet a* resides on the side of the *Vorstellungsrepräsentanz*, structuring infant perception as an oscillation between being and nothingness, making of the subject a material object where language and desire coalesce, and sometimes produce traumatic effects (the real).

One of these primordial *objets a* is the imaginary phallus. In the 1960s Luce Irigaray and other French feminists, all influenced by Jacques Derrida, labeled Lacan a phallocentric thinker. In the 1970s many American poststructuralist feminists have taken up these same views, mistaking Lacan's elaboration of his concept of the phallus for Freud's penis. By making the literal equation of penis = male = phallus, these feminists missed two points crucial to Lacan's innovations here. The phallus is only ever a penis in the imaginary order, the order in which the body is imagized. Moreover, all the *objets a* have the property of seeming detachable or separable from the body. It is because of this feature of the penis/phallus that Lacan described this symbol as a third term, neither male or female. By linking this misconception of penis/ phallus to Lacan's statement that there is a phallic signifier at the origin of law, language, and the unconscious, these feminists understandably thought we had returned to a Freudian biological reductionism. Lacan, on the contrary, thought he had stumbled on the perceptual confusion that had given rise in part to patriarchies at all. Indeed, he argued that

---

[14]Jacques-Alain Miller, "Remarks on the Teachings of Jacques Lacan," paper given to the Psychoanalytic Interest Workshop (directed by Peter Homans and Bertram Cohler) at the University of Chicago, March 1986.

[15]Aubert, *Joyce avec Lacan*, 40–41.

Ellie Ragland-Sullivan

Freud intuited this concept by saying that there is only one libido, that of the male. While poststructuralist feminists have linked this statement from *Séminaire*, book 20 (*Encore*), to Lacan's description of woman as "not all," represented by a minus sign, Lacan points out that Freud's enigmatic one libido refers to the phallus as the first countable signifier of difference.[16] Lacan's argument regarding woman has also been misread by many feminists as a simplistic dismissal of the female sex. Lacan's thinking here is complex as he argues that there is no one symbol for sexual difference that is symmetrical to the penis for children first interpreting their bodies. In this sense girls are not re-presented in the unconscious by one symbol, but are more diffusely equated with the Otherness that dwells on the side of unconscious "truth," with what is palpable and enigmatic but lacking as a certainty in conscious knowledge.

For Lacan, woman as a category is perceptually opposed to the phallic signifier. While the phallic signifier denotes the masculine (not necessarily a male), woman is associated with the problematic of the unconscious, with the knowledge of something unknown or unknowable within language and consciousness. But, argued Lacan, woman is not an essence. She is not *all*, the totality of being that would end all quests. Although woman is a signifier and can, thus, be represented as a class, she is not the source of plenitude delineated in myth (and, within that context, worshiped as a goddess, a wooden image, a person, and, conversely, denigrated, humiliated, and mistreated). The masculinist essentialization of woman in the name of the problematic of lack and repression is no favor, if one reads Lacan.

But woman is always associated with the corporeal, for the primordial maternal phantasmal *objet a* serves as the material lining (*doublure*) of the subject which infers a structure (ordering) in being. Where a *rencontre* has occurred, said Lacan—that is, a perceptual meeting between infant and image or sound—there is evidence of a priority because an "aftereffect" remains. But one cannot reconstitute the prior. It makes sense that woman, as primordial natural signifier, has a closer perceptual proximity to the desire that cannot be separated from the corporeal (gaze and voice as crucial as breast or feces). But Lacan has displaced Freudian desire from wish fulfillment to ontologize biology and libidinize philosophy. The Freudian thing has become Hegelian—"the time of the thing"—and Kantian—*das Ding an sich*. Hegel's time is turned into childhood time, inferred into adult life. Kant's *das Ding*

---

[16]Jacques Lacan, *Le séminaire*, book 20: *Encore* (1972–73), text established by Jacques-Alain Miller (Paris: Seuil, 1975), 75.

has become the negative kernel of real *jouissance* which limits a subject because it is both unassimilable and unsymbolized but exists as a knot in the Other; thus clearly, it is there all the same. "It"—the "thing"—is no longer an object, no literal breast, pleasure, fantasy, or instinctual drive. It is, instead, that closed-off part of being which is inseparable from knowing. "It" speaks as a real *savoir* on *jouis-sens* (bliss and suffering) and keeps subjects locked in double binds.

But what does any of this have to do with the mother or a materiality of language? In *Séminaire*, book 7 (*L'éthique de la psychanalyse*), Lacan argued that the Cathars had taken the problem of materiality and desire to its extreme in deciding that flesh and sexual temptation were the source of evil. In an effort to become pure—that is, spirit separated from body—they based their twelfth-century Catholic heresy on the interdiction of generation. If flesh is inherently sinful, they argued, then begetting more flesh perpetuates the devil as the creator of matter.[17] In retrospect such unorthodoxy becomes proof of the problem posed by generating desire out of elemental blocks of the mother's perceived (and felt) body. In Lacan's purview incest is no longer only a literal act but also the haunting images, identificatory nostalgia, sensory longings, and claustrophobic desires related to voices, words, images, smells, bodies. In this context the mother is the natural signifier for desire, while the father's name offers a measure of distance, the mediation of language, as a phallic third term of flight, escape, or mastery, away from a profound source of affect.

The Lacanian thing, then, is the subject's "truth" fading from the unconscious bank of material memories, the impasses of sexuality, that mark that subject. Truth limps, Lacan said, and speaks partially, in symptoms and enigmatic dreams, always in reference to the real fragments that underlie metaphorical substitutions. The *objet a* of desire points to slits and openings to infer "drive" into daily life in a continual metonymic movement. But Lacan's arguments for a materiality of being are strangely closer to the theological/philosophical quests of centuries past than they are to the modern-day materialisms that from the eighteenth century onward have characterized Western explanations of what constitutes matter, be they sensualist, economic, capitalist, cybernetic, sociobiological, or neurobiological. In *Séminaire*, book 7, Lacan pointed out that the issue of matter (*la vieille langue materielle*) is that around which all ancient philosophy turns. "All Aristotelian philosophy must be thought—and it is for that reason that it is so

[17]Jacques Lacan, *Le séminaire*, book 7: *L'éthique de la psychanalyse* (1959–60), text established by Jacques-Alain Miller (Paris: Seuil, 1986), 149–50.

Ellie Ragland-Sullivan

difficult for us to think it—according to a mode which never omits that *mater (la matière)* is eternal, and that nothing is made from nothing." Paradoxically, the only believers were the eighteenth-century materialists (La Mettrie's man machine, etc.). "Their God is matter" ("I am what I am").[18]

In *Séminaire*, book 7, Lacan also set up the basis for his later reinterpretation of Freud's death drive. "Very well, one can say that the step made by Freud at the level of the pleasure principle is this: It is to show us that there is no sovereign good [in Aristotle's sense of 'the good'], that the sovereign good which is *das Ding*, which is the mother, who is the object of incest, is a forbidden good, and that there is no other good. Such is the foundation, reversed by Freud, or moral law." This bedrock material—*la dite maternelle*—gives a timing to the maturation of desire and underlies all subsequent use of knowledge as the *Vorstellungen*, which "from the beginning and already [are] at the origin [and] have the character of a signifying structure."[19] This meaning is to be sought later not only in language but especially in the structure of desire, because whatever has structure has meaning in Lacan's view.

But if *la dite maternelle* is an irretrievable part of "la chose freudienne," should we not view the oedipal structure from another viewpoint, as a Derridean, Heisenbergian, Gödelian, or hermeneutic impasse? Should we not simply agree to accept Derrida's injunction that we deconstruct or Gödel's undecidability theorem or simply the chestnut of the liar's paradox, rather than Lacan's injunction to us to restructure, in part (or in parts)? One can easily argue that reconstruction involves only the clinic. But such an argument would ignore that Lacan's teaching postulates an unconscious subjectivity behind all knowledge and language which keeps all systems from complete closure. Moreover, the *objets a* speak and can be decoded in bits and pieces. To choose the neoskeptical deconstructive solution regarding first principles enjoins us to dismiss from theory what we have learned from Freud and Lacan about dreams, jokes, symptoms, fantasy, psychosis, intentionality, narcissism, the real, not to mention the tautology of discourse, and so on. Lacan (after Freud) taught us how to read back into the *savoir*, desire and *jouissance* that cycles and recycles within generational sets

---

[18]Ibid., 27, 21 January 1960, p. 146. In "On God and Grammar: 'God Is a Verb'" Claude E. Midgette describes how Moses questioned God as to his identity. In Exodus God told Moses to say to the Hebrew people: I AM has sent me to you" (3:14, Revised Standard Version). In Hebrew *Eheyeh asher Eheyeh* is written, *Eheyeh* being the first person of the imperfect tense of the verb "to be." Cf. also Nietzsche's "eternal return," and Shakespeare's *King Lear* when King Lear speaks to Cordelia, telling her that nothing comes from nothing.

[19]Lacan, *Le séminaire*, book 7, 16 December 1959, p. 85, 3 February 1960, p. 165.

of cultural and familial myths, ideals, names, and claustrophobic aspirations.

But if deconstructive feminisms do not, indeed, go far enough in assessing first-cause issues, has Julia Kristeva not solved the problem by viewing writing as a material act that is both transgressive and sexual? Although Kristeva has accepted the Lacanian idea that writing (and interpreting) appropriate desire, her texts, in my view, risk equating the unconscious with the symbolic. Any such equation of desire with language ignores Lacan's theory of the topology of the subject. As we have said, subject (unconscious) desire is not only substitutive but also positioned differently, often contradictorily, in the different orders. Who is speaking to whom and from where? Freud did not realize that desire was substitutive. Lacan did, but Lacan did not view desire as infinitely substitutive. In my reading of Lacan, desire, like writing or fantasies, fills up lack, making it appear that there is no lack. Thus, writing could not appropriate desire in a one-to-one way since writing is itself one more substitution that tries to re-present and negotiate the impasses of one's own desire aimed at the Other via others.

Lacan picked up where Freud left off, proposing a single and unifying first principle at the heart of human subjectivity.[20] The phallic signifier links language to repression and representation, giving rise to a logic of the signifier in which an unconscious signifying chain constitutes material inscribed in the other which builds a bridge between all conscious and unconscious life. The reason for choosing the word *phallus* becomes less susceptible of a sexist interpretation if one views language as playing both a material (causative) and functional role in the attribution of identity, correlated by the mother's desire in reference to the father's name. Although the inmixing of the imaginary and real in language give it "affective" body—materiality—the symbolic order separates human beings from other animals. That is, because a memory bank from which we draw our language and perceptions is subtracted from conscious knowledge and discourse—although not wholly absent as a referential base—the ego and grammar system can exist as seemingly autonomous entities because the causes of difference are hidden. Both language and ego seem to build a frame inside which one is framed. But by adding the theory that difference exists in reference to an invisible third term, whose effects are palpable, Lacan hypothesized that inside/outside distinctions are only imaginary monuments based on confusing the bodily organism with the imaginary images it spawns.

[20]Ellie Ragland-Sullivan, *Jacques Lacan and the Philosophy of Psychoanalysis* (Urbana: University of Illinois Press, 1986), 216.

Ellie Ragland-Sullivan

When poststructuralist feminists debunk Lacan for offering them nothing, they would do better to consider Lacan's topological concept of subject structure. Although Derrida's *différance* recognizes the absence of irretrievable traces within a present moment, such a concept paradoxically closes off the terrain it opens up by treating it merely hypothetically. Poststructuralist feminism is left holding a Heideggerian vase whose emptiness cannot be valorized, whose inscribed traces have no power. But what if the Derridean idea of an absence that is not really one were seen as yet one more mental construct that fills up a gap that is real-ly present, a gap whose symptoms appear in enigmatic statements, in affect, in anxiety, in dreams, in repetitions, in the vagaries of desire, in power plays and ploys, in the pluralisms of interpretation, and in the subjectivity of human perception and discourse? Any political theory that relies on either/or-but/and strategies as final words of a supposed nonmastery that is one, elevates pluralism to a sacred position of insight, much as classical Marxists elevated the "people" (*peuple, Volk*) to a similar position of supposed "ignorant wisdom." By using only strategies designed to dismantle language into traces, deconstructionists have done their work. But if one wants to know how language acts as a *living material* that spurs individuals to violence, narcissistic aggrandizement, love, and so on, then one cannot dismiss the inert powers of metonymy or the discourse structures to which it gives rise.[21] Metonymy enables metaphor to retain a double functioning—as ego, for example—because, Lacan maintained, opposites are never simply interchangeable, except as abstract attributes.

The third term—just out of the conscious grasp—determines that no element, whether similar or antithetical, can be reduced to the same, for the specificity of each person's being and knowledge issues from the concrete but not from hypothetical notions of the aesthetic. Lacan's theory of an overlap between the orders of the symbolic and the real declares that language never works only in a linear or simply oppositional way. Theoretical and practical consequences of a Lacanian psychoanalysis for feminism are that neither language, gender, power, patriarchy, nor the symbolic can be equated to each other in any one-to-one way. If they do not or cannot say why or how language exercises power or negotiates narcissism or desire, poststructuralist feminists are left in a phenomenological impasse where men and women are framed within a masquerade they can only describe but not really analyze. For instance, an equation of the feminine with the passive, receptive Nietzschean *page blanche* and the masculine with *écriture* or institutional-

[21]Lacan, *Le séminaire*, book 20, "A Jacobson," 19–27.

ism perpetuates the myth that the difference between the sexes is only a poetics and not a politics.

Rather than argue that the difference between the sexes makes no difference, Lacan declared that the difference is crucial in all aspects of personal and cultural life. Moreover, his formula of woman as "not all" does not equate her with Derrida's no-thing. Lacan hypothesized that sexual difference derives from a representational interpretation of one anatomical symbol that sends both men and women in search of ideals or totalities to complete a partial picture. The twist in Lacan's concept of the oedipal structure is new, although Lacan claims evidence for it in Freud's *Totem and Taboo* and *Moses and Monotheism*. The function of the symbolic father—identified with law—is to attenuate the desire of the mother as primordial omnipotent other.[22] The incest taboo, unexpectedly, does not arise from a moral horror at the idea of copulation with one's own mother, but from a "turning toward the father." Both sons and daughters first identify with the mother's body, being, and desire. As they begin to splinter this identificatory mirror of illusory Oneness, they are castrated, that is, they enter into the order of language and law. The mother and/or father who do not point a child away from identification with the mother place a major representational deficit in the unconscious: the foreclosure of a signifier for a father's name, a foreclosure that heralds psychosis. The incest taboo is, therefore, not a prohibition against the mother's body per se, but an injunction to identify with the cultural order, which represents difference or otherness or individuation.

The turn toward the father—*père-version*—is a normative orientation, a structuration of love and desire on the side of taboo (prohibition) rather than on the side of permission (access to the mother). In "Freud's Problem of Identification," Russell Grigg writes: "Love relates to the father by virtue of the father's being the vehicle of castration. This is what Freud proposes in *Totem and Taboo*. It is insofar as the sons are deprived of women that they love the father—a bewildering remark that is sanctioned by the insight of a Freud."[23] On the maternal side the primordial objects of desire resonate powerfully throughout life, and reappear as concrete fragments in poetry, painting, psychic or physical symptoms, as hallucinatory material in dreams or psychosis, and in fantasies. Thus, the primordial objects of desire are not themselves signifiers but libidinal material that surges forth in fantasies, words,

---

[22]Russell Grigg, "Freud's Problem of Identification," *Newsletter of the Freudian Field*, 1 (Spring 1987), 14.

[23]Grigg, "Freud's Problem of Identification," 20 n. 8. Cf. *Le séminaire*, book 23 (1975–76), unpublished; *Le sinthome*, published in *Ornicar?* (Winter 1977), 7.

and actions to create enigmas that give an unquantifiable quality to human re-presentations. Since the *objets a* are not the partial objects (of object-relations theory) that refer to a unified totality but objects that partially represent the function that produced them in the first place, these objects function in a way that escapes conscious understanding. Their relationship to the subject turns around an edge or a cut such as the lips, the anus, a glance, and so on.[24]

Such a concept of a materiality in language and identification is new. Indeed, how can a perceived image of an elephant or breast become concrete, a "letter" in the order of an object? Centuries ago Aristotle said that the first of the four "first causes" is the material one, what things are made of. Modern science claims to have answered Aristotle for all time by reducing matter to physically visible properties of biology (human beings) or physics (the universe). We are familiar with poststructuralist answers to Aristotle, with the idea that the translation of one language into another shows that the materiality of language is a figural or rhetorical issue, that the logos is the word. Lacan gave an answer to the problematic of first causes different from Derrida's. The symbol, redefined by Lacan as "an everlasting possession," is that which ultimately permits human beings to speak (and later write).[25] But it is not a second or double meaning. For Lacan the symbol is a "letter" in the order of an object, an irreducible unit of meaning. Everything in the unconscious is put there by symbolization and its effects. Thus, Lacan called symbols the lowest common multiples to which all language will later refer. It follows that primary symbols will play a crucial role in structuring (ordering) subject functions (narcissism, aggressiveness, desire, discourse intentionality, love and so on). The first symbols—re-presented images and effects—take on meaning in relation to objects of desire. First, imaginary and real material infers a materiality into language that will give it density, weight, and richness at the levels of effect and affect, where body and language are joined by the "letter" of *l'être*.

Language is material, second, because it can be transformed through the plasticity of its own metaphorical properties. Such transformations—substitutions—produce a metonymy that is language itself. Freud called this veering off of meaning the unconscious or repression. Lacan called it the littoral (where sea and coast meet). Third, language, in the shape of ideas, can change the world, and in this sense it has

[24]Bice Benvenuto and Roger Kennedy, *The Works of Jacques Lacan: An Introduction* (London: Free Association Books, 1986), 177, 176.

[25]Jacques Lacan, "The Function and Field of Speech and Language in Psychoanalysis," in *Ecrits: A Selection*, trans. Alan Sheridan (New York: Norton, 1977), 65.

political force. Finally, language is material because it is thought of as property that can be stolen as copyright laws and plagiarism cases indicate. Little children's squabbles over who owns a "favorite" song or story might offer further demonstration that language is material in the imaginary order. With these various ideas regarding a materiality of language Lacan has returned us to Freud's *Interpretation of Dreams* and pushed us forward to his own concept of a scansion of discourse. If, indeed, there is a primordial materiality of the subject that ancients, philosophers, theologians, cultists, and the romantics have chased since the beginning of recorded history, there may be a cause to consider Lacan's idea that human subjects are subjectivized by representations and desire long before they begin to imagine themselves as objectified by language and mind.

But subjects do not know they are material, other than biologically so. The phallic signifier divides the subject from conscious knowledge of its own roots. In the symbolic order, the phallus stands for social law and is seen in many cultures as a structuring cause—an encounter with the real—of which subjects are effects. Between the symbolic and the real one meets cultural desire regarding the masculine and the feminine. Between the imaginary and the symbolic phallic effects are felt as prohibitive words, as a superego. In this sense the phallus is a third term that stakes out the structure of an ideal ego, as well as the limits of anxiety and the causes of guilt. One could go farther and argue that the symbolic order is itself a third term that functions to smash imaginary fantasies and symbiotic collusions, opening the door to the play of retaliatory aggressivity in language, whether one refers to disagreements, derisions, or annihilative tactics.

When the phallus refers to an individual's unconscious desire, it joins the signifier on the side of the Other, although it is not "contained" within the Other except as an imaginary *objet a*. Lacan taught that subjects only have access to their repressed "truth"—cum unconscious desire—through the agency of a third term. When an analyst occupies this position, he or she is enjoined to function on the slope of the symbolic, not the imaginary. Only such "distance" can permit analysands to name their own unconscious desire—not some preconceived notion of the analyst's—and, then, to create new desire that suits them, rather than the analyst. One sees that language cannot be thought of as inherently patriarchal or matriarchal in this context. Only when a person's speech is correlated with desire, with law, with a voice or a gaze, does it take on overtones of sexual difference. One sees that Lacan did not teach that language was patriarchal, a system exclusive of women. Rather, he rethought the problematic of language, asking us to weigh its Pantagruelian properties. Not only did he transform it into living material that mediates desire, but he also gave it the paradoxical property of immunizing a subject against any "beyond" in his own knowledge and discourse. There is no metalanguage, said Lacan.[26]

If Lacan is correct in arguing that language alienates us, living us as if it were a mechanical god that cares little for our own "good," then any feminist psychoanalytic theory that wishes to change the order of things cannot ignore the scope of Lacan's arguments. The oppressiveness of the imaginary, the real of a hole in the Other, and the mediating potential of the symbolic (with its paradoxical alienating properties) must all be taken into account. By seeking to break out of imaginary impasses that characterize all group ideals, feminists will know how to position themselves toward the will to power or the demand for love that lurks behind the Nietzschean mask every person wears. The feminism I propose would find its power in a psychoanalytic study of first causes. It would avoid the exclusivity and rigidity of imaginary gluing that marks any dogma that grows out of a conviction of being right. Such a feminism would—as Lacan did—see the ego as an enemy to itself and to efforts to change things as well. Such a feminism would question the deconstructive Lacan currently in vogue with the psychoanalytic Lacan who cared about suffering and who elevated desire over reason and logos. The same man viewed the superego as "ferocious and obscene." He located the place of cure for psychic pain in an awakening and cultivation of the specificity of one's own desire.

But Lacan did not mean that anything goes. He taught that desire must be balanced by distance from one's childhood bogies and by developing the capacity to judge, by an ethics of psychoanalysis. Thus, the Lacanian feminism I describe would honor the Lacan respectful of the hysterics who beckoned Freud along the paths of the unconscious. Even though many of his followers made Lacan into their master, he placed his own discourse on the slope of the hysteric and the analyst. Indeed, his description of the "master discourse" points toward a use of language in which language becomes utilitarian and pragmatic insofar as its goal is masculinist and repressive: to deny the unconscious in its proximity to the feminine. Such denial is at the heart of patriarchy, as well as other discourses whose goal is closure, be it rejection of any Otherness in being or simply normative imaginary exclusivity.

If it is true, as Lacan taught, that the ego and language are themselves defenses against knowing what or who we are, one can see the implicit difficulties within—indeed the magnitude of—any struggle for personal or social freedom.

[26]Cf. Žižek, "Why Lacan Is Not a Post-structuralist."

4

Desire and Identification
in Lacan and Kristeva

Cynthia Chase

It is necessary to find the subject as a lost object. More precisely this lost object is the support of the subject and in many cases is a more abject thing than you may care to consider.

Jacques Lacan, 1966

En fin de compte je suis hégélien.

Paul de Man, 1982

The witty butcher's wife, or *la bouchère*, as Lacan calls her, is my favorite character—my favorite hieroglyph—in analytic literature. You may remember her from *The Interpretation of Dreams:* she is the witty hysteric who challenges Freud's theory of wish fulfillment with her dream that she wanted to give a dinner party but had nothing in the house but a piece of smoked salmon and her telephone was out of order and all the shops were closed.[1] *La belle bouchère*, the beautiful butcheress, and the beautiful stopper-upper:[2] Freud diagnoses

[1]Sigmund Freud, *The Interpretation of Dreams*, in *The Standard Edition of the Complete Psychological Works*, ed. and trans. James Strachey (London: Hogarth Press, 1953– 74), 4:146–51, hereafter cited in the text by page number.

[2]*Bouchère* carries both meanings: from *boucher*, masculine noun meaning "butcher," and from *boucher*, a transitive verb meaning to fill up (a gap), to stop (up), block, plug a hole." It is Catherine Clément, in *Vies et légendes de Jacques Lacan* (Paris: Grasset, 1981), who calls this patient of Freud's "la *belle* bouchère" (in part of chapter 3 subtitled "L'histoire de la belle bouchère, et le Desir de l'Autre"). This appellation implicitly links her case with the question of narcissism, which Freud in "On Narcissism: An Introduction" deems the characteristic form of object choice for "probably the purest and truest female type": the narcissistic woman, the beautiful woman (*Standard Edition*, 14:88– 90). Freud's description of feminine narcissism is one of his few departures from the characterization of feminine sexuality as a deficiency—as "penis envy." In naming the butcher's wife "beautiful," Clément is no doubt responsive to this aspect of Freud's essay

65

Cynthia Chase

her "need for an unfulfilled wish," Lacan her "desire for desire." That desire, no doubt, makes her memorable. You may remember her from Catherine Clément's *Lives and Legends of Jacques Lacan*, where she figures in a vivid and amused retelling of Lacan's reinterpretation of her dream in his essay "The Direction of the Treatment and the Principles of Its Power."[3] Lacan interprets the appearance of the smoked salmon in her dream as the fulfillment of the wish for identification with the phallus, with the signifier of desire. Lacan's flamboyant ritual gesture alludes to and repeats two others, those ritual gestures performed in the Eleusinian mysteries and at formal dinner parties, whereby the phallus, or *saumon à l'antique*, is revealed beneath a piece of gauze or a veil.[4] Clément's appropriation of this reading makes a striking ending to a story that begins with an instance of feminine "resistance" to a man's theory. What starts out as an ingenious dreamer's demurral to Freud's claim that all dreams fulfill wishes ends up as a celebrated tour de force of psychoanalytic theory: Lacan's claim that desire as such finds its signifier in the phallus, in a context reclaimed by a woman and a feminist (Clément) as evidence that Lacan draws his model of subjectivity from feminine sexuality. The witty butcher's wife, I submit, is a figure for the conversion of *resistance* to *theory*.[5]

As such she certainly provokes resistance, from theory or from those who would speak for theory, as well as from those who would speak for feminism. Coping with this figure, appreciating this character, self-indulgent as she seems precisely in her self-denials—she teases her husband to give her caviar sandwiches, she tells Freud, but also insists she doesn't want any—involves addressing two questions, denying oneself neither of them. One: How could the notion of a necessary

---

on narcissism, as well as to the fundamental link between the concept of narcissism and the problematic of desire and identification outlined in the story of the witty butcher's wife. (On the significance of Freud's figure of the narcissistic woman, see Sarah Kofman, *The Engima of Woman: Woman in Freud's Writings* [Ithaca: Cornell University Press, 1985].)

[3]Catherine Clément, *Lives and Legends of Jacques Lacan*, trans. Arthur Goldhammer (New York: Columbia University Press, 1983). Jacques Lacan, "La direction de la cure et les principes de son pouvoir," *Ecrits* (Paris: Seuil, 1966), "The Direction of the Treatment and the Principles of Its Power," *Ecrits: A Selection*, trans. Alan Sheridan (London: Tavistock, 1977), hereafter cited in the text by page number, the original text abbreviated *E*.

[4]Clément, *Lives*, 130.

[5]In "The Witty Butcher's Wife: Freud, Lacan, and the Conversion of Resistance to Theory," *MLN* 102 (December 1987), I elaborate ways in which interpretations of the witty butcher's wife reflect the resistance to theory within "theory" itself. Cf. Paul de Man, "The Resistance to Theory," in the volume of the same title (Minneapolis: University of Minnesota Press, 1986).

identification with the phallus or even the mere identification of the phallus as the signifier of desire form part of a feminist understanding of desire and meaning? This question has had groundbreaking responses from Juliet Mitchell, Jane Gallop, and Jacqueline Rose.[6] I would pose it again with regard not only to Lacan's work but to Julia Kristeva's, above all her retheorization of the mirror stage as "primary narcissism" involving an "immediate identification" with the imaginary father and "abjection" of the mother.[7] Two: how can such conditions for the emergence of the subject be understood as a genuinely *linguistic* predicament? You may remember the last two words: they're Paul de Man's.[8] Can such radically heterogeneous questions—But how is this feminist? and What is the linguistic predicament?—even be addressed in the same discourse? Strictly speaking, no doubt not, but I'm going to, for love of *la b.b.*

These questions come together, in fact, in reflection on three different readings of Hegel—Kristeva's, Lacan's, and Alexandre Kojève's. Lacan's reading of the dream of *la belle bouchère* belongs to the postwar reception in France of Hegel's *Phenomenology of Mind*, first translated and lectured on in the 1930s by Alexandre Kojève and Jean Hyppolite, and that reception of Hegel still orients Kristeva's interpretation of primary narcissism.[9] It is Lacan who first articulates a Freudian problematic in Hegelian terms. The inevitability of stating the universal category of the particular, the inevitability of stating an absolutely general "here" or "this" in the act of indicating a quite particular "here" or "this"—that analysis of the logical difficulty of the deictic or demonstrative function of language in chapter 1 of the *Phenomenology* underlies Lacan's account of desire, demand, and need. Those terms form the framework of Lacan's discussion of desire in the dream of *la belle bouchère*. Lacan interprets her relations toward her husband and her

[6]Juliet Mitchell, *Psychoanalysis and Feminism* (New York: Pantheon, 1974); Jane Gallop, *The Daughter's Seduction: Feminism and Psychoanalysis* (Ithaca: Cornell University Press, 1982); Jacqueline Rose, "Dora: Fragment of an Analysis," in *In Dora's Case: Freud, Hysteria, Feminism*, ed. Charles Bernheimer and Claire Kahane (New York: Columbia University Press, 1985), and the Introduction to *Feminine Sexuality: Jacques Lacan and the Ecole Freudienne*, ed. Juliet Mitchell and Jacqueline Rose (New York: Norton, 1983).

[7]Julia Kristeva, "L'abjet d'amour," *Tel Quel* 91 (1982), 91, 17–31; this text forms part of the first chapter of *Histoires d'amour* (Paris: Denoël, 1983). See also *Powers of Horror: An Essay on Abjection* (New York: Columbia, 1982)

[8]Paul de Man, *The Rhetoric of Romanticism* (New York: Columbia, 1984), 81.

[9]Alexandre Kojève, *Introduction to the Reading of Hegel: Lectures on "The Phenomenology of Spirit,"* assembled by Raymond Queneau, ed. Allan Bloom (Ithaca: Cornell University Press, 1980), hereafter cited in the text, published in French under the title *Introduction à la lecture de Hegel* (Paris: Gallimard, 1947).

woman friend in the light of those first desires and identifications that
Lacan carefully doesn't assimilate to the child's relations to mother and
father but that do imply specific relations to gender. Lacan does not
rewrite Hegel's analysis of the deictic function as a family romance.
Rather, he makes it possible and necessary to sketch the mediations
between the function he redefines as that of the *phallic* signifier and the
conditions of sexuality as they relate to gender. Those mediations are
sharply outlined in the recent work of Kristeva, which impinges in
another way too upon Hegel's analysis of deixis, for her interpretation
of primary narcissism casts it as an inaugural act of signification comparable to the deictic function and describes the tenuous conditions of
that inauguration. Rereading *la belle bouchère*'s dream as a replay of
primary narcissism, as I shall do here, sharpens its significance insofar
as such a reading brings out the critical meaning of Hegel's text,
namely, that meaning or signification depends on identification, on a
transference, a trope, with which the material conditions of language
are nonetheless incompatible.

Before considering how Kristeva's work inflects an essentially Hegelian account of the conditions of subjectivity, I want to describe how
Lacan's terms alter that account in changing the gender of the subject in
question. Among French readings of Hegel, Lacan's discussion of the
dream of the witty butcher's wife represents an important change of
style and a striking change of focus: from the master-slave dialectic
construed by Kojève as a fight between two men to a dialectic of desire
described by Lacan as an identification between two women.

Lacan's reading of Freud's interpretation of the dream of the witty
hysteric in chapter 4 of *The Interpretation of Dreams* recasts the concept of "anthropogenetic desire" elaborated in Kojève's introduction to
the reading of the *Phenomenology,* his "translation with commentary"
of Hegel's chapter 4, on the master-slave dialectic. Kojève begins by
defining not thought or contemplation but desire (in Hegel's text *das
Begehren*) as that which reveals man to himself as a subject, an *I*.
"Human desire, or better still, anthropogenetic desire, . . . is different
from animal desire . . . in that it is directed, not toward a real, 'positive,'
given object, but toward another Desire" (6). Kojève moves at once to
the unexceptionable example of "the relationship between a man and
woman." He writes, "Desire is human only if the one desires, not the
body, but the Desire of the other; if he wants 'to possess' or 'to assimilate' the Desire taken as Desire—that is to say if he wants to be 'desired'
or 'loved,' or, rather, 'recognized' in his human value" (6). What Lacan
will give new opacity in *his* phrase "the desire of the Other" was
invoked by Hyppolite as well as Kojève; Hyppolite wrote, in terms

luminously Hegelian in their abstraction, "The desire that constitutes the self can only exist if it is for itself an *object* of another desire. Thus the desire of life becomes the desire of another desire . . . [and] human desire is always *desire of the desire of another.*"[10] Kojève's distinctive gesture was to infer that "to speak of [such an] 'origin' of Self-Consciousness is necessarily to speak of a fight to the death for 'recognition.'" His move was to read literalistically the inference that starts off Hegel's section "Mastery and Slavery" and to subsume under that phase of the dialectic all the separate stages of consciousness of the *Phenomenology.*[11] How that inference—the deathly struggle for recognition—impinges on "the relationship between a man and a woman" was left to be worked out by René Girard, in *Deceit, Desire and the Novel.*[12] Kojève concentrates on the struggle for recognition that moves through the successive moments in which one man gives up the fight to preserve his life and so is constituted as the slave of the master; in which the master reaches an "existential impasse" since he is now recognized as master only by a slave, only by a thing, though his desire was directed not toward a thing but toward another desire; and in which, finally, the slave frees himself from the master through work, in which desire, "the negative-negating relation to the object, becomes a *form* of this object and gains permanence," a form in which "the working Consciousness" can "contemplate itself" (25).

Thus the desire that moves history, for Kojève, is the "desire for 'recognition.'" Lacan's reading of Freud on the dream of the butcher's wife echoes and inverts Kojève's key terms. The reading of the dream, the science of dream decipherment, shows, he writes, "that the dream is made for the recognition . . .—but our voice hangs fire before concluding—of desire. For desire, if Freud speaks truly and if analysis is necessary, is only grasped in the interpretation. But let us continue," Lacan goes on. "The elaboration of the dream is nourished by desire. Why does my voice fail to finish, *for recognition,* as if the second word was extinguished which, a little while ago the first, reabsorbed the

[10]Hyppolite quoted in Mark Poster, *Existential Marxism in Postwar France* (Princeton: Princeton University Press, 1975), 25.

[11]Cf. Poster, ibid. On Kojève's teaching of the *Phenomenology,* see also Michael S. Roth, *Psychoanalysis as History: Negation and Freedom in Freud* (Ithaca: Cornell University Press, 1987).

[12]René Girard, *Deceit, Desire, and the Novel: Self and Other in Literary Structure* (Baltimore: Johns Hopkins University Press, 1965). For another account of triagulated desire, see Eve Sedgwick, *Between Men: English Literature and Male Homosocial Desire* (New York: Columbia University Press, 1984). The shift in tonal register and conception of gender between Girard's book and Sedgwick's is even more exhilarating than the similar shift between Kojève's text and Lacan's.

other in its light" (260; *E* 623). A little while ago—in Lacan's previous sentence and in a previous controversial teaching, Kojève's—the opacity of desire was as if reabsorbed in the light of the word *recognition*; now—in this sentence, in this teaching—*recognition* is as if extinguished by the opacity of the word *desire*. Its opacity lies in the fact that desire is present in the dream as "fulfilled," not as revealed or recognized. The dream, Freud states, is a wish fulfillment, and as such it articulates a desire, writes Lacan, that is "is not assumed by the subject who says 'I' in his speech," since it is articulated in a mode with "no optative inflexion": "the aspect of the verb is that of the perfect, the fulfilled." "It is this ex-sistence"—Lacan wrenches that word of the moment into another shape, making it translate Freud's *Entstellung*, the dream's "distortion"—"it is this *Entstellung* of desire in the dream"— its articulation, its fulfillment—"that explains how the significance of the dream masks the desire that is present in it" (264; *E* 629). Such desire, identifying with signifiers, will not be a desire that reveals the subject to itself as "I." The goal of analysis cannot be "recognition," for Freud discovered the dream's structure, Lacan writes, "in a signifying flow . . . of which the subject does not even know where to pretend to be its organizer"; hence, "to make him *find* himself there as *desirer* is the inverse of making him *recognize* himself there as subject" (256; *E* 623).

Unlike the analysand's, the slave's subjection culminates in an "experience" of "value." Only in and by work," writes Kojève, "does man finally become aware of the *significance*, the *value*, and the *necessity* of his experience of fearing absolute power, . . . of the fight between Master and Slave and the risk and terror that it implies" (23). Other existentialist Marxists were alert to the dangerous hypostatization here. More radically, postexistential, *analytical* reading of Hegel questions the consistency between *value* and *meaning* ("significance") and between *meaning* and *value* (with its ethical overtones), as well as the dialectical conditions of experience. Kojève's conception of value is firmly tied to the experience of "recognition." He writes, "To desire a Desire is to want to substitute oneself for the value desired by this Desire. [It is] to desire that the *value* that I am or that I 'represent' be the value desired by the other: I want him to 'recognize' my value as his value. I want him to 'recognize' me as an autonomous value. In other words, all human, anthropogenetic desire—the Desire that generates Self-Consciousness, the human reality—is, finally, a function of the desire for 'recognition'" (7).

Lacan's interpretation of the witty butcher's wife rewrites the ending of this paragraph, swerves decisively between the point at which Kojève speaks of the desire to be the value desired by the other and the point at which he concludes that this "is necessarily to speak of a fight to the death for recognition." For Lacan this is rather to speak of the mechanism of identification and of feminine sexuality as identification with desire. Kojève conceives of human desire—the desire for desires rather than for things—as the desire to *be desired*, that is, to be *recognized* by the other, brought to consciousness and acknowledged by the other *as desirer*, as the one who has human desire. To attain that result involves the risk of one's mere life in a fight. The slave's work will ultimately attain the acknowledgment the slave gave up. Lacan's story of the emergent subject differs decisively from this scheme because, like Marx and Saussure, he understands "value" as exchange value or the condition of signification and sharply distinguishes it from the existential aim of "recognition." That "all Desire is desire for a value," as Kojève writes, means to Lacan that all desire is desire for the signifier that makes exchange, makes signification, possible: desire for the "absence" that is the practical, syntactical exclusion of the form of absolute value from the order of relative values or significations.[13] Freud's account of the witty butcher's wife's "need for an unfulfilled wish"—desire for a desire, desire for a lack or an absence—gives Lacan the occasion to displace Kojève's conception of anthropogenetic desire with his own. And this displacement involves a departure from Freud's manifest argument as well.

Freud deduces the butcher's wife's "need for an unfulfilled wish" from her remark that she has "asked her husband not to give her any caviar, even though she is crazy about it" (147).[14] She has dreamed that she wanted to give a dinner party, but the dream arranges the circumstances so that "I had to abandon my wish"; how then, she challenges Freud, can my dream be, as you claim they all are, a wish fulfillment? Freud masters the objection. He concludes from her attempt in waking life too to bring about a renounced wish—her wish for caviar—that the dream signifies an unconscious wish of another order. Her associations to the dream turn up the fact that her husband the day before had declared his plan to go on a diet and accept no more dinner invitations, making her aware of the link between dinner parties and gaining weight; and the same day a friend of hers, a thin friend—whom her husband always praises and whom she knows he is attracted to, though as a rule he doesn't like thin women—this friend asked her, "When are you going to ask us to another meal? You always feed one so well" (147). The

[13]That the phallus is, like money or gold, a "general equivalent" whose promotion to that role entails its exclusion from use is exhaustively argued in Jean-Joseph Goux, "Numismatiques," in *Freud, Marx: Economie et symbolique* (Paris: Seuil, 1973).

[14]Clément, 126.

dream then, Freud maintains, in telling the butcher's wife that she is unable to give a dinner party, fulfills her wish not to help her friend gain weight and so become more attractive to her husband. But "the same dream admits of another and subtler interpretation," he goes on. For in the dream the butcher's wife had identified herself with her friend; she dreamed not that her friend's wish but that one of her own wishes was not fulfilled. The dream displays the crucial mechanism of "identification." Freud concludes: "My patient put herself in her friend's place in the dream because her friend was taking my patient's place with her husband and because she (my patient) wanted to take her friend's place in her husband's high opinion" (150–51).

On a first reading it seems that for Freud both the "attempt to bring about a renounced wish" and the identification with the other woman are reducible to the patient's wish to keep her friend's wish unsatisfied and to ensure her own continued sexual satisfaction from her husband. Lacan does a further reading of Freud's two main insights about the case. For Lacan the "need for an unsatisfied wish" is irreducible and is the reason for, or another aspect of, the equally irreducible identification with the other. *La belle bouchère*'s identification with her friend is an identification with her friend's desire for desire. This thin friend, Freud happens to know, he tells us, grudges herself smoked salmon no less than the butcher's wife grudges herself caviar. "If our patient identifies with her friend," Lacan writes, "it is because she is inimitable in her desire for this smoked salmon—God damn it, if He doesn't smoke it himself!"(261, trans. mod.; 625–26).

The desire to desire, not the desire to be desired, is for Lacan constitutive of feminine sexuality. *La belle bouchère*'s husband is "a genital character"—Lacan spells this out. So, as Catherine Clément writes, "the wife is therefore presumably a 'satisfied' woman: but no, she isn't—that is precisely the point."[15] Here again we get "anthropogenetic desire," in a different style. Like "Man," for Kojève, the witty butcher's wife "doesn't want to be satisfied only at the level of her real needs," according to Lacan. "She wants other, gratuitous needs, and to be sure that they are gratuitous they must [not] be satisfied" (261).[16] Whence comes an interpretive, if not exactly an existential "impasse." Lacan writes: "So to the question 'What does the witty butcher's wife want?' we can reply, 'Caviar.' But this reply is hopeless, for she also does not want it." He goes on: "But that isn't all there is to say about her

[15]Clément, 128.
[16]Lacan, *Ecrits: A Selection*, 261. Through a remarkable printing error or error of translation, the "not" in this sentence is in fact omitted. See *Ecrits*, 625: "ne pas les satisfaire."

mystery. Far from imprisoning her, this impasse provides her with the key to the fields [la clef des champs], the key to the field of the desires of all the witty hysterics, whether butcher's wives or not, in the world" (261; *E* 625).

Capturing the exhilaration of accession to meaning in the very poise of his syntax, in a pivotal moment of his reading, Lacan merges two metaphors to suggest the dialectical movement that follows from the witty butcher's wife's "impasse." The impasse provides one with a key, with a pattern that gives access to an order of meaning. Or more exactly, or finally, the impasse provides one with "the key to the fields," "la clef des champs," the liberty to go wherever one will: it gives access to the very activity of symbolization or the signification of desire. How does this happen in the dream of *la belle bouchère?* As wanting and not wanting caviar comes to signify, first, not only identification with her friend and (this is Lacan's addition) with her husband but—in the production of the figure, the smoked salmon in the dream—identification with the signifier of desire. The impasse of wanting and not wanting that particular thing, caviar, functions like the impasse of indicating and not indicating a particular "here" or "this," the impasse in the attempt to assert the certainty of sense perception, analyzed in chapter 1 of the *Phenomenology.* Lacan's interpretation of the dream retraces the dialectical movement of the process of symbolization he reads in this first chapter and rewrites, most plainly in the essay "The Signification of the Phallus," in defining the interrelation of need, demand, and desire. The contradictory indication of caviar has the implications of the contradiction involved in the assertion of the truth of a particular sense perception. "To make such an assertion is not to know what one is saying, to be unaware that one is saying the opposite of what one wants to say. . . . And what consciousness will learn from experience in all sense certainty is, in truth, only what we have seen viz. the This as a *universal.*"[17] Such is the key, the meaning, to which the impasse of wanting/not wanting gives access: the universal or absolute nature of the demand (Lacan's term) to which needs are subjected simply in being articulated. "Demand annuls (*aufhebt*) the particularity of everything that can be granted by transmuting it into a proof of love" (286; *E* 690). *La belle bouchère*'s teasing about caviar annuls the particular and installs the universal: annuls the particular need and expresses the absolute demand, the demand for love. It is a demand for love from her husband, put in terms that also reveal it as an identification with the

[17]*Hegel's Phenomenology of Spirit*, trans. A. V. Miller (Oxford: Oxford University Press, 1977), 65.

friend whom her husband desires. Lacan associates demand and identification: "Demand . . . bears on something other than the satisfactions it calls for. It is demand of a presence or an absence—which is what is manifested in the primordial relation to the mother" (286; *E* 690)—the "primary *identification*" that is at stake, that is replayed, in *la b.b.*'s relation to her husband.

Lacan pushes beyond Freud's discussion of the dream to interpret that relation in terms that make it the means whereby *la b.b.*'s impasse becomes "the key to the fields" of desire, access to the very activity of symbolization. This is his reasoning: the desire for caviar signifies the desire for an unsatisfied desire; it is substituted for in the dream by the desire for smoked salmon, which signifies the dreamer's identification with her friend. And not only with her friend but with her husband. This is Lacan's genial invention. *La belle bouchère* identifies with her friend's desire, and she also identifies with the desire for her friend: she identifies with her husband's desire. Not only with the desire of the Other; with the other's desire for the other. "How can another woman be loved," she wonders, "by a man who cannot be satisfied by her (he, the man of the slice of backside)," the man not attracted by thin women? This is the question in its sharpened form, "more generally," writes Lacan, "the question of hysterical identification." And he concludes, "It's that question that the subject becomes, right here. In which the woman identifies with the man, and the slice of smoked salmon replaces desire for the Other" (262, trans. mod,; *E* 626).

Lacan thus locates the emergence of the subject in the moment of "inversion," his term, which has both a linguistic and a sexual sense. What is engaging about this reading is, in the first place, its culmination in a woman's desire for another woman, when, according to Clément, *la belle bouchère* " 'becomes' the question, [and] to answer it . . . places herself in the masculine position and desires the other woman as her husband does."[18] Equally engaging is Lacan's indication of the constitutive status and the dialectical logic of bisexuality, the motor of desire as the unending transformations between wanting to have and wanting to be. Yet what do we make of Lacan's assertion that *la belle bouchère*'s identification with her friend and with the desire of her friend means, finally, an identification with the signifier of signifiers, with the phallus?

My response turns on the status of that assertion in Lacan's argument. That the dreamer has identified with the signifier of desire constitutes the completion, in Lacan's story of *la belle bouchère*, of the dialectical logic of symbolization. To put it in the abstract terms of the

[18]Clément, 130.

essay "The Signification of the Phallus," although "demand annuls (*aufhebt*) the particularity of everything that can be granted," "the particularity thus abolished . . . reappear[s] *beyond* demand," with the emergence of desire as a function of signifiers. Demand, writes Lacan, is "demand of a presence or an absence" (286; *E* 691). What *is stated*, according to Hegel's account, is the *presence or absence* not of a particular here or this but of This as a universal, of objects as such. I think chapter 1 of the *Phenomenology* can be understood and is in effect understood by Lacan as an analysis of the nature of *reference*—as a demarcation of the referential status of language, the impossibility of having access in speech to *referents*, the inevitability of making reference to *signifieds*. Lacan's reflections on the phallic signifier arise in the light of the question: in the impossibility of access to referents, how does signification take place?

His conclusion about *la belle bouchère* seems to me to brush two different ways of thinking this problem. One sees this best in the paragraphs where Lacan worries the question this dream posed for Freud, the question of how it constitutes a wish fulfillment. The butcher's wife's dream fulfills a "need for an unfulfilled wish"; it manifests "desire for desire." But since *la bouchère*'s desire "is presented [in Freud's text] as that which is implied by her (conscious) discourse, reasons Lacan, "that is to say as preconscious, . . . one must go further if one is to know what such a desire means in the Unconscious" (258;*E* 622). What it means in the unconscious, he concludes, is identification with the phallus. This completes the *interpretation* of the dream, and Lacan's essay several times stresses that "desire is only grasped [only grasps itself: ne se saisit que] in the interpretation" (260; *E* 623). It is in this sense that "the dream is made for the *recognition* of desire." At this point in the text, in the passage I quoted earlier, Lacan wonders, "Why does my voice fail to finish" the phrase "for recognition," and he goes on: "For, in fact, it is not while one is asleep that one is recognized" and "The dream, Freud tells us, without appearing to be aware of the slightest contradiction, serves above all the desire to sleep. It is a narcissistic folding back of the libido and a disinvestment of reality" (260; *E* 623). The wish to sleep, introduced in the seventh, "metapsychological" chapter of *The Interpretation of Dreams*, is not a desire grasped in its interpretation. It is not a desire accessible to the query, repeated in Lacan's text without being answered, about the preconscious desire that must have a meaning in the unconscious, the question "[a meaning] for whom?" For no other sharing a dialogical space or a dialectical process with the subject as signifier. The notion of the wish to sleep disrupts the assumption of the meaningfulness of dreams. All that dream-work, all that trope production, all that condensation and displacement, presented and performed over six chapters, serves the wish of the preconscious *to go on being unconscious.* "Wish," in this context, indicates a determination of the order not of intention (unconscious intention) but rather of tendency. Whereas in fulfilling an unconscious wish discoverable through interpretation, the dream participates in the order of intention, desire, and meaning, in fulfilling the wish to sleep it serves not so much a desire as a need. Dreams are construed throughout Freud's work as covertly intentional, meaningful, interpretable structures, yet here they are also construed as the effect of necessity or probability. This bland assertion in chapter 7 brings out the *indeterminacy of the status* of the dream text, which is now construed *both* as interpretable and significative *and* as essentially nonsignificative. It is as the uncertain meaningfulness of dream-*text*-production, conceived as the tendency to maintain unconsciousness, that Freud's final chapter reencounters the enigmatic nature of a certain force, of *Trieb*, of the "drive."

The preconscious "wish to sleep" or tendency to go on being unconscious is essentially not meaningful or interpretable. Stress on its importance would put in question the assumption of the interpretability of preconscious wishes which guides Lacan from the butcher's wife's *pre*conscious "need for an unfulfilled wish" to her *un*conscious desire for the phallus. In serving above all the preconscious wish to sleep, dreams—like the instance that impels Freud to adopt his second topology: the unconscious ego—undo the pertinence of the distinction between consciousness and the unconscious, the distinction that orients "the direction of the treatment" toward "recognition" or recollection. But this distinction orients not only a treatment aimed at the recovery of memories of actual events or the reconstitution of a *referential* discourse. It orients as well Lacan's project of *interpretation* and treatment aimed at the recovery of primal *fantasies* or the production of a nonreferential discourse that signifies according to the universal rules of grammar. That the dream is such a discourse is Lacan's tenet of faith. "The desire of the dream is not assumed by the subject who says 'I' in his speech," he writes. "Articulated, nevertheless, in the locus of the Other, it is discourse—a discourse whose grammar Freud has begun to declare to be such" (264; E 629). Or again (toward the end of the essay): "Freud's discovery is homologous with in the first place considering as certain that the real is rational—. . . and then proving that the rational is real. . . . what presents itself as unreasonable in desire"—shall we interrupt to say such as identification with the phallus?—"is an effect of the passage of the rational in so far as it is real—that is to say, the passage of language—into the real, in so far as the rational has already traced its circumvallation there" (272; E 637).

I am charging Lacan, then, with the belief that although it is non-referential, signification takes place according to rules determined by a transcendental structure of meaning. Lacan's commitment to signification interferes with his reading of Freud's text. The opacity of desire touched on in the allusion to the wish to sleep, and to the dream as a "narcissistic" "disinvestment of reality," is passed over in this essay with interpretation maintaining belief in a grammar, the mutual determination of the rational and the real. The conclusion that *la belle bouchère*'s dream is an identification with the phallus takes its significance in Lacan's text from those grounds. A notion of the role of identification with the phallus might form a part of a *feminist* understanding of desire and meaning, could it undercut the structuralist conception of signification as ultimately *determined*. In Lacan's account, however, "The phallus is the privileged signifier of that mark in which *the role of the logos* is joined with the advent of desire" (287; E 692). In this context, to identify with the phallus is to invest in a system of meaning ruled by value, in language as a system of abstract values, signs with a determinate difference between signifier and signified guaranteeing the presence of meaning. Language so conceived is a system of preexistent positions in which gendered subjects find their assigned place.

These implications of structuralist thought are made conspicuous, and challenged, by the work of Julia Kristeva. In two essays published in *Tel Quel* in 1982, "L'abjet d'amour" and "Ne dis rien," Kristeva's critical reflection on structuralism takes the disquieting form of an attempt to provide a psychoanalytic explanation for the possibility of religious experience, specifically that of a God of love.[19] The possibility of a love without libidinal investment—not Eros but Agape, a "love without effort, merit, judgment, recompense, or other sign of the exercise of a Law," is ensured, she maintains, by "an archaic modality of the paternal function" associated with primary narcissism—a modality entirely distinct from the agency of prohibition, the supergo, heir of the oedipus complex.[20] Kristeva's recent work is vital, I suggest, even though it risks losing sight of Freud's discovery, in that it calls attention to an incipient theological character of the concepts she takes over from Lacan and Hegel and works to undo the structuralist assumption that

---

[19]Kristeva discusses the compatibilities and disparities of psychoanalysis and Christian belief in *Au commencement était l'amour: Psychanalyse et foi* (Paris: Hachette, 1985).
[20]Kristeva, "L'abjet d'amour," 25, my translation.

the structure of the sign is a given and a locus of the mutual determination of the rational and the real.

How does Kristeva reinterpret the desire of the Other, the desire of desire ultimately implying identification with the phallus, read by Lacan in *la belle bouchère*'s dream? She sets out to locate these conditions of desire and meaning in a still earlier moment or modality than the mirror stage preceding the symbolic function. She locates the condition of signification—the condition that sustains the structure of the sign, the gap between the signifier and the signified—in the modality of "primary narcissism," defined by Freud in "On Narcissism" and chapter 3 of *The Ego and the Id* not as original autoerotism but as a triadic structure composed when a "new psychical action" impinges on the autoerotism of the mother-infant dyad.[21] This "new psychical action" is a first differentiation of mother and infant in "an individual's first and most important identification, his identification with the father in his own personal prehistory. This . . . is a direct and immediate identification and takes place earlier than any object-cathexis."[22] That identification with the imaginary father, as Kristeva terms this instance, establishes and sustains the *gap* constitutive of the structure of the sign.

For Lacan as well as Kristeva, signification depends on "identification," on a transference, on a trope that sets up the distinction and relation between signifier and signified. Both of them, that is, presume the original and irreducible role of figure of rhetoric, of *Dichtung* (poetry) and not just grammar (not just a set of rules that work without interpretive reading), in the functioning of language. But Kristeva's text furthers reflection on the predicament implied in the dissolution of the distinction between a sign and a trope, and it does so by attending to the operation of *the mother's desire* in the transference that sets up the structure of the sign. Kristeva interrogates the claim that the transference onto the imaginary father is an *immediate* identification, a claim comparable, she suggests, to the assertion of the immediate presence to consciousness of the Absolute, read critically by Heidegger in his essay on the Introduction to the *Phenomenology*. The critical force of Freud's allusion to an "immediate identification" (if not of Hegel's conception of immediacy) is the implication that the signifying function does not in fact take place by means of dialectical mediation or the process of annulling the particular and preserving it "beyond," at a higher level, as Lacan describes the emergence of desire through need and demand. Rather, the signifying function would not achieve mediation or sublation, since it operates through figural and material dimen-

---

[21]Freud, "On Narcissism: An Introduction," in *Standard Edition*, 14:77.
[22]Freud, *The Ego and the Id*, in *Standard Edition*, 19:31.

sions impossible to mediate. Thus Kristeva terms the "immediate iden-tification" with the imaginary father a transference, a figural moment, which is indeed not truly mediated but in fact relayed, relayed by the signifiers of maternal desire, by the mother's signifying herself to the infant as having a desire other than that of responding to her infant's demand. Those maternal signifiers have the status, Kristeva implies, of what Paul de Man has called *inscription,* the materiality of traces not determinably perceivable as signs.[23]

La b.b. performs a reading of that inscription, of the mother's care, which Freud described as the universal seduction, the sexualization of the infant by gestures of care inflected by the mother's own sexuality. Kristeva's account of this, like Lacan's, provokes the question of what one is to make, as a feminist, of the description of a maternal role that consists in relaying an image of the father, associated moreover with the logos or with God. But it matters that this is not quite what her text describes. What the infant reads in maternal care, according to Kristeva, is the mother's desire for the phallus. The infant identifies with that desire: with the mother *cum* her desire, or the phallic mother. Imagi-nary father, phallic mother—same identity; Kristeva writes,

> The most archaic unity that we thus uncover, an identity autonomous to such a point that it attracts displacements [or transferences], is that of the Phallus desired by the Mother: it is the unity of the Imaginary Father, a coagulation of the Mother and her Desire. The Imaginary Father would thus be the mark that the Mother is not All but that she wants . . . who? what? The question is without response other than that which discovers the narcissistic void: "In any case, not me." The famous "What does a woman want?" is perhaps just the echo of a more fundamental interroga-tion: What does a mother want? The question runs into the same impos-sibility, bordered on one side by the Imaginary Father and on the other by a "not me." And it is from this "not me" . . . that a Self tries painfully to emerge.[24]

This passage situates in the question of feminine sexuality, of the mother's sexuality, the very condition of the production of a subject, the narcissistic void or wound. Compare this with the decisive moment in Lacan's story of *la belle bouchère:* "It's that question that the subject becomes, right here. In which the woman identifies with the man, and the slice of smoked salmon replaces desire for the Other" (262, trans.

[23]See Paul de Man, "Hypogram and Inscription," in *The Resistance to Theory* (Min-neapolis: University of Minnesota Press), 36–51. On inscription and prosopopoeia in Lacan and de Man, see Cynthia Chase, "The Witty Butcher's Wife: Freud, Lacan, and the Conversion of Resistance to Theory," *MLN* 102 (Dec. 1987), 898–1013.

[24]Kristeva, "L'abjet d'amour," 22, my translation.

mod.; *E* 626). Like another witty hysteric, Dora, the butcher's wife accedes to her status as a subject, that is, as a *signifier*, at the point at which she identifies with the man's desire for her friend's desire (that of her thin woman friend whose *desire* he must evidently desire, rather than her inadequate slice of backside), at the point, that is, at which she identifies with the *question* of feminine sexuality. At that point the phallus, the signifier of desire, replaces desire for the Other. Kristeva follows Lacan in conceiving identification with the phallus, with the signifier of desire, as the first key condition of the emergence of the subject. Lacan's story *la belle bouchère* situates this condition in her identification with her husband, which his essay implicitly associates with her "primary identification" with the *mother* insofar as both those relations take the form of "demand." The implication that her identification with the *man* replays her identification with the *mother* is reinforced and takes on a new twist under the impact of Kristeva's focus on primary narcissism, her rereading of that moment (that condition) of identification with the phallus. For *la belle bouchère*'s identification with her husband's *desire* could then be understood as a recapitulation of her identification with the mother's *desire*. The possibility of a signifier or of a subject is then situated in the identification with the desire *of* the mother, rather than with the desire *for* the woman. Such would be an account of the so-called preoedipal dimension of Dora's or the witty butcher's wife's case that would stress precisely the *questionable* nature of the maternal function, of "maternal" "desire," rather than counter Freud's and Lacan's insistence on desire's masculine identification with an insistence on the daughter's primary, unmediated identification with the mother's body.

But the crucial difference in recasting Lacan's story of *la belle bouchère* in the terms of the Kristevan story of *la b.b.* comes from another feature of Kristeva's account, from what she terms the mother's abjection. I said that *la b.b.* performs a reading of maternal inscription, or let me quote Neil Hertz's summary: "The infant . . . performs a double gesture: on the one hand linking itself, through a quasi-identification, with 'the archaic modality of the paternal function,' and, on the other, simultaneously rejecting 'that which could have been a chaos and which now begins to become an *abject*' (22), for it is only through this gesture of dismissal or abjection, Kristeva argues, that the place of the Mother can emerge as such, 'before becoming an object correlative with the desire of the *ego*'" (22).[25] The maternal inscription is read both as

[25]Neil Hertz, *The End of the Line: Essays on Psychoanalysis and the Sublime* (New York: Columbia University Press, 1985), 232. The relation between mother and infant as

the imaginary father and as the abject Mother: as (one) the differentiated unity of the sign, or as an instance described by Kristeva in effect as
a placeholder (maintaining the space between sign and sign, between
signified and signifier), and as (two) "that which could have been a
chaos and now begins to become an abject," or indeterminable differentiation. Kristeva's conception of the abject is a rethinking of the questionable nature of maternal sexuality and so has quite different significance from that implied in Lacan's account of primary identification or
of the mother as object of the demand for love, which is "demand of a
presence or an absence." The "demand of a presence or an absence"
annuls reference to a particular reality but is the signification of a
universal one. To emphasize the import of that signification, a sublation, is to compose the question of sexuality as a question of whether a
sign will be produced in a given case to correspond with what is, in any
event, an existing position in a structure of language, or "the rational
insofar as it is real," as Lacan writes (258; E 622). Kristeva's notion of
the "abject" instead associates the maternal not with the presence or
absence of the signified but with the significative status of the marks
that are read as signs. If the marks of maternal care must be *read* to
signify the mother's desire, Kristeva implies, they may not. They may
not signify. In such a case one faces a "narcissistic disorder," in diagnos-
tic parlance, with all the threats to normal functioning implied by the
"eclipse of the object" and the lapse of the paternal function that such a
condition involves. But just that case—the possibility that the inscription may not signify and the impossibility of determining, of deciding
other than in an act of reading, whether it signifies or not—is the
predicament implied in abjection or primary narcissism as such. The
predicament is that of the indeterminable significative status of the
sign.

The question raised with the maternal role as object of the demand,
for Lacan, is the question whether the signified will meet its signifier (in
desire), but the question raised by the maternal "abject," for Kristeva, is
the question of whether a trace (a rhythm, a pattern) signifies at all,
whether a regularity, an outline, is perceivable. The signification of the
phallus, then, is never guaranteed, and that is the burden of the subject's
constitution in terms of the question of maternal sexuality: the wound
of narcissism.

---

conceived by Kristeva becomes a figure for the relation between figure and grammar or
the cognitive and performative dimensions of language. On the conceptualization of
narcissism and the production of signification in de Man, Hertz, and Kristeva, see
Cynthia Chase, "Primary Narcissism and the Giving of Figure," in *Desire and Love: The
Work of Julia Kristeva*, ed. Andrew Benjamin (London: Routledge, 1989).

This might be read as well, I suspect, in other texts of Lacan, or in the text of another Lacan than the one I have positioned as a reader of Hegel still committed to the dialectical production of meaning. One could work out how the undoing of the significative status of the sign is involved in the materiality of the signifier which Lacan's late texts on feminine sexuality especially, perhaps, insist on. In her introduction to *Feminine Sexuality: Jacques Lacan and the Ecole Freudienne*, Jacqueline Rose presents a Lacan whose work "totally undercut[s] any . . . conception of language as mediation." Thus she writes, "Meaning can only be described as sexual by taking the limits of meaning into account, for meaning itself operates *at* the limit, the limits of its own failing. . . . Sexuality is the vanishing-point of meaning." Rose reads in Lacan's late writing the critique with which I have credited Kristeva: "Thus there is no longer imaginary 'unity' and *then* symbolic difference or exchange, but rather an *indictment* of the symbolic for the *imaginary unity* which its most persistent myths continue to promote."[26] To describe how the primary narcissism that sets up the structure of the sign involves abjection is to suggest the implications of the sheerly imaginary status of that unity-in-difference which is the condition of the symbolic. Kristeva describes the nature of such imaginary unity most suggestively, I think, in formulations that allude to the identification and abjection involved in narcissism not separately (on the one hand . . ., on the other hand . . .) but in the same breath. The passage I quoted earlier, for example, defines "the most archaic unity" as "the *coagulation* of the mother and her desire"—*coagulation* suggesting a clot and a wholeness made of dissolution. Kristeva's wording here evokes a violent dissolution of difference also powerfully evoked by Lacan: an indifference in the heart of desire.

I want to conclude an essay as speculative as this with an inference that reverts to the bathos of so-called ordinary experience. I have suggested reading Kristeva's essay as a reflection that would undercut the ultimately stabilizing impossibility of deciding between presence and absence or reality and fantasy or event and structure with the thoroughly *un*stabilizing impossibility of determining between the significative, marks determined by an encoding, and the insignificative, effects of sheer probability or chance. When she ascribes the possibility of the emergence of a sign to the moment of primary narcissism—to a transference onto an imaginary instance—Kristeva is describing the figural status of the sign. When she ascribes the condition of the sign's emergence to the existence of the mother not as object but as abject—

[26]Jacqueline Rose, *Feminine Sexuality*, 46–47.

the existence not of the maternal image but of maternal inscription—Kristeva is describing signs' materiality. Their material rather than phenomenal status, that they only *may or may not* be perceived (as signs), is crucial. For only as such are they *read*: they *can be signs* precisely because they may or may not be significative. That is what is called a text. I have been speaking here of maternal inscription, of the text of maternal desire or, more generally, the matter of feminine sexuality. To say that something *can be textual* precisely insofar as it *may or may not* be a text is also to say what I invite you to recognize from your own experience, that something *can be* sexual only insofar as it *may or may not* be. That is how I would interpret the stress on nonsexual love, or narcissism, of Kristeva.

5

Julia Kristeva Et Al.;
or, Take Three or More

Paul Smith

*By some strange oversight or act of inattention (no doubt the product
of the knowledge that I was one of only two men amongst the keynote
speakers), while writing my contribution to the conference from which
the present collection is drawn, I had imagined that the rubric under
which I was supposed to work was "Feminism, Psychoanalysis and
Literature." Thus, I began my writing with some sententious remarks
which were intended to provoke both me and my imagined audience.*

Whenever, over the last couple of decades, the terms of a conjunction
between feminism and literature have been incremented by the invocation of psychoanalytical theory, the result seems to have been difficult
to imagine as anything but an antagonistic and not always productive
disturbance. Indeed, psychoanalysis could be said to come always in
between the text and feminist politics, between feminist politics and
the text in such a way as to detract from both, disturb their specificity,
and inhibit their pairing.

In the most optimistic account of this three-fold articulation the
addition of psychoanalysis has maybe the effect of helping to forestall
the construction of any such uncompromising category as "feminist
literature," or even "literary feminism." And equally, feminist thinking has maybe the effect of forestalling what might otherwise have
looked like a natural pairing off of psychoanalysis and literature by
inserting between them the example of political consideration.

But these are, in a certain light, only preventative possibilities, inhib-
itive ones, and even they have not necessarily been fully realized. For
instance, it would seem fairly obvious by now that feminism's struggle
to infuse into psychoanalytical theory the breath of an efficacious poli-

tics has not been a major success. Feminist approaches in recent years to Lacanian psychoanalysis, for instance, have tended to become politically blocked in the question of subjectivity and in the seemingly intransigent problem of how to conceive of difference beyond the phallus. Or, and this may be to say the same thing, they have been thwarted by the obstinacy of psychoanalytic *universalist* theories of subjective construction. And Lacan's own stellar presence has on occasion instigated something like a Hollywood scenario for feminists, in which the romance of the male and female heroes takes preeminence over and misplaces whatever (if any) political issues might have been touched upon in the course of the narrative. And even beyond such dramas, much feminist psychoanalytical work has exhibited a quite conspicuous reluctance to work out an accommodation with what might be thought of as the rejected suitor, Marxism.

Thus the place (and usefulness) of psychoanalytical theory in feminist discourses seems, after twenty years or so, not altogether unproblematical. It's at least a double-edged affair: a question of power in which what is negotiated are competing heuristics and institutional traditions. If literature, as an institution, has the longest of these traditions, that's not to say that it has the most powerful. Indeed, literary tradition has been in many ways questioned by the intervention of psychoanalysis both within and without feminist discourse; ironically enough perhaps, it is now feminism which often comes to strengthen it again, even if in altered mode.

The institution of psychoanalysis has always been relatively more open to a feminist influence than have some other patriarchal forms. At least, the relation of psychoanalysis to feminist thinking has not necessarily been a problem primarily or simply caused by a constitutive or residual homocentric structure in psychoanalysis, but just as much by the inherent inability of psychoanalysis to construct for itself any but the scantiest tradition of political efficacy, or even political desire. Wherever we see a politicized psychoanalysis it has been the result of, for instance, the urgent need of Marxism for a supplementary methodology. The mutations which psychoanalytical theory undergoes in such a bonding are perhaps indication enough of its being unsuited to the task, but in any case it's certainly true that the desire to produce a politically orientated psychoanalytical theory has rarely arisen from psychoanalysis's own sense of itself and its desire.

I think, then, that it can be proposed that the recent history of this articulation—psychoanalysis, feminism, literature—has tended to be constituted mostly by a set of disturbances and problems in which cohabitation has proved possible only to the cost of one or other of the

Paul Smith

terms. And specifically, as a result of the difficulty that psychoanalysis makes for any political theory, feminism as politics has most regularly paid the price of the inmixing.

To say all this is a long way from intending to criticize feminist attempts to make the conjunction among psychoanalysis, literature, and feminism work; rather more I mean it as an at least tentative return to older complaints about psychoanalysis itself. In my view psychoanalysis has been quite properly the object of multifarious political critiques and, even before the flowering of post-structuralist varieties, had shown itself incompatible with other critiques of bourgeois capitalism. In short, psychoanalysis has shown itself amazingly resistant to political desire, and here my assumption will be that it still does. My suggestion is that some of the apparent impasses faced by feminism in relation to psychoanalysis can be read off from this fact and that many of the lineaments of the relationship are emblematised in the work of Julia Kristeva.

It hasn't, of course, always seemed like an impossibility to produce at best a simultaneity of the three elements, at worst a productive tension between them. Wherever the question has been one of how to maintain a political urgency and commitment within feminism while taking account of psychoanalytical thought, Kristeva's work has been indispensable and has, indeed, been exemplary in discussions about the potentials and possibilities of such a project. At least, I'm sure that I'm only one amongst many who, not too long ago, came to think of Kristeva's work as exemplary, salutary, problem-solving, and so on, by dint of its attempt to negotiate the terms of a cohabitation. Equally, that work often promised to formulate a conjunction which would also include Marxist thought.

However, I know I'm only one amongst many who are by now somewhat bemused, disturbed, or disappointed by recent twists in Kristeva's course. Something of what's at stake in her recent turn in the direction of anti-feminism and anti-Marxism (concomitant with her full embrace of the practice of psychoanalysis) can be glimpsed, for instance, in the clearly informed but equally clearly hostile questioning she underwent at the hands of British feminists quite recently. At a conference in London Kristeva presented some of the spadework for *Histoires d'amour* (the book to which I'm mostly going to address myself here); although the following exchange is not the most hostile that occurred, it does give a sense of the occasion.

> Jacqueline Rose: . . . your account of the political . . . is a relegation of the political to a marginal and inadequate arena of work. And in a sense your personal history . . . has a classical ring about it. It's the story of

somebody who became disillusioned with politics and those very big desires for change. . . . [This] leads to a move into a more personal, more individualised sphere.

  Kristeva: . . . it seems to me that if the artist or the psychoanalyst acts politically they act politically through an intervention on the individual level. And it can be a main political concern to give value to the individual. My reproach to some political discourses with which I am disillusioned is that they don't consider the individual as value.[1]

It would be a relatively simple exercise to adopt the tone of, say, a Terry Eagleton and merely dismiss as pathetically and irredeemably bourgeois Kristeva's claim for "the individual as value." However, my aim here is to address through Kristeva's example the problematic to which an exchange such as the one quoted contributes, to note Kristeva's own attempt to articulate our threefold conjunction, and especially to look at the ways in which the political has been and might in the future be treated in such a conjunction.

The first working title for my essay was "The Word Not Made Flesh," since I had intended to talk critically about how Kristeva's psychoanalytically informed notions of the subject and language had, after long elaboration, landed up with an absolutely idealist version of subjectivity and a nonmaterialist account of language. As I wrote, that discussion seemed to demand that I give a stronger sense of what other, more optimistic accounts had been offered by feminists. Thus, my second working title became "Kristeva Et Al.," and this title was intended to increase a discussion of other writers. This it ended up not doing exactly. It did, however, cover—provisionally at first—my explication of Kristeva's dealings with the question of subjectivity and language.

Et Al. (And [the] Other)

Kristeva's well-known notion of subjectivity, the poststructuralist moment par excellence, goes by the tag "the subject in process." The human subject is here posited as a series of shifting identities, held in check and in cohesion only by the arbitrary imposition of paternal law. The subject is, in Kristeva's related account, a crossing of what she calls the semiotic and the symbolic: the semiotic is the name for the processes of resistance and unifixity which continually both subvert and subvent the establishment and maintenance of symbolic cohesiveness in the subject. This, very crudely, is the idea that founds nearly all of Kristeva's meditations on subjectivity. At any rate it is the idea for

---

[1]Julia Kristeva, "Love Stories," in *Desire* (London: ICA, 1983), 27.

which, rightly or wrongly, she is best known, and it requires little elaboration here. However, I do want to elaborate on one aspect of Kristeva's theory of the "subject in process" which isn't often dealt with and which I think to be precisely the aspect that once allowed Kristeva to argue for the political consequences of the "subject in process."

It seems right—and Cynthia Chase elaborates finely on this in her contribution to this volume—that Kristeva's arguments around notions of subjectivity are heavily dependent on her reading of the Hegelian dialectic. In particular, they fall heavily around her reading of Hegel's notion of *negativity*, a term which Kristeva calls "the forgotten fourth term of Hegel's dialectic" and which she understands and exploits in a particular manner. This is the aspect of Kristeva's work with which I want to begin.

Hegel conceives of negativity (in *The Phenomenology of Spirit*, that is) as the very form of the mediation between self and other. It is the concept in Hegel which most closely describes heterogeneity itself in the dialectic or process of self-consciousness, and thus it acts as that which enables self-identity (the same) to distinguish itself from the other. Equally (dialectically), the other can be defined as that which is distinguished from the self by the mediation of negativity. In *Révolution du langage poétique*, Kristeva proposes that for Hegel heterogeneity is the force of a certain excess within the subject's forging of a conceptually unified and securing schema of self and other, and that such a force is more or less synonymous with notions of liberty and freedom. Heterogeneity figures in the dialectic in the shape of negativity, which "can be thought of as both the cause and the organisational principle of *process*. Distinguished from nothingness and also from negation, negativity is the concept which represents the indissoluble relation between an 'ineffable' movement and its 'singular determination'; it is the mode of mediation, that which exceeds those 'pure abstractions,' being and nothingness."[2]

Kristeva establishes here an approximate equivalence among these concepts (heterogeneity, freedom, negativity) and argues for their function as a disturbance across the constitution of the fixity of self and other. She then claims that "the Hegelian conception of negativity already prepares the ground for the possibility of thinking a materialist *process*"; thus she points out that in Lenin, for example, negativity comes to be seen as an actual material force, "the necessary and objec-

[2]Julia Kristeva, *Révolution du langage poétique* (Paris: Seuil, 1974), 101, my translations.

tive link between all aspects, forces, tendencies, etc., in the domain of given phenomena."[3] This is the component of the materialist dialectic which in the seventies Kristeva had wished to stress and preserve: the principle of heterogeneity, the "indissoluble" linkage of the dialectic, become objective process. Thus negativity is, as it were, the vehicle of Kristeva's semiotic, an objective force that will threaten and destabilise the conceptual unity of Hegel's own, more strictly identitarian logic.

Concrete instances of the subject in process through negativity are for Kristeva mostly written. Thus in an early and eloquent essay on Roland Barthes, Kristeva claims literature as the privileged (i.e., objective) instance of the "intersection of subject and history." This intersection, she says, is where "the ideological tearings in the social fabric" can most readily be discerned.[4] Such an emphasis on the special case of the literary text is a constant throughout Kristeva's work, and the disruptive, or "avant-grade" text is consistently seen as an especially privileged case in relation to other systems of representation in the social. The "avant-garde" text is the place where the legalistic or fixatory *structures* of the social (always seen as signifying systems in some way analogous to linguistic ones and dependent for their signification on the subject's accession to the symbolic) confront the repressed or marginalized *processes* of the subject in language. These latter processes, Kristeva claims, always constitute an excess, a something more, in relation to whatever juridical demands might historically hold them in check. In other words, the processes of literature are uniquely placed to illuminate and question the ideological.

This championing of "avant-garde" textuality becomes, as I take it, a symptom—perhaps also a cause—of what has happened to Kristeva's work in the eighties: the "avant-garde" has increasingly been posed as the model of the only kind of linguistic and then political dissidence possible in relation to a monolithic symbolic order. This happens as Kristeva turns her emphasis away from the mutually constraining dialectic of the semiotic and the symbolic. She undoes what she had earlier claimed as the "indissoluble relation" of negativity in the dialectic and moves instead towards the revindication of a putative priority and primacy of the semiotic. That's to say, she begins to expand the psychoanalytical basis for the semiotic/symbolic doublet and locates the semiotic much more determinedly in the preoedipal, where it is assigned both logical and ontological priority over the oedipal symbolic. This move is (perhaps) supposed to foreground the resistant and opposi-

---

[3] Ibid., 102.
[4] Julia Kristeva, *Desire in Language* (New York: Columbia University Press, 1980), 93.

Paul Smith

tional quality of the semiotic, but at the same time it has the effect of "individualizing" that force, making it transhistorical and dematerialising it—in other words, the semiotic is extricated from the closely worked historical and materialist dialectic of Kristeva's earlier work.

The same fate attends Kristeva's reworking of the notion of the semiotic in *Pouvoirs de l'horreur*, a reworking that comes in the form of the concept of the abject. The abject is something that "disturbs identities, systems, orders. Something that doesn't respect limits, positions, rules. The in-between, the ambiguous, the mixed,"[5] but it differs from the earlier notion of the semiotic in crucial ways.

First, whereas the semiotic and the symbolic were considered as existing in an indefeasible dialectic, the abject is a concept that is intended to displace the theoretical term to which it might be coupled, namely the psychoanalytically invested term *object*. In other words, the abject is a notion by which Kristeva can take up cudgels against what she sees as the overreliance of psychoanalysis on the role of the object in the construction of subjectivity. Whatever the success of her assault, it remains the case that abjection operates as a term of transcendence, outside the careful dialectical thinking at which Kristeva had previously so excelled.

Furthermore, the abject marks the painful difficulty of the subject's experience of being constructed in the semiotic/symbolic dialectic. Kristeva seems to want the term to stand, as it were, as the "repressed" of that dialectical explanation of subjectivity—"the repressed," whose return she attempts to foster. It stands as the moment when "the subject, tired of its vain efforts to recognise itself from the outside, discovers that its impossibility is its very existence [*être*]."[6] In this sense the abject can be understood as the registration of individual psychical pain and thus to contain a dimension that the semiotic did not.

Relatedly, the experience of the abject can be constituted as pain, difficulty, impossibility, and so on, precisely because it arises from the subject's registering or remembering its existence prior to the oedipal moment. The preoedipal is the object of the subject's primary repression; thus its "return" is traumatic. In claiming to recognize the marks of such a return in her analysands and in the history of cultural significatory artifacts Kristeva chooses to reify the existence of the *content* of primary repression, available in its imaginary, imagistic traces. This reification constitutes another difference in conception from the semiotic, whose paramount feature was its *process*.

[5]Julia Kristeva, *Pouvoirs de l'horreur* (Paris: Seuil, 1980), 12, my translations.
[6]Ibid.

In *Pouvoirs de l'horreur*, Kristeva attempts to chart a kind of social history of the traces of the abject—a history that turns out to be nothing less than a vindication of certain moments of abject difference within what Kristeva cheerfully indentifies as the Judaeo-Christian tradition, *I have just returned from the 1986 conference of the Institute on Culture and Society on the topic "The Third World under Erasure." There it was pointed out several times that this currently much-favoured term could have been invented only after 1948 and is thus not at all an innocent one with which to approach the history of the West.* when the symbolic law appears to repress the very condition of its own possibility. The immediate effect of this history (the details of which I will leave to the reader's own curiosity to familiarize herself or himself with) is to idealize the abject *because* of its having been repressed and demeaned, and in sympathy with its pained attempt to attain any degree of symbolisation.

As I suggested before, all of this entails the undoing of the carefully theorized dialectic that had previously obtained to the semiotic/symbolic pairing. The abject now is separated from any such dialectic and is thrown into a kind of Manichean struggle with its opposite, the fixed object (and the urge towards objectification) in the history of the West. My complaint is not of course that Kristeva has taken the side of the abject over the phantasms of an object-ruled psychoanalysis, nor do I want here to argue with the particular instances of the abject in her analyses (though that would be a possibility in a lengthier paper). Rather, I mean simply to bemoan the way in which the semiotic/symbolic doublet has been recast so that what had indicated a simultaneous inscription of struggle and mutual regulation now appears as something more akin to a dualism.

The difference, clearly, is that Kristeva's current work has abandoned the dialectical link of negativity which she had once struggled so hard to sustain, and the result is necessarily that the political impulse of her work changes. Kristeva once stated, with a hard-won dialectical poise, that our thinking could not proceed through any absolutisation of the thetic, nor through an undoing of the thetic by the fantasy of an atomizing irrationalism. Her work now seems to have a *parti pris* in the dreaded fantasy and moves toward a kind of stasis where the previous productivity of the semiotic is now fixed and embodied in the abject as pain, desperation, disillusionment, and inefficacy.

The final twist in this excision of negativity is in Kristeva's *Histoires d'amour*, the last chapter of which is devoted to a rhetorical reconsideration of the imaginary as the place from which not only psychic but also social crisis can be addressed and resolved, cured. I'm not altogether certain what Kristeva takes to be the nature of the current social crisis but she repeatedly alludes to one and claims that the explanation of its coming about can be discovered psychoanalytically through an account of the individual's alienation from the social. "The speaking being is a wounded being, with its discourse dumb from the disorder of love, and the 'death drive' (Freud) or the *'désêtre'* (Lacan) coextensive with humanity determines the discontents of civilizations, even if it doesn't justify them."[7] The psychical disorder in the "wounded being" is here taken, then, to "determine," to be the cause of social disorder and discontent. This is again a long distance from a dialectic whose mediation was always negativity and where the "wounded being" referred to here was always, more tendentiously, known as the "signifying subject" and was quite clearly not designated to become anything like the cause or origin of the discontents of civilizations. And so far as the subjective crisis itself is concerned, Kristeva's view now seems to be that this is "an inevitable discontent . . . [and] the existence of psychoanalysis reveals the permanence, the ineluctability of crisis" (347). Thus this cause of social discontent which is the subject is now given as itself in permanent crisis (and indeed, the words with which Kristeva ends the book are "Une crise permanente" (356).

This permanent crisis, the state of polyvalency and shifting heterogeneity in the subject, has clearly lost something from its earlier forms in Kristeva's expression, even though it stands in a certain relation of continuity to much of her earlier view of subjectivity. Notably, this new version installs the polyvalent subject as a cause of the social; the subject's own crisis, its suffering, is now no longer an oppositional quality by which the relatively fixed surface of the *doxa* is put under strain and stress. In other words, Kristeva's subject in crisis is no longer the other that both enables and undercuts, in its own suppression, the economy of the same. The two are no longer in a relation mediated by their shared heterogeneity.

What Kristeva now wants to do is to make a very different kind of virtue out of subjective malaise: instead of making it oppositional, she wants to make the subject (specifically, the analysand) understand and accept that its own crisis is not out of phase with the social but is more nearly the truth of the social. That's to say, the subject's response to crisis will have to consist in a transvaluation of it: stop worrying and love your crisis. This is almost a grotesque travesty of the old whipping boy of Lacanian analysis, ego psychology, which makes the analysand conform to a pregiven social world; but here the psychical entity that

---

[7]Julia Kristeva, *Histoires d'amour* (Paris: Denoël, 1983), 347, my translations, hereafter cited in the text by page number.

Kristeva wishes to "cure" actually produces, "determines," the social in the first place and thus it is only the imaginary, home of abject traces, and not the ego that needs to conform.

One of the possibilities that gets lost in this new Kristevan account of the subject is one which her earlier work had been particularly influential in opening: the possibility of what, in another language, might be called ideology critique, or the moment of not just finding but also critiquing the "tears in the social fabric." Rather than leaving space for uncovering the process by which an ideologically constructed social world conceals the subject's splits and gives the subject its coherent facade, Kristeva is now abjuring the social element of her work—and this precisely at the moment of crisis, the moment of decision, the critical moment—by transcendence and transvaluation, as it were. She now offers a theory of a childish subject that needs to be taken care of and needs to have its pain and suffering understood as transcending the import of the social of which it is nonetheless the cause and appropriate model. This theory of the subject establishes the social as explicable through the subject and renders any attempt to specify the political evidently useless.

The repetitive nature of my claims here and the rhetoric that carries them reflect my impatience with what I was finding in Kristeva as I was writing the first version of this paper. The impatience was also compounded by a certain distraction since I often work in front of the television and the "breaking story" on the cable news channels as I wrote was of the United States encroachment into the Gulf of Libya and the sinking of at least one Libyan partrol boat. I was also becoming more and more aware of the ineptitude of my attempts to structure my paper around the title that by now I had given the conference organizers: "Julia Kristeva Et Al.; or, Take Three or More." This title was intended to take advantage of an allusion that Kristeva makes in Histoires d'amour *to the movie* ET, Extra-Terrestrial. *Thus the title of my next section.*

Et Al. (ET, Alien)

The bearer of Kristeva's remodeled theory of subjectivity is a new Narcissus. In the final chapter of *Histoires d'amour*, again, Kristeva sets forth the manifesto of this new Narcissus. As I have suggested, about all that's left of the "subject in process" of Kristeva's early work is this narcissistic figure's polyvalency, and it is this remnant that I want to comment upon here.

93

Paul Smith

It would seem that part of Kristeva's intent in foregrounding this new narcissistic figure is to expand upon (even counter) psychoanalytical theory's basic explanations of the pain or the crisis in subjective experience. She claims in this regard that, with the orthodox Freudian notion of the death drive and the Kleinian concept of hate, psychoanalysis has pointed towards but has not sufficiently elaborated a satisfactory view of primary narcissism. For her, narcissism is preoedipal, certainly, but "not a screen, not a state, but a structure" (348). The claim appears to be that such a structure has not been well accepted in psychoanalysis as a founding and inevitable instability in which the subject is traversed by primal loss and the vacillatory experience of "tying and untying, fullness and emptiness" (348).

It might have been imagined that precisely this structure is what Lacan's work aims to express, but Kristeva elaborates it differently. For her the psychical scaffolding of this instability is constituted by, on the one hand, the subject's primary identification with "the father of individual prehistory" and, on the other hand, the simultaneous "fascination and repulsion" with/towards the archaic mother who is "neither subject nor object, a mother abject [*une mère-'abject'*]" (349). It is this figure of abjection which she has traced in *Pouvoirs de l'horreur* through some of its exemplars in Western history.

In conjunction with this tropical history, the preoedipal narcissistic structure that Kristeva proposes comes to look almost archetypal. It is less a process than a store of images, and it holds hard to the figure of a supposedly mobile narcissism by way of a paradoxically fixed formation that is almost essentialist: that is, beneath the "structure" resides the figure or image of a primal father and the archaic mother, rock-bottom tropes to which the subject cleaves and around which all experience and history is articulated.

The same criticism could be made of the more conventional accounts of oedipal structure, of course.

Kristeva's rhetorical purpose in constructing this "antiobject" imaginary for the abject is to be able to complain that in Western society and through the connivance of psychoanalytical theory narcissism has lost its proper place and importance in both the social and the psychic. In fact her Narcissus has been, it seems, "deprived of both substance and space" (348). She likens this new Narcissus to ET from Steven Spielberg's movie of the same name. At the end of *Histoires d'amour*, ET becomes the settled figure for all of the narcissistic subjects whose pain and suffering Kristeva wants to draw attention to: deprived of his proper space, ET shuttles from heaven to earth, neither at home not totally alien, neither human nor animal, neither adult nor child, neither articulate nor dumb. Everything, Kristeva claims, is closed off to this ET. But his problems might well be solved by a fifty-minute phone call to Paris so that he could be made to feel good about himself again, since Kristeva's practice sees "psychoanalysis as the opening of a way out of this closure, rather than its gatekeeper" (353).

Thus this new Narcissus, this ET, can be relieved of the necessity of position, as unimpressed by the lure of any utopian relation to the world as he is liberated from what might be called (almost in mimicry of an earlier Kristeva) the mono- or homotopia of a more orthodox narcissism. But despite her claims that ET has no substance or space, she is able to point out to him in enthusiastic terms the place where he might appropriately live: "This fin-de-siècle culture whose popular projects are jazz and rock. A culture where you write a novel just as you'd play jazz or rock. Where you can hear or think discourses from a base of the convulsive excesses of the people in these modern megapolises whose words appear as just provisional and inessential masks."[8] This culture, America, would seem appropriate to the subject whom Kristeva in *Histoires d'amour* advises to "stay floating, in empty moments, inauthentic and sewn by an invisible thread" (oo–oo). The superficial elements of the fluctuant, anchorless space of the U.S.A. probably haven't been so valorized since the era of abstract expressionism. And even a Pollock, a Rothko, or a poet like O'Hara by and large refrained from an absolute vindication of those cultural characteristics from which their work was drawn. Kristeva, on the other hand, appears to revel in the pleonasms of American culture, wanting to see a Joycean "work in progress" in its excesses.

Perhaps what is most distressing about this homologisation of the idealized ET-subject and its appropriate culture in a polyglot world of jazz, rock, abundant novels, and so on, is the political conclusion to which Kristeva is thereby led. Of America she says:

> Now that the Latin-American or Arab Marxist revolution groans at the gates of the United States, I feel myself closer to truth and liberty when I am working in the space of this embattled giant which is perhaps on the point of becoming a David facing up to the growing Goliath of the Third World.
>
> I dream that to the camp of this David, with all his faults and difficulties, our children will go.[9]

At this point my original manuscript was in severe danger of breaking off altogether. I felt a certain desperation that someone whose work I had for many years followed and admired for its ability to offer sophis-

[8]Julia Kristeva, "Memoires," *L'Infini*, no. 1 (1983), 54, my translations.
[9]Ibid.

ticated ways of thinking through the inequities of contemporary life and thought under capitalism should descend to this level of pronouncement. The sentiment of this last quotation would not be out of place in a Reagan administration press conference.

Desperation gave way to depression: the day after I had finished translating this small quotation from Kristeva, the news came that the United States had bombed Libya. There really seemed little point in talking any more about Kristeva. As a result of the bombing the rest of my paper for the conference remained quite patchy and unformed. At the conference I warned the audience that this was to be the case and of the ostensible reasons why. In retrospect, I'm also bound to recognize that my desperation and depression (that is, my irritation against Kristeva and the United States) was compounded by a discomfort of another kind. I had learned that the only other male keynote speaker at the conference, Andrew Ross, was planning to talk about Steve Fagin's video on Lou Andreas-Salomé and that his contribution wasn't likely to engage directly the issues that I thought the conference would bring up for feminist thinking.

The difficulty of speaking as a man near feminism is one with which I'm familiar and is still the topic of much debate, obviously. At the conference itself, however, it turned out that the topic did not come up—at least in any public forum that I heard. The reasons for this will probably remain obscure, but I think in that regard that it's worth paraphrasing a remark made publicly by Jane Gallop after my and Jerry Aline Flieger's presentations, to the effect that it had become rather unspectacular (Jane's word, I think!) to be talking, writing, and teaching about feminism, about psychoanalysis, and about their conjunction. The political situation that such a remark points to can perhaps be taken as a welcome one, but the fact that its consequences went unquestioned at this conference is probably a cause for concern.
It would seem that for Kristeva, America is something like the solution to the narcissist's crisis, presumably because it is avowedly the product of it. The United States is the appropriate space of a narcissism that has historically been repressed and marginalised. It is the narcissist's space of image, noise, disturbance, and logorrhea. If those terms seem to aptly describe the familiar Kristevan notion of the *chora*, that may well be because the *chora* acted as the intermediate term in Kristeva's path toward a reification of the semiotic: after the semiotic, the *chora*, and after the *chora*, the United States.

In this space where ETs can live, the society not so much of the Logos as of the logo, the fixed preoedipal figures that underpin the narcissist's vacillation can be vindicated also. "Pardon the stable Image but disinvest the transcendental Unity which assures its authenticity. Valorize the semblant, the seeming, the imaginary. Not the imagination of power, but a saturation of powers and counterpowers through imaginary constructions: phantasmatic, daring, violent, critical, demanding, timid . . . let them speak, and the ETs will live" (352). The ETs' speaking will be a *work in progress*, a kind of unleashed musicality of the preoedipal. In *Histoires d'amour* one of the places where Kristeva begins to elaborate her argument for this kind of musical speaking is in a chapter on Don Juan. This chapter follows the tradition of Rank and Klein in psychoanalyzing the Don Juan figure in his various literary and operatic manifestations. But what is of interest in Kristeva's account for my argument here is the way in which the musical/operatic version of the Don Juan legend takes a privileged preeminence over any literary ones. The rubric of one part of the chapter is very explicit and indicates Kristeva's path: "Narration and music: morality and infinity" (188). This is perhaps at first sight a rather strange couple of pairs to juxtapose, but the functions become clearer upon the realisation that Kristeva wishes to privilege musicality and infinity over morality and narrative. This move is basically the one I wish to question in the rest of this paper (if I have not evidently enough questioned it up until now). The assignation of narration to the realm of morality is an interesting one—especially, I'll suggest, for feminism.

In dealing with the Don Juan legend Kristeva claims that the fundamental narrative of the protagonist's counting and re-counting of women is of less interest than the state into which that narrative brings him. This numerical disregard of the women in the legend allows Juan to transcend the politico-ethical world (the *moral* world of the narrative) and to reach the narcissistic plane of the infinite and the musical. Like the artist himself, Don Juan is in quest of "the impossible identificatory object" (197), and this quest leads him away from morality—a realm of little usefulness in Kristeva's account—and toward "the baroque drunkenness of signs, to their original and musical inconstancy" (201).

For Kristeva the question to be asked of the Don Juan narrative is no longer one that would permit (for a crude example) a feminist explication and critique of the sexuality of men and its investment in the exchangeability of women. Such a critique, the germs of which are to be found already in both Rank and Klein, would begin with the narrative or the serial quality of Juan's re-counting and address its morality. That is to say, it seems to me that the necessarily *ethical* impulse of feminism would dictate that any feminist critique begin with the serial rather than the melodic characteristics of a story such as this one. It is in the place of the story's morality that its ideology can be located. I mentioned before that, in abandoning the dialectical mode of her earlier thought, Kristeva would now forgo the possibility of constructing the ideological critique that a feminist reading would lead towards and finally amount to. Here, in positing the oppositions narration/music, morality/infinity and opting for one side, Kristeva abandons even the possibility of such a reading.

There is a further difficulty with this fixing of her thought into opposed pairs. The musicality/infinity doublet that she sets up is not only no longer a process of resistance and subversion but has become a fixed and static image, a reified end unto itself. It relies finally upon the fixing of process into image—like the fixation of Don Juan himself on his dead father (and Kristeva's finding ET). My main point is that the deplorable turn of Kristeva's work of late might well be connected to the ossification of the process of signification into visual, musical, or, more properly, imagistic moorings. This "fixation" carries with it the hint of obsessiveness, the obsession of/in the imaginary with a prehistory of the self—its own prehistory—which can function to block out the structures of the political world. Thus the place of the oppositional subject, bearer of the mediation of negativity, now comes to be what can only be thought of as the epitome of the liberal subject—perhaps no longer the bourgeois individualist (even Kristeva cannot imagine that the North American multivalent and heterogeneous megapolises are peopled only by the bourgeoisie) but certainly the individualist.

Take Three

Although I didn't consciously recognise it until some time after I started writing this piece, the title to this section evidently alludes to a paper by Jacqueline Rose called "Julia Kristeva: Take Two." In this section I wanted to look at the work of two feminist writers whom I have long respected—Juliet Mitchell and Jacqueline Rose—and one whose writing was new to me but clearly politically motivated—Toril Moi—to see how they might have reacted to Kristeva's new course. My tactic was partly dictated by my discomfort at having produced what I think amounts to a fairly relentless attack on Kristeva, and I suppose that I intended either to subvent that attack with the authority of those three or to use them to find ways of mollifying the attack. The effort was only partially successful in that what follows tends to be more critical than I'd hoped. The difficulty of speaking as a man near feminism is still here, its major symptom (so far as I can tell) the

scarcely innocent effect of having chosen, as it were, between women.
But I hope that it's the case that choosing between women is not
tantamount to legislating between them.

The turns in Kristeva's political map are not, of course, confined to
the adoration of the American David. *Pouvoirs de l'horreur* contains a
quite outrageous revindication of Céline's virulently anti-Semitic writings (Kristeva says they constitute an apocalyptic music). The same
book also contains Kristeva's by now well-known description of feminism as "the latest power-hungry ideology." *Histoires d'amour* goes in
a direction that might be seen as even more damaging for feminism
because of the celebration of a form of idealising and abjectified love.
For those who have followed and admired Kristeva's work during the
last decades, and for feminists especially, there is in its current phase
clearly enough cause to become disillusioned. There has been no short-
age of attacks on this new political tone in Kristeva, such as those by
Terry Eagleton or Jennifer Stone, but despite the fact that I might well
want to agree with those attacks, I want to talk for now about a couple
of attempts by feminists to look with as much sympathy as possible at
the Kristevan spectacle: the final chapter of Toril Moi's *Sexual/Textual
Politics*, and Jacqueline Rose's essay "Julia Kristeva: Take Two."

The overall tone and intent of Toril Moi's book is guided by her belief
that there is in feminism an "absence of a genuinely critical debate
about the political implications of [feminism's] methodological and
theoretical choices."[10] Moi sees herself as installing the terms of such
a debate. However, her attitude towards Kristeva's recent political
choices is almost nonchalant. She remarks, rather coolly, and with the
wisdom of hindsight, that Kristeva's "development away from Marxism and feminism is not as surprising as it seems at first glance,"
apparently because Kristeva's thought was always tinged with "anarchist tendencies" and anarchist tendencies are just libertarianism and
libertarianism is nothing but a symptom of bourgeois individualism.
Moi's book is, of course, concerned to salvage from feminist theory a
specifically anticapitalist and not merely antibourgeois politics, and so
she is not particularly put out of the joint by Kristeva's turn, preferring
to think of it as a predictable unveiling. Her reasons for being cool about
it all are that she wants to be able to claim that Kristeva's "most
valuable insights draw at times on highly contentious forms of subjectivist politics."[11]

[10]Toril Moi, *Sexual/Textual Politics* (London: Methuen, 1985), xiii.
[11]Ibid., 168–69.

Paul Smith

*How often, I wonder, has this form of argument been made to vindi-
cate the thought of one's favourite French theorist?*
At any rate, Moi's ability to defend Kristeva in this way and within the
framework of her own stated desire to repoliticise feminism suggests to
me a kind of ambivalence about collectivist and subjectivist politics
which is underscored by her conclusion to this chapter on Kristeva, and
thus also to her book: a long quotation from Derrida where, in a manner
not too unreminiscent of Kristeva's privileging of the avant-garde, he
dreams of a future, "a multiplicity of sexually marked voices. I would
like to believe in the masses, this indeterminable number of blended
voices, this mobile of non-identified sexual marks whose choreography
can carry, divide, multiply the body of each individual."[12]

Moi talks about this quotation as "utopian," but in a way she's wrong
to do so: it has a place, which is precisely the narcissistic imaginary
productions of poststructuralism, now more or less nicely institution-
alised. Thus Moi, pretending her work to be guided primarily by the
need for an anticapitalist feminism, ends her book with the rhetoric of
an entirely typical poststructuralist public policy utterance, and her
utopia is finally totally nonmaterialist. Rather, it is the common vision
of a dance of voices: the vision that, for instance, guides the current fad
amongst theorists for versions of Bakhtin and the vision that could
aptly act as a rubric for Kristeva's own celebration of the polylogical
text and so on.

*It might not be insulting enough to suggest that Kristeva in fact leads
the American literary theoretical field by just a head.*

Jacqueline Rose's essay likewise suggests that Kristeva's passage was
to be expected, but for reasons quite different to Moi's. Rose questions
the very basis of the many other readings of Kristeva which have
latched onto the idea of the semiotic as part of a liberatory heuristics of
subjectivity and signification. Rose denies that Kristeva tended toward
the anarchic, and she quite rightly stresses that Kristeva never unproblematically embraced the kind of libertarianism of which Moi thinks to
have caught sight. Rather, Kristeva has seen the subject as constructed
simultaneously in the semiotic *and* the symbolic. Working "towards an
at least partial symbolisation of the repressed," Kristeva had managed
to maintain the sense that the subject and the social were forever
dialectically intertwined.[13]

Rose's essay grants that from such positions Kristeva has recently

[12]Jacques Derrida, quoted in Moi, *Sexual/Textual Politics*, 173.

[13]Quotations from this essay are from an unpublished manuscript: page references are
therefore not given. I thank Jacqueline Rose for letting me see the essay, which is now
published in her excellent book, *Sexuality in the Field of Vision* (London: Verso, 1986).

been moving towards the prioritising of the semiotic as a fixed and stable origin, as I have been pointing out, and she shows that Kristeva's tendency to homologise the semiotic with the feminine has proved to be a risky undertaking from the start. However, at the same time, she tries to rescue Kristeva from the kinds of political charges that can be made against her. For instance, in regard to the homologisation of the semiotic with the feminine, Rose suggests that this tack has the virtue of allowing an investigation and critique of that "hideous moment when a theory arms itself with a concept of femininity as different, as something other to the culture as it is known, only to find itself face to face with, or even entrenched within, the most grotesque and fully cultural stereotypes of femininity itself."

Thus for Rose the importance of Kristeva's work resides precisely in its questioning or examination of feminism as a political practice, and this importance is summed up at the end of her article. Kristeva's work "gives us the measure of the difficulties when politics tries to open itself up to the ravages of the unconscious mind." Clearly the form of the sentence here gives priority and privilege to psychoanalysis as the perhaps immovable obstacle—the further truth—against which any political thought must eventually come a cropper: the investigations of psychoanalysis must continue in despite of any loss of political point. Rose's formulation almost makes it sound as if it's politics' *fault* not to be able to open itself to the ravages of the unconscious mind, whereas I want to suggest that it might equally be psychoanalysis's problem that it has been chronically unable to politicize itself.

Both these pieces of writing, then, in their different ways, attempt to assess Kristeva's work from a sympathetic angle. Faced with Kristeva's embourgeoisification, Moi counterposes a generic literary poststructuralist shibboleth, and Rose conducts a defence of metapsychological theory. The one privileging the literary and the other the psychoanalytical, neither actually construes an obstacle to Kristeva's newfound political positions. The problem, it seems to me, is that in both accounts the political aspect of Kristeva's work remains something that might be excused or excised or covered over, when in fact it is crucially intertwined with her particularised versions of subjectivity and her use of psychoanalysis in general. Here again the three terms of the threefold conjunction with which I began seem impossible to articulate together without loss—and especially without loss of radical political urgency.

This situation is one about which Juliet Mitchell occasionally complains in her book around the three terms, *Women: The Longest Revolution*. Mitchell says little there about Kristeva directly, except to ask a very basic but still, I think, signally unanswered question: "One needs to ask why Kristeva and her colleagues, while producing very interesting ideas, choose exclusively masculine tests and quite often proto-fascistic writings as well." Mitchell goes on to point out in her habitual commonsensical manner that "disruption itself can be radical from the right as easily as from the left."[14] These comments occur as a kind of repetition of what I take to be one of Mitchell's main points in this book, that the notion of the subject-in-process, the postmodernist drifting and turning in heterogeneous dreams, is an answer to no political question that feminism might have raised. Against all this Mitchell wants to retain a consideration for what Kristeva has increasingly ignored: the process of narrative and its morality, the story of development and growth, the specificity of histories. "I do not think that we can live as human subjects without in some sense taking on a history; for us it is mainly the history of being men and women under capitalism."[15]

Or More

Kristeva's current postures provoke the need for reconsiderations that could proceed in various directions. In the wake of her return to a particularised view of the imaginary and as a result of her concomitant abandonment of feminism, there may be space to reconsider, for instance, more experienced feminist sojouners in the imaginary. I'm thinking of someone like Luce Irigaray, whose celebrated retreat into the imaginary is in the service of a conceptual revolution for feminism. Irigaray has actually attempted to construct a conceptual schema arising from what she sees as the logic of the imaginary order, using its somatic and conceptual shape to configure a certain kind of negativity and freedom. Kristeva has attacked this project, assigning it to what she calls the second stage of feminism—the first stage had been constituted in "virile militancy," and the second stage tries to "exhume, under the cover of idylls between women, the ravages of sadomasochism."[16] Kristeva's current concept of the imaginary is as a mere receptacle, filled with preoedipal figures and supplemented by the excrescent images of a media-bound society (and it's forgotten that these are still, in terms of real power, produced predominantly by men). Kristeva calls upon us to valorise this version of the imaginary, and the ideal American home that it has produced for itself.

[14]Juliet Mitchell, *Women: The Longest Revolution* (London: Virago Press, 1984), 292.
[15]Ibid., 294.
[16]Kristeva, *Histoires d'amour*, 349.

At this point in writing the original text I stopped and went to see a movie. It was Joyce Chopra's Smooth Talk, *and I recall in particular one line of the dialogue. A somewhat stern mother says to her teenage daughter something like, "I look you straight in the eye and all I see is a head filled with trashy daydreams." That line, it seemed to me, might have been worked into my text in a way more elegant than this!*

Beyond such a reconsideration of the more traditional, as it were, feminist uses of the imaginary, an equally productive countering of Kristeva's kind of political turn might be the adoption of the kind of tactic that Juliet Mitchell usually uses. Working from the assumption of the heuristic efficacy of narrative and the both personal and social histories she continually delves into, Mitchell manages to maintain some of the time-honoured affinity of psychoanalysis with the literary, but at the same time her work sustains the question of the relation of psychoanalysis to political thought and action and its potential to help explicate social and political histories. For Mitchell there is always a superabundance or an overdetermination of questions to be asked, and their commonality is in history and their common tool is narrative. For Kristeva, on the other hand, narrative turns out to be useful only in so far as it crystallises into static figures, decomposes into music, displaces morality into indecidability. This is not to say that there is no history for Kristeva, but rather that when she investigates it she does so only through figures, forms, and tropes whose only real history is a formalistic, intradiscursive one that leads her to collapse the complex (hi)story of subjectivity to ciphers, figures of polyvalency like ET. A materialist sensibility no longer supplies the urge to question, to analyse, or to embrace dialectics and overdetermination but has been changed into a demand for simple acceptance and thence supplies the paradoxically static figure of vacillation.

In the constrast that I'm drawing I don't at all mean to idealise Mitchell's work or hold it up as offering the right answers to the question of how to maintain the terms of the conjunction of feminism, psychoanalysis, and literature. Indeed, Mitchell's tactic is not really to offer answers at all but rather to display and organise the questions. What I want to stress is that, through her sense of the overdetermination of and within histories, Mitchell keeps in tension an *excess* of questions, and through her sense of the centrality of narrative as a term that resides right along side psychoanalysis, feminism, and literature, she avoids the traps of privileging any one of those terms at the expense of the others.

In the conjunction, then, among feminism, psychoanalysis, and literature, there is a continual disturbance, and evidently different effects are gained from differing dispositions, different privileging of the terms.

Paul Smith

What I've wanted to say here is that in my view Kristeva's current work constitutes a kind of limit; that her work has come to the point where the results of juggling the three terms are no longer politically useful; that perhaps the crisis in the conjunction can be eased not by rejecting psychoanalysis (I don't at all mean that) but by reemphasising for the sake of political efficacy the conjunction between any and each of the terms with what I take to be their tutelary term, narrative. At this juncture perhaps history has as much to tell us, women and men, as much to tell us as prehistory.

This version of the text was finished during the 1986 celebrations of independence in the United States, not too many days after the Supreme Court had voted to uphold a Georgia antisodomy law and Congress had voted to give the Nicaraguan Contras a hundred million dollars to carry on their war against the government and people of Nicaragua. Some of the most offensive media coverage of the Fourth of July celebrations featured various resident aliens and naturalized citizens offering their paeans to the American ideals of freedom and democracy.

6

Veiling over Desire:
Close-ups of the Woman

Mary Ann Doane

Psychoanalysis has consistently been suspicious of the realm of the visible, intimately bound as it would seem to be to the register of consciousness. The psychical layer Freud designated perception-consciousness is frequently deceived, caught from behind by unconscious forces which evade its gaze and which are far more determinant in the constitution of subjectivity. Stephen Heath goes so far as to specify the birth of psychoanalysis as a rejection of vision as a mode of organizing and apprehending psychical phenomena. Freud's most important move, from this perspective, lies in the displacement from the "look" to the "voice," from the visible to language. Charcot analyzed hysteria with the aid of a series of photographs depicting women in various stages of the disease. For Heath, this series of photographs is a prefiguration of the cinema—a cinema that is thus placed ineluctably on the side of the pre-Freudian. Freud rejected the photographic techniques of Charcot in favor of the analytic session in which contact with the patient was achieved through speech, association, interpretation of linguistic lapses. According to Heath, "Charcot sees, Freud hears. . . . Psychoanalysis is the anti-visible; significant in this respect, moreover, are Freud's distrust of projects for rendering analysis on the screen and, conversely, the powerful social desire to bring that same analysis into sight, the fascination of so many films with psychoanalysis."[1] The visible and its relation to knowledge are problematized in psychoanalysis, ensured in the cinema, polarizing the two discourses. In much of film theory, psychoanalysis becomes the superior, intelligent discourse of which cinema is the symptom, the guilty mechanism of that cultural constitution and reconstitution of subjectivity as imaginary coherence and security.

[1]Stephen Heath, "Difference," *Screen* 19.3 (1978), 58.

Mary Ann Doane

On the other hand, the fascination with psychoanalysis on the part of film theory is linked to the centrality and strength of its reliance on scenarios of vision: the primal scene, the "look" at the mother's (castrated) body, the mirror stage. Psychoanalytic theory would appear to be dependent upon the activation of scenarios with visual, auditory, and narrative dimensions. Yet, the visible in no way guarantees epistemological certitude. Insofar as it is consistently described as a lure, a trap, or a snare, vision dramatizes the dangers of privileging consciousness. In Lacan's analysis of the eye and the gaze, the gaze takes on an unconscious dimension and is significant in that it "escapes from the grasp of that form of vision that is satisfied with itself in imagining itself as consciousness."[2] There is a hole in the visible. What consciousness and the cinema both fail to acknowledge in their lust for plenitude is that the visible is always lacking. This failure is then subject to formulation by psychoanalysis as the elision of castration. According to Lacan, "To go from perception to science is a perspective that seems to be self-evident. . . . But it is a way that analytic experience must rectify, because it avoids the abyss of castration."[3] This abyss is most evident, of course, in the scenario whereby castration anxiety is generated as an effect of the look at the woman, a scenario in which what is involved is the perception of an absence rather than a presence, a negative perception or, in effect, a nonperception. For what the subject confronts is the woman's "nothing-to-see." At first glance, then, sexual differentiation in psychoanalysis seems to hinge on the visibility or invisibility of the sexual organs, the phallus taking on prominence because it is most easily seen. Yet, the phallus actually becomes important only insofar as it might be absent, it might disappear; it assumes meaning only in relation to castration. Vision remains precarious. As Jacqueline Rose points out, the phallus must be understood in its relation to vision as a "seeming" or an "appearing" rather than as an essential value: "The phallus thus indicates the reduction of difference to an instance of visible perception, a *seeming* value. . . . And if Lacan states that the symbolic usage of the phallus stems from its visibility (something for which he was often criticized), it is only in so far as the order of the visible, the apparent, the seeming is the object of his attack. In fact he constantly refused any crude identification of the phallus with the order of the visible or real."[4]

[2]Jacques Lacan, *The Four Fundamental Concepts of Psychoanalysis*, ed. Jacques-Alain Miller, tran. Alan Sheridan (Harmondsworth, Eng.: Penguin Books, 1979), 74.
[3]Ibid., 77.
[4]Jacqueline Rose, "Introduction—II," *Feminine Sexuality: Jacques Lacan and the Ecole Freudienne*, ed. Juliet Mitchell and Jacqueline Rose, trans. Jacqueline Rose (New York: Norton, 1982), 42.

Such a position seems to justify situating psychoanalysis as a meta-language with respect to the cinema, which forces its spectator to consent to the lure of the visible. For the classical cinema is the opposite of psychoanalysis in that it depends on the axiom that the visible equals the knowable, that truth resides in the image. Yet, although it is clear that psychoanalysis does not trust the visible, denies its appeal to certitude, and does not, in effect, believe in love at first sight, neither does the cinema at all moments. An investigation of these moments of slippage between vision and epistemological certitude in the cinema can illuminate something of the complexity of the relations between truth, vision, and the woman sustained by patriarchy. For the subtextual theme recurrent in filmic texts, which resists the dominant theme whereby vision is constantly ratified, is that appearances can be deceiving. And surely they are most apt to deceive when they involve a woman. The seductive power attributed to the figure of the femme fatale in film noir exemplifies the disparity between seeming and being, the deception, instability, and unpredictability associated with the woman. While the organization of vision in the cinema pivots around the representation of the woman—she is always aligned with the quality of to-be-looked-at-ness—it is also the case that in her attraction to the male subject she confounds the relation between the visible and the knowable.

A site where the classical film acknowledges the precariousness of vision and simultaneously seeks to isolate and hence contain it is the close-up of the woman, more particularly, the veiled woman. For the veil functions to visualize (and hence stabilize) the instability, the precariousness of sexuality.[5] At some level of the cultural ordering of the psychical, the horror or threat of that precariousness (of both sexuality and the visible) is attenuated by attributing it to the woman, over and against the purported stability and identity of the male. The veil is the mark of that precariousness. Clearly, one can trace a poetics or theoretics of the veil in the texts of literature, psychoanalysis, and philosophy as well as the cinema, but in the cinema it is most materially a question of what can and cannot be seen. Only the cinema need give the uncertainty and instability of vision visible form. Ultimately, however, the cinematic activation of the veil serves to demonstrate that doubting the visible is not enough. Psychoanalysis's distrust of the visible is not a guarantee of its use-value for feminism, of an alternative

[5]My analysis is restricted to the usage of the trope of the veil in Western discourse. It seems to me that a quite different problematic informs, for instance, the relation of the Algerian woman to the veil. See Malek Alloula, *The Colonial Harem*, trans. Myrna Godzich and Wlad Godzich (Minneapolis: University of Minnesota Press, 1986), especially chap. 2, "Women from the Outside: Obstacle and Transparency," 7–15.

Mary Ann Doane

and noncomplicit conceptualization of sexual difference. In fact, a psychoanalytic discourse, a philosophical discourse, and a cinematic discourse are more likely to converge at certain points in attaching the precariousness of vision (in its relation to truth) to the figure of the woman or the idea of the feminine—or to make it ineluctably bound up with sexual difference.

Despite the perhaps apocryphal Billy Bitzer story in which D. W. Griffith's purported discovery of the close-up is resisted as a violent fragmentation of the human body ("We pay for the whole actor, Mr. Griffith. We want to see *all* of him."),[6] the close-up has become crucial in the organization of cinematic narrative. And with the formation of a star system heavily dependent upon the maintenance of the aura, the close-up became an important means of establishing the recognizability of each star. At moments it almost seems as though all the fetishism of the cinema were condensed onto the image of the face, the female face in particular. Barthes describes this phenomenon in relation to the face of Garbo: "Garbo still belongs to that moment in cinema when capturing the human face still plunged audiences into the deepest ecstasy, when one literally lost oneself in a human image as one would in a philtre, when the face represented a kind of absolute state of the flesh, which could be neither reached nor renounced."[7] The scale of the close-up transforms the face into an instance of the gigantic, the monstrous: it overwhelms. In the dystopia of *Blade Runner*, a giant video close-up of an Oriental woman oversees, haunts the Los Angeles of the future. The face, usually the mark of individuality, becomes tantamount to a theorem in its generalizability. In the close-up, it is truly bigger than life. The face is that bodily part not accessible to the subject's own gaze (or accessible only as a virtual image in a mirror)—hence its overrepresentation as *the* instance of subjectivity.[8] But the face is not taken in at a glance, it already problematizes the notion of a pure surface since it

[6]Lillian Gish, in *The Movies, Mr. Griffith and Me* (Englewood Cliffs, N.J.: Prentice-Hall, 1970), 59–60, cited in Stephen Heath, "Screen Images, Film Memory," *Edinburgh '76 Magazine*, no. 1, "Psycho-analysis/Cinema/Avant-garde," (1976), 36.

[7]Roland Barthes, *Mythologies*, trans. Annette Lavers (New York: Hill and Wang, 1972), 56.

[8]This notion that the face is the most intense manifestation of subjectivity is also proposed in Béla Balázs's analysis of the close-up, and here it is tinged with essentialism: "Facial expression is the most subjective manifestation of man, more subjective even than speech, for vocabulary and grammar are subject to more or less universally valid rules and conventions, while the play of features, as has already been said, is a manifestation not governed by objective canons, even though it is largely a matter of imitation. This most subjective and individual of human manifestations is rendered objective in the close-up." *Theory of the Film: Character and Growth of a New Art*, trans. Edith Bone (New York: Dover, 1970), 60.

points to an interior, a depth. The face is the most *readable* space of the body. Susan Stewart traces the process by which the face becomes a text.

> If the surface is the location of the body's meaning, it is because that surface is invisible to the body itself. And if the face reveals a depth and profundity which the body itself is not capable of, it is because the eyes and to some degree the mouth are openings onto fathomlessness. Behind the appearance of eyes and mouth lies the interior stripped of appearances. . . . The face is a type of "deep" text, a text whose meaning is complicated by change and by a constant series of alterations between a reader and an author who is strangely disembodied, neither present nor absent, found in neither part nor whole, but, in fact, *created* by this reading. Because of this convention of interpretation, it is not surprising that we find that one of the great *topoi* of Western literature has been the notion of the face as book.[9]

The face, more than any other bodily part, is *for* the other. It is the most articulate sector of the body, but it is mute without the other's reading. In the cinema, this is evidenced in the pause, the meaningful moment of the close-up, *for the spectator*, the scale of the close-up corresponding less than the scale of other shots to the dictates of perspectival realism. And this being-for-the-gaze-of-the-other is, of course, most adequate as a description of the female subject, locked within the mirror of narcissism. Stewart suggests why it is the woman who most frequently inhabits the close-up in various discourses of the image.

> Because it is invisible, the face becomes gigantic with meaning and significance. . . . The face becomes a text, a space which must be "read" and interpreted in order to exist. The body of a woman, particularly constituted by the mirror and thus particularly subject to an existence constrained by the nexus of external images, is spoken by her face, by the articulation of another's reading. Apprehending the image becomes a mode of possession. We are surrounded by the image of the woman's face, the obsession of the portrait and the cover girl alike. The face is what belongs to the other; it is unavailable to the woman herself.[10]

Lacan also refers to this idealist *"belong to me* aspect of representations, so reminiscent of property."[11] From this perspective it is not at all

---

[9]Susan Stewart, *On Longing: Narratives of the Miniature, the Gigantic, the Souvenir, the Collection* (Baltimore: Johns Hopkins University Press, 1984), 127.
[10]Ibid., 125.
[11]Lacan, *The Four Fundamental Concepts*, 81.

surprising that the generalized social exchange of women should manifest itself in the cinematic institution as a proliferation of close-ups of the woman—established as the possession of the gaze of a man through glance-object editing.

What is most intriguing here, however, is the frequency with which the face of the woman in the close-up is masked, barred, shadowed, or veiled, in which a supplementary surface is introduced between the camera or spectator and the contents of the image. When attempting to decipher the rationale of the veil, it is crucial to acknowledge that it has at least several different functions. The veil serves as a form of protection—against light, heat, and, of course, the gaze. To "take the veil" is to become a nun, to seclude oneself in a convent. Most prominently, perhaps, the veil's work would seem to be that of concealing, of hiding a secret. Garbo, as a well-known instance, has recourse to the veil in order to conceal an aging and disintegrating beauty. In Helma Sanders-Brahm's *Germany Pale Mother*, an idyllic mother-daughter relationship is broken by the postwar return of the father, and the resulting neurosis of the mother is evidenced by a paralysis of one side of her face, which she desperately attempts to conceal. Here, the veil is used to hide the scar of historicity, etched upon the woman's face as a hysterical symptom. In Fritz Lang's *Secret beyond the Door*, a marginal female character uses a scarf to veil a facial scar obtained when she saved the male protagonist's son from a fire. The scar acts as a reminder of the deed, and the woman uses it to maintain an emotional hold over the man. At a certain point in the film, however, she is caught without the veil, and it is revealed that she has no scar (its disappearance, she guiltily explains, is a result of plastic surgery obtained years before). The veil in this instance functions to hide an absence, to conceal the fact that the woman has nothing to conceal, to maintain a debt, and thus to incite desire.

Yet, in all these instances of concealing, covering, hiding, or disguising, the veil is characterized by its opacity, its ability to block the gaze fully. When it is activated in the service of the representation of the seductive power of femininity, on the other hand, it simultaneously conceals and reveals, provoking the gaze. The question of whether the veil facilitates vision or blocks it can receive only a highly ambivalent answer inasmuch as the veil, in its translucence, both allows and disallows vision. In the cinema, the magnification of the erotic becomes simultaneous with the activation of objects, veils, nets, streamers, etc., which intercept the space between the camera and the woman, forming a *second screen*. Such a screen is no longer the ground of the image but its filter. This is particularly the case in the films of directors who are

explicitly and insistently associated with the photography or the nar-
rativization of the woman—directors such as Max Ophuls and Joseph
von Sternberg. In the first image of Marlene Dietrich as Concha Perez in
Sternberg's *The Devil Is a Woman*, the sight of her face is doubly
obscured by a filigreed mask that surrounds her eyes and an elaborate
tufted veil that encages the head (figure 1). The disguise is partially
motivated by the mise-en-scène, the carnival, which also authorizes the
masking of the figure of her potential lover in the reverse shot (figure 2).
He, however, has a supplemental, political motivation for concealing
his face. Very vaguely situated as a "revolutionary" who is sought by
the police, he is hiding his identity to avoid detection. But his disguise
does not change throughout the film; it at least has the attribute of
stability, anchored as it is by the desire to hide. The various disguises,
masks, and veils of the Marlene Dietrich character, on the other hand,
take on the arbitrariness of the signifier in their apparent lack of any
motivation beyond that of pure exhibitionism, pure show. The tropes of
the mask, fan, and veil are here the marks of a dangerous deception or
duplicity attached to the feminine (figures 3, 4, 5, 6, 7). In *Dishonored*,
Dietrich assumes a masquerade when she works as a spy for her country—this is an honorable disguise—but in the beginning of the film
when she is literally found in the streets and at the end when she reverts
to the status of prostitute, she is veiled. And the excess and incongruity
of the veiled woman is condensed onto her gesture of lifting the veil to
apply lipstick as she faces a firing squad.

In Sternberg's films, politics is generally an afterthought, but it is
always there, lurking in the background, articulating a discourse of
femininity with a discourse of power. In *The Scarlet Empress*, a seductive, provocative femininity is the pure distillation of power in the
figure of Catherine the Great. In a scene with a powerfully situated
priest who offers her political aid, Catherine claims, "I have weapons
that are far more powerful than any political machine," and this statement is followed by the gesture of raising a veil to her face so that only
the eyes are visible (figure 8). In a subsequent scene, Catherine's antagonistic idiot husband has her surrounded by his Hessian troops and uses
his own sword to play dangerously with the bodice of her dress. Her
response is to take the veil of the earlier scene and push it over his sword
(figure 9). In this and other scenes, the politico-military realm is baffled
by femininity. The film produces a fantasy of power in which femininity conquers the sword and becomes the foil to the phallus. Yet, the
limits of that alleged feminine power are also represented by the iconography of the veil. In a scene in which Marlene Dietrich once again
appears to demonstrate her control over the male, she literally plays

Mary Ann Doane

Figure 1

Figure 2

Figure 3

Figure 4

Figure 5

Figure 6

Figure 7

Figure 8

Mary Ann Doane

Figure 9

Figure 10

Figure 11

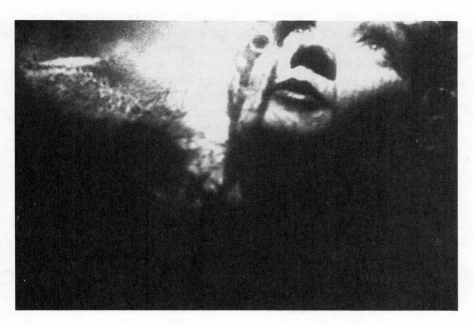

Figure 12

Mary Ann Doane

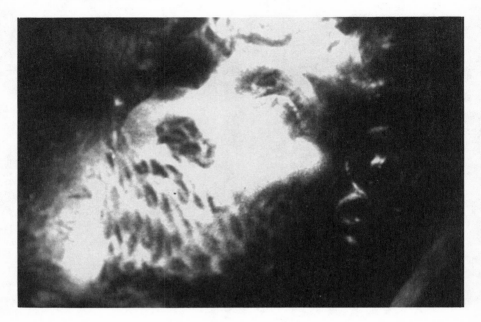

Figure 13

with the veil (figure 10) as she instructs one duped male lover to travel down a secret passage from her bedroom in order to admit his rival. But in the course of the scene, the camera moves closer and closer to Dietrich, she gradually lies back on the bed, and the veil covers the screen (figures 11, 12, 13). The film traces a movement from a moment where the woman controls the veil, moves in and out of its folds in order to lure the male, to a tableau where her very stillness mimics her death in representation, her image entirely subsumed by the veil.

Apart from any intradiegetic motivation, the woman is veiled in an appeal to the gaze of the spectator. And the veil incarnates contradictory desires—the desire to bring her closer and the desire to distance her. Its structure is clearly complicit with the tendency to specify the woman's position in relation to knowledge as that of the enigma. Freud described female sexuality as "still veiled in an impenetrable obscurity."[12] In the discourse of metaphysics, the function of the veil is to

12Sigmund Freud, *Three Essays on the Theory of Sexuality*, trans. James Strachey (New York: Basic Books, 1975), 17. The original is: "Die Bedeutung des Moments der Sexualüberschätzung lässt sich am ehesten beim Manne studieren, dessen Liebesleben allein der Erforschung zugänglich geworden ist, während das des Weibes zum Teil infolge der Kulturverkümmerung, zum anderen Teil durch die konventionelle Verschwiegenheit und Unaufrichtigkeit der Frauen in ein noch undurchdringliches Dunkel gehüllt ist." *Gasammelte Werke* (London: Imago, 1942), 5:50.

make truth profound, to ensure that there is a depth that lurks behind the surface of things. The veil acts as a trope that allows one to evade the superficial, to complicate the surface by disallowing its self-sufficiency. But what the veil in the cinema makes appear to be profound is, in fact, a surface. The function of the veil here is to transform the surface of the face into a depth, an end in itself. While the face in Stewart's analysis is a kind of "deep text," revealing a "depth and profundity which the body itself is not capable of," the addition of a veil as secondary or surplus surface results in the annihilation of that depth which hides behind the face. The veil, in a curious dialectic of depth and surface, reduces all to a surface that is more or less removed, more or less accessible. It is not a privileged depth, interiority, or psychology of the woman which is inaccessible but her sexualized, eroticized, and perfected surface, the embodiment of pure form. Thus, the woman comes to confound the topology of Western metaphysics, its organization of space and hierarchization of depth and surface in their relation to truth. This process has not gone unrecognized. In a temporary deviation from this discussion of the cinema, I would like to explore some of the ramifications of this confused topology in certain texts of philosophy and psychoanalysis.

Nietzsche's attempt to dismantle a philosophy of truth and to undermine the security of knowing produced what is perhaps the most striking analysis of the veil—an analysis that coincides with the beginning of a sustained philosophical attack on metaphysics. And the woman figures prominently there. Furthermore, two recent texts, by Derrida (*Spurs*) and Irigaray ("Veiled Lips"), return to Nietzsche's text in order to extricate a logistics of the veil. Nietzsche both reinscribes and criticizes philosophy's tropological system linking the woman, truth, and the veil. In his writing there is quite definitely a sense in which the movement of truth resembles the veiled gesture of feminine modesty. The veil produces the differentiation between surface and depth required by truth but it also presupposes the necessity of concealing and hence the moral opposition between decent and indecent. Nietzsche extends the metaphor of clothing in the preface to the second edition of *The Gay Science:* "We no longer believe that truth remains truth when the veils are withdrawn; we have lived too much to believe this. Today we consider it a matter of decency not to wish to see everything naked, or to be present at everything, or to understand and 'know' everything."[13] By securing truth's position as a question of decency vs. indecency as it concerns the clothed or unclothed state of the body, Nietz-

---

[13]Friedrich Nietzsche, *The Gay Science*, trans. Walter Kaufmann (New York: Vintage Books, 1974), 38, hereafter cited in the text.

sche aligns it more surely with the figure of the woman—a woman who refuses to or cannot or ought not be known. In preparation for this disclaimer of the desire to know (i.e., to unveil) the truth, Nietzsche alludes to a poem by Schiller, "The Veiled Statue at Saïs," in which a young man, "impelled by a burning thirst for knowledge," travels to Egypt and confronts a veiled statue of Isis.[14] He is told that the veil conceals the very form of truth but also that there is a divine decree prohibiting its disturbance. The youth transgresses, pulls aside the veil and looks, and the sight of truth—head on—induces death. There is no "other space" to counterpose to Plato's cave. The philosophical gaze must be blocked, indirect, difficult. Reminiscent of the structure of fetishism in which the gaze finds itself consistently displaced in relation to the horror of absence, this gaze also aligns or misaligns itself with the body of a woman, in this case, Isis, the sorrowing wife and eternal mother.

Nietzsche's claim to philosophical superiority in this preface rests on his attempt to differentiate between the "we" ("we, artists") of the passage and "those Egyptian youths who endanger temples by night, embrace statues, and want by all means to unveil, uncover, and put into a bright light whatever is kept concealed for good reasons" (38). On the contrary, Nietzsche allies himself with the Greeks who knew how to "stop courageously at the surface, the fold, the skin, to adore appearance, to believe in forms, tones, words, in the whole Olympus of appearance. Those Greeks were superficial—*out of profundity*" (38). The real does not lurk behind the surface: it resides on that surface or exists as a play of surfaces. In this valorization of the surface, Nietzsche elaborates an antihermeneutics whose ultimate aim is the collapse of the oppositions surface/depth, appearance/reality. Nietzsche would like to distance himself from the enterprise of metaphysics.

Yet, this demolition of the dichotomy of surface and depth in relation to truth does not signify the definitive loss of the category of deception. As one of Nietzsche's commentators, Eric Blondel (who characterizes Nietzsche's "ontology" as feminine or gynecological) points out, in his philosophy "the notion of a truth *beyond* appearance, underneath or behind the veil, is rendered null and void. It is certainly true that life deceives us with her ambiguous apparitions: but she deceives us not because she conceals an essence or a reality beneath appearances, but

---

[14]*Works of Frederick Schiller* (New York: John D. Williams, n.d.), 5:197–99. Although the celebrated temple of Isis (or Neith, who is often confused with Isis) at Saïs no longer stands, Plutarch writes that it contained this inscription: "I am all that has been, that is, and that will be. No mortal has yet been able to lift the veil which covers me." See *New Larousse Encyclopedia of Mythology*, trans. Richard Aldington and Delano Ames (New York: Prometheus Press, 1968), 37.

because she has *no* essence and would only like to make us think that she does. Her 'essence' is to appear."[15] Deception, from this point of view, is not defined as the noncoincidence or incompatibility of surface and depth (appearance and the truth), but as the very posing of the question of truth and its hiding place—the gesture indicating truth's existence. Deception, far from distorting truth, operates a double negation by, as Derrida will point out in another context, concealing the secret that there is no secret. Furthermore, it is not accidental that in the quotation from Blondel the pronoun *she* plays such a major role in delineating the operation of this mode of deception. For in Nietzsche's view, woman epitomizes the pretense of essence. Her great talent lies in the area of deception or dissimulation, in what would appear to be the very opposite of truth: in giving herself, as Nietzsche says in *The Gay Science*, she "gives herself for" (317), that is, plays a part, produces herself as spectacle. In *Beyond Good and Evil* Nietzsche compares her to the actor who dons a mask for every occasion and whose "essence" is ultimately subsumed by the mask. Confronted with the demands of a vocal feminist movement, Nietzsche seeks shelter in the idea that woman does not *want* truth, reinforcing her association with dissimulation.

> We may in the end reserve a healthy suspicion whether woman really *wants* enlightenment about herself—whether she *can* will it—
>
> Unless a woman seeks a new adornment for herself that way—I do think adorning herself is part of the Eternal-Feminine?—she surely wants to inspire fear of herself—perhaps she seeks mastery. But she does not *want* truth—her great art is the lie, her highest concern is mere appearance and beauty.[16]

The desire to know can only be a new piece of clothing for the woman, a new surface, something with which to play at seduction. Only this will make feminism palatable for Nietzsche.

[15]Eric Blondel, "Nietzsche: Life as Metaphor," in *The New Nietzsche: Contemporary Styles of Interpretation*, ed. David B. Allison (New York: Dell, 1977), 157.

[16]Nietzsche, *Beyond Good and Evil*, trans. Walter Kaufmann (New York: Vintage Books, 1966), 163. I should point out that Nietzsche prefaces these—and other even more disparaging—remarks about woman in section 232 of *Beyond Good and Evil* with what might be interpreted as a disclaimer at the end of section 231: "After this abundant civility that I have just evidenced in relation to myself I shall perhaps be permitted more readily to state a few truths about 'woman as such'—assuming that it is now known from the outset how very much these are after all only—*my* truths" (162). It is not clear, however, to what extent this statement really does function as a disclaimer since truth, for Nietzsche, is certainly not generalizable in any event. The will to knowledge is a form of the will to power and to state that something is simply "*my* truth" is a way of staking out a territory (and a "perspective") in relation to this willing. The text on woman is not necessarily undermined thereby.

Mary Ann Doane

Deception and dissimulation are not negative categories in Nietz-sche's work, since they align themselves with the work of the anti-metaphysical philosopher. Nevertheless, they also place the woman as the privileged exemplar of instability. Luce Irigaray criticizes Nietzsche for situating femininity as "the simulacrum which introduces the false into the true": "So she who is always mobile renders him the possibility of movement in remaining, for him, the persistence of his being. Truth or appearances, according to his desire of the moment, his appetite of the instant. Truth and appearances and reality, power . . . she is—by virtue of her inexhaustible aptitude for mimicry—the living support of all the staging/production of the world. Variously veiled according to the ep-ochs of history."[17] Derrida is more generous to Nietzsche, claiming that his alliance of the woman with the artist or the actor represents an instance of his determined antiessentialism. In this sense, she becomes the ruin of philosophy, which Derrida can only approve: "There is no such thing as the essence of woman because woman averts, she is averted of herself. . . . And the philosophical discourse, blinded, found-ers on these shoals and is hurled down these depthless depths to its ruin. There is no such thing as the truth of woman, but it is because of that abyssal divergence of the truth, because that untruth is 'truth.' Woman is but one name for that untruth of truth."[18] Woman is truth only insofar as it diverges from itself, is not reducible to the evidence of self-presence, multiplies its surfaces, and produces frames within frames. Always "averting," it is anything but straightforward. Just like a woman. For Derrida, woman incarnates the mise-en-abŷme structure of truth.

This deception attributed to the woman does not, however, connote hypocrisy on her part. Her dissembling is not a conscious strategy. She has no knowledge of it or access to it as an operation. And this uncon-sciousness of the woman, her blindness to her own work, is absolutely necessary in order to allow and maintain the man's idealization of her, his perfection of her as an object. According to Nietzsche, "Given the tremendous subtlety of woman's instinct, modesty remains by no means conscious hypocrisy: she divines that it is precisely an actual naive modesty that most seduces a man and impels him to overesti-mate her. Therefore woman is naive—from the subtlety of her instinct, which advises her of the utility of innocence. A deliberate *closing of one's eyes to oneself*—Wherever dissembling produces a stronger effect

[17]Luce Irigaray, "Veiled Lips," trans. Sara Speidel, *Mississippi Review*, 11.3 (1983), 98, 118.

[18]Jacques Derrida, *Spurs: Nietzsche's Styles*, trans. Barbara Harlow (Chicago: Univer-sity of Chicago Press, 1979), 51, hereafter cited in the text.

when it is unconscious, it *becomes* unconscious."[19] The philosopher-voyeur sees quite well that the woman "closes her eyes to herself." She does not *know* that she is deceiving or *plan* to deceive; conscious deception would be repellent to the man and quite dangerous. Rather, she intuits or "divines" what the man needs—a belief in her innocence—and she *becomes* innocent. Closing her eyes to herself she becomes the pure construct of a philosophical gaze. Becoming unconscious of any knowledge she might have concerning truth as dissimulation, as surface, she becomes instead its representation, its idea. As Derrida points out, "It is impossible to resist looking for her" (71). Woman is situated as the substrate of representation itself, its unconscious material.

In this way, Nietzsche deprives the woman of subjectivity. Or it could be said that women attain subjectivity only when they become old, and the recurrent image of the old woman in Nietzsche's work corroborates his own philosophy. For the old woman knows more than the metaphysicians: "I am afraid that old women are more skeptical in their most secret heart of hearts than any man: they consider the superficiality of existence its essence, and all virtue and profundity is to them merely a veil over this 'truth,' a very welcome veil over a pudendum—in other words, a matter of decency and shame, and no more than that."[20] A woman is granted knowledge when she is old enough to become a man—which is to say, old enough to lose her dissembling appearance, her seductive power. And even then, it is a kind of "old wives" knowledge, not, properly speaking, philosophical. For the most part, the figure of the woman is the projection of Nietzsche's own epistemological desires, his will to *embody* the difficulties, the impossibilities of what remains a tantalizing truth. This is how the woman comes to represent a variety of often contradictory notions: truth, dissimulation, superficiality, even "calm." Overcome in *The Gay Science* by the philosophical tumult of ideas, Nietzsche envisages the woman as a sail floating in the calm distance: "When a man stands in the midst of his own noise, in the midst of his own surf of plans and projects, then he is apt also to see quiet, magical beings gliding past him and to long for

[19]Nietzsche, *The Will to Power*, trans. Walter Kaufmann and R. J. Hollingdale, ed. Walter Kaufmann (New York: Vintage Books, 1968), 425.

[20]Nietzsche, *The Gay Science*, 125. Despite this access to a knowing subjectivity, the old woman is, like the young one, often treated by Nietzsche as a metaphor for truth; she no longer knows it but represents it (and "truth" here is Nietzsche's despised truth of the metaphysicians). Two examples from *The Gay Science:* "Humanity! Has there ever been a more hideous old woman among all old women—(unless it were 'truth': a question for philosophers)?" (339) and the verse "Up north—embarrassing to tell— / I loved a creepy ancient belle: / The name of this old hag was Truth" (357).

their happiness and seclusion: *women*" (124). But if one gets too close to the sailboat, the magical silence is broken by the chattering, babble, and incoherency of the woman:" The magic and the most powerful effect of women is, in philosophical language, action at a distance, *actio in distans;* but this requires first of all and above all—*distance*" (124). Proximity reduces her (its) value. She (it) can seduce only from a distance. Or behind a veil. Nietzsche here gives us the mise-en-scène of the philosophical hypostatization of Woman.

Woman as a truth that is difficult to win, as semblance, as the mistress of the lie and dissimulation, or as seductive deceiver, as residing in the realm of appearances—there is no doubt that Nietzsche invokes "worn" metaphors in the service of an antitraditional, antimetaphysical discourse in an attempt to collapse the opposition between appearance and reality and, consequently, that he revalues such notions as "appearance," "surface," and "dissimulation." But the worn metaphors carry with them a problematic haze of associations and the revaluation of the woman image is not always distinguishable from idealization. One is forced to ask why it is the woman who must represent either truth or its fading, its disappearance, especially in relation to an erotics of the veil.

The veil poses difficulties for both Nietzsche and Derrida insofar as it drags along its metaphysical baggage, but neither of them will reject the trope altogether. According to Derrida, Nietzsche recognized the fragile structure of truth in its relation to the veil and both refuse to perform the gesture of either veiling or unveiling. Derrida prefers the image of *suspending* the veil: " 'Truth' can only be a surface. But the blushing movement of that truth which is not suspended in quotation marks casts a modest veil over such a surface. And only through such a veil which thus falls over it could 'truth' become truth, profound, indecent, desirable. But should that veil be suspended, or even fall a bit differently, there would be no longer any truth, only 'truth'—written in quotation marks" (59). To suspend means to hang from a single point of support in space, to interrupt, to defer. The woman perpetually defers the question of truth. It remains, precisely, suspended. In *Spurs*, the term *woman* functions as a point of comparison to style, writing, inscription, particularly inasmuch as the notion of "writing" in Derrida's work always signifies the undoing of metaphysical oppositions. The attempt is clearly to introduce a division between any question of the woman and an ontological question. Nevertheless, it is still the woman who figures the very resistance to the ontological question:[21] "The

21Derrida does insist that he is dealing with the question of the woman rather than her figure—"It is not the figure of the woman precisely because we shall bear witness here to

question of the woman suspends the decidable opposition of true and non-true and inaugurates the regime of quotation marks which is to be enforced for every concept belonging to the system of philosophical decidability. The hermeneutic project which postulates a true sense of the text is disqualified under this regime" (107). In a quite Nietzschean gesture, Derrida takes up and employs the worn-out tropes of femininity—instability, indecisiveness, dissimulation—and yet injects them with a new and more positive value for the sake of his philosophical operation. The woman is used to destabilize the hierarchy of values of metaphysics, and the eroticism of the operation is not lost. The voyeurism continues: "It is impossible to resist looking for her."

Nietzsche manipulates and works within the problematic wherein the woman is a trope of truth. Yet, believing in truth is, from his point of view, a common mistake of philosophers. The woman, on the other hand, who represents truth, has no use for it herself. Derrida reiterates this idea in claiming that the philosopher must emulate the woman, who does not believe in truth or castration. He locates three types of proposition about the woman in Nietzsche's text. In the first, the woman is a figure of falsehood, against which the man measures his own phallogocentric truth. Here, she is castrated. In the second proposition, she is the figure of truth but plays with it at a distance through a guile and naïveté that nevertheless ratify truth. Here, she is castrating. In the first two types of proposition in Nietzsche's text, the woman is "censured, debased and despised." Only the third type of proposition is conceived outside the bind of castration. Here, the woman is an "affirmative power, a dissimulatress, an artist, a dionysiac" (97). Derrida succinctly outlines the desire of Nietzsche: "He was, he dreaded this castrated woman. He was, he dreaded this castrating woman. He was, he loved this affirming woman" (101). And Derrida would like to be Nietzsche being the woman. According to Irigaray, "Ascribing his [Derrida's] own project to her, he rises from the abyss—or the *abyme*."22 Woman-truth, woman-lie, woman-affirmation—it is quite striking that the woman comes to represent all these things, as though affirmation, the most highly treasured category, could somehow not be *thought* except in and through the figure of the woman. She enables the philosophical operation, becomes its support.

In Derrida's text, the woman no longer figures the veiled movement of truth but the suspended veil of undecidability. She comes to repre-

---

her *abduction,* because the question of the figure is at once opened and closed by what is called woman" (41). Still, I would argue that the woman in Derrida's text serves to figure a question—whether of truth or of the figure. Her function is clearly tropological.

22Irigaray, 105.

sent the limit to the relevance of the hermeneutic question. Derrida's skepticism about that question, about the project of interpretation in general, is focused in his consideration of Nietzsche's marginal unpublished note, "I have forgotten my umbrella." For its secret, its hidden meaning beneath the veil of a surface, may be that it has no secret. The note is therefore like the woman insofar as "it might only be pretending to be simulating some hidden truth within its folds. Its limit is not only stipulated by its structure but is in fact intimately con-fused with it. The hermeneut cannot but be provoked and disconcerted by its play" (133). The woman becomes even more tantalizing, desirable, and like the umbrella, something you do not want to forget. The veil ensures that this is not a question of visibility, of the visible as a guaranty or measure of certitude. For, as Derrida admits, "Nietzsche himself did not see his way too clearly there" (101). Nevertheless, he managed. In both Nietzsche's and Derrida's texts, the woman becomes the site of a certain philosophical reinvestment—this time in the attempt to deconstruct truth. She remains the fetish of philosophy.

From this point of view, Lacan's appeal to the trope of the veil might seem more desirable for feminist theory inasmuch as it hovers around not the woman but questions of representation and the phallus. Yet, it is still contaminated a little by the problematic of truth and deception or fraud. The veil is the privileged content of the trompe l'oeil constituted by painting: it fools or deceives the human subject. In the story of Zeuxis and Parrhasios invoked by Lacan, Zeuxis, challenged by his rival, Parrhasios, produces a painting of grapes which attracts birds who attempt to pick at them. But when Zeuxis demands that Parrhasios draw aside the veil that covers his painting, he is startled to find that the veil itself is painted. Lacan uses the story to establish a distinction between the "natural function of the lure" (the painted grapes) and that of trompe l'oeil (the painted veil): "If one wishes to deceive a man, what one presents to him is the painting of a veil, that is to say, something that incites him to ask what is behind it."[23] This painting elicits the desire to touch, to transgress the barrier of representation and to posit its "beyond" or "depth," prompted by the extent to which the surface posits something "other." Plato's objection to painting is, therefore, not based on its illusion of equaling its object but on the fact that the "*trompe-l'oeil* of painting pretends to be something other than what it is" (112). Lacan's analysis of the story constitutes a complication of vision, marking it with absence so that the picture takes on the mechanism of language.

[23]Lacan, *The Four Fundamental Concepts*, 111–12, hereafter cited in the text.

In the process, vision is destabilized; it becomes less sure, precisely because it is subject to desire. Parrhasios's painting demonstrates that "what was at issue was certainly deceiving the eye (*tromper l'oeil*). A triumph of the gaze over the eye" (103). *Gaze* here signifies the excess of desire over geometral vision or vision as the representation of space through perspective. In the geometral relation of perspective, the subject is centered as the master of representation; visual space is mapped and controlled. The gaze, on the other hand, indicates that the "I," no longer master of what it sees, is grasped, solicited, by the depth of field (that which is beyond). Zeuxis, subject to desire, seeks to know what is beyond the surface/veil. The trick is that the surface is all there is to be seen. There is dissimulation or deception here, but as in Nietzsche's text, it does not consist of a distortion of the truth behind appearances but a mere gesture toward that "beyond."[24] And while, according to Nietzsche, it is the woman who exemplifies the instability of the visual and the pretense of essence, in Lacan's analysis it is representation—the picture—that pretends to be something other than what it is.

This theoretical move, however, is not in fact a desexualization of the dialectic of appearance and reality, the veil and the beyond. For behind the veil lurks the phallus. The gaze and desire are in tandem because the field of the visible always registers (is always inhabited by) a lack: "The subject is presented as other than he is, and what one shows him is not what he wishes to see" (104). The gaze is hence the *objet a* in the scopic dimension. Symbolic of lack, it is clearly inscribed in a phallic order. Furthermore, in Lacan's work the veil itself is, most strikingly, reserved for the phallus. Torn from the woman's face, it is located elsewhere. I am thinking, of course, of the often quoted statement in which Lacan claims that "the phallus can play its role only when veiled." For Rose, this appeal to veiling is evidence of Lacan's demotion of the realm of the visible: "He constantly refused any crude identification of the phallus with the order of the visible or real and he referred it instead to that function of 'veiling.' "[25] The disorganization of the field of perception—its destabilization—is attributed not to the woman but to the phallus. Now it is certainly possible to develop the argument that the phallus is not a masculine category, that it is a signifier and not equivalent to the penis (the consistent strategy of those who argue that Lacanian psychoanalysis is useful for feminism), and therefore that we are not con-

---

[24]It should be noted that Lacan does not annihilate the "beyond" of appearance (as Nietzsche often seems to want to do) but dematerializes or desubstantializes it by locating the gaze there: "I shall take up here the dialectic of appearance and its beyond, in saying that, if beyond appearance there is nothing in itself, there is the gaze" (103).

[25]Rose, "Introduction—II," *Feminine Sexuality*, 42.

fronted with a situation in which the psychoanalyst snatches the veil from the woman in order to conceal his own private parts. Far from being exhausted by its masculine status, the phallus would appear to be to some degree feminized in Lacan's text. The woman's relation to the phallus is that of "being" rather than "having" and the mother is sometimes "phallic." Or one could subscribe to Jane Gallop's analysis of the grammatical categories of gender and note that the phallus, in a slip of the type, is modified by "la" rather than "le" or that "voile" as Lacan uses it, is both feminine (as "sail") or masculine (as "veil"). For in "The Agency of the Letter in the Unconscious," Nietzsche's sailboat in the distance glides through Lacan's text and becomes the privileged example of metonymy: "thirty sails." As Gallop points out, " 'Voile' for 'sail' is derived from 'voile' for 'veil,' and it may be just this sort of slippage between a masculine and a feminine term that is at play in Lacan's notion of the phallus, which is a latent phallus, a metonymic, maternal, feminine phallus."[26]

But even Gallop acknowledges that "the masculinity of the phallic signifier serves well as an emblem of the confusion between phallus and male which inheres in language, in our symbolic order,"[27] and concludes her reading of "The Meaning of the Phallus" with a return to the penis (the knot). It might be useful, then, to turn our attention to an examination of what the role of the phallus is and therefore why the veil is necessary. The phallus takes on meaning in relation to the differential function of language and the corresponding structure of signifier/signified. The entire sentence reads, "All these propositions merely veil over the fact that the phallus can only play its role as veiled, that is, as in itself the sign of the latency with which everything signifiable is struck as soon as it is raised (aufgehoben) to the function of the signifier."[28] The veil over the phallus points to the necessity of a division between the latency of the signifiable and the patency—the materiality—of the signifier, a splitting in language as well as a splitting of subjectivity. The phallus, as the signifier with no signified, indicates the perpetual deferral of meaning, its failure to coagulate. Behind the veil, which must remain in place, lies a series of linked terms: lack, the gaze, the *objet a*, the phallus. There is no doubt that Lacan attempts to disrupt the spatialization of the classical philosophical dialectic between surface and depth, appearance and being. The "beyond" is a function of desire and hence deessentialized but not entirely negated. Rather, the sur-

[26]Jane Gallop, *Reading Lacan* (Ithaca: Cornell University Press, 1985), 131.
[27]Ibid., 140.
[28]Lacan, "The Meaning of the Phallus," in *Feminine Sexuality*, 82.

face/depth dichotomy is reformulated as a splitting, a fracture, necessitated by the subject's relation to language and the unconscious. If there is a truth in Lacanian psychoanalysis it is a truth of language and the contribution of language to the constitution of subjectivity. But it is a truth that, like Nietzsche's, is particularly evasive, slippery. For that which is latent—the signifiable—is also always deferred, out of reach, subject to a metonymic displacement. Like a woman, the phallus—in a perpetual demonstration of the inadequacy of language with respect to meaning—plays its role only when veiled. Neither the woman nor the phallus seems to be capable of completely escaping the problematic of truth, even if it is defined in its very inaccessibility, in its resistance to the purely visible, or as belonging to the order of language. Whether or not the phallus is feminized, truth, in the Lacanian text, insofar as it concerns a question of veiling, is usurped for the phallus, no longer figured explicitly through the woman, who nevertheless comes to represent an absolute and unattainable state of *jouissance*. Both Derrida and Lacan envy the woman they have constructed.

There is, at one point in *The Gay Science*, a reference to a female figure who might disturb or disconcert this phallocentric staging of truth (or its destabilization) and representation with respect to veiling and unveiling. It is a reference Nietzsche does not develop. He writes, "Perhaps truth is a woman who has reasons for not letting us see her reasons? Perhaps her name is—to speak Greek—*Baubo?*" (38). There is nothing more about Baubo, only this vague reference to her name in relation to truth and what it allows or disallows in the realm of vision. The translator and editor, Walter Kaufmann, adds, however, a footnote which transforms Nietzsche's remark into something of a dirty joke: "*Baubo:* A primitive and obscene female demon; according to the *Oxford Classical Dictionary*, originally a personification of the female genitals." In Greek mythology, Baubo is a minor character in the story of Demeter, the goddess of fertility, whose daughter Kore (renamed Persephone after the abduction) was stolen and raped by Hades, lord of the underworld. Demeter fled Olympus and wandered throughout the world for years in the guise of an old woman, searching for her daughter. One day, as she was resting in the shade of a tree in Eleusis, Baubo offered her a drink of barley water and mint. In her grief, Demeter refused the drink and in response Baubo lifted her skirts to reveal her pudenda. A drawing of a boy's face (Iacchus—a mystic name for Dionysus) appeared on the lower part of her body, and Baubo, with a gesture of her hand, made it seem to grimace, provoking Demeter to laugh, breaking her mourning. The laughter freed Demeter, and she accepted the drink from Baubo. Afterward, she managed to free her

Mary Ann Doane

daughter Persephone from the underworld for three-fourths of the year. In the remaining one-fourth, when Persephone resides with her husband in the underworld, Demeter's sadness is reflected in the coldness and barrenness of the earth.

In Peter Wollen's brief but fascinating analysis of the myth, Baubo's exhibitionism is interpreted as a potential alternative to the castrating display of the Medusa: "[Baubo's] display is to another woman and its effect is to provoke laughter and to end grief and mourning (brought about by mother-daughter separation at the hands of a man, Pluto). . . . Demeter is shown the "Truth," but is it just a joke? It is not shameful, not horrifying, but funny, comical, laughable." The laugh, outside the semantic and "on the edge of language," breaks the hold of a phallogocentric grammar.[29] Sarah Kofman also interprets Baubo as a figure who resides outside the regime of phallocentrism, undermining its logic. Through a number of links, including the inscription of Dionysus's face on Baubo's body, Kofman makes the claim that Baubo is a feminine double of Dionysus. And Dionysus, nude but also the god of masks, "erases the opposition of veiled and non-veiled, masculine and feminine, fetishism and castration."[30] Both Wollen and Kofman point out that the story of Baubo is told in the texts of the early church fathers. Kofman observes that these texts are censored and qualified with obscurities, seemingly confirming the notion that Baubo exemplies the marginalization of the woman's story as well as the woman's genitals within a patriarchal discourse.

In an extremely short text, "A Mythological Parallel to a Visual Obsession," Freud also invokes the myth of Baubo, but the specificity of the feminine gesture of unveiling the genitals and the inscription upon the female body are lost.[31] Freud's male patient is obsessed with an image of his father's body, minus chest and head, but with the facial features represented on the abdomen. Freud recognizes the parallel with the myth of Baubo, but his analysis centers on the son's anal eroticism and his resistance to and caricature of the father (the *Vaterarsch-Patriarch*).

[29]Peter Wollen, "Baubo," *subjects/objects*, no. 2 (1984), 121, 123.

[30]Sarah Kofman, "Baubô: Perversion théologique et fétichisme," in *Nietzsche et la scène philosophique* (Paris: Union Générale d'Editions, 1979), 297. Although I agree with much of Kofman's specific analysis of Baubo, that analysis takes place within the context of a more extended investigation of Nietzsche's use of the figure of the woman (and the question of his misogyny) with which I would take issue. In a reading inspired by Derrida, Kofman makes what is essentially an apology for Nietzsche hinge almost entirely on the figure of Baubo as she is linked to Dionysus (clearly a valorized name in Nietzsche's text).

[31]Sigmund Freud, "A Mythological Parallel to a Visual Obsession," *Collected Papers*, trans. Joan Riviere (New York: Basic Books, 1959), 4:345–46.

The myth of Baubo finds an interesting—and similarly porno-graphic—echo in Lacan's work. Lacan is fascinated with anamorphosis and its inverted use of perspective. In *The Four Fundamental Concepts* he makes it the center point of a large part of his analysis of the gaze and claims that it is evocative of that which "geometral researches into perspective allow to escape from vision" (87). Anamorphosis gives a glimpse of this excess; its fascination is a fascination with the annihila-tion of the subject. But the scenario he constructs to illustrate ana-morphosis, immediately before the better-known analysis of Hans Hol-bein's painting *The Ambassadors*, is rather strange, almost fantastical, and, like the myth of Baubo, invokes a notion of body-writing: "How is it that nobody has ever thought of connecting this [anamorphosis] with . . . the effect of an erection? Imagine a tattoo traced on the sexual organ *ad hoc* in the state of repose and assuming its, if I may say so, developed form in another state. How can we not see here, immanent in the geometral dimension . . . something symbolic of the function of the lack, of the appearance of the phallic ghost?" (87–88).[32] The preferred space of inscription for anamorphosis becomes the phallic organ. The apparently alternative conceptualization of the female genitals in Baubo's story is here recuperated, revamped. For the male subject's body allows him to do it better. Lacan, envious of the woman, appropri-ates her picture-making activity, her body-writing, and inscribes it on the phallus. After all, anamorphosis would seem to prefer a masculine space, as in the Holbein painting.

Yet, Lacan has to go into certain contortions to write on the penis/phallus. When the metaphor of writing is invoked, the phallus is usu-ally conceptualized as the tool that writes, the pen, rather than the surface of writing. Lacan seems to be uncomfortable with the specifica-tion of the penis/phallus as mere ground, space for inscription (a tradi-tionally "feminine" characterization). Perhaps this is why the reference to the phallic organ as the site of anamorphosis is so brief, laconic, and almost immediately displaced by the analysis of the Holbein painting. Here the phallus is no longer the ground for anamorphosis but its

[32]Anamorphosis, although it does point to that which escapes geometral vision, re-mains within the problematic of that vision, for it is still a question of rays of light—the straight line and the mapping of space rather than sight. Specific to vision, as far as Lacan is concerned, is light as refracted, distorted, diffused. He often uses words such as "pulsatile," "irradiation," "the play of light, fire," "dazzling," etc. In this sense, he sometimes seems to divorce the gaze from the phallic function: "But it is further still that we must seek the function of vision. We shall then see emerging on the basis of vision, not the phallic symbol, the anamorphic ghost, but the gaze as such, in its pulsatile, dazzling and spread out function, as it is in this picture [*The Ambassadors*]" (89). At other times the gaze, in its operation as lack or as *objet a*, clearly plays the role of the veiled phallus.

Mary Ann Doane

central figure. The phallus is *in* the picture, the picture no longer *on* the phallus, allaying any fears about the complete feminization of the phallus, particularly since the mise-en-scène of the Holbein painting is so insistently masculine.

The male theorist's relation to the woman, in general, seems to oscillate between fear and envy of the feminine. Lacan attributes to the phallus qualities formerly specified as feminine: veiled, it connotes visual instability, deception. The phallus symbolizes the failure of meaning, the fact that it is mere semblance. If "the status of the phallus is a fraud,"[33] as Rose points out, it is fraudulent in much the same way as woman represents untruth or dissimulation in Nietzsche's text. Lacan reverses the usual terms of sexual difference in relation to the visual field. In Nietzsche the precariousness of vision is incarnated in the woman, while the man is a point of stability (in relation to the will to know, to philosophize, if not in relation to knowledge itself—Derrida's "It is impossible to resist looking for her"). In Lacan, the necessary destabilization or deception of the visual is a function of the phallus, while the woman, in some sense, comes to represent the immediacy and security of the visible. This immediacy is a result of the *jouissance* attributed to her: "As for Saint Theresa—you only have to go and look at Bernini's statue in Rome to understand immediately that she's coming, there is no doubt about it. And what is her *jouissance*, her *coming* from? It is clear that the essential testimony of the mystics is that they are experiencing it but know nothing about it."[34] As Stephen Heath points out, the "more" of the woman's *jouissance* in Lacan's work compensates for the absence she represents in relation to the scenario of castration.[35]

And one could add that the price to be paid for visual immediacy and the "more" of *jouissance* is the absence of knowledge. Lacan explains that while the woman is "not all" in relation to the phallic function and is "excluded by the nature of things which is the nature of words," she nevertheless has a supplementary *jouissance*.

> There is a *jouissance* proper to her, to this "her" which does not exist and which signifies nothing. There is a *jouissance* proper to her and of which

[33]Rose, "Introduction—II," *Feminine Sexuality*, 40.

[34]Lacan, "God and the *Jouissance* of the Woman," in *Feminine Sexuality*, 147. Stephen Heath is quite critical of the immediacy of the image in this passage as well as the use of a photograph of Bernini's statue of Saint Theresa on the cover of the seminar volume from which the passage is taken—*Encore*: "It might be added, moreover, as a kind of working rule, that where a discourse appeals directly to an image, to an immediacy of seeing, as a point of its argument or demonstration, one can be sure that all difference is being elided, that the unity of some accepted vision is being reproduced." "Difference," 53.

[35]Heath, 53.

she herself may know nothing, except that she experiences it—that much she does know. . . . As I have said, the woman can love in the man only the way in which he faces the knowledge he souls for. But as for the knowledge by which he is, we can only ask this question if we grant that there is something, *jouissance*, which makes it impossible to tell whether the woman can say anything about it—whether she can say what she knows of it.[36]

Jouissance presupposes a nonknowledge or even an antiknowledge. It is linked to the realm of the mystics and hence, at the very least, divorces the register of knowledge from the register of discourse. The woman cannot say what she knows; that knowledge may exist, but it always resides elsewhere. Since psychoanalysis, however, is in itself a form of antiepistemology insofar as the unconscious subverts the possibility of a stable knowledge, the woman here becomes emblematic of the subject who is duped by the unconscious, of the nonknowledge of the subject. It is almost as though there were an obligatory blind spot as far as the woman is concerned which is compensated for by an *over*-sight, a compulsion to see her, to image her, to make her revelatory of something.

Nietzsche's woman, closing her eyes to herself, and Lacan's woman, who doesn't know (who has *jouissance* without knowledge), have something in common. Yet, knowledge, like truth, is a peculiar term in the work of both Nietzsche and Lacan. The subject's position outside of knowledge is not necessarily to be lamented. In these theories, therefore, it is a question not so much of depriving the woman of subjectivity (a term psychoanalysis problematizes in any event) as of making her a privileged trope, a site of theoretical excess, an exemplar of the philosophical enterprise. Derrida positions the woman as affirmative and Dionysiac, the figure of undecidability and the point of impasse of the hermeneutic question. Clearly, Lacan's theoretical assumptions about subjectivity and his strategic moves distance him significantly from Derrida's deconstructive efforts, and their differences should not be minimalized, but Lacan's phallocentrism and Derrida's antiphallocentrism (or hymen-ism) ultimately occupy the same discursive register as far as the fate of the woman is concerned. Is there that much difference

---

[36]Lacan, "God and the *Jouissance* of the Woman," 144, 145, "A Love Letter," in *Feminine Sexuality*, 159. Lacan's generalizations about *the* woman are qualified by his insistence upon crossing through the definite article: "*The* woman can only be written with *The* crossed through. There is no such thing as *The* woman since of her essence—having already risked the term, why think twice about it?—of her essence, she is not all" (144). It is a strange qualification of generalization, however, which qualifies by imposing another generalization. It only *seems* less totalizing because of its negative formulation ("not all").

Mary Ann Doane

between the affirmation beyond castration of the Derridean woman and the *jouissance* of the Lacanic woman? *Affirmation* and *jouissance* both indicate a certain "beyond" in their respective theories, a beyond that seems to represent, interestingly, the very limit of what is theorizable.

The theoretical limit is tantalizing, seductive in its very inaccessibility. But the term that seems most adequately to describe the relation of the philosopher/psychoanalyst to the woman here is envy. And it is Lacan who gives us a clue to a possible deciphering of this envy. The scenario he invokes in order to depict envy as a way of looking is that of the child at the mother's breast. "The most exemplary *invidia*, for us analysts, is the one I found long ago in Augustine, in which he sums up his entire fate, namely, that of the little child seeing his brother at his mother's breast, looking at him *amare conspectu*, with a bitter look, which seems to tear him to pieces and has on himself the effect of a poison." Lacan claims that this envy has nothing to do with the child's desire for what the brother has—the milk or the breast or the mother as possessions. In this sense, it differs from jealousy. Rather, "such is true envy—the envy that makes the subject pale before the image of a completeness closed upon itself, before the idea that the *petit a*, the separated *a* from which he is hanging, may be for another the possession that gives satisfaction, *Befriedigung*."[37] Lacan initially interprets the envy as that of brother for brother—male subject for the apparently total gratification and contentment of another male subject. But the fact that it is an "image of a completeness closed upon itself" which prompts the envy would seem to suggest instead that it is the woman— the mother—who is the object of the envy. For in psychoanalytic theory the woman is depicted in her narcissistic self-sufficiency as the being who most fully embodies a "completeness closed upon itself." In effect, what the male subject of theory here envies is the woman whom he has constructed as inhabiting a space outside his own theory— nevertheless supporting that theory through her very absence. "You only have to go and look" to see that she is not of this world. As Lacan himself points out, the Latin *invidia*—envy—is derived from *videre*, to see. What we witness here is the displacement of vision's truth to the realm of theoretical vision. The psychoanalyst sees immediately that to see the woman is to envy her, to recognize that what she represents is desirable. The "seeing" is often on the side of the theory that hopes to disengage itself from the visible, from the seeing/seen nexus.

The idea that the visible is a point of crisis seems to be conveniently forgotten when theory contemplates its own limits. On the whole,

[37]Lacan, *The Four Fundamental Concepts*, 116.

however, Lacan's analysis of vision, hovering around the "phallic ghost" and lack, does seem to emphasize the precariousness of vision, as Rose suggests. But it is not always necessary to be able to see or to be able to see clearly in order to maintain the given symbolics of a patriarchally ordered sexual difference. Distrusting the visible or geometrical optics and valorizing anamorphosis for its departure from a pictorial realism or its annihilation of the centered subject of perspective do not suffice. This insufficiency is, once more, demonstrated by the function of the veil, where the philosophical and the cinematic organization of vision in relation to desire appear to coincide. The veil's curious dialectic of vision and obscurity, of closeness and distance, is evidenced, again, in Sternberg's work, which, in its sheer concentration upon the surface of the image, recapitulates many of the themes and difficulties of the philosophical discourse. Although Sternberg is fond of interposing veils, screens, and streamers between the camera and Marlene Dietrich, he would also like to get as close to her as possible. Early in *The Scarlet Empress*, in her marriage scene, Catherine appears, predictably enough, in a wedding gown (figure 14). What is not predictable, however, is the insistence of the camera upon positioning itself closer and closer to her face as the scene progresses, until the very texture of the veil becomes marked (figures 15, 16, 17). An even more striking instance of this tactic occurs later in the film. Catherine has just given birth to a baby boy, heir to the throne. She lies in a bed surrounded by veils and is presented with a gift, a necklace, from the queen (figure 18). Again, as she examines the necklace the camera reduces its distance from her (figures 19, 20). As Sternberg's camera gets closer to the woman, she almost disappears, the outline of her face grows indistinct, and her place is taken by the surface or texture of the image, the screen.

As the camera increases its proximity to the veil, the veil and the screen it becomes seem to become the objects of desire. The veil mimics the grain of the film, the material substrate of the medium, and becomes the screen as surface of division, separation, and hence solicited transgression. This gesture, mimicking the grain of the film, *might* be viewed as deconstructive par excellence, for it indicates the woman's status as the substrate of representation. The woman is revealed as no longer simply the privileged object of the gaze in the cinema but the support of the cinematic image. Yet, I would argue that the marking of the image in this way, the foregrounding of the grain, the positioning of the woman as screen—all of this merely heightens the eroticism, makes her more desirable, stimulates the envy of the filmmaker ("Marlene is me," Sternberg once said). The image of Dietrich indicates that even when the woman is no longer fully visible, she is the support of its

Figure 14

Figure 15

Figure 16

Figure 17

Figure 18

Figure 19

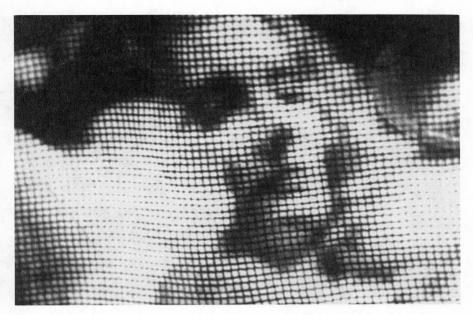

Figure 20

seduction of the spectator, its provocation. And I think one could ask similar kinds of questions about the desire of the philosopher or the psychoanalyst who appeals to the woman as a form of theoretical proof—the desire to reveal her status as support, substrate of truth/ untruth or representation, and simultaneously to maintain her "operation," because she can indeed be so representative of so many things even if she doesn't understand them herself. The question is why the woman must always carry the burden of the philosophical demonstration, why she must be the one to figure truth, dissimulation, *jouissance*, untruth, the abyss, etc., why she is the support of these tropological systems, even and especially antimetaphysical or antihumanistic systems.

It is not surprising that the confused topology of Western metaphysics finds a perfect site for its inscription in a classical cinema that organizes its appeals to scopophilia around the figure of the woman as distanced surface. That topology takes on the burden of defusing the philosophical insecurity associated with the instabilities, the contradictions, and the limits of its own discourse—defusing them by projecting that instability in relation to truth onto the woman.[38] It is at once

[38]For a similar argument see Michèle le Doeuff, "Cheveux longs, idées courtes," in *L'imaginaire philosophique* (Paris: Payot, 1980), 135–66.

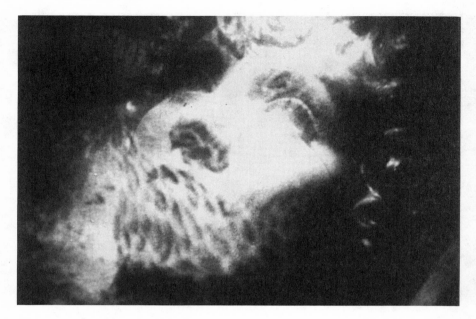

Figure 21

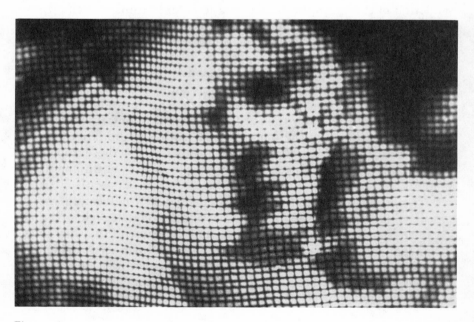

Figure 22

more striking and more disconcerting, however, that the antihumanist and antimetaphysical discourses associated with poststructuralism are inexorably drawn to the same necessity of troping the woman (although here she is revalued and becomes the signifier of what is most desirable in theory—or at its limits).

It might be useful to imagine what Dietrich's return look might be, from behind the veil (figures 21, 22). Usually, the placement of a veil over a woman's face works to localize and hence contain dissimulation, to keep it from contaminating the male subject. But how can we imagine, conceive her look back? Everything would become woven, narrativized, dissimulation. Derrida envies that look. He loses himself in her eyes. It would be preferable to disentangle the woman and the veil, to tell another story. As soon as the dichotomy between the visible as guaranty and the visible as inherently destabilized, between truth and appearance, is mapped onto sexual difference, the woman is idealized, whether as undecidability or *jouissance*. The necessary incompletion or failure of the attempt to leave behind the terms of such a problematic is revealed in the symptomatic role of the woman, who takes up the slack and becomes the object of a desire that reflects the lack that haunts theory. What I have attempted to suggest here is how we might begin to understand the philosophical and psychoanalytical envy of the woman through examination of a desire that always only seems more visible in the cinema.

7

The Everyday Life of Lou Andreas-Salomé:
Making Video History

Andrew Ross

I

Anyone who sets out to write a history of the concept of everyday life would have to account for the respective discoveries of Sigmund Freud's *Psychopathology of Everyday Life* (published in 1901) and Henri Lefebvre's *Everyday Life in the Modern World* (published in 1961). Freud's book, the least theoretical of all his major works, is little more than a dazzling series of anecdotes, micronarratives, or other illustrations of Freudian slips—all manner of parapraxes, errors, the forgetting of names and words, slips of the tongue and the pen, bungled actions, etc.—each exemplifying how the languages of everyday life are informed by the unconscious. The narrative space of these anecdotes is private and, of course, bourgeois. In effect, the social function of the anecdote is to make common, or public, sense of a private experience or event, while the effect of the Freudian slip itself is to invite us to interpret that event as historically specific, as contingent upon a personal history and the logic of meanings specific to that history alone. The psychopathology of everyday life, then, demonstrates how everyday life is consequent upon the repression of a *particular* history.

By contrast, Lefebvre's book is concerned with the *spectacle* of public, or popular, space. Of course, this is not simply a historical difference (*Critique de la vie quotidienne* does appear sixty years later than Freud's book, and in this respect, it is clearly addressed to a different set of social relations). For Lefebvre is writing within a Marxist philosophical tradition that proclaims itself to be antibourgeois and antiindividualistic, a tradition that he nonetheless chastises for its transcendentalism and its long and critical neglect of everyday life. Lefebvre maintains that the colonizing logic of capital has advanced into every sphere of everyday life. In fact, in a society of controlled consumption, everyday life has become the chief "province of organization" for capital, the very sphere in which the production and reproduction of capitalist social relations takes place. In exploring the ways in which everyday life helps to make society appear coherent to the individual, Lefebvre performs the classical task of ideology critique, the task of showing that apparently universal and natural forms—the basic rhythms of everyday life: cooking, lovemaking, relaxing, vacationing—in fact support a particular set of power relations in a particular time and place. In effect, it is the routine immobility of everyday life that masks the giddy acceleration of capital, hell-bent on change, accumulation, and quick turnovers.[1]

Although neither of these books espouses the rhetoric of discovery, each seeks to present a new strategy of knowledge, the "stuff" of transformation, where before there was only know-how or the various technologies by which everyday life helps us to negotiate survival.[2] But this knowledge, which is intended to augment and transform, if not replace, know-how, is not simply presented in the grand metaphysical manner

[1]Henri Lefebvre, *Everyday Life in the Modern World* trans. Sacha Rabinovitch (New Brunswick, N.J.: Transaction Books, 1984). Lefebvre begins this book by invoking a time and a cultural moment when everyday life, for the first time, was not unavoidable, when, in fact, everyday life erupted into literature in Joyce's *Ulysses*. What is notable about Lefebvre's reading of Joyce's exhaustive inventory of one day in the life of Leopold Bloom is how it all too quickly becomes a "symbol of universal everyday life." The history of a single day becomes the history of the whole world: Dublin becomes Ithaca, Atlantis, all cities, and an everyday man becomes both quotidian and heroic, historical and cosmic: Bloom, Ulysses, all men and all god-men. For the modernist, everyday life is invoked in order for it to *negate* itself through imagery, symbolism, and allegory. In this respect, the modernist text of everyday life is like Jung's psychotic, who "suffers the reminiscences of mankind." Postmodernist everyday life appears, in its solidity and facticity, as a necessary and unavoidable particularity. More generally, however, the fact that representations of everyday life can be seen to differ historically (from James Joyce to Alain Robbe-Grillet, from Freud to Lefebvre) raises the question that has long plagued debates about the politics of psychoanalytical theory. How can the categories of psychoanalysis help to constitute a politics, when these categories are generalizing and resistant to historicization, when, in effect, these categories can appear to lend themselves to the universalizing work of ideology? One of the possible responses to this question, today, would be to further explore the concept of everyday life. Everyday life history is no more "real" as history than the grand narratives that have traditionally been supported and supplied by psychohistorians. As a historical practice, however, the concept of everyday life represents interests that are more germane to the "everyday" affect of psychic life.

[2]In *The Practice of Everyday Life*, trans. Steven F. Rendall (Berkeley: University of California Press, 1985), Michel de Certeau uses the term *know-how* to describe people's survivalist *knowledge* of everyday life; people are "the renters and not the owners of their own know-how" (171). Certeau's description of oppositional resistance to this "official" version of know-how depends upon various strategies of poaching or reappropriating these forms for an earlier "artisanal" sense of know-how.

of disclosing or revealing a realm of reality behind appearances. Every-day life is not, in this respect, merely a pale copy of Being. Nor can it be made to submit to any grand narrative of becoming—Heraclitean, He-gelian, or Marxist—if only, as Lefebvre points out, because it is made up of recurrences, or cycles of repeated and time-honored activity.[3]

On the contrary, both Freud and Lefebvre remind us that everyday life is both constituted by and dependent upon the repression of a knowl-edge we already know but which is unconscious; in Freud's case, it is the knowledge of our own psychic history, and in Lefebvre's case, the hidden knowledge of power relations which ideology secretes about our person. What is more significant about this knowledge, however, is the way in which it is bandied about in the interplay between *narrative* and *spectacle*.

In Freud's case the stories we tell each other, if we are prepared to look and listen, are seen to be shot through with the spectacle of the unconscious at work (seemingly effortless work: the unconscious does not sweat). But his spectacle is neither immobile nor does it submit to any narrative logic; one does not know what will come next in its backward-moving chain of determinations, and besides, it all takes place (if one can use that location) in the present tense of the uncon-scious. In the case of Lefebvre, the spectacle of our consumer space is offset by the stories that each sign or commodity is likely to divulge, under the right interpretive pressure, about the material conditions of its production. We could say that these stories are micronarratives about existing power relations; at least they are not microversions of the grand narrative of Marxist necessity.

What can we conclude? That we are transfixed, on the one hand, by the Freudian spectacle of the unconscious staging itself, and that we are moved, on the other, by the Lefebvrian stories about ideology revealing itself, *but* that we submit, nonetheless, for the most part of everyday life, to the dominant forms of spectacle and narrative, in other words, to the spectacular lure of the commodity and the anecdotes of power? Perhaps this way of putting it achieves little more than to point out that spectacle and narrative have no meaning in themselves, as forms or discourses, and that they can be appropriated accordingly; but this point, it seems to me, cannot be emphasized too much, especially in the context of the last decade of feminist film theory and its debate about the thesis that narrative and spectacle in classical Hollywood cinema are the conventional instruments of oppression for women. Rather than quote from Laura Mulvey's well-known "Visual Pleasure and Narrative

[3]Lefebvre, 18.

Cinema," the source of this debate, let me cite instead this observation of Lefebvre's, from a different political context, about everyday life:

> Everyday life weighs heaviest on women. . . . they have their substitutes and they are substitutes; they complain—about men, the human condition, life, God and the gods—but they are always beside the point; they are the subject of everyday life and its victims or objects and its substitutes (beauty, femininity, fashion, etc.) and it is at their cost that substitutes thrive. Likewise they are both buyers and consumers of commodities and symbols for commodities (in advertisements, as nudes or smiles). Because of their ambiguous position in everyday life . . . they are incapable of understanding it.[4]

We could be kind to Lefebvre and read his last statement in the following way: "women understand everyday life only insofar as they are prepared to be masculinized by this understanding," which is to say, of course, that a large part of everyday consumer life is constructed for and around a masculine point of view, even for female consumers. Even at that, however, one is reminded of a similar kind of formula from an earlier, more orthodox stage of Marxist thought: the "masses" are incapable of understanding revolution unless they take up the position of the proletariat, the privileged subject of revolution. And in recent years, we have seen the "masses" feminized in Jean Baudrillard's theories of mass culture. In a mass democratic culture, the "masses" are under two contradicting obligations: first, to be democratic subjects, that is, to have political opinions, to vote, to make responsible decisions, to produce, to consume, and second, to be objects of power, that is, to be submissive, inert, passive, and conformist. When the "masses" refuse this double role (like Lefebvre's women, who are "incapable of understanding" everyday life), they are practicing what Baudrillard, citing Hegel, calls the "eternal irony of femininity . . . the irony of a false fidelity to the law, an ultimately impenetrable simulation of passivity and obedience . . . which in return annuls the law governing them."[5] For Baudrillard's "masses" and for Lefebvre's women, resistance arises only out of the lowest common denominator of political activity— passivity, or the refusal to be political.

[4]Ibid., 73.

[5]Jean Baudrillard, *In the Shadow of the Silent Majorities; or, The End of the Social and Other Essays*, trans. Paul Foss, Paul Patton and John Johnston (New York: Semiotext[e], 1983), 33. Tania Modleski discusses this quotation in an examination of the relation between theories of mass culture and theories of the "feminine," in "Femininity as Mas(s)querade: A Feminist Approach to Mass Culture," in *High Theory, Low Culture*, ed. Colin McCabe (London: Macmillan, 1986).

Andrew Ross

II

It is to Baudrillard, moreover, that we owe the recent perception that the society of the spectacle has run its course. He has argued that the theatricality or fictionality of the commodity image, with its staged distance and its promise of another scene of reality—somewhere else— is now impoverished. Baudrillard's portrait of the simulacrum incarnates the myth of instantaneity generated by today's video technologies of everyday life. Baudrillard's relation to the screen ironically answers to Walter Benjamin's call for a holy war against the auratic distance which the art cult maintains between audience and object or image. While the spectacle demands that we look, but nothing else, that we do not get involved, the simulation already implies our interactive participation in its utterly visible medium. Benjamin wanted the audience to come closer, to reestablish sensuous contact with the image. Now Baudrillard tells us that our sensitivity, the response of our senses, is already simulated for us by and on the screen.

As video technology comes to consummate its relationship with the computer, the prospect of cybernetic omnipotence will join this already potent myth of instantaneity, this immediate access to events and data which television cultivates and manages through its conventional genres. Oppositional questions of popular response and technology appropriation will be transformed. Already the new forms assumed by these questions have turned our available language inside out: How can we desire the realities we simulate by trying to simulate the realities we desire?

In the same way, the introduction of video technology has been a double source of anxiety and opportunity for avant-garde artists. The twenty-year history of "video art" as an art medium with its own specificity has prompted an anguished call to order from the endangered species of the avant-garde filmmaker. Hollis Frampton, for one, voices the now-familiar complaint: "Since the birth of video art from the Jovian backside (I dare not say brain) of the Other Thing called television, I for one have felt a more and more pressing need for precise definitions of what film art *is*, since I extend to film, as well, the hope of a privileged future."[6] To furnish the complaint with its full historical scope, the impulse behind it could be traced back to Gotthold Lessing's *Laokoon*, the book that ushered in the Enlightenment demand for

---

[6]Frampton, quoted by David Antin in "Video: The Distinctive Features of the Medium," in *Video Art* (Philadelphia: Institute of Contemporary Art, University of Pennsylvania, 1975), 58.

generic specificity not only among the arts but also, some would say, among the spheres of public life itself: law, morality, science, art.[7] But if Frampton's complaint begs the question of specificity, this could equally be said of critics who have, in fact, sought to legitimize video art as a definitive new art form either by specifying its "difference" from television or by placing it within a history of avant-garde experimentation, which jealously guards its inoculated distance from the contagious discourses of popular culture. (It is hardly surprising, in this respect, to find the early history of video art dominated by the work of performance artists, pursuing their organicist concern with expressions of body-centered resistance to technology into the mainstream of the new medium.)

To reduce the prickly question of "art" specificity to its material coordinates, however, we can say that video art's conditions of cheap production and limited consumption, its channels of distribution, and even its range of cultural reference *tend* to be markedly different from those of television; the technology, however, is essentially the same, and the imminent perfection of high resolution will virtually neutralize the visual differences between the "look" of film and the "look" of video and television. Why was it not called "television art?" Because, as Amy Taubin points out, the moment of its origin was one in which artists' grants were being liberally awarded, and "video art could hardly have been so ungrateful as to call attention to its bad bloodlines."[8] The result, however, is that exhibition and distribution has been restricted to the ghetto of art museums and alternative art spaces; video art must be viewed in depressing, art-purist rooms with uncomfortable chairs in a milieu that is quite remote from the everyday-life environments fashioned around television technology.

Surely in this age of cable and cheap production, the golden technological opportunity for independent artists to enjoy access to popular channels of communication, cannot be too far away. Even if video art succeeds in breaking out of the ghetto of PBS and public access the problem will still be to hold on to ways of exposing the material conditions of televisual cultural expression, for in matching everyday life with everyday technology, television creates the "artificial paradise" of a *present tense* that is resistant to most of the ways in which history can make its presence felt in our everyday lives. This "present tense" of television celebrates the technological myth of instantaneity. In the

[7] The best-known and most accessible presentation of this point of view is that of Jürgen Habermas in "Modernity—an Incomplete Project," in *The Anti-Aesthetic: Essays on Postmodern Culture*, ed. Hal Foster (Port Townsend, Wash.: Bay Press, 1983), 3–15.

[8] Amy Taubin, "Room without a View," *Village Voice*, 8 September 1987, p. 49.

case of television, it is a myth with its own history, a prehistory of prewar technological innovation and the Golden Age of "live" productions in the 1950s, followed by the postlapsarian age of second-rate production we enjoy today.[9] With the development of the outside broadcast, satellite link-ups, and the possibility of endless live coverage of the object world, television has consumed our future as efficiently as it has learned to "forget" our past, while its only available references to its conditions of production are increasingly reserved for Lettermanesque contexts in which guarantees of "live" authenticity are required—those "errors," interruptions, and technical gaffes that "prove" the spontaneity of live broadcasting, both inside the studio and on outside broadcasts. David Antin has described how similar production "crises" are regularly staged and selectively presented in video artists' tapes. Far from expressing materialist-inspired resistance to the symbolic grain of the medium, these carefully dressed errors, Antin claims, are to be interpreted as marks of authenticity, in the heroic tradition of the abstract-expressionist drip.[10]

Where television introduces these malfunctions to advertise its claim to provide complete, public visibility, however socially managed, video art exploits them to reclaim its vanguardist heritage through acts of private, expressionist abandon. If only to erode this separation of public and private cultural sectors, video must take responsibility for addressing the cultural effects and possibilities inherent in the technology it shares with television. If the televisual "present tense" is coming to be our only lived sense of a "public sphere," then its reign of soft terror over our everyday commodity life must be fully examined.

This concern about immediacy, for example, is one of the topics addressed by Laura Kipnis's videotape *Ecstasy Unlimited: The Interpenetration of Sex and Capital.*[11] Her work provides an analysis of the various myths of instantaneous access (to truth, liberation, happiness, etc.) which the sexual revolution of the sixties promised to women and which have become powerful commodity myths today. The projected object of these myths is an enlightened body, universal in perceiving the rationality of its demands for sexual autonomy. Accordingly, Kipnis's tape explores the heavily advertised universality of this claim and reveals the deep structure of its other political referent—the universality of the commodity form itself.

[9]Mimi White, "Television: A Narrative Ahistory," a paper presented at National Humanities Center, March 1987.

[10]Antin, 62.

[11]Laura Kipnis, *Ecstasy Unlimited: The Interpretation of Sex and Capital,* distributed by Electronic Arts Intermix, New York, and the Video Data Bank, Chicago.

From Laura Kipnis, *Ecstasy Unlimited*

From Laura Kipnis, *Ecstasy Unlimited*

Andrew Ross

From Steve Fagin, *Virtual Play*

In contrast to this orthodox strategy of demystifying the symbolic body, Steve Fagin's tape *Virtual Play*[12] takes on an equally necessary project in speaking to the imaginary body, the body which fails to cohere in response to the doxical pressure of everyday life but which is nonetheless constructed out of a lived experience of time and its affective character. There is nothing essentialist about this body; nor is it immune in any way to the shapes of ideology, for it is constructed out of the history of its memories of images; images culled from photographs, films, and television.[13] What is libidinally retained from this lifetime of images? And how does it historically personalize our otherwise official acquiescence in the spectacles and narratives of the present tense?

III

In his last book, Roland Barthes, the most celebrated modern reader of the imaginary, described the early days of photography in terms of the

[12]Steve Fagin, *Virtual Play: The Double Direct Monkey Wrench in Black's Machinery*, distributed by Video Data Bank at the Art Institute of Chicago. Fagin's and Kipnis's tapes were both shown at the Normal conference on feminism and psychoanalysis.
[13]Jean-Louis Schefer has written such a phenomenology of the "interior body" in *L'homme ordinaire du cinéma* (Paris: Gallimard, 1980).

painful transformation of a subject into an object: "In order to take the first portraits (around 1840) the subject had to assume long poses under a glass roof in bright sunlight; then a device was invented, a kind of prosthesis invisible to the lens which supported and maintained the body in its passage to immobility."[14] This prosthesis would function, as Barthes puts it, as "the corset of my imaginary essence," the technological means of producing *another* body for the camera. More generally, it is of course an objective correlative for the camera itself, the most recent advance, in 1840, in man's technological crusade to shape the world in his own image. And in the last two decades, psychoanalytical theory has helped to write the entire history of cinema and the cinematic apparatus in terms of a prosthetic completion of subjectivity, a technological extension that labors to complete the phenomenological centrum.

With the advent of video technology, the pain of prosthetic surgery has dissipated, even though the terrorism it harbors for the subject-cum-object has retained some of its power. The uncanny distance, for example, between our own body-being-filmed and the video body that answers to our every gesture on the screen is hardly a comforting one; it is probable that most of us will first have experienced this phenomenon of the two "live" bodies in the presence of a surveillance camera in a bank, store, or airport. In video, nothing is made up, nothing is added to the world, and nothing substitutes for a lack, for the prosthetic function of video lies in its claim to simulation. No longer a corset of the imaginary, video is an organ of the symbolic, resolving the crises of everyday subjectivity by persuading us that division only ever produces a repeated, duplicated, or simulated body, and never a different body.

The spectacle of the prosthesis is a famous part of the image repertoire of psychoanalytical history itself. Every late photograph of the immaculately barbered Freud records, in the immobility of its poser, the absent presence of the surgical prosthesis with which the roof of his mouth had been repeatedly reconstructed. In a letter to Lou Andreas-Salomé in 1924, Freud meditates upon the "small-scale war" he had been waging against this "refractory piece of equipment": "Reflecting on the fine but yet not entirely acceptable sentences in which you discussed the relationship of man to his body, I ask myself what you would say to the analogous relationship to a substitute such as this, which tries to be and yet cannot be the self. This is a problem which arises even in the case of spectacles, false teeth and wigs, but not so

[14]Roland Barthes, *Camera Lucida: Reflections on Photography*, trans. Richard Howard (New York: Hill and Wang, 1981), 11.

insistently as in the case of a prosthesis." Freud goes on to praise his own prosthesis for holding up so well but then observes how " 'Nature' tends to lull us into a false sense of security before administering the *coup de grace;* which of course on the other hand is one of her ways of being merciful."[15] Here Freud personifies Nature in his selective sense of the entropic "nature" of the death drive, which, it could be argued, was the nearest he ever came to a conception of nature as unquestionable, essential, or irreducible. Even here, however, nature's mercy can only be demonstrated in the failure of the subject's defenses against failure, a failure of the "false sense of security" promised by each prosthetic extension of the ego as an advancement over the deficiencies of the natural body.

The letter to Salomé goes on to link this failure of the psychic and physiological economy with the failing economy of his own psychoanalytic practice, financially curtailed by the prosthetic blow to Freud's "working capacity." The context of this observation, moreover, is the responsibility Freud expresses toward the financial upkeep of Lou Andreas-Salomé, even in the face of his own unemployed sons' struggle against poverty. As if to illustrate her own maxim—"men do battle, women give thanks"—Salomé reports, three months later, on the outcome of one of these regular installments of Freud's generosity: "The result of this [gift] is that my wonderfully thin and light fur coat, which is several decades old, suddenly declared that its bare patches, on account of which it had been put out of circulation, could and must be repaired, whereupon I actually sent it to a furrier in Hanover." Salomé thanks Freud for "having seduced [her] to this" (mid-Nov. 1924, p. 141.)

In this role as the kept mistress of psychoanalysis, she responds as she would have to any other male benefactor of the time by renewing her cosmetic contract with "Nature." Unlike Freud's discreet, invisible battle against bodily decay, waged through internal reconstruction, Salomé's imaginative attention must be to the external reconstruction of her second skin, a prosthetic covering whose furry texture advertises its origins somewhere else, in a more "natural" realm of nature. Years later, after surgery to remove a cancerous breast, she ironically reaffirms the ideological link between nature and falsity. Placing some padding under her silk dress to substitute for her lost breast, she quips to a friend: "Nietzsche was right after all. Now I do have a false breast."[16]

[15]*Sigmund Freud and Lou Andreas-Salomé: Letters,* ed. Ernst Pfeiffer, trans. William Robson-Scott and Elaine Robson-Scott (London: Hogarth Press, 1972), 8 August 1924, p. 137, hereafter cited in the text.
[16]Quoted by H. F. Peters in *My Sister, My Spouse: A Biography of Lou Andreas-Salomé*

Salomé's furs, themselves symptoms of all the bourgeois hysterics who had passed through Freud's rooms, are probably best known to us from photographs of assembled groups at various psychoanalytic congresses from Weimar in 1911 onward. Attention in these photographs oscillates between the grand rhetorical presence of the furs and the stiff, antithetical pose of Freud himself. Salomé's "glamour" bespeaks its structuring function in this group; it has no relative autonomy. Juliet Mitchell has succinctly described this position in the following way. Because "there was no alternative non-patriarchal culture," she writes, "Lou Andreas-Salomé tried to create such a culture in her own person, but what she achieved was in a sense a glorious parody of the masculine vision of women. . . . The feminine culture that Lou created in her person was the masculine ideology writ large; personally independent of men, she could only fashion herself within the terms of the choice this male vision offered . . . [as] superwoman to Nietzsche's superman."[17] If Mitchell's diagnosis explains, perhaps, why Salomé's celebrated historical role in the lives of Nietzsche, Rilke, and Freud is almost too *perfectly* drafted in terms of its anecdotal imaginary, we ought to recognize that such a diagnosis forever resigns her to her position as a victim of history (a victim of her time). While Mitchell's observation is unlikely to be seriously challenged, we ought, at least, to examine some of the structural components of that so-called victim's position.

Documented history, for example, comments on the highly privileged and deeply ambiguous effects of Lou Andreas-Salomé's role in the lives of these men. Nietzsche, for one, announced shortly after meeting her that she "was prepared like none other for that part of [his] philosophy that has hardly yet been uttered."[18] In other words, she appeared to him as his last chance not only to construct an ideal bride but also to acquire a true philosophical heiress and successor into the bargain. For her pains, however, in becoming disentangled from Nietzsche's plans for her future, Salomé was to become the living butt of his most bitterly misogynist attacks in *Also Sprach Zarathrustra* and other works, just as she became the model for the destructive vamp in Frank Wedekind's *Lulu*.

(New York: Norton, 1962), 292. Peters earlier quotes from one of Nietzsche's letters: "In a letter he once called her 'his fate.' *Quel goût!* This thin, dirty, evil-smelling little monkey with her false breasts—a fate!" (146).

[17]Juliet Mitchell, *Psychoanalysis and Feminism* (Harmondsworth, Eng.: Penguin, 1975), 430.

[18]*The Freud Journal of Lou Andreas-Salomé*, trans. with an introduction by Stanley A. Leavy (New York: Basic Books, 1964), p. 6.

As for Freud, there was no one more privileged in his eyes.[19] During the brief period Salomé spent in Vienna with the Inner Circle, Freud went so far as to extend to her the role of a Tiresias, from whose bisexual point of view the fractious, internecine quarrels of the psychoanalytical movement at the time of Adler and Rank's secession could be judged in abeyance. He wrote to her, "One cannot help feeling a covert desire to find out how the whole thing might look to another person, to a judge male or female, and I confess that it is to you that I would most gladly have entrusted such an office." (29 July 1914, p. 17).

In saying this, Freud, characteristically, was risking nothing. For Salomé's deep-seated views on the psychology of the sexes had long since hardened around a principle that would determine each stage of her practical involvement with psychoanalysis: "Men do battle, women give thanks." Indeed, their favorite private joke was that Freud had given psychoanalysis to Lou as a "Christmas present," a tribute to her gratitude which was repeatedly repaid in their long years of correspondence, not least in her final monograph on psychoanalysis, published under the title *My Thanks to Freud.* To his protestations of modesty, designed, in vain, to persuade her to change this title, she responded that all of her psychoanalytical work had "been wholly derived from the man who bears this name [Freud]; what it would have been as purely factual knowledge without this human experience I simply cannot imagine (I am a woman after all.)" (mid-July 1931, p. 196). Freud described the monograph as "an involuntary proof of [her] superiority over all of us . . . a true synthesis, not the nonsensical therapeutic synthesis of our opponents" (ca. 10 July 1931, p. 195). In this way, then, were monuments fashioned out of a woman's thanks.

So too, in a letter of 1916, Salomé relates her regret that she had not stood up at the end of one of the celebrated Wednesday meetings at Freud's house to "thank psychoanalysis for the fact that it leads us away from the isolated work at our desks into vital activity and into a kind of brotherhood." She goes on to justify the currently fratricidal state of that brotherhood: "If only . . . the hallmark of psychoanalysis—honesty to oneself and to others—remains untarnished, then—at least in a woman's eyes—all is well, and it is a joy to see even 'brothers' thus

---

[19]In his biography of Freud, Ernest Jones wrote of Andreas-Salomé as one of a succession of women "of a more intellectual and perhaps masculine cast," to whom Freud was attracted. "Such women several times played a part in his life, accessory to his men friends though of a finer calibre, but they had no erotic attraction for him. The most important of them were first of all his sister-in-law Minna Bernays, then in chronological order: Emma Eckstein, Loe Kahn, Lou Andreas-Salomé, Joan Riviere, Marie Bonaparte." *Sigmund Freud: Life and Work* (London: Hogarth Press, 1955), 2:469.

engaged in mutual conflict" (30 June 1916, p. 47). Here Salomé directly alludes to her "fraternal world-view," which she claimed was the product of growing up in a family of brothers; when she left Russia, she "looked on all the world as if it were populated by brothers alone" and vowed that "this was responsible for the openness and trustfulness I have had toward all men in my life, and it has never been deceived."[20] In the case of Freud, at least, this statement was quite true, if only because he recognized her relation to the project of psychoanalysis—her "woman's eyes"—as an optimum point of view. Hers was the place from which Freud wanted the whole psychoanalytical enterprise to be viewed. That this point of view was also a vanishing point is made nowhere more manifest than in Freud's complaint that he had trouble lecturing when she was absent from the audience, because it was to her person that he addressed himself, "my point of fixation," as he put it (2 March 1913, p. 13). Accordingly, Freud believed that there was never any danger of her "misunderstanding" his arguments; she was an " 'understander' par excellence," casting a synthesizing light from her privileged vantage point upon his work (25 May 1916).

By contrast, Freud characterizes his own work as so many leaps in the dark, reproducing in the following flight of rhetoric yet another of these uncanny prefigurations of what film theorists have recently explored in discussions of the cinematic apparatus suggested by psychoanalytical accounts of voyeurism and fetishism:

> I have to blind myself artificially in order to focus all the light on one dark spot, renouncing cohesion, harmony, rhetoric and everything which you call symbolic, frightened as I am by the experience that any such claim or expectation involves the danger of distorting the matter under investigation, even though it may embellish it. Then you come along and add what is missing, build upon it, putting what has been isolated back into its proper context. I cannot always follow you, for my eyes, adapted as they are to the dark, probably can't stand strong light or an extensive range of vision, but I haven't become so much of a mole as to be incapable of enjoying the idea of a brighter light and more spacious horizon, or even to deny their existence. (25 June 1916, p. 45)

If Lou Andreas-Salomé was indeed the only bright star on Freud's "more spacious" technicolor horizon, then it was because she was already serving a function the Hollywood screen goddesses would soon come to consecrate—that of securing a complete object world for an incomplete subject. For example, in the year she spent in Vienna in 1912–1913, Lou

[20]*The Freud Journal*, 93.

did more than her fair share of ministering to the wounded. Freud perpetually assured her that she was the only "synthesizer" of his work, that she "could put everything in order and show that it was quite possible to be comfortable," whereas he viewed his own "eternal ambivalences" as evidence that he was "prepared to leave everything higgledy-piggledy" (9 May 1931, p. 193). In this way was Lou the operative housewife of the psychoanalytical movement.

In addition, she was playing the role of go-between in attending both the Wednesday meetings and Adler's renegade group encounters; in doing this she had special dispensation from Freud to "make use of an artificial psychic split,"[21] but she was to remain silent about her double role. So too, she acted as lover-cum-mediator in the ménage-à-trois with Freud and Viktor Tausk, his only serious intellectual rival in the movement, a man hurried on to suicide by the psychological humbling he suffered at Freud's side, just as Paul Rée, the Schopenhauerian positivist, had been suicidally smitten by the various sublimitations of his desire in the earlier ménage-à-trois he had shared with Lou and Nietzsche.

And in yet another capacity, this time as theorist and analyst within the movement, Salomé was to become the most confirmed essentialist interpreter of the thesis that "anatomy is destiny" by proposing an autonomous female psychology based entirely upon the perception of physiological differences. As a result, her best-known work, on narcissism, grew out of her interest in and focus upon the undifferentiated preoedipal subject and the moment of protonarcissism which she considered to be the truly natural state of human activity; after this ideal moment adult sexuality could only be promiscuous enjoyment of "the partner inside [oneself]."[22] For Salomé this thesis was particularly significant for women: "Woman's only cultural attainment [is] that she isolates sexuality from her experience less than man is able to do." This "erotism," this act of *fidelity* to her sexuality, which is her "only cultural attainment," is proof of her "masochistic organization," which she cultivates with "all the strength of her civilization." Hence the woman who is unfaithful is a woman who has not conserved sufficient energy to lavish on morality; "she saves nothing," writes Salomé in a memorable sentence, "out of the erotism of the hour that might serve to build houses, but into it she has put everything that ever was called loneliness."[23]

[21]*The Freud Journal*, 41.

[22]Quoted in Rudolph Binion, *Frau Lou: Nietzsche's Wayward Disciple* (Princeton: Princeton University Press, 1968), 343

[23]*The Freud Journal*, 81.

Given the racy history of Salomé's many love affairs, it is no surprise to find that Rudolph Binion, her most exhaustive biographer (or, rather, psychobiographer) to date, extends this discussion of fidelity and intimacy into an analysis of her everyday life as it is revealed in journals and correspondence. Binion's book, moreover, is prefaced by a series of ridiculous comments by Walter Kaufmann, the Nietzsche scholar, who recalls how he had wondered, at first, whether Salomé was important enough to merit such a large book. In fact, the book only passes muster in Kaufmann's eyes because "it throws new light on a great many interesting men" (for example, it makes a "major contribution to the study of Nietzsche's life and character"), while it proves beyond all doubt that Lou, like Nietzsche's notorious sister, Elisabeth, "falsified the story" of her relationship with Nietzsche. For Kaufmann, the ultimate merit of the book is that it shows how all Lou's later friendships were nothing but "repeated attempts to cope with her rejection by Nietzsche." Kaufmann, moreover, is quick to credit Salomé with the kind of "pathology of brilliance" that can blend fact and fantasy.[24] Binion himself goes farther along this path in claiming that Salomé's accounts of herself, which have passed for factual, are really fanciful through and through; "all of her work," he says, "is one distorted *journal intime*, with the distortions largely wishful."[25] Nevertheless, Binion is willing to grant that "she did tell every last truth about herself at least once in some misleading context or another." His final dilemma, of course, is that, in exposing Lou's "infidelity" not only to others but also to herself, he feels he has been exercising the "conscience of a scholar" and not that of a gentleman."[26]

By contrast, H. F. Peters, an earlier male biographer, had managed to avoid what Anaïs Nin in *her* preface to his book calls the "double standard in biographies of women." Nin urges readers to use their imagination to interpret Salomé's life "in the light of woman's struggle for independence," even though Lou was not a feminist herself and, as Nin puts it, actually, struggled *against* "the feminine side of herself in order to maintain her integrity as an individual."[27]

For Kaufmann, then, history and biography are objective ways of clarifying and testifying to concepts like documentary truth and fidelity to experience. For Nin, history and biography are always unfaithful anyway: they must be constantly rewritten, even if fantasmatically, in the heat of political commitment. Mutually exclusive as these claims

---

[24]Walter Kaufmann, Foreword to Binion, *Frau Lou*.
[25]Binion, 25.
[26]Binion, x.
[27]Anaïs Nin, Preface to Peters, *My Sister, My Spouse*, 9.

appear to be, neither, on its own, can make autonomous sense of the everyday presence of history in our lives, for everyday life cannot afford to distinguish in such a categorical way between documentary and fantasy. Instead, it draws upon whatever is historically available to provide us with a more or less fixed sense of the unalterable, of a pattern or rhythm of events that is so necessary to all people that it even precedes the stage of popular negotiation and contestation that produces meaning. Everyday life is a highly organized, conventional system of experience, a system where narrative, spectacle, and interpretation have already done much of their respective work *before* we recognize them for what we think they are. Perhaps it is only by reviving epistemological chimeras like fidelity or falsity that history can save its often inhuman face and reclaim its authoritative privilege to stand apart from popular corruptions of the stories it tells.

IV

Denying history this privilege, is one of the working assumptions of Steve Fagin's *Virtual Play*, a videotape "dedicated to Lou Andreas-Salomé" in the grand benefactory tradition to which she herself so graciously submitted. The dedication, however, is no act of Pygmalion-esque devotion; it is made in the spirit of Salomé's own glorious bad faith: "To memories I shall ever be true, to persons never." Of course, this is itself a manifesto to which neither the video nor Lou herself could ever be true, but that is a starting point rather than the concluding logic of *Virtual Play*'s investigation of the various ways in which the history of Salomé's "everyday life" might be represented to us now, against the grain of the video's present tense. Fagin's tape works hard and fast. Its panorama of detailed tableaux appear as so many *disjecta membra* put to work at anecdotalizing and deanecdotalizing the imaginary and sometimes narrative space that makes up this "film about a woman who . . ."

Much of this "work" or interrogative activity is directed against the flimsy partition that conventionally divides memory from experience or, if you like, memories from history. Given the chance, ideology will harden any sense impression into a husk of factual attention; in this respect, daydreams, memories, reminiscences, anecdotes, and documentary histories are all subject to the same ideological process even if they are assigned different ranks as representational categories of truth. What is more important, however, than Fagin's irreverent polemical scrutiny of these categories is his attention to the real power of our imaginary participation in the mythical construction of history. If, like Lou and Tausk on their truant visits to the cinema, Fagin does indeed prefer what the fragmented voice-over calls "the reflective glory of the imaginary" to the "petrified remains of the symbolic," it is because he sees that there is no easy passage beyond that choice, least of all as far as visual images are concerned. As a model of the Taj Mahal slowly burns against the backdrop of Ansel Adams's *Yosemite Half-Dome,* a terse Syberbergian voice-over elegiacally intones the "collapse of the image-repertoire." Even after the iconoclasts have done their work, even after the apocalyptic destruction of the imaginary in the worst "porno-graphic nightmare," the "afterglow" of the spectacle lingers on: "The end of sight does not mean the end of vision." The symbolic cost of "twilighting" the imaginary is suggested in a following scene, shot in an urban wasteland presided over by giant antislumlord graffiti: ARSON FOR PROFIT. A distant figure crosses and recrosses the picture plane, describing the mnemonic system she has constructed to help her to remember a list of names required for the scene. For each name to retain its place in the system, it must be associated or attached to elements in other symbolic systems: kinship (a maternal grandmother), verbal puns, or a personal history of desire (to live in a coffin, like Sarah Bernhardt). Remembering any of the names is a symbolic victory, but it is only achieved in the imaginary, by invoking the cumbersome psycho-pathology of images, puns, and associations which patches together the symbolic.

But it is the *real,* the "third term," that *Virtual Play* invokes when it addresses "even the most innocent spectator" in the first tableau: "The third term, which makes for geometry, functions as the vanishing point of the picture and serves as a measuring point of subjectivity." This "third term" is the proof of our silent majority as spectators, because it defines our legitimate (or "virtual") position as consenting witnesses or participants in the making of history through images. In this respect, Fagin's work clearly subscribes to the new *realism* about history that has nothing to do with literalism and everything to do with acknowl-edging the complex role of fantasy and representation in the construc-tion of historical narratives and images. Historians of every stripe have had to shoulder this new responsibility toward the "desire" of their subject. No longer, like Walter Benjamin's *flaneur,* strolling with classi-cal restraint among the goods on display, but more like Poe's restless "man in the crowd," whose peregrinations, Benjamin writes, land him "at a late hour in a department store where there are still many customers. He moves about like someone who knows his way around the place. . . . [He roams] through the labyrinth of merchandise as he had once roamed through the labyrinth of the city."[28]

In *Virtual Play*, this same restless, nomadic motion is thematized as Odyssean, steering a charmed but confused course around the commoditylike lure of the siren images and memories that make up the film's case history. A simulated underwater scene seems to speak directly to this sense of thwarted purpose. Traces of recent mermaid activity are detected on the seabed: "shards, a mural, even some skin." Have the mermaids been stripped bare by some overeager tourist? Perhaps. At any rate, they are not the kind of mermaids we expect; those committed to "serving man, permitting passage through their mystery so he can gain access to his truth." In fact, it turns out that these mermaids have no body at all, and they travel as a couple, not alone or in schools. In short, they are no more a source of "feminine" truth than they are a source of disorder. Besides, everything is out of sync: the timing of our arrival, the displaced scene of instruction, the narrator's lack of an epic voyager's confidence.

The suggestion of similar failures is epidemic in the video. Throughout *Virtual Play* there are images and jigsaw pieces that will not fit; displaced sensory impressions; unanswered questions; simultaneous narrative accounts, like those of Lou and Elizabeth, that do not match up; interrupted anecdotes; misinterpreted comments—all set alongside games of chance, jokes, riddles, lies, and aphasic messages. Fagin exploits every available technology of falsification, displacement, and misrepresentation, and he draws, in classical *bricoleur* fashion, upon everyday materials and discourses to do it. Even the "most innocent spectator" will suspect that *Virtual Play* has learned many of the lessons of the last decade of avant-garde filmmaking, and is equally well versed in the psychoanalytic theories of representation which have inspired these films.[29]

What is most striking is the ingenious treatment in *Virtual Play* of the way in which everyday life is shot through with the psychopathological effects of memories and fantasies of history. In this respect, the primary difficulty or failure which *Virtual Play* addresses is that of

---

[28]Walter Benjamin, *Charles Baudelaire: A Lyric Poet in the Era of High Capitalism,* trans. Harry Zohn (London: Verso, 1973), 54

[29]A good, exhaustive review of these features of *Virtual Play* can be found in Margaret Morse's discussion of narrative in "Shaking and Waking," *Afterimage* (November 1985). Also see Peter Wollen's interview with Fagin in *October* (Fall 1987).

From Steve Fagin, *Virtual Play*

Andrew Ross

From Steve Fagin, *Virtual Play*

present-tense enunciation. It is important to emphasize this point, if only because we might otherwise be tempted to trace the film's own force field of infidelity to the "magnetic" source of Lou Andreas-Salomé herself—to a woman, again, as a decentering cause of instability and unrest, both in her own life and times and now, in our fantasmatic reconstructions of this glamour girl of the psychoanalytical movement.[30] But the *realism* of *Virtual Play* lies in its willingness to acknowledge the power and fatal attractiveness of these historical fantasies. It no more denies this attraction than it seeks to construct a more "authentic" picture of Salomé, while it suggests that this is as

[30]In an article that runs through some of the problems Salomé's case history poses for feminist recuperators today, Biddy Martin sums up the importance of coming to terms with Salomé's own essentializing of "failure": "The danger, of course, is that such an emphasis on feminine difference matches the historical definitions of patriarchal societies in which 'woman' has been identified as essentially amoral and narcissistic, and women have been held to the forms of control constructed and justified in those terms. Certainly, Salomé's arguments are formulated from within the ideological and social constraints of her time and are ridden with biological analogies and essentialist explanations. However, it is not necessarily the truth-value of her work that interests us, but the ways in which our historical knowledge, our conceptions of sexual differences, and our approach to language are opened up by the difficulty of placing her, by her undecidability." "Feminism, Criticism and Foucault," in *New German Critique* 27 (Fall 1982), 29.

much a man's problem as it is an integral cause of women's cultural oppression in the theaters of history.

Fagin's video emphasizes that there are no easy escapes from this movie-theater-cum-prison-house of the male imaginary. Salomé herself wrote that freedom "is released in us . . . not when our ego says 'I desire'—but: 'Here I stand, I can do no other.' "[31] *Virtual Play* does not take a stand, nor does it repudiate the power of desire. When case histories are no longer trials, for the analyst and subject alike, then the question with which the tape ends will no longer be implausible and utopian; it will be rhetorical: "If the camera had remained perfectly still, what would have been seen?"

[31]Quoted in Peters, 146.

8

Feminism, Psychoanalysis, and the Heterosexual Imperative

Shirley Nelson Garner

At its incipience, psychoanalysis defined the "mature" and "normal" woman as heterosexual and ready for or a participant in marriage and the family in the role of wife and mother. Its aim—though unspoken, unacknowledged, and perhaps unknown—was to socialize women to suit the ends of patriarchy as we know it in the Western world. Sharing the biases of the white middle class, it has tended to discourage celibate or lesbian women and has more or less ignored postmenopausal women. Its boundaries have been much narrower than those of feminism. As I see it, feminism puts the biologically female and culturally feminine at the center of experience and looks at the world from that perspective.[1] It is interested in woman's state and also in her prospects and potentialities. It would argue for variety in the patterns of women's lives, as a matter of choice or necessity. We may not be white or middle class. We may choose to live alone, together, or with men. We cannot help but grow old.

I want to consider here psychoanalytic attitudes toward lesbianism, particularly as those have or have not changed in the last decade or so. I am especially interested in the efforts of psychoanalysis to take into account lesbian existence other than in terms of arrested or aberrant sexual development. Though I believe that no woman is an island, that in some sense what happens to one of us happens to us all, psychoanalytic response to lesbianism engages me as a heterosexual woman not only as it affects other women but as it affects me. Since lesbianism is emblematic of "women together,"[2] it represents the feminist challenge

---

[1] I am indebted to Martha Roth for the shape of this definition.

[2] "Women together" is Virginia Woolf's phrase; see *Night and Day* (1920; rpt. New York: Harcourt, Brace, 1948), 101.

to patriarchal values in the clearest form. Even when lesbians are not in fact free from the impositions of patriarchal structures, metaphorically they are often taken to be so. Though homosexual himself, E. M. Forster could tell Virginia Woolf that he "thought Sapphism disgusting: partly from convention, partly because he disliked that women should be independent of men."[3] All of us who claim the name "feminist" must accept that for many people, "feminist" is a code word for "angry, man-hating lesbian." Our identity is connected with that stereotype. For those of us who wish to continue to use psychoanalytic theory as clinical practitioners, patients, or literary theorists, it is important for us to understand how it is or is not responsive to lesbian existence. So long as it takes that reality into account only through its historical biases, it cannot be truly responsive to women, particularly those who define themselves as feminist.

When we speak of psychoanalysis, we are, of course, speaking of different experiences. Some of us know it as practitioners, many of us know it as patients, and still more of us know it as readers of its researchers and theorists, who may or may not be practitioners of psychoanalysis. I use *psychoanalysis* here not only to mean the practice of what is frequently called "classical psychoanalysis" but also to describe the psychoanalytically based therapies that derive from it. Patients' experiences of such therapies vary markedly. A lesbian friend recounts her experience of treatment by a male psychiatrist, a student of Erik Erickson, who was trained in and practiced classical psychoanalysis as well as psychoanalytically based therapy; he did not try to "cure" her of her lesbianism or treat it as problematic in any way. When she discussed her lesbianism with him at the outset, he told her that he did not look upon homosexuality as a problem unless a patient did. When she and her lesbian partner later sought a psychiatrist who would see them as a couple, they interviewed several who clearly would not have been helpful to them. Ultimately, they chose a woman therapist with conventional training, who, they felt, treated their difficulties as a lesbian couple without any of the traditional biases. At the same time, I read about a lesbian's vastly different experience with the psychiatric establishment in a recent issue of *Hurricane Alice,* a feminist review I help to edit. Twenty-seven sculptures, titled *Still Sane,* by Persimmon Blackbridge and Sheila Gilhooly, recount Gilhooly's experience of coming out as a lesbian and being admitted to a mental institution as a result. A text that accompanies one of the sculpture reads, "*I told my shrink that I didn't want to be cured of being a lesbian. He said that just proved how sick I was. He said I need shock treatment. . . . 19*

[3]Quentin Bell, *Virginia Woolf: A Biography* (New York: Harcourt, Brace, 1972), 2:138.

Shirley Nelson Garner

shock treatments and I still didn't want to be cured of being a les-bian."[4] What these two stories suggest is that the aims of feminism and psychoanalysis may be, on the one hand, complementary or coincident or, on the other, at war with each other. Psychoanalytic practice may offer us sympathy or abuse.

Contemporary theories of psychoanalysis still labor under the weight of Freud's ideas. So compelling is his notion of the Oedipus complex as an explanation of male psychology and sexual development—at least in a patriarchal culture[5]—that it has carried along his less convincing and unconvincing ideas of female sexual development. His privileging of male sexuality leads him, at best, to misunderstand female sexuality, at worst, to deny it. It is to his credit that he often confesses that he does not understand female sexuality, that it is a mystery to him.[6] While Freud acknowledges the essential bisexuality of human beings, his theories, in fact, reinforce the heterosexual demands his society imposed on both women and men. As is revealed in Freud's letters to Wilhelm Fliess, his relationship with his colleague and friend was circumscribed by his own homophobia. His clinical practice reveals this bias as well. His study of Dora is a case in point. Freud seems unable to recognize the strength of Dora's attraction to Frau K., attributes to Dora heterosexual desires she probably did not have, and encourages her in a particularly corrupt and undesirable heterosexual alliance.[7]

When I began to read Karen Horney, who very early on questioned the bases on which psychoanalytic notions of female psychology rested, I was struck by her deference to Freud and his disciples, her reasonable-ness and considerable patience. Reading her for the first time in the early seventies, I thought the care and precision with which she ad-dressed Freud and his followers over and over, point by point, concern-ing penis envy, for example, made her writing sound almost like a parody of an academic paper. Straight-faced, she quotes Karl Abraham:

[4]Quoted in Jenny Miller, "Creating a Mad Culture," *Hurricane Alice* 3.1 (1985), 1.

[5]Luce Irigaray remarks on the congruence of values implicit in psychoanalytic dis-course and those "promulgated by patriarchal society and culture, values inscribed in the philosophical corpus: property, production, order, form, unity, visibility . . . and erec-tion." *This Sex Which Is Not One,* trans. Catherine Porter with Carolyn Burke (Ithaca: Cornell University Press, 1985), 86, Irigaray's ellipses.

[6]Juanita H. Williams catalogs Freud's frequent references to the mysteriousness of female psychology in *Psychology of Women: Behavior in a Biosocial Context,* 3d ed. (New York: Norton, 1987), 34. See also Zenia Odes Fliegel's essay "Women's Develop-ment in Analytic Theory: Six Decades of Controversy," in *Psychoanalysis and Women: Contemporary Reappraisals,* ed. Judith L. Alpert (Hillsdale, N.J.: Analytic Press), 4–15.

[7]See the essays of Suzanne Gearhart, Toril Moi, and Maria Ramas in *In Dora's Case: Freud, Hysteria, Feminism,* ed. Charles Bernheimer and Claire Kahane (New York: Columbia University Press, 1985). All comment on Dora's homosexual attractions.

"Many females, both children and adults, suffer either temporarily or permanently from the fact of their sex." (Can we imagine psycho-analysts saying or paying attention to a comparable statement: "Many males, both children and adults, suffer either temporarily or perma-nently from the fact of their sex"?) Horney responds with only a touch of reprimand: "The conclusion so far drawn from the investigations— amounting as it does to an assertion that one half of the human race is discontented with the sex assigned to it can overcome this discontent only in favorable circumstances—is decidedly unsatisfying, not only to feminine narcissism but also to biological science."[8] Writing in the 1920s, she was obviously required to take such statements as Abra-ham's seriously. The deference to Freud and his ideas and to those who followed him is in some respects deserved. He was the father of Hor-ney's discipline; much of what he discovered and created was valuable and has remained so. But ideas about female psychology, such as those surrounding penis envy, have held on tenaciously not only because they were Freud's but also because they surfaced in a culture that so wishes to believe in the superiority of men to women, to protect the sources of male power.

Beginning as they must, with Freud, students of psychoanalysis work through case studies and theoretical essays and papers that are not helpful in understanding the psychology of women, that share the culture's biases against them. They confront an even more serious prejudice against homosexuality. Unlike Freud, Horney seems disin-terested and dispassionate when she considers homosexuality. Yet if it is not "abnormal" in her thinking, it represents, at best, a marginal accommodation for female sexuality. But it is not a subject that often interests her. Many of the matters she is concerned with are relevant to all women. She continually argues that society, rather than biology, accounts for those things, penis envy, for example, which psycho-analysts have taken as biologically determined. When her concerns are not those of all women, she is interested mainly in those that pertain to heterosexual women. I would argue, however, that to maintain that all human beings have bisexual potentialities, on the one hand, and to marginalize a homosexual resolution of sexual desires, on the other, is to make it less possible, probably impossible, to understand either male or female sexuality in specific cases or generally.

I want to turn to our time, when psychiatrists and other theorists should find it easier to work outside the prejudices that hampered those

[8]Karen Horney, *Feminine Psychology*, ed. Harold Kelman (New York: Norton, 1967), 37, 38.

writing before the late 1950s and early 1960s. As Susan Krieger in her review essay in *The Lesbian Issue: Essays from Signs* describes the earlier literature based on medical and psychoanalytic expertise, it depicts lesbians "as pathological: sick, perverted, inverted, fixated, deviant, narcissistic, masochistic, and possibly biologically mutated, at best the daughters of hostile mothers and embarrassingly unassertive fathers." She traces the beginning of a different view to the late 1950s and after, when a growing number of sociologists, social psychologists, and psychiatrists started to take issue with "the assumptions of the pathological models. They offered new evidence and corrective interpretations and suggested that lesbianism was neither a sexual nor a social disease but, rather, a life-style choice linked with a sense of personal identity."[9] This literature, much of it published since the middle of the 1970s, has encouraged a reversal of the pathological paradigms and provided a shift toward the view of lesbianism as normal. A central influence in the emergence of this literature, Krieger asserts, was the founding of the *Journal of Homosexuality* in 1974 by researchers and clinicians who opposed the medical model. She cites Charlotte Wolff's *Love between Women* as standing alone at the beginning of the decade. The theorists that I want to look at have had the advantage of writing during this change in thinking.

After the midseventies, several American feminists published books that deal with female sexuality, focusing particularly on women in their roles as mothers and child rearers. In 1976 Adrienne Rich's *Of Woman Born: Motherhood as Experience and Institution* and Dorothy Dinnerstein's *The Mermaid and the Minotaur* appeared, followed by Nancy Chodorow's *Reproduction of Mothering: Psychoanalysis and the Sociology of Gender* in 1978. All these books are informed by psychoanalytic theory but differ from Freud in concentrating on the preoedipal period and the child's early relationship to the mother. They see woman's femininity (patriarchally defined) and her capacity for nurturance as consequences of her experience as exclusive child rearer. Reproducing these traits in her daughters, she passes on her strengths as well as those capacities that determine her subordinate position in society. Because Nancy Chodorow is more fully in dialogue with psychoanalytic theorists than Dinnerstein or Rich and because her work has been taken up in America by both psychoanalysts and feminists as well as literary critics, I want to look at her notions of women's sexuality as they are relevant to her treatment of lesbianism.

[9]Susan Krieger, "Lesbian Identity and Community: Recent Social Science Literature," *The Lesbian Issue: Essays from Signs*, ed. Estelle B. Freedman, Barbara C. Gelpi, Susan L. Johnson, and Kathleen M. Weston (Chicago: University of Chicago Press, 1985), 225.

Chodorow's thesis, stated succinctly in her introduction, is that "women, as mothers, produce daughters with mothering capacities and the desire to mother. These capacities and needs are built into and grow out of the mother-daughter relationship itself." Woman's role in mothering is responsible for "sexual asymmetry and inequality."[10] For the psychoanalytic underpinnings of her argument, Chodorow looks beyond Freud and his followers to the "cultural school" psychoanalysts (such as Erich Fromm, Karen Horney, and Clara Thompson) as well as object-relations theorists (such as Alice and Michael Balint, John Bowlby, and W. R. B. Fairbairn). She bases her arguments concerning the reproduction of mothering on the persuasive assertion of the object-relations theorists that the child's "social relational experience from earliest infancy is determining for psychological growth and personality formation." These theorists dispute the view of Freud and the ego psychologists that "the biological requisites of the leading erotogenic zone (oral, anal, phallic, genital) determine the form of the child's object-relations." They claim, instead, that "with the possible exception of an 'oral' stage, the accession to experienced primacy or preoccupation with other 'erotogenic zones' is a result of particular social interactions concerning these zones" (47–48).

Chodorow maintains that current child-care arrangements are responsible for the particular characteristics of the girl's Oedipus complex. Though coming from object-relations theory, she reaches a conclusion about sexual development that echoes that of Helene Deutsch, who, of course, follows in Freud's direction:

> A girl does not turn absolutely from her mother to her father, but adds her father to her world of primary objects. She defines herself, as Deutsch says, in a relational triangle; this relational triangle is imposed upon another inner triangle involving a girl's preoccupation alternatively with her internal oedipal and internal preoedipal mother. Most importantly, this means that there is greater complexity in the feminine endopsychic object-world than in the masculine. It also means that although most women emerge from their oedipus complex erotically heterosexual—that is, oriented to their father and men as primary *erotic* objects (which the psychoanalysts seem not so sure of)—heterosexual love and emotional commitment are less exclusively established. Men tend to remain *emotionally* secondary, though this varies according to the mother-daughter relationship, the quality of the father's interaction with his daughter, and the mother-father relationship. (167)

[10]Nancy Chodorow, *The Reproduction of Mothering: Psychoanalysis and the Sociology of Gender* (Berkeley: University of California Press, 1978), 6–7, hereafter cited in the text.

Though Chodorow draws on a different line of psychoanalytic theorists to corroborate her thesis, she is in continual disagreement with Freud. Her tone does not convey Horney's calm attitude of respect, but she still feels the need to give Freud considerable space. In her chapter "Freud: Ideology and Evidence," she affirms the ways in which many of Freud's theories of female sexual development serve patriarchal aims. She points out that in Freud's system the girl's change of sexual object "is important only because it is the way a girl becomes heterosexual" and that "the change from activity to passivity and the shift of primary organ of sexual gratification from clitoris to (or back to) vagina are necessary for the requisite heterosexual stance." She adds, further, that "this change of object prevents the most threatening form of incest to men—that between mother and daughter" (157). These observations would seem to invite some consideration of lesbianism, but that comes later in the book and seems brought forth only to be dismissed: "Deep affective relationships to women are hard to come by on a routine, daily, ongoing basis for many women. Lesbian relationships do tend to recreate mother-daughter emotions and connections, but most women are heterosexual. This heterosexual preference and taboos against homosexuality, in addition to objective economic dependence on men, make the option of primary sexual bonds with other women unlikely— though more prevalent in recent years" (200).

Adrienne Rich responds to Chodorow's treatment of lesbianism. Hearing the evasiveness in her statement that lesbian relationships have become more prevalent in recent years, Rich asks: "Is she saying that lesbian existence has become more visible in recent years (in certain groups?), that economic and other pressures have changed (under capitalism, socialism, or both?), and that consequently more women are rejecting the heterosexual 'choice?'" She declares that Chodorow "leads us implicitly to conclude that heterosexuality is *not* a 'preference' for women; that, for one thing, it fragments the erotic from the emotional in a way that women find impoverishing and painful." Rich concludes that Chodorow's book "participates in mandating" heterosexuality.[11] Though I think Rich's phrasing is too strong, Chodorow clearly distances herself from what she is saying in two important respects. When she writes that women's primary erotic and emotional relationships may be disparate, she does not consider the effect such a disparity must have on women. This is surely an unhappy separation of Eros and feeling; yet Chodorow describes it without a clear sense that it

---

[11]Adrienne Rich, "Compulsory Heterosexuality and Lesbian Existence," *Signs* 5 (1980), 636.

is so. More important, she does not pursue the implications of her argument. If women's and men's primary attachments are both to the mother, why do women turn toward men? What Chodorow says is simply that "most women are heterosexual" and then refers to "this heterosexual preference." What is the source of this heterosexuality, or is it a mystery? Rich says that male power forces heterosexuality upon women, that it is a means of "assuring male right of physical, economical, and emotional access."[12] What Rich sees is that the "logic" of psychoanalytic models centering on the importance of the preoedipal period in the formation of our relationships argues in the case of women for homosexual rather than heterosexual attachments. Chodorow runs headlong into this "logic" and cannot work herself through or around it.

In preparing to write this essay, I reviewed several editions of a psychology textbook on my office bookshelves, *Psychology of Women: Behavior in a Biosocial Context*, by Juanita H. Williams. The book was published by Norton in 1974, reprinted in 1977, published in a second edition in 1983 and a third in 1987. Between the first edition and the latest, the discussion of lesbianism has been considerably expanded. In the first edition, there is a short section on the subject included in the chapter "Sexuality"; in the second edition, it is extended. Unlike birth control, for example, the subject does not receive a whole chapter; yet, the author presents lesbianism positively. Interestingly enough, Williams cites Rich's article and phrases for her readers' consideration Rich's question, "Why are most women heterosexuals?"[13] In the third edition, "Lesbian Identity" is a section unto itself. It draws heavily on feminist scholarship and reiterates Rich's question.

Two years before the publication of Rich's *Of Women Born* and Dinnerstein's *The Mermaid and the Minotaur*, Luce Irigaray published in France *Speculum of the Other Woman*, followed in 1977 by *This Sex Which Is Not One*, both of which were translated into English and published in 1985 by Cornell University Press. A practicing psychoanalyst, Irigaray is concerned to show how female sexuality has been seen through men's eyes, understood according to phallocentric values, and written, or rather *erased*, through phallocentric discourse. It is Irigaray's intention to undo the whole system: to disrupt male theories and constructions by writing female desire into language, an act requiring a new form of discourse. Though her work has been repudiated by Lacanians in France, feminist scholars in America, particularly those in

---

[12]Ibid., 647.
[13]Juanita H. Williams, *Psychology of Women: Behavior in a Biosocial Context*, 2d ed. (New York: Norton, 1974), 241, 3d ed. (1987), 409–10.

Shirley Nelson Garner

foreign language departments, hold it in esteem. Now that it has been translated, it has been more widely read. Up to now, it seems to have had a negligible effect on the psychoanalytic establishment in America.

In *This Sex Which Is Not One*, Irigaray, like Chodorow, is engaged with Freud, and her audience is clearly the predominantly male psychoanalytic establishment as well as feminists and others interested in female sexuality. She answers the questions "Why do you begin your book with a critique of Freud?" (actually a reference to *Speculum*) and "Must we go over this ground one more time?" by suggesting that many of Freud's ideas persist to the detriment of women and implying that she does need to go over the old ground again. What interests me is that through her argument with Freud and the psychoanalytic establishment, she also begins to shape a counterdescription of woman's desire. Her title is rich in meaning, but the central image comes from female genitals. While she demonstrates how woman's sexuality and desires have been written from a phallocentric perspective, she also asserts against it another vision:

> This organ which has nothing to show for itself also lacks a form of its own. And if woman takes pleasure precisely from this incompleteness of form which allows her organ to touch itself over and over again, indefinitely, by itself, that pleasure is denied by a civilization that privileges phallomorphism. The value granted to the only definable form excludes the one that is in play in female autoeroticism. The *one* of form, of the individual, of the (male) sexual organ, of the proper name, of the proper meaning . . . supplants, while separating and dividing, that contact of *at least two* (lips) which keeps woman in touch with herself, but without any possibility of distinguishing what is touching from what is touched.
>
> Whence the mystery that woman represents in a culture claiming to count everything, to number everything by units, to inventory everything as individualities. *She is neither one nor two.*[14]

Irigaray continually emphasizes that woman's sexual pleasures are plural:

> The pleasure of the vaginal caress does not have to be substituted for that of the clitoral caress. They each contribute, irreplaceably, to woman's pleasure. Among other caresses . . . Fondling the breasts, touching the vulva, spreading the lips, stroking the posterior wall of the vagina, brushing against the mouth of the uterus, and so on. To evoke only a few of the most specifically female pleasures. Pleasures which are somewhat misun-

[14]Irigaray, *This Sex Which Is Not One*, 26, hereafter cited in the text.

derstood in sexual difference as it is imagined—or not imagined, the other sex being only the indispensable complement to the only sex.

But *woman has sex organs more or less everywhere.* She finds pleasure almost anywhere. Even if we refrain from invoking the hystericization of her entire body, the geography of her pleasure is far more diversified, more multiple in its differences, more complex, more subtle, than is commonly imagined—in an imaginary rather too narrowly focused on sameness. (28)

What I find important here is that sexual pleasure is described as residing *within* a woman. It cannot come from *outside* unless the capacity for it exists *inside.* The one who caresses is not designated, so that the experience described may be autoerotic, homosexual, or heterosexual.

Irigaray suggests that there are many areas in which the premises of psychoanalysis may merit questioning and that female sexuality is only one of them. Raising a number of questions with regard to women's sexuality, she suggests answers that indicate the male bias of psychoanalytic perspective. For example, she asks: "*Why has the alternative between clitoral and vaginal pleasure played such a significant role?*" and responds with another question: "Is it informed by the *standardization* of this sexuality according to *masculine parameters* and/or by criteria that are valid—perhaps?—for determining whether autoeroticism or heteroeroticism prevails in man? In fact, a woman's erogenous zones are not the clitoris or the vagina, but the clitoris and the vagina, and the lips, and the vulva, and the mouth of the uterus, and the uterus itself, and the breasts . . . What might have been, ought to have been astonishing is the *multiplicity of genital erogenous zones* (assuming that the qualifier 'genital' is still required) in female sexuality" (63–64).

One of the questions she asks concerns lesbianism: "*Why is the interpretation of female homosexuality, now as always, modeled on that of male homosexuality?*" Finding the psychoanalytic premise in Freud's "Psychogenesis of a Case of Homosexuality in Women,"[15] she notices that "the female homosexual is thought to act as a man in desiring a woman who is equivalent to the phallic mother and/or who has certain attributes that remind her of another man, for example her brother." She continues, "Why should the desire for likeness, for a female likeness, be forbidden to, or impossible for, the woman? Then again, *why are mother-daughter relations necessarily conceived in terms of 'masculine' desire* and homosexuality? What is the purpose of this misreading, of this condemnation, of woman's relation to her own original desires, this nonelaboration of her relation to her own origins?

[15]Sigmund Freud, *The Standard Edition of the Complete Psychological Works,* ed. and trans. James Strachey (London: Hogarth Press, 1953–74), 18:147–72.

Shirley Nelson Garner

To assure the *predominance of a single libido*, as the little girl finds herself obliged to repress her drives and her earlier cathexes. Her libido?" (65). Later on, she objects at length to Freud's envelopment of female homosexuality into a "masculinity complex" and concludes that female homosexuality eludes psychoanalysis (193–97). Like women's sexuality generally, it is eclipsed.

The insistence of the dialogue with Freud in all these writers—Horney, Chodorow, Irigaray—as I listen to it, suggests the urgency of a repeated dream or the continual dramatization of a traumatic experience. The form of their discourse suggests an engagement with a psychoanalytic establishment that must seem at its center intractable. What I hear in Luce Irigaray that is hopeful is an effort to see anew, to think, imagine, and write woman differently. She suggests a possibility for reimagining female sexuality that could encompass female homosexuality without a negative cast. But what we have is still a beginning that asserts itself mainly in opposing and putting questions.

When I looked at psychoanalytic attempts to consider lesbianism, specifically in the work of clinicians and theorists who tended not to view it negatively, I went to Charlotte Wolff's *Love between Women* (1971), mentioned positively in Krieger's article and referred to me by a lesbian colleague. A psychiatrist and fellow of the British Psychological Society, Wolff bases her work on her clinical practice with lesbians between 1930 and 1950 and a particular study in which she looked mainly at nurses, secretaries, civil servants without university educations, writers, artists, and typists living in England. There were also a few women from professions of higher status—doctors, lawyers, professors, and the like—and a few skilled workers. She asked her subjects to write their "emotional autobiographies," participate in a lengthy interview with her, and answer a questionnaire.[16]

The underlying premise of Wolff's book is that "the one and only way to equality and progress in human as well as love relationships lies in the expression of the whole bisexual nature of every man and woman." Without any apparent anxiety, Wolff comments, "In society where bisexuality could be fully expressed and accepted, the family as we know it would be broken up" (81). Acknowledging that in such a society lesbianism would look different, and hence her assumption that psychology does not stand apart from the society in which it exists, she sees her task as explaining lesbianism in her current milieu. Unlike the other theorists with whom I have been dealing, Wolff is not particularly engaged with the psychoanalytic establishment. She refers to various

---

[16]Charlotte Wolff, *Love between Women* (New York: Harper and Row, 1971), 117–18, hereafter cited in the text.

theorists, to give credit or to depart from them, but her main effort is to describe lesbianism as she understands it. Though she states her main psychoanalytic disagreements with Freud, she gets over these quickly and focuses on his notion that human beings are essentially bisexual. In other words, she takes what she wants from him and seems by and large to forget the rest.

After discussing reasons for the prejudices against lesbianism, she begins to expound her own "theory" of it. She sees its main feature as intense emotion: "Emotion is the life centre of lesbian love" (17). Lesbians experience such emotional intensity, according to Wolff, because they can reconnect with the primary feelings of love they had for their mothers and because it is required to join in a relationship so forbidden. Without intense feeling, lesbians would be more likely to remain within the bounds of a repressive society.

One of the things I find refreshing about this book is the positive way Wolff views those aspects of lesbian existence that psychiatrists often read negatively. While traditionally a less than stable gender identity, which lesbians are often seen to have, might be interpreted as problematic, Wolff holds an opposite position: *"The retention of the capacity to change feminine into masculine feelings and attitudes, and vice versa, is one of the assets of female homosexuality, because it makes for variety and richness in personal relationships"* (52). In a rather stunning reversal of commonly held heterosexual attitudes, she argues for the "sexual virility" of lesbians:

> The marrying type of girl is frequently sexually inadequate or even frigid, while one who is homosexual has a better chance of being sexually alive. It is interesting to note that almost all homosexual women whom I interviewed were tomboys as children. This holds good for the more masculine as well as the more feminine lesbian. Both types, if one can differentiate them at all, showed sexual *virility*. Before they realised their true libidinous preference, they had, with few exceptions, sexual contact with men. Although many found heterosexual intercourse less enjoyable than homosexual love-making, they were, as my statistics show, living out their bisexual nature. Many of them were married, and a number of these realised their homosexuality only after years of marriage.
>
> I have no doubt that lesbianism makes a woman virile and open to *any* sexual stimulation, and that she is more often than not a more adequate and lively partner in bed than a "normal" woman. It is her virility and aggressiveness that enable her to subject herself to heterosexual intercourse without feeling humiliated. (64–65)

She further ascribes to lesbians a hardy independence: "The lesbian has never accepted the status of an object. It is in this rejection of female inferiority and masquerade that she steps outside the 'eternal' habits of her sex. . . . Whatever their physical type, educational level, temperament or mentality, all homosexual women are *one* in their rejection of bondage to the male. They refuse to be the second sex" (79).

Wolff does not depict the lesbian's existence as unproblematic, however. She describes it as typically clouded, with an edge of "resignation and sadness" (16), which may be the result of childlessness, a wish for union with the mother that can never be fulfilled, and her status as an outsider. The other side of the positive aspects of the lesbian's emotionalism, all of which Wolff sees as a result of social pressures rather than intrinsic, are emotional instability and hence unreliability, a tendency toward paranoia, and a "conflict between integrity and adaptation" (90).

The main defects of this book are Wolff's failure to argue as convincingly as she might because of her tendency to overgeneralize, whether she is speaking of the positive or the negative aspects of lesbianism. On balance, she presents a rather monolithic and dichotomized picture of lesbian existence. She is, further, still dependent on models she wishes to cast aside. Though she puts "normal" in quotation marks, she continually juxtaposes the lesbian and "normal" woman; this habit of diction tends to reinforce the opposition rather than to change it. Though she writes positively about the lesbian's pleasure in "sameness" and her efforts to reestablish her primary bonds with her mother, she persists in talking about "emotional incest," which cannot help but undercut a relationship she intends to validate. While she largely rejects the biological bases on which Freud's theories rest, she does not seem to separate sexual aims from reproductive aims—hence her sense that childlessness is necessarily a source of sadness (she leaves aside the fact that lesbians need not be childless).

Her response to three lesbian autobiographies represents the kind of ambivalence and division I find in her. Her comments after each are divided into two sections: a "psychological interpretation" and a "personal impression." In one instance, her "psychological interpretation" concludes dismissively and seems to fall into a pathological model; yet her "personal impression" is generous and seems intended to see her subject whole:

> Miss Y. . . . is painfully shy, but once put at her ease, she shows intelligence and a witty, sharp edge to her conversation. I am sure that she has high principles in behavior and action. She lives up to the rare virtues of steadfastness, loyalty and stability in human relationships. She would never let anybody down, nor betray a confidence. A social misfit, not by necessity but through her up-bringing, she has not found a professional or

social place in accordance with her abilities. She compensates for her professional frustration through her interest in the theatre and literature. She identifies with those who are unfortunate through physical handicaps or other defects, and applies a practical religion: she goes and helps them. (257–58)

Wolff's case histories lack the rich psychoanalytic detail Freud gave to such studies as "The Psychogenesis of a Case of Homosexuality in Woman" or his case history of Dora, in part because of her method; but they also highlight how narrowly Freud worked toward establishing heterosexual identification or the lack of it.

Though I find Wolff's book seriously flawed, I also find it provocative. Many of its defects, like those of Freud's work, stem from its effort to break new ground. I would have found *Love between Women* as helpful as the more traditional psychoanalytic texts I used to help me describe a latent lesbian relationship in Virginia Woolf's *Night and Day*.[17] It would have helped me to understand, for example, how it might be different to love someone whom a person experienced as same rather than other and how the women characters in the novel value sameness.

Charlotte Wolff's work is not typical, however, for we do not tend to find comprehensive efforts to examine lesbianism or studies that reflect psychoanalytic experience in depth. What we find instead are studies that look at a number of subjects with regard to certain aspects of personality or behavior. These tend to emphasize the similarities between lesbians and heterosexuals and reinforce the sense that lesbians are "normal" in the same respects as others. Lesbians are not necessarily emotionally disturbed; they have no more psychological disorders than anyone else and no different ones. In one study, for example, "when young single women who identified themselves as lesbians were compared with a group of heterosexual counterparts, no differences in psychological adjustment were found. Even with respect to life styles, when the women were questioned about living situations, roles, friendship patterns, drinking, drugs, and suicidal behavior, the only differences between the groups were related to sexual orientation."[18]

As Krieger describes the directions of these studies, they tend to

---

[17]See my essay " 'Women Together' in Virginia Woolf's *Night and Day*," *The (M)other Tongue: Essays in Feminist Psychoanalytic Interpretation*, ed. Shirley Nelson Garner, Claire Kahane, and Madelon Sprengnether (Ithaca: Cornell University Press, 1985), 318–33.

[18]Williams, 2d ed., 242–43. Williams omits a description of this study from the third edition of her book, presumably because she sees contemporary researchers as "no longer concerned with the issue of assumed pathology" (3d. ed., 405).

view the lesbian individual in a social context—in terms of her relationships in couples, institutions, communities, and a larger society—rather than in isolated individual terms or in relation to a family of origin. They consider lesbianism to be a matter of total personal identity rather than primarily a sexual condition, and they view it as subject to choice and as changeable in definition rather than as something that is a given. In the broadest sense, then, the shift that has occurred may be described as one that moves us from thinking about lesbianism in terms of deviance, narrowness, simple causation, isolated occurrence, and fixed nature to thinking of it in terms of normality, diversity, multiple influence, social context, choice, and change.

The biases of these studies—in their sample populations as well as researchers—are those of the educated white middle class. An increase, according to Krieger, "in the number of women researchers has been accompanied by an emphasis on the similarities between lesbians and other women, while the increasing number of lesbian researchers has encouraged an emphasis on the positively valued norms evolving among lesbians with regard to identity, relationships, and community—norms that differ from those of heterosexual culture."[19]

Psychoanalytic investigations of lesbianism still tend to be marked, however, by the pathological notions and heterosexual biases with which they began.[20] I was interested to see Juanita Williams imply in the conclusion of her section on lesbianism that her readers should look beyond psychology for an understanding of lesbianism: "The growth of research interest in lesbianism and the interpretations of its meaning by feminist scholars in psychology, anthropology, history, and literature are beginning to bring lesbianism out of the shadows of obscurity and defamation. This movement, born out of feminism and gay activism, has the promise of bringing us to a greater appreciation of the sexual diversity that has always been observable among earth's people."[21]

What seems to have developed in psychoanalysis as in psychoanalytic literary criticism is a kind of double track. I recently attended a workshop titled "Changing Views of the Psychology of Women: Implications for Psychotherapists" at the Hamm Clinic, a psychiatric clinic in the Twin Cities. The principal speaker, Dr. Teresa Bernardez,

[19]Krieger, "Lesbian Identity," 226–27, 228.
[20]See Stephen F. Morin, "Heterosexual Bias in Psychological Research on Lesbianism and Male Homosexuality,"*American Psychologist* 32 (1977), 629–37, for a discussion of the ways in which such biases are revealed.
[21]Williams, 2d ed., 245, 3d ed., 411.

Professor of Psychiatry in the College of Human Medicine at Michigan State University in East Lansing, gave two addresses: "Prevalent Disorders of Women: Depression" and "Gender-based Countertransference of Male and Female Therapists." Bernardez was educated in Buenos Aires and completed a psychiatrist residency at the Menninger School of Psychiatry, after which she received postgraduate education in adult psychiatry at Menninger Foundation and psychoanalytic training at the Topeka Institute for Psychoanalysis. From the outset, she said, she knew she would have to modify the strictures of her training to treat patients according to their needs. She was never simply uncritical of psychoanalytic methods, but she recounted her early unwitting participation in the socialization of women for their feminine roles in patriarchal society. Gradually, she realized that women had to be treated as members of an oppressed group. A therapist could not simply act upon her psychiatric training without filtering it through her consciousness that conventional psychiatric therapy reinforced the repression of women. She also saw that women from various ethnic groups could not be treated the same as white, middle-class women, that a therapist needed to be aware of the values of the culture from which her patients came. When I asked her whether she found that lesbian and heterosexual women are equally subject to depressive illness, her answer was revealing. She said that she thought so, but could not answer definitively. In East Lansing, she said, there is a very active lesbian community, and lesbians tend, according to her, to prefer therapists within that community. As a heterosexual woman, she is not a preferred therapist of lesbians. The lesbians who come to see her do so because she is reputed to be good at dealing with particular mental problems. Her main source of information about lesbians is from lesbian therapists who are her colleagues. Bernardez is in the process of writing a book on the psychology of women, and from all I could gather from hearing her, it will be an intelligent book with feminist values. But it is also clear that she will have less firsthand clinical experience of lesbians than of other women and, therefore, must necessarily write about them less fully and specifically. Unless she collaborates with a lesbian therapist, she will have limited access to information she needs to write a complete account of women's psychology.

The recently published *Lesbian Psychologies: Explorations and Challenges* offers a rich account of lesbian experiences, including identity, relationships, problems, and therapies. Edited by the Boston Lesbian Psychologies Collective, the book contains essays by psychologists, social workers, counselors, and others. Noticeably, no contributor to the collection is a medical doctor or describes herself as a psychoanalyst.[22] Though some psychoanalysts and psychiatrists, especially women, are beginning to write women's experience into their field, their efforts to deal with lesbianism apart from traditional disciplinary prejudices are rudimentary.[23]

When I look at *The Lesbian Issue,* the collection of essays from *Signs* concerning lesbianism, I notice that none of the writers of the essays combines an interest in lesbianism with an interest in psychoanalysis. The only essay that relates the two is Krieger's review essay "Lesbianism Identity and Community," which deals with psychology as a discipline and to which I have frequently referred. Of the essays in *The (M)other Tongue: Essays on Feminist Psychoanalytic Interpretation,* the two that deal with forms of lesbian experience, Martha Noel Evans's "Writing as Difference in Violette Leduc's Autobiography, *La Batarde,*" and my essay, " 'Women Together' in Virginia Woolf's *Night and Day,*" depend on psychoanalytic theory less than most of the essays in the anthology. At the same time, when Alma H. Bond, a psychotherapist writes about Virginia Woolf, she seems to define Woolf's lesbianism as problematic. Looking at her competitive relationship with her brother and what Bond perceives as her mother's distance, Bond comments, "No wonder Virginia Woolf left behind her a history of homosexuality, her continuing attempt to reunite with the early mother."[24]

If I consider the recently published anthology *In Dora's Case,* it seems clear that psychoanalytic critics have become sensitive to heterosexual biases, for several essays in that anthology recognize such failures in Freud's reading of Dora's case. And we have also become alert to recognizing lesbianism in the margins, as the essays in *The (M)other Tongue* demonstrate. Yet psychoanalytic theory does not offer us sufficient material to help us understand and write about lesbian experience as we encounter it in literature or in life. We must collect that analysis in bits and pieces, here and there, and look to references outside the mainstream of psychoanalytic theory or criticism. At the moment, we

[22]*Lesbian Psychologies: Explorations and Challenges,* ed. Boston Lesbian Psychologies Collective (Urbana: University of Illinois Press, 1987).

[23]In *Psychoanalysis and Women,* Alpert includes an essay titled "Lesbian Choice: Transferences to Theory," by Ruth-Jean Eisenbud. Though Eisenbud separates herself from traditional analysts in her attitudes toward lesbians, her essay is mainly taken up with describing her own change of perspective and discussing sources of lesbianism that she sees as having negative aspects. The contributors to Alpert's collection have all had psychoanalytic training and tend to be professors in psychoanalytic institutes or to have private practices. They tend to hold Ph.D. degrees; only one is an M.D.

[24]Alma H. Bond, "Virginia Woolf: Manic-Depressive Psychosis and Genius: An Illustration of Separation-Individuation Theory," *Journal of the American Academy of Psychoanalysis* 13 (1985), 202.

are likely to find more help in other disciplines and the arts. *Lesbian Psychologies* will be an important resource. It remains to be seen whether psychoanalysis will be able to accommodate itself to feminism, to give its energies wholeheartedly to understanding lesbianism without seeing it as disease or deficiency, or to examining it at all. This task is, I think, inextricably linked with coming to understand the psychology of women generally.

LITERARY
TEXTS

9

Entertaining the Ménage à Trois:
Psychoanalysis, Feminism, and Literature

Jerry Aline Flieger

A Troublesome Trio

R eading Freud has taught us that three can most definitely be a crowd; an importune third party always acts as an obstruction to gratifying solutions. Lacan's "return to Freud" bears the same message: however blissful the "Imaginary" dream of a twosome may be, the oedipal triad or Symbolic threesome is a recipe for conflict. The psychoanalytic feminist literary critic might be inclined to agree: the very appellation "psychoanalytic feminist literary critic" is already unwieldy, with at least one too many qualifiers to be aesthetically manageable and with at least two of these terms—psychoanalytic and feminist—being practically guaranteed to alienate many traditional readers.

Out in the Real world of academe, moreover, we quickly learn that the precarious position of the psychoanalytic feminist literary critic is not just a matter of aesthetics but an economic and political concern as well, since our choice of this particular practice may threaten our status in the profession, if not (at tenure time) our very right to "profess." In other words, in professing a feminist and psychoanalytic approach to literature, we must not only surmount the complexities and difficulties posed by the literary work, but we must also arbitrate between sometimes seemingly contradictory systems—simultaneously apologizing to other feminists for our use of "patriarchal" theory and to other psychoanalytic theorists for our revision of that orthodox theory—even while we confront a larger intellectual community, which is often downright hostile to one or both of our theoretical interests. We are well aware that three is an awkward number as we struggle to "entertain" three complex traditions and modes of thought—the psychoanalytic, the literary, the feminist—none of which, of course, is monolithic: just as there have always been many concepts of literature and many veins of literary criticism, there are also of course many competing "schools" of psychoanalysis and many rival notions of feminism, on both sides of the Atlantic.

To further complicate matters, each of the three parties in this quarrelsome triangle has historically manifested a problematic relation with the other two. We could say, for instance, that psychoanalysis and feminism have entertained a love-hate relationship characterized by a highly ambivalent mutual fascination. The much-discussed hostility of feminist pioneers—Shulamith Firestone, Simone de Beauvoir, Betty Friedan, Kate Millett—to Freudian doctrine has been answered by a number of rebuttals (Juliet Mitchell's work is the best-known example) which have blasted traditional feminists for their misreadings of Freud and have argued compellingly for the crucial importance of psychoanalytic theory—penis envy and all—for a critique of patriarchal culture.[1] On the other hand, Lacanian analyses of the relationship between psychoanalysis and feminism have tended to foreground the attraction between the two theories. Jane Gallop's work, for example, has cast the relationship in familial terms as an oedipal struggle between feminist daughters and founding fathers (Freud and Lacan), often carried on in the name of the mother, who remains the disputed object of affection and reverence, as well as a certain hostility.[2]

Psychoanalysis and literature, the second couple in our theoretical triangle, have hardly had a less complicated history. Their relationship might be considered not so much an ambivalent love-hate relationship as a long-standing flirtation, or even an affair, which is still going strong even without the blessing of more traditional (hence "legitimate") elements of literary scholarship. From the earliest period of psychoanalysis, in which Freud chose Sophocles' *Oedipus Rex* as the emblem of the psychic drama of subjectivity, to the recent Lacanian readings of *Hamlet* and *The Purloined Letter* as emblems of the function of the signifier, the psychoanalytic master narrative of love and murder has looked to literature for its inspiration, imagery, and even its technique. For Freud himself, of course, is an accomplished storyteller, able to involve his reader in the psychoanalytic detective story, the search for the answer to the riddle of the sphinx. And Freud is also the first psychoanalytic literary theorist and critic, in his discussion of the sources of poetic art

[1]Juliet Mitchell, *Psychoanalysis and Feminism* (New York: Random House, 1974).
[2]Jane Gallop, *The Daughter's Seduction: Feminism and Psychoanalysis* (Ithaca: Cornell University Press, 1982).

("Creative Writers and Day-dreaming" [1908]) and in his reading of J. Vilhelm Jensen's novel *Gradiva* as evidence of the analogous nature of the analyst's task and the writer's work.[3] On the other hand, psychoanalysis has exerted a considerable influence on the themes and techniques of modern literature—surrealism provides perhaps the most obvious example of influence of psychoanalytic material on a literary movement—and Sigmund Freud himself seems to have evolved into a fascinating literary character not only in the recent best seller *The White Hotel* but in his own recently published unabridged letters, which have given rise to much speculation, often highly literary in nature, over the enigmatic man accused, among other things, of *"the seduction of truth"* (the title of Jeffrey Masson's "exposé" of the beginnings of psychoanalysis). Of course, the "affair" between literature and psychoanalysis, like all great passions, has had its problems, notably the stern parental resistance on the part of the literary establishment and the psychoanalytic establishment alike to the unorthodox union between "scientific" and "aesthetic" concerns.

Finally, if we look at the third couple of our critical threesome—feminism and literature—we encounter yet another complicated relationship, but this one differs markedly from those of the other two pairs. For feminism and literature do not seem to be engaged in a power struggle motivated by love and hate, nor do they seem as historically "intertwined" as psychoanalysis and literature. Their relationship, especially as concerns contemporary feminism and modern literature, seems to be more of an ethical and social alliance dictated by a moral imperative: literature and literary studies, as humanist activities, are quite simply and obviously incomplete when they omit the perspective of one half of humanity. Thanks in large part to the agency of women's studies programs, feminism and literature seem to be experiencing a marriage of sorts, but it is an open marriage, whose contract includes the right of experimentation and growth.

There is a growing awareness, even in establishment circles, that the literary process must solicit the participation of women writers and critics and at least tolerate feminist analysis, not simply in the liberal spirit of fair play or affirmative action but for the very legitimation of literature as a humanist endeavor. For much the same reasons, feminism turns to literature, albeit somewhat critically, as a sometime ideological ally (in the study of women writers, feminist fiction, and alternative genres, for example) and a rich source of insight, even while

[3]Sigmund Freud, *Delusions and Dreams in Jensen's "Gradiva"* (1907), *The Standard Edition of the Complete Psychological Works* (London: Hogarth, 1953–74), 9:1.

insisting on the right to criticize the patriarchal bias of the canon. Insofar as literature and the arts express what is human, a humanist ideology like feminism looks to the literary work for confirmation, example, inspiration, even while it criticizes the androcentrism that grounds and consecrates the study of Great Western Writers. Of course, in spite of the growing reputation and respectability of women's studies and feminist analysis, the academic establishment still seems to harbor some uneasiness about the contamination of literary purity by social and sexual concerns and often attempts to quarantine feminist studies in women's studies programs, in the name of academic standards and the promulgation of the canon ("Of course we'd love to teach women writers in our great writers course, but alas, we hardly have time to get to the truly great writers as it is"). If feminism has managed to effect an alliance with literature which legitimates the feminist enterprise, thanks to the effort of feminist scholars, traditional literary criticism nonetheless seems to look askance at this alliance, entertaining the suspicion that literature in its relation to feminism is perhaps engaged "below its station."

The question, then, for those of us who identify our own literary practice with psychoanalysis and feminism, is how to entertain a mé-nage à trois whose critical axes are characterized by ambivalence and a certain mutual incompatibility. Indeed, since it is our own work that stages this drama, this "entertainment" entails a kind of identity crisis in our own critical practice, for we ourselves to some degree identify with and occupy each of the three rival loci. How do we, as readers of literature, "manage" to appreciate the work, in the French sense of the term *ménager*, with a reading at once sensitive and critical, without resorting to a reductive view of literature as symptom or an overly antagonistic view of literature as ideological vehicle of patriarchal culture? How do we, as feminists, manage this sensitive literary appreciation without losing sight of the political and ethical agenda of feminism, without being compromised by the patriarchal ideology that inhabits psychoanalysis, and without being taken in by the Kantian notion of aesthetic privilege which would exempt the literary work from mundane (and political) concerns? How do we, as psychoanalytic theorists, manage to avoid "repression" of Freud's most virulent and difficult discoveries—of sexuality and of the unconscious—as we try to reconcile the feminist ethic of conscious activist involvement with a belief in unconscious agency? How does unconsciousness raising tally with consciousness raising? If, as feminists, we are mistrustful of authority as "phallic" and if, as psychoanalytists, we are all too aware of how ethics may be underwritten by an unchartable desire, by what authority and by what criteria do we critique and prescribe? Is the feminist-humanist project (as the Parisian antifeminist feminists contend) at odds with a critique of the phallogocentric assumptions of humanism?

These are difficult questions, to be sure. But only by playing host to these problematic issues can we hope to begin to negotiate the difficult theoretical triangle, itself oedipal in nature. (Is feminism not an unruly upstart that challenges the paternal law of Freudian theory for possession of the beloved "body" of literature?) The obstacles confronting the psychoanalytic feminist literary theorist are many, but the potential rewards are great—the politicization of aesthetics, the enrichment of the literary process by the perspective of one half of the human species, engaged as agents, rather than as literary, psychological, and sexual objects. Our task, then, is to negotiate something like "the successful passing of the Oedipus complex" (to use Freud's own term), which will enfranchise the woman writer and reader as protagonist-subject, even while it avoids the twin oedipal temptations to kill the Fathers of theory and to succumb to the seductive (Imaginary) promise of fulfillment, an overly indulgent union with a body of literature experienced as maternal corpus. (This is perhaps the temptation of a certain separatist or cultural feminism, which celebrates women's language, women's writing, and female poetics to the exclusion of all "great" works and all traditional aesthetic categories.) In order to begin to realize the promise of psychoanalytic feminist literary theory, we need to look first at the many connections, the points of convergence and shared interest—or disputed territory—intersections that Freud would call "nodes," those "knots" linking psychoanalysis, feminism, and literature and marking their meeting space or common ground.

The Tie That Binds: "Trying" Intersections

The nodal points connecting psychoanalysis, feminism, and literature—although intricate and complex—may for purposes of discussion be clustered around several general rubrics: first, the interest in human subjectivity and its relation to act of writing (what is a human subject, a woman subject, a woman writer); second, the interest in the unconscious (as agent of the human psyche; as ideology; as agent of the literary text); third, a preoccupation with language (as structure of the unconscious; as vehicle of patriarchal culture; as medium for the work of art); fourth, an interest in the notion of human activity as "symptom" or sign of something not explicitly stated (as symptom of repression; as effect of patriarchy; as work of art). Each of these nodes, has, of course, already been the site of a great deal of imaginative work by feminist critics working with psychoanalytic theory. I want first to comment briefly on the direction of this work, arguing against a tendency in feminist theory toward overemphasis on the maternal function or essentialization of femininity itself. I want to suggest, as others have done (Jacqueline Rose, Jane Gallop, Alice Jardine, Gayatri Spivak, Claire Kahane) that a "return to Freud" which owes much to Lacan but which remains critical of the androcentrism of Freud's theory, a return to Freud which emphasizes some of the earliest work (on jokes, dreams, parapraxis, as well as the celebrated Dora case) and which draws upon later cultural essays as well (*Totem and Taboo, Moses and Monotheism, Beyond the Pleasure Principle*) may serve as the ground for a new feminist thematics and a retelling of the oedipal narrative as "passed along" to us by Freud and Lacan as well.

Feminist psychoanalytic theory has, it seems to me, taken up three different stances in the family scene of psychoanalysis—a scene that is of course itself oedipal in nature, requiring that each generation of readers and interpreters of psychoanalytic doctrine take a position vis-à-vis the founding father. The first stance, typified by the work of Juliet Mitchell, has been that of a dutiful daughter, whose task is to interpret psychoanalytic theory in a manner not too unpalatable to feminism. Mitchell and other "daughters" of Freud, and of Lacan as well—and I think we all participate in these activities—tend to do several things: to point out Freud's own discomfort with the rigid categories of masculine and feminine; to emphasize that Freud's account of human subjectivity is descriptive rather than prescriptive; and to argue that Freudian theory is essential to an understanding of the psychological and ideological underpinnings of patriarchy. Feminist Lacanians often take a more radical position, contending that Lacan's insistence on the privilege of the phallic term undercuts "phallic conceit" and exposes it as a ruse, a covering of castration, the divided subjectivity of all human beings. As I have said elsewhere, these daughterly readings are often ingenious and extremely useful to a feminist reconsideration of psychoanalysis, but they frequently seem to concede too much to the overvenerated founding fathers, dealing in alibis designed to let Dad off the hook of his own "phallic conceit."[4]

---

[4]The term is taken from Gallop, *The Daughter's Seduction*, chap. 2, "Of Phallic Proportions: Lacanian Conceit." And see my essay "(What) Does Woman Want?" in *Psychoanalysis and ...*, ed. Richard Feldstein and Henry Sussman (New York: Routledge, 1989).

The second familial stance of psychoanalytic feminism is reaction against this phallic conceit and this paternal authority. Mother's daughters (Luce Irigaray is perhaps the best example of this tendency) turn away from their theoretical father(s) in a kind of affirmative action that seeks to rehabilitate the preoedipal, the maternal, and the Imaginary, at the same time engaging in a search for a female language (the "[m]other tongue") characterized by fluidity and openness and grounded in female anatomy.[5] From the positing of a women's language, it is a short step to the elaboration of a female poetics (the "gynesis" that is the focus of Jardine's work) that represents the other of the phallic or monologic (Kristeva's term) system. The value of the approach of these mother's daughters is the highly affirmative nature of their stance, their elaboration of the heretofore repressed "maternal subtext" (Coppélia Kahn), and their search for a uniquely female creative subjectivity. Yet such theorizing risks the fetishization of the female body and sometimes tends to privilege maternity at the expense of sexuality or even to equate female creativity with maternity (as Kristeva sometimes seems to do), coming full circle to the worst of Freud. Indeed, the privileging of the Imaginary may neglect the Symbolic altogether, promoting the old fiction of unified subjectivity, experienced in a golden "semiotic" age of infant fusion with the mother. Similarly, the mystification of women's language as the locus of cosmic incoherence (in the work, for example, of Chantal Chawaf), overlooks the question of women's complicity and responsibility in history, reconsigning women to a role at worst passive or separatist (as when "Psych et Po" rejects the notion of equality as a phallic term), at best indirect and manipulative (as in Irigaray's concept of "mimicry," or nonsubmissive submission).[6]

Thus much of feminist psychoanalytic theory today seems to propose what is finally the old oedipal impasse between father and mother, system and silence, structure and anarchy. Yet all the feminist writers to whom I have alluded, and many others as well, suggest a third possible position at the oedipal intersection—beyond simple submission or rebellion—the stance of which I have elsewhere called the "prodigal daughter."[7] She is a daughter who acknowledges her heritage, or rather, like the prodigal child of the biblical account (a "son"), she

---

[5]See The (M)other Tongue: Essays in Feminist Psychoanalytic Interpretation, ed. Shirley Nelson Garner, Claire Kahane, and Madelon Sprengnether (Ithaca: Cornell University Press, 1985).

[6]Luce Irigaray, This Sex Which Is Not One, trans. Catherine Porter with Carolyn Burke (Ithaca: Cornell University Press, 1985).

[7]In my paper "The Female Subject: What Does Woman Want?" presented at the 1985 MLA Convention Forum on Psychoanalysis and Literature.

goes beyond the fold of restrictive paternal law, only to return. But unlike the prodigal son, who returns repentant, this daughter returns enriched, for she is *prodigal* in the second sense of the word as well: lush, exceptional, extravagant. To be prodigal in this way is to alter the law, to enlarge its boundaries and recast its meaning (even in the biblical parable, let us recall, the prodigal is forgiven his outlandish behavior and reassimilated, thereby changing forever the limits of the permissible). Thus the Law to which the prodigal daughter accedes is an altered law.

The prodigal daughter of psychoanalysis, I suggest, is engaged in a rereading of female "illness," such as hysteria, casting the hysteric simultaneously as cultural heroine and as victim of the patriarchal symbolic (as Naomi Schor's work on *Eugénie Grandet,* for example, suggests), whose very illness is a testimony to the persistence and ingenuity of female desire, which *will* speak when repressed, even if only in somatic symptom. For many feminists today, Dora and Anna O. are the prodigal daughters par excellence, who either refuse the patriarchal version of their illness or actively participate in the invention of their own cure, forever transforming psychoanalytic "law."

The prodigal daughter of today (Mitchell and Rose are both examples) insists on the cultural nature of Freud's and Lacan's discoveries, even when the fathers themselves are blind to it. One of the most promising efforts at this kind of cultural interpretation is found in the work of Luce Irigaray, who analyzes Claude Lévi-Strauss's findings concerning the cultural position of women as objects of exchange circulated among men—or, in Lacanian terms, as a Signifier to be valued and exchanged in language—with an eye to securing "a place for women within sexual difference" rather than eschewing cultural transaction altogether because of its heretofore sexist character. Such an effort entails the recasting of psychoanalytic law, a rerouting of Oedipus via cultural theory. For as Irigaray points out, Lévi-Strauss demonstrates that woman is not only an object of exchange but a speaking subject as well; she might make use of her unique position and double perspective to critique and reshape culture.[8] The prodigal daughter's own situation at the node between intersubjective culture and intrasubjective psyche—a position perhaps first decribed in Lacan's concept of analysis as a triangular "knot," operating in three dimensions[9]—permits her to recast the oedi-

---

[8]Luce Irigaray, "Women on the Market," in *This Sex Which Is Not One,* 170–91.

[9]Jacques Lacan's concept of the Borromean knot was introduced in the Seminar of 1973 and elaborated throughout the seminars. See Stuart Schneiderman's *Jacques Lacan: The Death of an Intellectual Hero* (Cambridge: Harvard University Press, 1983), 33–38.

pal drama (Oedipus as heroine) and to suggest that "her" "oedipal" position at the intersection may not be doomed to a tragic outcome.

How then can we transfer the prodigal uses of psychoanalysis to our own practice as readers and interpreters of literature? I suggest that we take yet another detour—a long-circuit that requires a return to Freud via Lacan—rather than opt for the shortest distance between the two points. For some of the more direct routes to feminist pscyhoanalytic theory—such as the grounding of female subjectivity and female language in female anatomy or the celebration of female subjectivity through the substitution of a mythological heroine (Antigone) for the hero of Freud's version (Oedipus)—may prove to be short-circuits or dead ends of sorts, rather than short cuts. While such efforts do provide a rich source of imagery and female prototype, insofar as they also tend to produce versions of human experience which rival traditional androcentric narrative, they risk valorizing sexual difference to the point, paradoxically, of confirming Lacan's dead-end "conclusion" that "there is no sexual relation," no real communication or shared experience between genders.[10] The feminist psychoanalytic reappropriation of subjectivity should of course make new myths and continue to explore the questions of "what woman wants" and what she is from perspectives neglected or insufficiently explored by the male psychoanalytic establishment. But such efforts need to be combined with a retelling of Freud's own master narrative, a recasting of the oedipal scenario with a greater flexibility in "roles" played by both genders. Freud's own writings—and particularly his early psychoanalytic writings in the first decade of the century—provide ample material from which to restage the oedipal drama and to suggest that Freud's later, more biologically deterministic readings may themselves be symptoms of the repression of earlier findings. This, of course, is the argument of much of what is called "French Freud," and indeed, in spite of the phallocentrism of much of Lacan's "return to Freud," the Lacanian emphasis on shifting gender identity, the dispersion of the subject in intersubjectivity, and the importance of locus rather than gender as determinant of subjectivity, is a reading of Freud which can be enormously useful in retelling the human drama of love, murder, sacrifice, and accommodation.

Return to Freud: Recasting Oedipus

We are all familiar with Freud's master plot, the tale of Oedipus to which he first alludes in *The Interpretation of Dreams* and which

[10]Lacan deals with the "question of woman" in the Seminar of 1973.

becomes the grounding for all of psychoanalytic theory. Even when Freud is not explicitly alluding to the story of Oedipus, this narrative paradigm insists in his work. Freud relates the same story—and indeed seems to have lived it—over and over again, depicting a tripolar relationship in which children rebel against a father figure, who "lays down the law" concerning incestual gratification with a forbidden object. The same "plot" seems to play itself out in works as diverse as *Jokes and their Relation to the Unconscious* (1905), *Totem and Taboo* (1912), *Moses and Monotheism* (1933), and in various descriptions of the transference phenomenon in analysis. In each of these variants, the gender roles appear more or less stable: a masculine subject-protagonist finds an impediment to infantile gratification in the person of authority and, paradoxically, is initiated into the human order by the very figure who first poses an obstacle to his desire. Even in the late works, the father lives on as the superego, or conscience, which aids the ego in its struggle to wrest itself from the inchoate and undifferentiated id, the curiously transformed "maternal" element in the ego-id-superego triangle. Jocasta, in the latest formulation, "returns" unmasked as a *threat* to subjectivity, growth, and human order, a tempting territory to be dominated and civilized (Freud: "where id was, ego shall be").

Lacan retells the same story as the drama of the human subject's entry into the Symbolic order, occasioned by submission to paternal law and enforced, as in Freud's account, by the threat of castration. But whereas for Freud this threat is, among other things, a literal threat, a prohibition against masturbation, for Lacan it is a matter of symbolic castration, which every human being undergoes as the price for acquisition of language and access to the human community. For Freud as for Lacan, however, the essence of the great human cultural achievement, repeated by every human child, is the management of the potentially lethal oedipal triangle, thanks to an act of Symbolic substitution, in which the human child identifies with and imitates the father, renouncing the wish to take his place ("I want a girl, just *like* the girl, who married dear ole Dad"). The child Oedipus avoids the fatal outcome by finding a substitute love object, obeying the incest taboo (symbolized for Lacan in the name-of-the father) and paying his Symbolic debt—whose payment he will in due time exact from his own progeny. In the successful negotiation of the oedipal drama—as Lévi-Strauss's and Luce Irigaray's work has underscored—the two male rivals become allies, and patriarchal law is cemented by an exchange of an appropriate female love object. The father, after all, "gives his daughter away" to the Son-in-Law, who has renounced the competition with his own father for the females of his tribe. Both generations give up incestuous pleasure in the cultural practice of exogamy in order to become father-and-son-*in-Law*.

This exogamy, as Lévi-Strauss has shown, is the very foundation of culture, depending upon that patriarchal "traffic" in women which allows man, as subject-protagonist, to get beyond the stifling incestuous family circle. The cultural dimensions of the oedipal tragedy discussed by Lévi-Strauss and subjected to feminist analysis by Luce Irigaray were, of course, first analyzed and narrated by Freud himself, whose *Totem and Taboo* (1913) mythifies the primal scene in which the sons murder the father-chieftan who possesses the women of the tribe. Freud's founding myth of human culture is taken up in turn by Lacan, for whom the "Symbolic debt" is, among other things, the repressed knowledge of that first patricide, the crime of the species which can be expiated only by submission to patriarchal law. The debt to the slain father is paid up, for Lacan, in the assumption of the name-of-the-father, that paternal metaphor which both bears witness to and suppresses the "original" crime. In Lacan's version of Freud's myth, the linguistic-symbolic order itself, which founds cultural transaction, is a function of legitimacy in its fullest patriarchal sense, as an act of exogamous trade of female-as-Signifier by male-subject-traders. In the most extreme formulation of this aspect of Lacanian theory, woman becomes a mere category of language, who exists *only* as Signifier and with whom "no sexual relation" is possible.[11] It is thus hard to imagine how Freud's master cultural narrative could be *less* flexible in terms of gender roles and the insistence upon female subordination as well as the secondary nature of female subjectivity than it is in *Totem and Taboo*, and in Lévi-Strauss's and Lacan's uses of this narrative. The law of female submission and objectification seems "written in stone."

Yet when we look at Freud's later work *Moses and Monotheism* (1933), which both repeats elements of the earlier narrative and at the same time tells the story of the origin of patriarchal law itself—literally written in stone by God the Father and handed from God to Moses—we find fascinating hints of ambivalence in gender roles and functions. For in Freud's version of the Exodus story just as in *Totem and Taboo*, traces of the oedipal plot remain clear (the patriarch Moses is murdered by his "children," the Jews, who, even while repressing the memory of their crime, continue to expiate their filial sin by their observation of Moses' law and veneration of his name); yet in this later narrative, the

[11]Jacques Lacan, Seminar xx, 1972–73, "God and the *Jouissance* of the Woman," trans. in *Feminine Sexuality: Jacques Lacan and the Ecole Freudienne*, ed. Juliet Mitchell and Jacqueline Rose, trans. Jacqueline Rose (New York: Norton, 1982), 137–48.

Jerry Aline Flieger

gender of the principal players and the notion of the "identity" of Moses
himself are not nearly as clear as they are in the stories of Oedipus and
in the primal myth of *Totem and Taboo*. Moses remains a masculine
figure, to be sure, the original patriarch, but in Freud's startling interpretation of biblical legend, Moses is an *alien*, an Egyptian of *illegitimate* royal birth and thus the product of a pantheistic culture that
worships female principles of fertility and rebirth and expresses itself in
the "dream-language" of imagistic hieroglyphs, which Freud discusses
elsewhere as the source of ambivalence itself.[12] The monolithic "identity" of the Jewish father—his phallic "legitimacy"—is undermined in
Freud's retelling of the oedipal legend. The second "player" in the
oedipal drama is of course the Jewish people, in its infancy, which
acquires its identity as the "chosen people" with its entry into law. But
in contradistinction to the role of subject-protagonist in the oedipal
drama—which is played by one distinct male figure—and in the story
of *Totem and Taboo*—where the "protagonist" is a group of tribal
sons—the "subject" of *Moses and Monotheism* is both plural and non-
gender-specific, a whole people. As for the third player or function in
the oedipal drama, which is of course the maternal player/function who
tempts the protagonist to rebel against the father (Jocasta in *Oedipus
Rex*; the tribal women in *Totem and Taboo*), we might say that "her"
role is filled by the idol—the golden icon—which instigates the wild
orgiastic revelry, the illegitimate behavior, of the Jewish people during
Moses' sojourn on the mountain. This tempting mother symbolizes
pantheism, disorder, disobedience, pleasure, plurality—a graven *image*
rather than a written *word*—like the Oriental culture, inscribed in
hieroglyphs, from which the Jewish people seeks to differentiate itself
in triumphant exodus. Interestingly, however, not even this gender
identity—of the tempting (maternal) icon—is stable, in spite of its
association with female elements, for the image is a golden *calf* of
indeterminate gender (rather than the fertile, milk-giving cow). Yet the
icon clearly represents the other of monotheistic law: in this recasting
of Oedipus, then, the father competes *with* the mother, not *for* the
mother ("the Lord thy God is a jealous God"), requiring an act of
obedience and identification on the part of the subject-protagonist, who
is called upon to renounce the incestuous temptation of the maternal
body. In the latest of Freud's master narratives of culture, then, we find
that the players in the oedipal drama are inhabited by a curious instability of gender: the Patriarchal narrative of the triumph of law is
haunted by doubt concerning the legtimacy of the lawgiver himself.

[12]Sigmund Freud, "The Antithetical Sense of Primal Words" (1910), *Standard Edition*,
11:155.

Entertaining the Ménage à Trois

I want to turn now from Freud's master oedipal narratives—the stories of Oedipus, *Totem and Taboo*, and Moses—to his discussions of several kinds of intersubjective interaction: the transference in analysis, the joking transaction, and the act of play—for each of these three models of interaction suggests further complications of the oedipal scenario and enables the rereading of the oedipal narrative in a feminist perspective, in which the role of protagonist is not restricted to or confused with the male gender.

Opening the Triangle: The Language Game Replayed

Freud himself was the first to comment upon the Oedipal dynamic of the analytic situation, referring to his method in an early letter (1906) as a "cure by love."[13] In later papers on "transference-love" (1912 and 1915), Freud extended the notion of the neurotic origin of the transference to the experience of normal love, indicating that "all feelings of sympathy are sexual in origin" and thereby suggesting that all analysis is an essentialized replay of normal (infantile) love relations.[14] In his last work, *An Outline of Psychoanalysis* (published posthumously in 1940), Freud insists that the transference is a *replay* of the original oedipal drama, in which the patient sees in the analyst "the return, the reincarnation of some important figure out of his childhood or past," who is generally "one or the other of the patient's parents, his father or his mother," onto whom he "transfers" the earlier affect and with whom he may replay the earlier drama in an act of "aftereducation" which resolves earlier conflicts.[15] Now the powerful position of the analyst in this drama is obvious. The therapist is parent, original love, and authority object. But this position is strikingly multivalent, overdetermined by multiple roles (analyst as authority and love object, father and mother, object of love and source of fear). Freud insists on the complications of the analyst-patient relationship, echoing to some degree his earlier statement that "four people are present in every sexact," because of the overdetermined nature of human sexuality itself.[16]

---

[13]See Ernest Jones, *The Life and Work of Sigmund Freud* (New York: Basic Books, 1955), 2:434.

[14]Ibid., 253.

[15]Freud, *An Outline of Psychoanalysis* (1940), *Standard Edition*, 23:141–207. The notions of transference and aftereducation are discussed in pt. 2, chap. 6, "The Technique of Psycho-analysis."

[16]Jones quotes Freud's letter to Wilhelm Fliess (1:315), in which Freud also writes: "You are certainly right about bisexuality," that is, about the fundamentally bisexual nature of all human beings.

Jerry Aline Flieger

For in the later formulation of the transference, Freud insists that both parties are at once agents and objects, transferents and transferees, masculine and feminine. Thus, even Lacan's description of analysis in the celebrated "schéma L" is merely a "return to Freud" and to Freud's own concept of the complicated and overdetermined schema that underlies every act of love. The essence of the transference is a drama of shifting power plays, in which players occupy different positions and assume different gender roles not only successively but simultaneously.

Indeed, Freud's own apprenticeship in the psychoanalytic method can be seen as his learning to relinquish the naturally dominant position of the analyst in favor of a more passive role. For Freud's analytic experience taught him, above all, *not* to intervene or to impose interpretative authority but rather to lend a "free-floating" attention to the analysand's narrative. Even Freud's much discussed departure from the early "seduction theory" as an explanation for the etiology of hysteria might be considered in this light, for whereas Freud's very early work with hysterics might be said to emphasize the objectified and passive status of the patient (as "seduced" victim, who—as the famous painting of Jean Martin Charcot's lecture on hysteria manifests—is offered up to the curious and somewhat lurid gaze of the onlooking male analyst who directs her cure), his later explanation of the imaginary origin of the pscyhic drama tends to give his patient the active, creative role of psychic subject, who "leads the analyst on" with her tales, a latter-day Scheherazade who captivates her accomplice in the countertransference. For the analysand, in this later understanding, is above all a storyteller, and the analyst, however powerful, is an audience, a reader, a recipient. Both positions contain aspects of power and passivity—which Freud sometimes elides with the concepts of masculinity and femininity—and both positions imply mutual implication and mutual vulnerability.

Of course, Freud's celebrated aborted analysis of Dora (1905) has often been read as just such a complicated play of transference and countertransference and of bisexuality of analyst and analysand alike. Many of the essays in Claire Kahane and Charles Bernheimer's recent anthology on the Dora case, for instance, emphasize the femininity of Freud's position, his identification with his patient, and his position of vulnerability in the abruptly terminated analysis, in which he is sent packing like a mere servant with barely two weeks' notice.[17] Charles

[17]Charles Bernheimer and Claire Kahane, eds., *In Dora's Case: Freud, Hysteria, Feminism* (New York: Columbia University Press, 1985).

Bernheimer's essay insists that the place of the analyst is as uncertain as that of the analysand, while Claire Kahane and others stress Dora's own uncertain gender role, attested by her attraction to both Frau K. and Herr K., as well as to Freud himself. All the essays in this collection, and in other treatments of the Dora case, stress the fictional and narrative aspects of transference, in which the detective work and the love plots are intertwined.

Now it is interesting to note that Freud's work on Dora appeared at about the same time as two other important and interesting works: *Three Essays on Sexuality* (1905) and *Jokes and Their Relation to the Unconscious*, published in the same year and composed concurrently with the essays on infantile sexuality. For if it is the case, as Kahane, Bernheimer, Madelon Sprengnether (in her essay "Enforcing Oedipus," in the same collection) have argued, that the Dora case can be read as a symptom of Freud's repressed "femininity," as well as a repression of the knowledge of Dora's "masculinity" or homosexuality (a repression or repudiation occasioned by Freud's own countertransference, his love for Dora), it is nonetheless evident that *Three Essays* represents an implicit recognition of bisexuality in all human subjects and that *Jokes and Their Relation to the Unconscious* occupies a middle ground, *implying* a certain flexibility of gender and overdetermination of sexual position, of masculine and feminine, even while skirting the (uncomfortable) issue. It is to the latter text that I want to turn now, as a particularly apt example of the recasting and replay of Oedipus which may yield a rereading useful for a feminist-psychoanalytic interpretation of the literary process and other kinds of human interaction as well.

Jokes and Their Relation to the Unconscious—like Freud's treatment of Oedipus, like *Totem and Taboo*, like *Moses and Monotheism*, like the Dora case—is built around a narrative that is also a paradigm or scenario, a model for human interaction. And on the most obvious level, as is the case with all the other narrative scenarios, the gender roles in its scenario *seem* straightforward and unambiguous; indeed, as I have written elsewhere, Freud's description of the genesis of the joke reads like a boy-meets-girl drama.[18] In brief, Freud's primal joke scene unfolds thus: a male subject-protagonist (pole one, the joke maker) desires a female object (pole two, the joke's butt), but she resists his advances because of the presence of a third person, another male (pole

[18]Flieger, "The Purloined Punchline: Joke as Textual Paradigm," in *Lacan and Narration*, ed. Robert Con Davis (Baltimore: Johns Hopkins University Press, 1984). This essay, which originally appeared in *MLN*, contains a longer discussion of Freud's joke theory as related to a theory of textuality.

three, the joke's audience), who, incidentally, desires her also. Frustrated and angry at the female's resistance and at the second male's presence, which has interrupted his wooing, the joke maker concocts a (dirty) joke at the expense of the female, which he tells to the second male. The two males thus receive a substitute gratification of their amorous desire, which exacts enjoyment out of exposing or embarrassing the female. It is hard to imagine a situation more oedipal than this (obstructed) triangle of desire and this solution, in which "father" and "son" (pole three, the hearer-obstructor, and pole one, the protagonist-joker) experience something like the "successful passing of the Oedipus complex," resulting in an alliance and identification that—like the tribal "traffic" in women which is the outcome of *Totem and Taboo* and the subject of Lévi-Strauss's and Luce Irigaray's work—is a profoundly *social* bond. The scenario of accomplices "exposing" a desirable female and sharing their "discoveries" brings to mind, as well, the famous painting of Charcot displaying his toothsome female hysteric patient, breast bared, to a circle of male colleagues (Freud, of course, among them). While Freud, of course, does not make this association, even as he declines to observe the oedipal nature of the scene of rivalry and symbolic/substitute gratification (and violation) he depicts, it is clear to his reader that yet another version of the same old apparently sexist, off-color story of Oedipus, is being put forward as a paradigm for a universal creative human activity: that of joking.

At first encounter, Freud's account of joking as prohibited oedipal desire would seem to be so blatantly sexist and gender-fixed as to be of little apparent use for a feminist understanding of this process. But the fact remains that Freud is describing an activity—joking and joke making—which is engaged in by every human being, regardless of gender. He is, moreover, talking about a larger phenomenon than joking. As I have said elsewhere,[19] this paradigm is applicable to all kinds of text making and creative activity. What is really being described is the human being's capacity for sublimation of sexual desire in many kinds of constructive social "intercourse." If Freud chooses to couch his parable in patriarchal garb—perhaps because this particular scenario is most instantly recognizable to his reader, also situated in patriarchal culture—this by no means signifies that the process (of joking, of signifying, of creating) is only open to males. Freud himself, of course, must have been aware that women have the capacity to joke and to be aggressive; thus, even if this scenario, like the others, fails to spell out the role of the female subject, potential or actual—just as Freud's anal-

[19]Ibid.

ysis of Dora's case elides her point of view—the notion of female subjectivity and of female as creative actor is nonetheless implied in the choice of a universal human activity (joking, loving, creating) as subject for commentary and analysis.

Yet rather than engage in an argument for the right of the female subject to assume the active role of the male protagonist-joker-creative in Freud's scenario, that is, the right of a female subject to "act like a man," it is perhaps a better feminist strategy to attend to the flexibility and multivalence inherent in Freud's own paradigm, recognizing that everyone in Freud's oedipal joke scene is at once active *and* passive, desiring *and* desired, even male *and* female, to use gender-bound terms. In the joking circuit, all players are implicated, and no one emerges unscathed, "uncastrated" or "unviolated." Pole one, the "male" joker, exerts power over his exposed victim and over his captive audience as well, whom, as Freud emphasizes, he *"bribes"* into complicity by the lure of shared pleasure.[20] This same third party, on the other hand, even though he is "used" by the joke maker and "taken in" by the joke process ("used" and "taken in" are the terms of the *Standard Edition,* as translated by James Strachey), nonetheless exerts considerable power over the joke maker (156).[21] For this third party is an absolutely indispensable element in the circuit, as Freud underscores. Without an audience, complicit in the hostile sexual put-down, there is no joke. It is in this respect that the analogy with the literary process, or text making, is most apparent. The writer, like the joke maker, needs an audience, which he or she must "captivate" and persuade, in order to fulfill the pleasure transaction of text making. (Freud himself touches on these issues in the essay "Creative Writers and Daydreaming," written in 1908, in which he likens the writer's art to a kind of disguise of personal libidinal fantasy, a "veiling" of "egotistical wishes" that the writer must make palatable to the reader.) Thus both "male" parties, the joke (or text) maker and the audience (or reader), occupy positions that are both powerful and mutually vulnerable, active and passive. But what of the second party, the "female" object, exposed in the joke and "shared" by the two complicit jokers? Her passivity and objectification seem obvious enough, but is there power inherent in her position as well?

In reading Freud's scenario of symbolic violation, we need to take note of the imaginary nature of the gratification of desire: the joking

---

[20]Sigmund Freud, *Jokes and Their Relation to the Unconscious* (1905), *Standard Edition,* 8:100, hereafter cited in the text.
[21]"I [the joker] am making use of him [the hearer] to arouse my own laughter."

transaction is a symptom or compromise formation, a substitute grati-fication of the original desire. It is the object's *refusal* or inaccessibility that occasions the joke transaction itself: her actual inviolability gives rise to the joker's creative solution. Furthermore, as Freud himself notes, the butt of the joke, the "offended party," more often than not removes herself from the joke transaction as well, leaving the room (100).[22] Thus, paradoxically, the joke's "object," who exerts a fascina-tion and thus a considerable power over the two other principals in the triangle, who desire her, is perhaps the least "scathed" by the joke process, which is, among other things, a testament to her inaccessibil-ity. The symbolic importance of the joke "object," moreover, must not be underestimated. "She" is the signifier of human desire, which (as Lacan's writings insist) is always by definition a surplus, a leftover quotient, an excess above and beyond "need."[23] It is inherent in the nature of human desire to be elusive and excessive, ceaselessly re-motivating the long-circuit of human social intercourse.

Freud himself underscores the profoundly social nature of joking, which always involves a pact of two transactors at the expense of a third and which, furthermore, always occasions its own repetition in an unending chain of scenarios of oedipal desire. In a fascinating footnote to his text (139), Freud comments on the *compulsion* the hearer feels to repeat a good joke to someone else ("he must tell it to someone else") and speculates that this is a kind of psychic vengeance for his own "use" by the joke master who has taken him in. The hearer, Freud writes, "damps down his annoyance" by resolving to tell the joke to someone else later on. Just as the protagonist of the oedipal familial drama compensates himself for his submission to human law and hu-man renunciation by reenacting the drama in his own (marital) family circle, just as the "sons" of *Totem and Taboo* become in turn the "chieftains" of a new generation, just as the Jewish people of *Moses and Monotheism* codify and hand down the law to successive generations, just so the joke's recipient acts in obedience to what Freud calls "that something which remains over" (143) and feels compelled to "commu-nicate the idea," thus bringing "the unknown process to an end" (143). But of course, no end is in sight, for the next "dupe" in the comic chain (obedient to the ancient slogan of farce, which declares that each player in the human drama must in turn receive his/her comeuppance: "à

---

[22]Ibid., 100: Freud tells us that the offended lady leaves the room, "feeling ashamed," increasing the pleasure of the two male allies.

[23]For a discussion of the difference among need, demand, and desire in Lacan's writings, see Anthony Wilden, *The Language of the Self* (New York: Dell, 1975), later reissued by Johns Hopkins University Press.

trompeur, trompeur et demi") will in turn be called upon to pay the symbolic debt of *désir*. The triangle is always a foursome, looking to the next link in the chain, the next "subject" of the next triangular passion play.

It is perhaps not necessary to insist upon the obvious association of this scenario, and all the oedipal scenarios, with the compulsion to repeat analyzed in Freud's celebrated later essay *Beyond the Pleasure Principle* (1920). For the parallels with the joke scenario are evident, particularly in the oft-discussed *fort-da* game observed and reported by Freud and analyzed as a paradigm for the activity of infant play: the protagonist, who, like the joker, finds himself in the grips of the oedipal dilemma (the mother has been called away by "social demands," the equivalent of the paternal prohibition of incest), comes to terms with an unpleasant deprivation or frustration by restaging the situation in play.[24] Thus, like the joker (and like the writer), he finds a substitute gratification of unassuaged desire, thanks to his own creative inventiveness. Of course, the child must also act as his own "audience" as well, which she or he does thanks to the opportune presence of a mirror. In any case, the "audience" of child's play materializes in a later passage in the same essay (18:11), which bears a striking resemblance to the structure of transmission of the joke (in which the "victimized" hearer retells the joke to the next dupe in line). In the second play situation described by Freud, a child who has been examined by a doctor (much to his displeasure), later "plays doctor" on another (usually younger or weaker) child, thus depriving pleasure from mastering an initially traumatic experience. In this instance, of course, two of the roles in the initial oedipal joke scenario are played by the new "victim," who is both exposed butt of libidinal desire and "audience" of the player's game. Or it might be more accurate to say that the "object" of desire—the female in the joke scene, the absent mother in the play scene—has in this instance become entirely abstract and is no longer an "object" at all but merely a situation of powerfulness or passivity experienced by the protagonist *himself* as "violated" object. In this perspective, the oedipal triangle is no longer the primal scene or paradigm but merely one particularly concrete instance of an even more universal human experience of desire, privation, and powerlessness, in which gender is no longer the primary factor. In this restaging of Oedipus, done by Freud himself and underscored by Lacan (who takes the *fort-da* scene as the archetype of human entry into the symbolic register), "violation" is, if

---

[24]Sigmund Freud, *Beyond the Pleasure Principle* (1920), *Standard Edition*, 18:2, hereafter cited in the text.

Jerry Aline Flieger

anything, more central than "castration," and the "solution" for all human subjects is the same: social interaction and creative play.

If we look, moreover, to Derrida's reading of Lacan's reading of Freud's reading of play, we find yet another example of destablization and overdetermination of gender and gender roles in all human play.[25] For Derrida takes issue with Lacan's insistence on the symbolic aspects of the *fort-da* scene, pointing out that the imaginary register is every bit as important (thanks to the play with the mirror image) and stressing, as have Fredric Jameson and others, that these two "stages" are not stages at all but intertwined registers of human activity. Such readings provide an important assist, in my view, to feminist efforts to recuperate the Imaginary register not as a maternal preoedipal "stage" that merely precedes the all-important paternal oedipal symbolic but as a crucial mode of human interaction which coexists and intertwines with the Symbolic at all moments of human life.[26] Derrida's reading of *Beyond the Pleasure Principle*, furthermore, like many feminist readings of Freud's analysis of the Dora case, tends to emphasize Freud's own involvement in the situation he observes and describes and insists that there is no position of exemption from desire in any intersubjective circuit, that all players are links in a desiring chain.

This is also the upshot of Jacques Lacan's celebrated reading of Poe's detective story *The Purloined Letter*, which describes just such a desiring chain along with the stigma of the "letter" (signifying castration, passivity, even the shock of surprise, as in the joke scenario) is transmitted from "victim" to "victim."[27] In this reading, the letter is Signifier of desire, the Symbolic nexus of language, which (again, like the joke in Freud's essay) will always circulate in search of the other to whom it is addressed. Lacan's reading of Poe—like Derrida's reading of Freud and Freud's own reading of the activities of joking, playing, and writing (described in "Creative Writers and Daydreaming" as yet another gratification of desire addressed to the other in a social circuit)—foregrounds the fundamentally *perverse* nature of human signification, if we use Freud's own notion of perversity as deflection from original goal and substitutive gratification (*Three Essays on Sexuality*, 1905). By such a definition, indeed, writing would be a highly "perverted" activity,

[25]Jacques Derrida, "Coming into One's Own," in *Psychoanalysis and the Question of the Text*, ed. Geoffrey H. Hartman (Baltimore: Johns Hopkins University Press, 1978), 114–48.

[26]See, for example, Naomi Schor, "*Eugénie Grandet:* Mirrors and Melancholia," in *The (M)other Tongue.*

[27]Jacques Lacan, "Le séminaire sur 'La lettre volée,'" *Ecrits* (Paris: Seuil, 1966), 19–75, trans. in *French Freud*, ed. Jeffrey Mehlman, *Yale French Studies* 48 (1972), 38–72.

fulfilling libidinal desire by "veiling" what Freud calls the "egotistical wishes" of the writer and enticing a third party to act as reader by the bribe of the pleasure of literary form.

The pleasure circuit of the literary process (like those of joking and play) is destined to be repeated in a widening social nexus of readers: it is, by definition, that act of repetitive play which most actively solicits the other. It is by nature, moreover, a long-circuit—as the work of Peter Brooks, for instance, points out—in which metonymic desire intentionally extends and complicates narrative plot.[28] The main point, however, is that according to Freud's own view of it as "compromise-formation" or symptom of desire, the literary text may be considered to be a "letter in circulation," which is at once metaphoric in nature—as symptom of the repressed tragic conflict between law and desire—and metonymic in function, driven by a never-assuaged *désir* addressed, like the purloined letter, to the other it both reaches and misses.

This view of textuality is useful for a feminist understanding of literary processes because of its emphasis upon the social aspects of intersubjective exchange: every human subject lays claim to his or her humanity by a *textual* process (with *text* understood etymologically as a weaving or web), a speaking or writing of desire *deflected* from the original short-circuit of the incestuous family foyer and diverted to the larger audience beyond. And as recent feminist reappropriations of Dora and other psychoanalytic "heroines" have demonstrated, such a circuit need not be a commerce in female objects. For in saying no to the circle of males who handed her over (from her father to Herr K. to Freud), Dora asserts her own voice and her own access to the position of subject, however transient, complicated, and overdetermined that place may be, however "framed" by other text acts, past and future.

Freud as Entertainer: Rethinking the Ménage à Trois

This long-circuit, then, which brings us back to Freud via Lacan by way of Dora and a whole cast of other players, insists upon Freud as literary creator and as literary actor, caught in the text of desire which his work describes. In Freud's own practice, of course, analysis itself can become a literary event (witness the spellbinding detective plot of Dora), the pretext of narrative, the case "history," which, having first captured Freud's own "free-floating attention," now works to captivate

---

[28]Peter Brooks, "Freud's Masterplot: Questions of Narrative," in *Literature and Psychoanalysis*, ed. Shoshana Felman (Baltimore: Johns Hopkins University Press, 1982), 280–300.

Jerry Aline Flieger

a new audience, thanks to Freud's own skill as master narrator and stylist. And in his narratives, we might say (borrowing from Lacan) that Freud himself "returns to Freud," each of his "histories" being framed and overdetermined by others, in an intertextual chain where the notion of "mastery"—sometimes equated with activity or masculinity— is undercut time and again by what Freud often calls the threat of "castration" but which manifests itself in many of his narratives as universal human experience of the obstruction of desire or the limitations of personal power, which often only masquerades in patriarchal garb as a "phallic" castastrophe.

Our own long-circuit, then, our own detour, which seeks to revisit the oedipal scene in order to manage our own critical "ménage" of psychoanalysis, feminism, and literature, brings us back to Freud's text, by way of those intersections or nodes of our triple perspective (the nature of subjectivity, of textuality, and of subjectivity as textual). But Freud's text is not an end point but a signpost, which points the way outward, beyond the oedipal impasse and the enclosure of intrapsychic subjectivity, at last indicating the way toward the intersection of the Symbolic and the Imaginary with the Real, the social, and the political. Our situation at the crossroads of literature, psychoanalysis, and feminism, while sometimes baffling and difficult, allows us to entertain a critical perspective that is not tunnel vision, that does not ignore the "Real."

For example, our critical perspective enables and indeed solicits the retelling of the oedipal story from "forgotten" perspectives: the perspective of the mother as subject (as in Marianne Hirsch's treatment of Jocasta in the oedipal scene or the work of Susan Suleiman on the dilemma of mother as writer, or the well-known work of Kristeva on the "maternal text")[29] and also the perspective of the father, who, in spite of his importance in the oedipal drama as lawgiver and as slain rival, nonetheless tends to be treated in psychoanalytic convention as a role or object rather than as a subjective voice in his own right. The work of Jane Gallop, for one, attends to the father as a desiring subject, caught in the incestuous web of the countertransference, and Madelon Sprengnether's essay on "enforcing Oedipus" discusses Freud's own fatherly "interest" in the oedipal interpretation of Dora's illness.[30] In

[29]Marianne Hirsch's paper on Jocasta—"Why Didn't My Mother Recognize Me?"— was first presented at the 1985 MLA Convention Forum on Literature and Psychoanalysis. Susan Suleiman's essay "Writing and Motherhood" appears in The (M)other Tongue. Essays on the semiotic mode and the maternal text by Julia Kristeva have been translated in Desire in Language: A Semiotic Approach to Literature and Art (New York: Columbia University Press, 1980).
[30]In The (M)other Tongue, 51–71.

such readings, mother and father are no longer simple functions or objects of desire; they are desiring agents who are themselves subject to the law they transmit. And giving a voice to these heretofore forgotten agents is, among other things, a feminist practice that seeks to grant full subjectivity to the other.

In addition to this rereading of the human oedipal drama from the neglected vantage point of the other, feminist psychoanalytic literary work encourages an opening of the eternal triangle to a broader human circuit. When Jane Gallop, for instance, pays attention to the forgotten fourth party in the Dora case—the governess—she opens the case to socioeconomic concerns beyond that of the family foyer. When Barbara Johnson points out the forgotten fourth corner in Derrida's "framing" of the Lacanian triangle, she opens the literary text (Poe's *Purloined Letter*) to an unending intertextual chain of reference.[31] This kind of work—which opens a closed triangular circuit onto a never-ending social nexus—entails a rereading of the act of reading itself, understood as an excessive phenomenon, which always solicits and implicates the extratextual other. Fredric Jameson's work—although it unfortunately does not incorporate an explicitly feminist perspective—is nevertheless in the same vein. His study of the work of the "political unconscious" in the text transforms the generational oedipal struggle (described by writers like Bloom and de Man as a source of unending conflict, an inescapable "anxiety of influence") to the notion of ideological transmission, in which economic and social conditions may make a difference.[32] And whether or not political writers like Jameson and Edward Saïd acknowledge their own debt to feminist psychoanalysis, it seems clear that the notion of a "political unconscious" is central to feminist analysis of patriarchy, even in its most popular form—the "consciousness-raising" group.

Most important, the feminist use of psychoanalysis is committed to making a difference, to raising hell along with consciousness, rather than to confirming orthodox views of the eternal patriarchal oedipal conflict, promulgating itself from generation to generation. Feminism, like psychoanalytic therapy itself, looks to repetition with a difference, to a restaging of "the same old story" with radical implications for the

[31]Jane Gallop's essay on Dora appears in *The Daughter's Seduction* and *In Dora's Case*. Barbara Johnson's essay "The Frame of Reference: Poe, Lacan, Derrida," appears in *Literature and Psychoanalysis*.

[32]See Fredric Jameson, *The Political Unconscious* (Ithaca: Cornell University Press, 1981); Harold Bloom, *The Anxiety of Influence: A Theory of Poetry* (New York: Oxford University Press, 1973); and Paul de Man, *Blindness and Insight: Essays in the Rhetoric of Contemporary Criticism* (Minneapolis: University of Minnesota Press, 1983), particularly the essay "Literary History and Literary Modernity," 142–65.

self and society. Indeed, a feminist psychoanalytic reading of the literary process alters the terrain of both literary studies and psychoanalysis, transforming Freud's notion of aesthetic processes as nonessential functions divorced from "vital need" to a notion of aesthetics as the links in the signifying chain that is the very essence of human being. Thus our critical ménage à trois—psychoanalysis, feminism, literature—opens inevitably to a fourth term of social significance and action, informed by an "intertextual" understanding of historical processes and giving a free play to difference and heterogeneity. Once they have entertained a feminist perspective, psychoanalytic literary critics must learn to entertain a new concept of entertainment itself. After Freud meets up with Dora, after Oedipus meets up with the Sphinx, the answer to "her" riddle will never again be contained in the monosyllable "man."

Constructing Female Sexuality
in the Renaissance:
Stratford, London, Windsor, Vienna

Carol Thomas Neely

I

Feminist criticism of Shakespeare, though less than twenty years old, has gone through a number of phases and now seems in the midst of a particularly difficult coming of age—one tied to controversies in feminism, feminist theory, and critical theory generally. In 1976 Juliet Dusinberre, in *Shakespeare and the Nature of Women*, maintained that English Renaissance drama reflected a feminism catalyzed by the Protestant Reformation and Elizabeth's rule. She found gains for women manifested in their improved legal situation and educational opportunities, in cross-dressing on the stage and off, and in vigorous defenses of women, some by women themselves, a new development in the literature of the controversy about women. In 1983 Lisa Jardine in *Still Harping on Daughters*, drew on similar material to declare that the drama of the period reflected its misogyny, representing powerful women negatively to justify their cautionary and inevitable suppression. This suppression, said Jardine, expressed and assuaged anxieties about the wider cultural changes characteristic of the Renaissance. These contradictory analyses, the interpretations of dramatic texts issuing from them, and the methodologies from which they derive have been much criticized and disputed.[1]

---

[1]Juliet Dusinberre, *Shakespeare and the Nature of Women* (New York: Barnes, 1975); Lisa Jardine, *Still Harping on Daughters: Women and Drama in the Age of Shakespeare* (Totowa, N.J.: Barnes, 1983). Earlier versions of this essay were delivered at Oberlin College, at the Conference on Feminism and Psychoanalysis, and circulated to a seminar,

Carol Thomas Neely

By 1980 Dusinberre's ideas were already being debated by the contributors to *The Woman's Part: Feminist Criticism of Shakespeare*, and Jardine, in her book, criticizes first-generation American, psychological/New Critical feminists like many of those represented in *The Woman's Part* for divorcing the plays from their cultural context and for naïvely assuming that the women characters reflect or reveal the nature of women in that period or our own. Along with Jardine, English cultural materialist critics and American new historicist critics in anthologies like *Political Shakespeare* argue that instead of looking at characters' actions, freedom, fantasies, we must historicize the plays and examine their textual strategies, the material conditions of their production, and the ideologies they embody and sustain. In such readings, women and female sexuality may become the site of larger cultural conflicts and a means to the end of talking about them.[2]

Meanwhile, deconstructive and semiotic critics in *Alternative Shakespeares* and *Shakespeare and the Question of Theory* imply that the new enterprise of feminist criticism demands radically new methods, that we must abandon liberal-humanist notions of formal unity in the text, mimesis, and unified subjectivity. Instead, they argue, we must deconstruct the text's unity and the ideological bias of a critical tradition that produced this ideal. In Jacqueline Rose's reading of *Hamlet*, for example, woman—female sexuality—becomes a site of absence, mystery, and contradiction, a central textual problem that points toward "a failure of integration within language and subjectivity itself." As with some historicist readings, women matter insofar as they stand for something else.[3]

"Images of Gender and Power in Shakespeare and Renaissance Culture," at the Third International Shakespeare Congress, West Berlin, 1–6 April 1986. I am indebted to the participants on these occasions for their useful and stimulating comments, questions, and interactions.

[2]Carolyn Ruth Swift Lenz, Gayle Green, and Carol Thomas Neely, eds., *The Woman's Part: Feminist Criticism of Shakespeare* (Urbana: University of Illinois Press, 1980); Jonathan Dollimore and Alan Sinfield, eds. *Political Shakespeare* (Ithaca: Cornell University Press, 1985). This elision of women into culture has been formulated most cogently by Madelon Sprengnether during discussion at the Seminar on Gender and Power at the Shakespeare Congress in Berlin. If Renaissance social critics displaced anxiety about cultural change onto women, perhaps contemporary literary and social critics displace anxiety about gender relations onto wider cultural relations. For a discussion of the development of feminist criticism of Shakespeare, see my "Feminist Criticism in Motion," in *For Alma Mater: Theory and Practice in Feminist Scholarship*, ed. Paula Treichler, Cheris Kramerae, and Beth Stafford (Urbana: University of Illinois Press, 1985), 70–77. For an extended discussion of the marginalization of feminist criticism by poststructuralist theory, see my "Constructing the Subject: Feminist Practice and the New Renaissance Discourses," *English Literary Renaissance* 18 (Winter 1988), 5–18.

[3]John Drakakis, ed., *Alternative Shakespeares* (London: Methuen, 1985); Patricia Par-

In this essay, I examine psychic and social structures in relation to each other without privileging either. I wish to clarify how female sexuality is constructed and deployed in Renaissance cultural discourse and for what purposes. I want to understand what conditions—of period or texts—allowed for and determined the representation of powerful women and positive female sexuality in Shakespearean drama. Neither the social dynamics of the period nor its constructions of female sexuality explain the plays, and the plays do not mirror the period in any straightforward way. But the social context and sexual dynamics in the period and in the plays can tell us, in their points of correspondence and contradiction, something about how it was with woman/women in the Renaissance.

I have not abandoned my conviction that the plays had an author, that their author was Shakespeare, that their positions in his canon are important—indeed that this author and these positions are among the most relevant cultural contexts in which we can place the plays. I do not think that character need be subsumed entirely under "textual strategies," that "desire" or "sexuality" can be satisfactorily explained as simply an aspect of class conflict, or that individual subjectivity is absolutely controlled by the dominant ideology. Cora Kaplan, in "Pandora's Box," shrewdly delineates how humanist feminist criticism and socialist feminist criticism each includes a crucial element the other ignores—that is, sexuality and material conditions. With her, I advocate a feminist criticism that is psychoanalytic and materialist, that takes into account subjectivity and class and sexuality: "Class and race meanings are not metaphors for the sexual or vice versa. It is better, though not exact, to see them as reciprocally constituting each other through a kind of narrative invocation, a set of associative terms in a chain of meaning. To understand how gender and class—to take two categories only—are articulated together transforms our analysis of each of them."[4] Such a criticism, although difficult to theorize because it resides in the contested territory between psychoanalytic and materialist criticism, strives to preserve interaction between sexuality and material conditions, whereas other approaches subordinate one or the other. I begin to attempt it here by interweaving Renaissance discourses on female sexuality, documentary material on women's lives in Strat-

---

ker and Geoffrey Hartman, eds., *Shakespeare and the Question of Theory* (London: Methuen, 1985); Jacqueline Rose, "Sexuality in the Reading of Shakespeare: *Hamlet* and *Measure for Measure*," in *Alternative Shakespeares*, 118.

[4] Cora Kaplan, "Pandora's Box: Subjectivity, Class and Sexuality in Socialist Feminist Criticism," in *Making a Difference: Feminist Literary Criticism*, ed. Gayle Green and Coppélia Kahn (London: Methuen, 1985), 148.

Carol Thomas Neely

ford, discussion of Elizabeth's and James's self-representations and the symbolism of the Garter ceremony with two comedies that are anomalous in the Shakespearean canon, *The Merry Wives of Windsor* and *Measure for Measure.* I explore how their anomalousness is connected with their constructions of female sexuality, their representations of gender relations, and their cultural contexts.

II

Female sexuality is at the center of Renaissance definitions of female gender roles. The source of women's power, it demands their subordination. Female sexuality is necessary for men to satisfy their desires and to fulfill their gender role requirements appropriately—to marry, procreate, and pass on money and property to their children. But it is potentially uncontrollable or unobtainable; it reminds men that they are all vulnerable mother's sons, that all children are potentially illegitimate. Because of this threatening necessity woman in all Renaissance discourses is defined as different from, the opposite of, and inferior to man.[5] According to the medicine and biology derived from Aristotle, the female is colder and moister than the male and hence weaker, stupider, less courageous, and less complete: "In all genera in which the distinction of male and female is found, Nature makes a similar differentiation in the mental characteristics of the sexes. . . . Hence woman is more compassionate than man, more easily moved to tears, at the same time is more jealous, more querulous, more apt to scold and to strike."[6] In Scholastic and Renaissance theories of reproduction, male and female reproductive systems and contributions are mirror images of each other; paradoxically they are exactly identical and completely opposite: "The spermatic vessels in women do nothing differ from those in men in substance, figure, composure, number, connexion, temper, original and use but only in magnitude and distribution. . . . For their Testicles, they differ little from mens but in quantity. For they are lesser and in figure more hollow and flat, by reason of their defective heat which could not elevate or lift them up to their just magnitude."[7] Since human beings all pass through female-

[5]The primary source for the following discussion is the comprehensive examination of the construction of women by the discourses of theology, medicine, ethics, politics, and law in Ian MacLean, *The Renaissance Notion of Woman* (Cambridge: Cambridge University Press, 1980).

[6]Aristotle, *Historia animalium* 9.1, quoted in MacLean, *Renaissance Notion,* 42.

[7]*The Workes of that Famous Chirurgian Ambrose Parey,* trans. Thomas Johnson

ness on the way to maleness, and since in generation, the hotter male seed or the colder female seed may predominate, resulting in a boy or a girl, sexual identity is both fixed and problematic, both inevitable and in need of control.

In theological discourse, as in medical, women, Eve's daughters all, are both strictly subordinated and potentially dangerous. Eve, who fell first, is both more and less responsible for the fall than Adam: her weakness partly excuses her. Nevertheless, for the Fall all women must suffer Eve's curse, which is, significantly, physiological and psychological and social—pain in childbirth, sorrow, and subjection to their husbands.[8] By theology then, and by law as well, women are defined and contained through their place in the marriage paradigm—as maidens, wives, or widows. These roles are in turn defined by the mode of sexuality appropriate to them: virginity for maidens, marital chastity for wives, and abstinence for widows. Hence, what Joan Kelly calls "the social relations of the sexes": women's economic, legal, and cultural status in relation to that of men,[9] rest on male constructions of women's sexuality and sexual roles. The reiterated admonitions in the prescriptive literature that women should be chaste, modest, silent, and obedient are directed to a single end. Modesty, silence, and obedience all ensure chastity.

None of these discourses, however, was monolithic; all were disputed, qualified, denied. There was a growing body of medical evidence that women were not colder or moister than men, that their uterus did not wander or have a sense of smell.[10] There was debate over whether Eve and Adam shared responsibility for the Fall, whether men and women were equal before God. Growing out of new medical definitions and changing theology was the ideal of companionate marriage, which held that men and women could be companions and friends as well as partners in procreation. As notions of sexual difference altered, constructions of gender difference became less fixed, perhaps, although they did not disappear. I am interested in asking what room for maneuvering there was within these definitions of women and in looking at

---

(London: Thomas Cotes, 1634), 889, quoted in Stephen Greenblatt, "Fiction and Friction," *Shakespearean Negotiations: The Circulation of Social Energy in Renaissance England* (Berkeley: University of California Press, 1988), 79. In his essay, Greenblatt explores contradictory Renaissance theories of reproduction and their implications for Renaissance attitudes toward gender boundaries.

[8]MacLean, *Renaissance Notion*, 17–18.

[9]Joan Kelly, *Women, History, and Theory: The Essays of Joan Kelly* (Chicago: University of Chicago Press, 1984), 1–18.

[10]MacLean, *Renaissance Notion*, 40–41.

Carol Thomas Neely

how and for what purpose literature represents both the constraints and their disruption. The nature of the constraints and the resistance, of course, differs according to women's class, age, marital status, economic circumstances, geographical location, family structure, and in the plays also according to the pressures of source, genre, audience.

III

In order to look at the differences in construction and manipulation of gender roles in the period and in the plays, I will look briefly at women in Shakespeare's family in Stratford (women for whom, accidentally, there is a fairly substantial body of documentary evidence, available in the background of biographies of Shakespeare) and at Queen Elizabeth. These examples, drawn from different places on the social scale, can suggest something of how women both lived within and unsettled the predominant discourses about them.

The Stratford women's lives are discontinuous, on the one hand, with institutional discourses such as theology and prescriptive literature such as marriage handbooks and, on the other hand, with the representations of women in drama.[11] Certain kinds of women are more prominent in the Stratford documentary records than in the plays and their lives are less stereotypical than those in the prescriptive literature. In the plays, the women are mostly aristocratic; in Stratford, they are, of course, middle-class.[12] Shakespeare's plays are replete with

[11]This section of the essay is derived from my extended discussion of the women in Stratford in "Shakespeare's Women: Historical Facts and Dramatic Representations," in *Shakespeare's Personality*, ed. Norman Holland, Sidney Homan, and Bernard J. Paris (Berkeley: University of California Press, 1989). The main biographies from which this material is drawn are Edmund K. Chambers, *William Shakespeare: A Study of Facts and Problems*, 2 vols. (Oxford: Clarendon, 1930), vol. 2; Mark Eccles, *Shakespeare in Warwickshire* (Madison: University of Wisconsin Press, 1961); and Samuel Schoenbaum, *William Shakespeare: A Compact Documentary Life* (London: Oxford University Press, 1977).

[12]There is much debate about whether there were classes at all in Elizabethan England (see Peter Laslett, *The World We Have Lost Further Explored*, 3d ed. [New York: Scribners, 1984], 22–53) and about whether conventional views of the middle class in the period are mythical (see Jack H. Hexter, *Reappraisals in History: New Views on History and Society in Early Modern Europe* [Evanston, Ill.: Northwestern University Press, 1963], 71–116). Nonetheless, I use the term "middle class," along with two Renaissance terms, "middling sort" and "middling ranks," in the absence of any more satisfactory. In reference to Shakespeare's family in Stratford, I use it to distinguish them from the aristocracy and from servants and laborers. In discussing *Merry Wives of Windsor*, I use it as well to distinguish the Pages and Fords (and the doctor Caius and the parson Evans), as they distinguish themselves and are distinguished by others, from, on the one hand, titled aristocracy—like Slender, who is "gentleman born" and "well-landed" (1.1.7; 4.4.85), and

men without women, children without mothers, and single men. The Stratford environment is rich with mothers who have many children and women without or between men—masterless women. Whereas in Shakespeare's drama, women are few, short-lived, and not very fertile, the women in Shakespeare's family in Stratford are characterized by considerable prominence, longevity, and fertility. For example, Shakespeare's mother, Mary, outlived John Shakespeare, dying in her late sixties; his sister, Joan, outlived her husband by thirty years, dying at seventy-seven; Anne Hathaway outlived Shakespeare by seven years, dying at sixty-seven; both of his daughters (probably) outlived their husbands, and Shakespeare's granddaughter Elizabeth outlived her first husband by twenty-three years.

The pattern of marriages and the nature of women's participation in them, as revealed in the documentary records, are also more flexible than they are in the plays. The drama often represents marriage as the triumph of romantic love and as a clean break, a decisive separation of children from parents, a decisive subordination of witty heroines to insipid heroes, and a conclusive resolution of generational conflict. The plays minimize the function of marriage as institutionalized transfer of title, line, property, and money through generations and the complicated negotiations among the couple, the parents, the church, and the state which regulated these matches. In contrast, marriages in Stratford have three salient features: (1) couples in the middling ranks often seem to have taken the initiative themselves, entering into matches to which parents subsequently acceded without much fuss; (2) although licenses were often required to ensure compliance with the complicated restrictions of ecclesiastical or secular courts, punishment for failure to follow the regulations seems to have been minimal; (3) age at marriage varied considerably, with most couples marrying late (as is true in general for the period but not for the plays). Shakespeare and Anne Hathaway had to obtain a license to bypass the required thrice asking of the banns in church, which would have delayed the wedding too long. They were then able to be married in November before the long period when weddings were liturgically prohibited. Their wedding by license, Anne's bridal pregnancy (their first child Susannah was born in May), and Anne's age (twenty-six, eight years older than Shakespeare) seem, in the

---

Fenton, who is "too great of birth" (3.4.4) though poor—and from, on the other hand, servants or itinerants. Those I call middle-class in the play are landed and wealthy or have professional status but are not titled and not ordinarily identified with the court. This class is not fixed, is not necessarily conscious of itself as such, and it is not distinguished by its relation to the means of production.

context of custom, statistical norms, and the Stratford documentary records, fairly typical for their class and locale.

The women in Stratford are the object of fewer rigid prescriptions regarding their sexuality than are the women in the plays. While this relative freedom made them vulnerable, it also allowed them to defend themselves against slander, which was less damaging than in the plays. Shakespeare's wife Anne was pregnant when she married. His married daughter, Susannah Hall, it was reported—bawdily—by one John Lane, Jr., "had the running of the reins [that is, venereal disease] and had been naught with Rafe Smith at John Palmer."[13] She sued Lane for slander; he did not appear and so was excommunicated. Shakespeare's son-in-law, Thomas Quiney, confessed to getting Margaret Wheeler with child (the incident occurred before his marriage; the trial for it six weeks after); his penance to wear a white sheet in front of the church was remitted and he was fined only five shillings, perhaps because mother and child both died in childbirth. The contingencies of everyday life in Stratford clearly did not demand or allow stringent regulation of female sexuality. Evidence from other locales similarly shows women to have been frequent objects of sexual defamation, accused by husbands, friends, and lovers of being "spanyell hoors" or "noughtie paks," but just as often they successfully defended themselves against these accusations or ignored the courts' attempts to regulate their behavior.[14]

Under different circumstances, Queen Elizabeth, although she could not completely escape the sexual and gender roles expected of Renaissance women, brilliantly manipulated (and hence problematized) them in order to maintain her power and alleviate the anxieties generated by her anomalous status as a woman ruler. She manipulated her presumptive marriageability to secure allies and favorites but refused to marry and encouraged idealized worship of herself as a perpetually virgin queen. She represented herself in her speeches to Parliament in whichever gender identity the occasion demanded, now constructing herself as a powerful prince with authority over her people, now as their nur-

---

[13]Lane, quoted in Schoenbaum, 289.

[14]Quoted from Lisa Jardine, " 'The Moor, I Know His Trumpet': Problems with Some New Historicist Readings of Shakespearean Female Figures," paper circulated to seminar, "Images of Gender and Power," Shakespeare Congress, Berlin, 1986. See also Susan D. Amussen, "Gender, Family, and the Social Order, 1560–1725," and David E. Underdown, "The Taming of the Scold: The Enforcement of Patriarchal Authority in Early Modern England," both in *Order and Disorder in Early Modern England*, ed. Anthony Fletcher and John Stevenson (Cambridge: Cambridge University Press, 1985), 196–216, 116–36; and R. G. Quaife, *Wanton Wenches and Wayward Wives: Peasants and Illicit Sex in Seventeenth-Century England* (New Brunswick, N.J.: Rutgers University Press, 1979), esp. chap. 6.

turing mother, now as bride to England, now as vulnerable woman.[15] This skillful manipulation of contrasting and, indeed, contradictory gender roles is seen most obviously in her well-known Armada speech at Tilbury: "I have the body of a weak and feeble woman but I have the heart and stomach of a king, and of a King of England too." Toward the end of her reign, her power assured, she refers to herself less and less often as princess or queen, more and more often as prince or as the "Monarch and prince sovereign," emphasizing her sovereignty and deemphasizing her sexuality and gender.[16]

IV

The sexuality of small-town, middle-class married women and Elizabeth's chastity and power are connected with each other in unexpected ways in *The Merry Wives of Windsor,* the Shakespearean play in which women's power is most persistent and least contained and in which their status in most like that of the Stratford women.[17] It is also the only play set in contemporary England and the only comedy that deals with the middle class and in which wives are protagonists. The very title of the play telegraphs its double anomalousness. The protagonists are married women whose sexuality, motherhood, and marriages are at issue; the play is in striking contrast to Shakespeare's other comedies, which achieve happy endings in part by the elimination of mothers and by projecting marital consummation into the future, after the plays' ends. Windsor is a thriving bourgeois town, and the detailed reference that gives the locale dramatic substance is reminiscent of the Stratford records—petty rivalry and threatened litigation, class conflicts and class mobility, lineage and coats of arms, marriage and dowries, the education of children. There is no other play in which the economic, social, class, and ethnic status of the characters is so clearly delineated and so much to the point. There are also wider and not well explained topical references, for example, to the order of the Knights of the Garter and its installation ceremonies in Windsor Castle.

---

[15]Allison Hirsch, "Queen Elizabeth I and the Persistence of Patriarchy," *Feminist Review* 4 (1980), 45–56; Leah Marcus, "Shakespeare's Comic Heroines, Elizabeth I, and the Political Uses of Androgyny," in *Women in the Middle Ages and the Renaissance: Literary and Historical Perspectives,* ed. Mary Beth Rose, (Syracuse, N.Y.: Syracuse University Press, 1986), 135–53.

[16]Quotations in Marcus, 138, 140.

[17]This discussion of *Merry Wives of Windsor* is an expansion and revision of a brief discussion of the play with a somewhat different focus which forms the conclusion of my "Shakespeare's Women."

Carol Thomas Neely

The play is unique in two other ways as well. It signals its author and
its place in the Shakespeare canon by including characters from another
Shakespeare work—one probably written about the same time. Falstaff,
Mistress Quickly, and others from *I Henry IV* and *II Henry IV* are in
Merry Wives both the same as and different from what they are in the
Henry plays—as if registering their transition from history to comedy,
from the reign of Henry IV and V to that of Elizabeth and calling
attention to their creator's sleight-of-hand. Finally, surprisingly, the
play comes down to us accompanied by an apocryphal but irresistible
story about the circumstances of its production. The title page of the
1602 Quarto claims that the play had been acted before the queen, and
Nicolas Rowe relates in his 1709 biography that Queen Elizabeth
wished Shakespeare to "shew" Falstaff "in love."[18] He follows John
Dennis who claimed in 1702, "This Comedy was written at her Command, and by her direction, and she was so eager to see it Acted that she
commanded it to be finished in fourteen days; and was, afterwards, so
Tradition tells us, very well pleased at the Representation."[19] "Tradition" thus records or invents gender and social relations of the play's
production which are unique in the canon and which connect the play's
explorations of women's power, social class, and genre with Elizabeth's
bifurcated identity; she is both a powerful monarch—the comedy is
written "at her Command"—and a conventional woman who wants to
see Falstaff "in love." These multiple anomalies raise the issue of the
relationships between the play's representations of female sexuality, its
Windsor setting, its focus on the middling sort, its transplanted characters, its allusions to Elizabeth and to the Garter ceremonies. What does
the wives' "merriness" and "honesty" have to do with the larger social
relations of the play and the period?

I think the play can incorporate, without anxiety or containment,
witty and manipulative married women who control all the men, a
remarkably cheeky and insubordinate daughter who chooses her own
marriage partner, male transvestism (represented nowhere else in the
canon), and the parallel and complete humiliation of both Falstaff, the
would-be cuckolder, and Ford, the imaginary cuckold, because all these
motifs function to protect the crucial possessions of the middling
rank—money, land, and marital chastity—and to ensure the continuity
of middle-class values, values represented as consonant with Eliza-

[18]Quoted by H. J. Oliver, ed. *The Merry Wives of Windsor*, Arden Edition (London:
Methuen, 1978), 45.
[19]Dedication to *The Comical Gallant*, quoted by Oliver, *Merry Wives*, 44. All Shakespeare citations are from *The Complete Signet Shakespeare*, gen. ed. Sylvan Barnet (New
York: Harcourt, Brace, Jovanovich, 1972).

beth's sovereignty. The overt and threatening sexuality and wit of the women and the misogyny they generate are mitigated by the construction of sexuality as a social and socially useful commodity, by the women's self-regulation, and by the appropriation of the power and chastity of Elizabeth in the service of the stability and harmony of the citizens of Windsor.

Certainly, the women's wit, their friendship, and their independence are represented as threatening, and as threateningly associated with their "natural" sexual assertiveness. So Mistress Quickly's description of Mistress Page implies through her puns on "will" and "kind": "Do what she will, say what she will, take all, pay all, go to bed when she list, rise when she list, all is as she will. And, truly, she deserves it; for if there be a kind woman in Windsor, she is one" (2.2.113–16). The men respond with conventional assumptions about the sexual frailty of women. Falstaff's would-be cuckoldry exploits these suppositions. He imagines himself a successful colonizer who will mine the "gold and bounty" of the wives: "They shall be my East and West Indies, and I will trade to them both" (1.3.68, 70–71). Ford, the conventional jealous misogynist, likewise exploits his wife's imagined frailty, railing against "married mankind," cursing "All Eve's daughters" (4.2.21–22), and, disguised as Brooke, participating gleefully and voyeuristically in his own cuckolding.

The women defend themselves wittily, successfully, and to applause from those who would exploit their sexuality. They are allowed to do so because they are "honest" as well as "merry" (4.2.100) and because this defense of chastity is likewise a defense of the Windsor middling sort against the aristocratic outsiders who would exploit its sexual and financial resources. Because the wives' allegiance to their chastity, their husbands, and their class remains secure, they are given free rein to humiliate Falstaff. He is dumped into the river in a basket of dirty laundry for his pretensions to aristocratic panache, dressed as an old woman and beaten for his pretence of youthful phallic potency, and pinched and frightened by Windsor fairies for his exploitation of lust, for his fantasy of "boarding" women—punishments that fit his attempted transgressions of sexual, marital, and class boundaries. He is then forced to declare himself an "ass" and beg pardon of the women and Windsor. Ford is everywhere identified with his apparent rival and is similarly deceived and humiliated for his analogous misconstruction of his wife's sexuality. Like Falstaff, Ford must apologize, promise reform, and beg for pardon, subordinating himself to his wife's will: "Pardon me, wife. Henceforth do what thou wilt. / I rather will suspect the sun with cold / Than thee with wantonness" (4.4.6–8).

Carol Thomas Neely

The older women's schemes are thwarted only by the Pages' daughter, Anne, who has the last word about her marriage, a triple inversion in a world in which men supposedly had authority over women, parents over children, the old over the young. By acting independently, Anne, like the wives, protects herself from those who would exploit her sexuality and marriageability for economic or social ends—Justice Shallow, Slender, Dr. Caius, her mother and father. The play carefully distinguishes Fenton, her choice of suitor, from the others by having him declare his love in verse, specifically renouncing economic motives for sexual ones: "Yet, wooing thee, I found thee of more value / Than stamps in gold or sums in sealèd bags; / And 'tis the very riches of thyself / That now I aim at" (3.4.15–18). The play validates the couple's elopement by marrying off the other suitors to transvestite brides—actually peasant boys.

Within the securely married community of Windsor, male transvestism is not a threat but a joke that upholds class and gender boundaries. It is used to mock and expose men who would exploit the supposed weakness of women to make them sex objects, while pretending a desire and potency they lack. Hence, Falstaff is dressed as the old woman of Brainford to reveal his misrepresentation of his own sexuality and his attempt to misuse women's. Hence, Caius and Slender find themselves married to boys, in mockery of their desire for money and status, their demand for wifely subordination, and their sexual inadequacy. Since the boys are adolescent and Falstaff is old, their transvestism does not threaten the sexuality or masculinity of the Windsor husbands. Only pseudomanhood is humiliated.

Alterations in the nature, status, and function of the characters who migrate from history to comedy likewise contribute to the changed genre, different status of women, and domestic ideology of *Merry Wives*. In the history plays, Falstaff was banished for his exploitation of political power. In the comedy, he preys on those below him in class, not above; his pretensions are sexual, not political; and he attacks a different kind of honor. Because the values he mocks in the comedy are too uncontested for his wit to gain sympathizers or to be effective, he is invited home to dinner instead of being banished. Unlike Falstaff, who loses power, Mistress Quickly gains it. In *I Henry IV* she is the hostess of the Boar's Head Tavern, laughed at for her bawdy malapropisms; in *II Henry IV* she is explicitly a bawd and is increasingly exploited by Falstaff. In *Merry Wives* her act has been cleaned up; though still a widow, she is now a respectable housekeeper for Dr. Caius: "I may call him my master, look you, for I keep his house; and I wash, wring, brew, bake, scour, dress meat and drink, make the beds, and do all myself. . . .

And to be up early and down late" (1.4.91–99). Her new respectability is intended sharply to distinguish her role as go-between and matchmaker from that of bawd in the *Henry* plays. Although she makes money from her arrangements, she does not exploit the women but aids them to deceive Falstaff (who deceived her in the history plays). Although without family or property, she is fully integrated into middle-class Windsor and furthers its goals—in her roles as housekeeper, go-between, and the fairy queen in the final pageant.

This last role belongs, in the iconography of the period, to Queen Elizabeth. In the pageant, Quickly, the housekeeper, is whimsically elevated to protective queen as she commands the fairies to attack Falstaff for his lust and invokes their care for Windsor Castle, the chairs of the Order of the Garter, the emblems and coats of arms. The references to the castle and the order, as well as the identification of Mistress Quickly with that other "radiant queen," Elizabeth, chaste mother of England, domesticate and appropriate the power of Elizabeth and her court. They identify Elizabeth, her castle, and her Order of the Garter (whose knights included among them foreigners, as Windsor society does) with the values of bourgeois Windsor—property, good housekeeping, lineage, and, especially, honesty. Pistol commands the cleaning of the castle, and Mistress Quickly urges her fairies, the townspeople of Windsor, to bless the castle with their values, exorcising "sluttery"—slovenliness and promiscuity:

> *Pistol:* Cricket, to Windsor chimneys shalt thou leap
> Where fires thou find'st unraked and hearths unswept,
> There pinch the maids as blue as bilberry.
> Our radiant queen hates sluts and sluttery. . . .
> *Quickly:* Strew good luck, ouphs, on every sacred room,
> That it may stand till the perpetual doom,
> In state as wholesome as in state 'tis fit,
> Worthy the owner, and the owner it.
> The several chairs of Order look you scour
> With juice of balm and every precious flow'r.
> Each fair instalment, coat, and several crest,
> With loyal blazon, evermore be blest. (5.5.45–48, 59–66)

The fairies are also ordered to emblazon on the grass the garter and its motto, *Honi soit qui mal y pense*, "In emerald tufts, flow'rs purple, blue, and white— / Like sapphires, pearl, and rich embroidery, / Buckled below fair knighthood's bending knee" (5.5.72–74), making it a part of nature, of the park, of their own exorcism of lust. This use of the garter recalls the unauthenticated but widely believed story of the origin of the emblem. When the original garter, dropped by the Countess of Salisbury (or, in some versions, by the queen) and picked up by Edward III, drew snickers from his knights as a bawdy emblem of illicit sexuality, the king defiantly transformed it from an emblem of promiscuity and dishonor into one of fidelity, power, and high honor.[20] The invocation of the garter emblem in opposition to Falstaff's lustful thoughts and false assumptions about women is exactly apropos; he is punished for his "evil" thoughts with the "ills" of pinches, torches, and humiliation. The garter here, as at its origin, becomes a symbol of the marital chastity that is secured and celebrated in the play. *The Merry Wives of Windsor*, therefore, fulfills Elizabeth's "Command" in curious ways. It appropriates Elizabeth's representation of her power to support her subjects' values, mocking courtly love and celebrating a marital chastity the opposite of her virginity and a communal harmony not dependent on the sovereign. The play seems both to satisfy and to subvert Elizabeth's desire for a "Representation" of "Falstaff in love."

From its inception, the Order of the Garter embodied religious, military, and armorous service, binding its knights to their sovereign. Elizabeth skillfully used the imagery and symbols of the institution to blur divisions within her kingdom and to symbolize and promulgate unity of various kinds. By leaving the statutes of the order virtually unchanged but altering its religious services to conform to Protestant observances, by appropriating the Catholic Saint George as the emblem of the Protes-

---

[20]This is the popular version of the origin and symbolism of the garter, first advanced by Polydore Vergil in *Anglicae historiae* (1570) and repeated with variations by other chroniclers. An alternative tale that argues for narrower military symbolism and hence is more acceptable to some commentators is that Richard I, inspired by Saint George, led his soldiers to victory in battle by having each tie a leather thong or garter on one leg as a symbol of unity. Others say that the garter was, more generally, a symbol of the unity of the knights with the sovereign and of the country behind Edward III at the time of his claim to the French throne. Elias Ashmole, *The History of the Most Noble Order of the Garter* (London: A. Bell, 1715), 119–28, works hard to "rectifie" (126) the "vulgar" story and argues for the exclusively religious and military significance of the order and its symbol: "There is not the least conjecture to countenance the Conceit of such a Feminine Institution" (120). But during Elizabeth's reign, most commentators record the origin myth neutrally or positively and defend the double symbolism of the garter. See, for example, George Puttenham, *The Arte of Englishe Poesie*, 1598, facsimile ed. (Menston, Eng.: Scholar Press, 1968). In this work dedicated to and in praise of Elizabeth, Puttenham commends Edward's device as a model for princes: "He also justly defended his owne integritie, saved the noble womans good renowne, which by licentious speeches might have been empaired, and liberally recompenced her injurie with an honor, such as none could have bin devised greater" (86). Readings of the garter's origin and symbolism provide a kind of barometer for attitudes toward women and toward the ruler. See the extensive notes in Nicolas Harris Nicolas, *The History of the Orders of Knighthood of the British Empire*, 2 vols. (London: John Hunter, 1842), 1:17–21, for quotations and a summary of attitudes toward the origin story.

tant nation, and by electing many foreign princes, both Catholic and Protestant, as knights, Elizabeth used the order and its ceremonies to smooth over religious divisions.[21] By delaying elections to the order while encouraging aspirants and sometimes personally investing those elected, the queen assured herself of loyalty and service from both knight-companions and those hoping to become knight-companions.[22] By moving the Garter feast from Windsor to London (the last feast held at Windsor during her reign was in 1572) and by allowing ever-increasing numbers of spectators at its rituals, she made the order a national symbol and encouraged identification between the court and the citizens of London.[23] It seems likely as well that the two emblems of the order—the elegantly jeweled garter and the George—a medal showing Saint George slaying the dragon—could aptly symbolize Elizabeth's carefully manipulated dual identity as virgin queen and warrior king and reinforce her association with honor in both its masculine and feminine senses.

In *The Merry Wives of Windsor*, Shakespeare, following Elizabeth's lead, emphasizes the garter's social and amorous implications and de-emphasizes its religious and military symbolism; he brilliantly transforms the garter, a rich symbol of the queen's chastity and national unity, into an emblem of the chastity and unity achieved by the community of Windsor. Those of foreign origin, like Caius and Evans, are united with natives, gentry with yeomen and professionals, men with women, the older with the younger generation. (Earlier, in the bilingual puns of the language lesson in act 4, scene 1, the Latin tongue works together with the vernacular.)[24] Conflicts and differences are blurred or concealed through the rituals of the final act as they are through the Garter ceremonies themselves. The effect of the allusion to the garter is to appropriate its symbolism for Elizabeth's subjects, representing their achievement at the local level of the harmony and unity for which

[21]Roy Strong, *The Cult of Elizabeth: Elizabethan Portraiture and Pageantry* (London: Thames and Hudson, 1977), 167–68, 176–83.

[22]Nicolas, *History*, suggests that Elizabeth's claim to have lost the list of Suffrages in 1586, and her refusal to attend the Scrutiny in 1587 because she did not have on the mantle of the Order were pretexts to avoid electing knights to vacant stalls; he claims that this avoidance is "part of Elizabeth's favourite system of government. Every vacant Honour or Office secured the fidelity and zeal of numerous candidates and she preferred relying on the hopes of many expectants, than upon the gratitude of the few who could be appointed" (1:199).

[23]Strong, 168, 172.

[24]Similarly, French and English are bawdily merged in the language lesson in *Henry V*, prelude to the marriage of Kate and Henry in which the union of France with England, achieved on the battlefield, is secured by and represented through the sexual union of the marriage.

she stands at the national level. Both of these harmonies rest, but in different ways, on women's control of their sexuality and on men's trust in this control: *Honi soit qui mal y pense.*

V

In Windsor sexuality is sufficiently and successfully regulated by the women, the family, and the town's inhabitants. Although there are a Justice and a Parson in the cast, and although the law and the church are viewed as possible means to secure order in Windsor, neither these institutions nor the ruler prove necessary to maintain the integrity of family, class, and community.

In *Measure for Measure,* everything has changed. This comedy, Shakespeare's last, is as anomalous as *Merry Wives,* but for different reasons and under different circumstances. *The Merry Wives of Windsor* may have been written for Elizabeth and performed before her. The first recorded performance of *Measure for Measure* was at court on 26 December 1604 with James I perhaps in attendance. The setting is not small-town Windsor but a fictionalized large city, Vienna, which bears close resemblance to London.[25] It is the only comedy full of the details of urban life. Its scenes take place not in homes and parks but within public, institutional spaces and at their boundaries: the palace, the courtroom, the nunnery, the prison, and especially the streets. In Vienna, there is no Windsor Park, no green world to offer escape and reconciliation. Its substitutes, Mariana's moated grange and Angelo's garden, are places of containment or corruption, not of communal rejuvenation. Vienna's ruler, the Duke, is not absent but ubiquitous; his power is not invoked but imposed. In no other comedy is the ruler so central or his connection with and regulation of sexuality so thoroughgoing. Many critics have seen in him some allusion to James, although the purpose and effects of this allusion are much disputed.[26] I

---

[25]In his discussion of the play's date, J. W. Lever, ed., *Measure for Measure,* Arden Shakespeare (London: Methuen, 1965), xxxii–xxxiii notes that the plague, brawls, war, executions, poor trade, and brothel closings alluded to in the play were all features of London in 1603–4.

[26]Lever, *Measure for Measure,* xxxiii–xxxiv; David L. Stevenson, *The Achievement of Shakespeare's "Measure for Measure"* (Ithaca: Cornell University Press, 1966), 134–66. Leonard Tennenhouse, *Power on Display: The Politics of Shakespeare's Genres* (New York: Methuen, 1986), 147–59, and Marilyn Williamson, *The Patriarchy of Shakespeare's Comedies* (Detroit: Wayne State University Press, 1986), 74–110, both situate *Measure for Measure* in the context of disguised ruler plays, disorderly social conditions, and James's strategies for consolidating power but read the representation of Vincentio

suspect that the representation of Vincentio predicts or interrogates the possibility of James's absolutism rather than alluding to or reflecting its actuality; James had been in power for little more than a year when the play was probably first performed in the summer of 1604.

In Vienna there are no unified communal, class, or family interests. Even characters of the same rank, family, or institution are divided against each other as well as against opposing ranks or factions. The Duke countermands Angelo's order to kill Claudio. Escalus countermands Angelo's order to have Pompey whipped. Froth and Pompey corrupt Elbow's wife. Lucio refuses to bail Pompey and slanders the Duke. Kinship neither unites individuals nor controls sexuality, for there are no intact families. Because Juliet and Mariana have no parents and no dowries, their virginities are lost, their marriages postponed. Angelo, Claudio, Lucio, and even Froth (2.1.123–25) have no fathers, and in the absence of parental restraints, economic motives, or community pressure, male sexuality is unregulated.

Male desire in the play is represented as inevitable, ungovernable, and degrading not only by the plot but by all the male characters as well—by Elbow, Pompey, Lucio, Angelo, the Duke, and even Claudio: "A thirsty evil, and when we drink, we die" (1.2.133). The men's attitudes toward sexuality are virtually indistinguishable from one another. Manhood can be achieved only by means of women's "vice," by female "shame" (3.1.137, 139), and hence is invariably contaminated. Because male sexuality is unrestrainable and degrading and there are no communal controls over it, prostitutes must serve it, and upper-class women, at first, must be protected from men by seclusion: Isabella in a nunnery, Mariana in the moated grange, and Juliet, too late, in prison.

But Vienna's reform cannot be accomplished by the eradication of prostitution and the incarceration of virtuous women. Sexuality, to perform its socializing and perpetuating function, cannot be just suppressed by the law but must be manipulated, channeled, redeemed. For the Duke's desired control and reform to be achieved, women must leave their protected places and expose themselves to sexual assault. Having lost their maidenheads, they must be married to guarantee not just procreation but legitimate offspring. Whereas in *Merry Wives* female sexuality was an invulnerable center of value, regulated by the community, *Measure for Measure* constructs it as contradictory: as

differently. For Tennenhouse, the portrayal authorizes and mythologizes absolutist monarchical authority in response to social and political threats to James's power (155–56, 159), whereas Williamson believes the representation of the Duke is "ambiguous," "subversive," and contradictory (105–110).

vulnerable to male invasion, as dangerously contaminating, and as necessary.[27] In the earlier comedy, female sexuality is identified with and expressed through love, family, and property—all institutions that require it and concretely depend on it. In this play, it must be regulated by the state, which tries to subsume these means. The conservative, abstract discourses that constitute religion, law, and rule, however, represent and exploit female sexuality in contradictory ways.

In the play Vincentio's ubiquitous power fills a vacuum left by the absence of the forces that regulated sexuality in Windsor (as in other romantic comedies). Representing the church, the law, and the state, he embodies their contradictory constructions of female sexuality and female roles as well as the conflicts among them. In his attempts to reform sexuality in Vienna, he merely reinstitutes the problems. When, effecting the play's conclusion, he shifts roles once again from ruler to suitor, from "ghostly" father to potential husband, he merely introduces further contradictions,—which are perhaps inherent in patriarchy's simultaneous positioning of men as rulers (who must regulate sexuality in the state) and fathers (who must participate in it as well as regulating it in the family).

Because men's roles are contradictory, women's are as well. All the institutions/discourses of the play (as of the period) need women, on the one hand, to confirm their power and necessity and, on the other hand, to ameliorate their excesses and failures—in effect, to confirm and subvert them simultaneously. Religious discourse needs women, Eve's daughters, to accept their responsibility for the Fall and their sexual frailty *and* to atone for man's fallen condition by suffering marriage, obedience to their husbands, and procreation. Juliet confesses to the Duke disguised as friar, as religious discourse requires, that her sexual act was "offenseful" and that she repents a "sin of heavier kind" than Claudio. But she also interrupts and rejects her confessor's lecture on her sinfulness to affirm that she rejoices in her repentance: "I do repent me, as it is an evil, / And take the shame with joy" (2.3.25, 28, 35–36). The legal system requires women to embody the Christian virtue of mercy so as to affirm the law's rectitude while alleviating its rigidity. Isabella, while acknowledging the validity of the "blow of justice" (2.2.30), begs Angelo for Christian mercy toward her brother and the Duke for a mercy compatible with justice toward Angelo in the last scene. The ruler and the state, to ensure legitimate heirs and social order and continuity, require women to be chaste and obedient wives.

[27]For additional discussion of female sexuality, see Carol Thomas Neely, *Broken Nuptials in Shakespeare's Plays* (New Haven: Yale University Press, 1985), 99–101.

But the women mystify the operations of the institution of marriage by "violent and unruly" love (3.1.243) like that of Mariana who "crave[s] no other, nor no better man" than Angelo for a husband (5.1.427). Together the women effect the redemption of the institutions of a fallen world: through the joyful shame of illegitimate pregnancy, the "lawful mercy" and "foul redemption" of the bedtrick (2.4.111–12), and the embrace of marriage to an unworthy husband: "They say, best men are molded out of faults; / And, for the most, become much more the better / For being a little bad" (5.1.441–43). The Duke's manipulations compel the women out of isolation and into their "destined livery" (2.4.137). But the men remain recalcitrant—inflexible and resistant to Christian virtue, romantic love, and comedic reconciliation. They do not ask the women for forgiveness; they do not express love; they resist legal marriage, preferring the rigor of law, the sentence of death.

The Duke, in his triple role as friar-confessor, deputizer of Angelo as judge, and disguised ruler, unites the institutions of the church, the law, and the state and reveals the failures of each to regulate the sexuality it constructs. His attempt, as friar, to impose internal restraints is unnecessary, since everyone already feels guilt; if, like Barnardine, they do not, they cannot be brought to do so.[28] The Duke's attempt is unsuccessful because this guilt does not result in abstinence or mercy but, as with Angelo, in prostitution and rape. The law, whether harshly or permissively administered, likewise fails to restrain sexuality. First, penalties are either too severe to be administered, like Angelo's, or too lenient to be a deterrent, like those in effect at the beginning of the play. Second, sexual offenses are difficult to discover or prove: Claudio's and Juliet's fornication is punishable only through the evidence of pregnancy. Third, offenders are too numerous to apprehend or punish: "If you head and hang all that offend that way but for ten year together, you'll be glad to give out a commission for more heads" (2.1.236–38). The Duke can rule successfully only when he withdraws from the dukedom and operates in disguise.

Since the Duke himself continues to act through the very institutions that fail to regulate sexuality, those that see women as both sexually frail and sexually desirable, his machinations have the effect of reinstituting the problems of the play. He himself becomes identified with the offenses he tries to regulate.[29] When his bedtrick arrange-

[28]Jonathan Dollimore, "Transgression and Surveillance in *Measure for Measure*," in Dollimore, *Political Shakespeare*, 81.

[29]Richard P. Wheeler, *Shakespeare's Development and the Problem Comedies* (Berkeley: University of California Press, 1981), 121–26, argues that, although the play protects the Duke from the sins he regulates, his connection with them is repeatedly implied.

Carol Thomas Neely

ments position him as a bawd ("the maid will I frame and make fit for his attempt" [3.1.255]), he tries to dissociate himself from the role by a hyperbolic attack on Pompey (3.2.20–28). Lucio soon identifies the Duke with the brothel's customers (3.2.115–30), an identification he angrily rejects. Finally, his proposal to Isabella is a repetition of Angelo's earlier coercion—at best an exchange of material property for sexual property and at worst analogous to rape.

In the last scene of the play, the women, rehearsed by the Duke, stage sexual frailty, Christian mercy, and social subordination, but the play leaves these roles unreconciled. They move into their prescribed places as wives, but both "merriness" and "honesty" are absent. Mariana bluntly expresses her degradation in the bedtrick and describes Angelo's faults. Juliet is silent upon Claudio's rebirth; her child remains unborn and unacknowledged. Isabella is silent in response to the Duke's proposal of merger: "Whereto, if you'll a willing ear incline, / What's mine is yours and what's yours is mine." And Kate Keepdown, who has borne his child and must now marry Lucio, remains silent as throughout. But her offstage presence, her child, and her enforced marriage to Lucio without her consent expose the identical methods and goals of all the marriages; illegitimate sexuality is used to enforce legitimate marriage, erasing the distinctions between legitimate and illegitimate, chaste and unchaste, wife and punk, which the institutions and the Duke (and the play) wish to construct. Without these distinctions, the men's sexuality remains uncontrolled and unsatisfied, their movement into marriage passive, sullen, or politic. *Measure for Measure* in effect produces a happy ending, legitimate marriages, and an ordered state, but by exposing the mechanisms whereby these are produced, the play unsettles responses to them. In the last scene, in his abrupt role shifts, his mostly bogus rhetoric, his curious scramble to do and undo, the Duke cannot fill the vacuum but reveals it, represents it.

In the last scene of *Merry Wives of Windsor*, theatricality employed by the community restores order, graciously appropriates Elizabeth's power, and uses it to ritualize domestic values centered on marital chastity. In the last scene of *Measure for Measure*, authority overtly employs theatricality to contain fornication through marriage. The power of James is appropriated to reveal its mechanisms, its contradictions and its limits. In each of the plays the power of the sovereign operates through and is defined by women, sexuality, and marriage.[30]

[30]Cf. Michel Foucault's formulation of the relationship between power and sexuality in *The History of Sexuality*, vol. 1: *An Introduction*, trans. Robert Hurley (New York: Vintage Books, 1980): "Sexuality is not the most intractable element in power relations, but rather one of those endowed with the greatest instrumentality: useful for the greatest

But whereas in *Merry Wives of Windsor*, the family, chaste marital sexuality, and merry wives affirm Elizabeth's benign housekeeping and its gratuitousness, in *Measure for Measure*, the power of the ruler is represented as necessary and effective but insufficient; it regulates sexuality by prescribing marriage, but it is severely limited in the social harmony, psychological satisfaction, and aesthetic pleasure it can produce.

The Duke can arrange consummation and enforce marriage, but he cannot compel desire or assent—not the characters' and not ours. No examination of the text of the play, however detailed and subtle, and no exploration of the historical context, however substantial, has persuaded readers, playgoers, or critics that the play ends satisfactorily. We cannot know what Isabella desires in response to the Duke's proposal. We cannot know whether James saw the play, whether he viewed it as approbation or slander. We cannot know whether Shakespeare desired to write a comedy that deconstructs comic form, that represents the unsatisfying and unsatisfiable workings of desire, that placates or subverts the power of his ruler. The play's impasse derives from its representation of female sexuality as paradoxically essential and fatal, voluntary and enforced, central and subordinated. This view of female sexuality is embedded in all the forms of Renaissance discourse—and persists today. But then as now, these contradictions are not always so starkly represented. The contrasted role of women in *Merry Wives of Windsor* and *Measure for Measure* suggests that positive representation of women's power and sexuality is possible when this power operates within and upholds the family and the community and when the ruler's power, in the play and outside of it, is assumed rather than contested. Especially, perhaps, it is possible when the power of a female ruler is appropriated on behalf of female subjects whose dramatic existence she has "commanded." In this instance, the playwright Shakespeare commands both his own (former) subjects and his queen's emblem of power.

---

number of maneuvers and capable of serving as a point of support, as a linchpin, for the most varied strategies" (103).

The Anathematized Race:
The Governess and *Jane Eyre*

Mary Poovey

This essay deals with two subjects that have become sites for the conjunction of psychoanalytic and feminist interest in the last few years: *Jane Eyre* and governesses. But rather than turn the psychoanalytic screw of interpretation again upon either of these subjects, I want to treat the whole problem a little differently.[1] By stressing the conjunction between *Jane Eyre* and the historical problem of the governess, I want to change the scene of interpretation from the individual (author, character, or text) to the historically specific class and gender system to which both Brontë's novel and the problematic governess belong. I want to suggest that only such a change can enable psychoanalytic practice to examine the social construction of sexual difference, and that only such a focus provides a basis for psychoanalysis to be political—that is, to be feminist. To join feminism and psychoanalysis, I think we need a third term—history. This essay, then, is a case study of how history can give psychoanalysis some basis for a feminist practice, for a politics of the unconscious.[2]

Even though governesses had been employed by the English upper classes at least since the sixteenth century, as an occupational group, governesses attracted widespread concern only in the 1830s and 1840s.[3]

[1]For recent discussions of the governess, see Shoshana Felman, "Turning the Screw of Interpretation," *Yale French Studies* 55/56 (1977), 94–207; and Jane Gallop, *The Daughter's Seduction: Feminism and Psychoanalysis* (Ithaca: Cornell University Press, 1982), 141–48. Bibliographies for *Jane Eyre* can be found in *Jane Eyre: An Authoritative Text*, ed. Richard J. Dunn (New York: Norton, 1971); and *Jane Eyre*, ed. Margaret Smith (London: Oxford University Press, 1973).

[2]For a discussion of the politics of the unconscious, see Stephen Heath, "Difference," *Screen*, 19. 3 (1978), esp. 74.

[3]See M. Jeanne Peterson, "The Victorian Governess: Status Incongruence in Family and

The attention the governess received was both sociological and literary: the difficulties of her position—the scarcity of jobs, her anomalous social rank, and wages too low to provide for periods of unemployment—were widely publicized in periodicals; at the same time fictional governesses began to appear as heroines who married their way out of work.[4] Without question, governesses did experience hardships and occasionally married well, but modern historians agree that the number of governesses was actually small and the degree of attention they received was disproportionate to their plight.[5] The 1851 Census of Great Britain lists 25,000 governesses, for example, at a time when there were 750,000 female domestic servants, whose working conditions and wages were often more debilitating but markedly less lamented than the distress of the governess. The most interesting analysis of this discrepancy to date is M. Jeanne Peterson's assessment of the governesses' incongruous social position; I want to elaborate Peterson's argument by suggesting that this social incongruity attracted so much attention when it did at least partly because the economic and political turmoil of the "hungry forties" drove members of the middle class to demand some barrier against the erosion of middle-class assumptions and values. Because of the place they occupied in the middle-class ideology, women, and governesses in particular, were invoked as bulwarks against this erosion.[6] In order to see what assumptions intersected in the governess, I want to examine the position she occupied within the system of representation that organized both class and social relations and that extended across the discourses of the middle class. By looking at how two different middle-class discourses constructed and worked through the governess problem differently, I will make visible at least some parts of this representational system and

---

Society," in *Suffer and Be Still: Women in the Victorian Age,* ed. Martha Vicinus (Bloomington: Indiana University Press, 1972), 5; Stanley J. Curtis, *History of Education in Great Britain* (London: University Tutorial Press, 1950), 171–75; and Wanda F. Neff, *Victorian Working Women: An Historical and Literary Study of Women in British Industries and Professions, 1832–1850* (1929; reprint, New York: Humanities Press, 1966), 153–74.

[4]For a list of additional periodical essays about governesses, see Neff, *Victorian Working Women,* 269–70. For discussions of governess novels, see Neff, 153–74; Jerome Beaty, "*Jane Eyre* and Genre," *Genre* 10 (Winter 1977), 619–54; and Robert A. Colby, *Fiction with a Purpose: Major and Minor Nineteenth-Century Novels* (Bloomington: Indiana University Press, 1967), 178–212.

[5]Peterson, "The Victorian Governess," 4; and Martha Vicinus, *Independent Women: Work & Community for Single Women, 1850–1920* (Chicago: University of Chicago Press, 1985), 23, 26.

[6]Peterson, "The Victorian Governess," 3–19.

the kinds of contradictions middle-class writers articulated only to deny or displace.

The periodical essayists of the 1840s justified the attention they devoted to the distressed governess by emphasizing the central role she played in reproducing the domestic ideal. As a teacher and example for young children, they argued, the governess was charged with inculcating domestic virtues and, especially in the case of young girls, with teaching the "accomplishments" that would attract a good husband without allowing the sexual component of these accomplishments to get the upper hand. The governess was therefore expected to preside over a contradiction central to the domestic ideal—the contradiction between the moral (asexual) woman and woman the incarnation of (sexual) desire. The governess presided over this contradiction both in the sense that she was meant to police the emergence of undue assertiveness or sexuality in her maturing charges and in the sense that she was expected not to display willfullness or desires herself.[7] Theoretically, the governess's position neutralized whatever temptation she, as a young woman herself, might have presented to her male associates; to gentlemen she was a "tabooed woman," and to male servants she was as unapproachable as any other middle-class lady.[8]

If the governess was asked to stabilize the contradiction inherent in the middle-class domestic ideal by embodying and superintending morality, then she was also expected to fix another, related boundary: that between "well-bred, well-educated and perfect gentlewomen," on the one hand, and, on the other, the "low-born, ignorant, and vulgar" women of the working class.[9] The assumption implicit in these con-

---

[7]For a discussion of the increasingly problematized conceptualization of Victorian children, see Mark Spilka, "On the Enrichment of Poor Monkeys by Myth and Dream; or, How Dickens Rousseauisticized and Pre-Freudianized Victorian Views of Childhood," in *Sexuality and Victorian Literature,* ed. Don Richard Cox (Knoxville: University of Tennessee Press, 1984), 161–79.

[8]The phrase "tabooed woman" comes from Lady Eastlake (Elizabeth Rigby), "*Vanity Fair*—and *Jane Eyre,*" *Quarterly Review* 84 (1848), 177. See also "Hints on the Modern Governess System," *Fraser's Magazine* 30 (November 1844), 573.

[9]*The Governess; or, Politics in Private Life* (London: Smith, Elder, 1836), 310. One of the few departures from the conceptualization of the governess as "genteel" appears in an article titled "The Governess Question," *English Woman's Journal* 4 (1860), 163–70. In this essay, the author argues that the governess's position is not considered genteel and is never likely to be elevated in status. "Whatever *gentility* may once have attached to the profession of the governess has long since vanished, and it is impossible to name any occupation, not positively disreputable, which confers so little respectability,—respectability in the worldly sense. . . . The governess, however well-conducted, remains a governess; may starve *genteely [sic]*, and sink into her grave friendless and alone" (163, 170). This is an explicitly polemical article, however, "addressed to parents, who, not

junctions, as in the middle-class preference for governesses from their own class, was that only "well-bred" women were morally reliable. In this reading of contemporary affairs, the unfortunate circumstances that bankrupted some middle-class fathers were critical to the reproduction of the domestic ideal, for only such disasters could yield suitable teachers for the next generation of middle-class wives.

One reason the governess was a figure of such concern to her middle-class contemporaries, then, was simply that she was a middle-class woman in a period when women were considered so critical to social stability. Especially in the "hungry forties," women became both the focus of worries among working-class men about competition for scarce jobs and the solution advanced by middle-class men for the social and political discontent hard times fostered. If only women would remain in the home, said men of all classes, work would be available to men who needed it and both the family wage and morality would be restored. The assumptions implicit in this argument are that morality is bred and nurtured in the home as an effect of maternal instinct and that if lower-class women were to emulate middle-class wives in their deference, thrift, and discipline, the homes of rich and poor alike would become what they ought to be—havens from the debilitating competition of the market.

A second reason the governess was singled out for special attention was that she did not seem to be fulfilling this critical social task. In fact, contemporaries openly worried that the governess was not the bulwark against immorality and class erosion but the conduit through which working-class habits would infiltrate the middle-class home. One source of this anxiety was the widespread belief that more tradesmen's daughters were entering the ranks of governess, therefore heralding the "degradation of a body so important to the moral interest of the community."[10] Against such "degradation," middle-class commentators proposed a range of defenses, including most of the solutions formulated to end the governesses' plight.[11] Whatever their practical value, all the suggested remedies functioned to defend the class barrier that was also assumed to mark a moral division; even the Governesses'

---

having the means of giving their daughters any fortune, seem seized with an epidemic madness to make them governesses" (163). It is, in other words, designed to discourage lower-middle-class women from entering the governesses' ranks by disparaging the social status of this work.

[10]The phrase about "degradation" appears in [Sarah Lewis], "On the Social Position of Governesses," *Fraser's Magazine* 34 (April 1848), 414. See also "Hints on the Modern Governess System," 581.

[11]See Eastlake, "*Vanity Fair*," 180; "Hints," 573, 580; "Social Position," 413–14.

Benevolent Institution reinforced the distinction between ladies "with character" and other women by providing the former with a separate residence and source of charity.[12]

A second source of the anxiety about governesses surfaces in discussions of the hardships of their situation. As these hardships were most vividly imagined, they were not primarily physical or economic but emotional; the threat they posed was to the governesses' self-control and, even more ominous, to her sexual neutrality. This danger surfaces most explicitly in fictional representations of the governess, and I will pursue it in a moment in relation to one of the most famous governess novels of the period, Charlotte Brontë's *Jane Eyre*.[13] In articles about the governess, allusions to her sexual susceptibility are more indirect, but precisely because of this indirection, they point to the governess's place in the complex system of associations in which the domestic ideal was also embedded. Two of the figures to which the governess was repeatedly linked begin to suggest why her sexlessness seemed so important—and so unreliable—to her contemporaries. These figures are the lunatic and the fallen woman.

The connection contemporaries made between the governess and the lunatic was, in the first instance, causal. According to both the author of the 1844 "Hints on the Modern Governess System" and Lady Eastlake's 1847 review of the Governesses' Benevolent Institution's annual report, governesses accounted for the largest category of women in lunatic asylums.[14] Lady Eastlake attributes this unfortunate statistic to the "wounded vanity" a governess suffers, but the author of "Hints" connects this "wound" more specifically to sexual repression. Citing "an ordinary case," this author describes a young girl trained for her governess position in "one of those schools which are usually mere gymnasia for accomplishments and elegant manners." There her "animal spirits" are indulged, and her youthful "elasticity" becomes a "craving for pleasures." Once she leaves the school, however, and takes up her governessing work, this "craving" is subject to the frustration and denial her position demands.

---

[12]Peterson also makes this point. See "The Victorian Governess," 17.

[13]For an autobiographical report of a governess's sexual vulnerability, see Ellen Weeton, *Miss Weeton's Journal of a Governess,* ed. Edward Hall, 2 vols. (New York: Augustus M. Kelley, 1969), 1:209–327. The sexual exploitation to which the governess was potentially exposed does surface obliquely at the end of an 1858 essay in the *English Woman's Journal.* "Depths of horror," the author (Jessie Boucherett) warns, "into which men cannot fall" await the unemployed governess ("The Profession," 13).

[14]See Eastlake, "*Vanity Fair,*" 177, hereafter cited in the text as *VF;* and "Hints," 573, hereafter cited as H.

She must live daily amidst the trials of a home without its blessings; she must bear about on her heart the sins she witnesses and the responsibilities that crush her; without any consent of her will, she is made the *confidante* of many family secrets; she must live in a familial circle as if her eyes did not perceive the tokens of bitterness; she must appear not to hear sharp sayings and *mal-a-propos* speeches; kindly words of courtesy must be always on her lips; she must be ever on her guard; let her relax her self-restraint for one moment, and who shall say what mischief and misery might ensue to all from one heedless expression of hers? (H 574)

If the allusion to some mischievous "expression" hints at the governess's latent feelings, this author will not elaborate the nature of these feelings; instead, the writer turns to the "nervous irritability, dejection, [and] loss of energy" that result from repressing them (H 575). The "twisted coil of passion and levity may be moved into sobriety by the help of forbearance and long-suffering," but too often the very girls who have sprung up "like plants in a hot-house" fade before their "bloom" is gone. "It is no exaggeration to say that hundreds snap yearly from the stalk, or prolong a withered, sickly life, till they, too, sink, and are carried out to die miserably in the by-ways of the world" (H 575, 574).

The image of the short-lived or barren plant elaborates the causal connection between the governess and the lunatic by metaphorically tying both to a vitality stunted, silenced, driven mad by denial and restraint. This vitality may not be explicitly represented as sexuality here, but its sexual content *is* present in the images to which this last phrase alludes. The representation of the governess "carried out to die miserably in the by-ways of the world" metonymically links her to the victim of another kind of work that was also represented as "white slavery" at midcentury—the distressed needlewoman "forced to take to the streets."[15] The two figures are even more strongly associated in being two of the three symbols of working women for the early and mid-Victorian public; the third was the factory girl.[16] Significantly, both of the working-class members of this trio were specifically linked by

[15]The phrase "white slavery" is the title of a letter published in the *Times* of London and cited by Barbara Leigh Smith Bodichon, *Women and Work* (London: Bosworth and Harrison, 1857), 17. The phrase "needlewomen forced to take to the streets" was used by Henry Mayhew in his 1849–50 *Morning Chronicle* series on London "Labour and the Poor" (see *The Unknown Mayhew: Selections from the Morning Chronicle, 1849–50*, ed. E. P. Thompson and Eileen Yeo [Harmondsworth, Eng.: Penguin Books, 1973], 200).

[16]See *The Woman Question: Social Issues, 1837–1883*, vol. 2 of *The Woman Question: Society and Literature in Britain and America, 1837–1883*, ed. Elizabeth K. Helsinger, Robin Lauterbach Sheets, and William Veeder, 3 vols. (New York: Garland, 1983), 115.

middle-class male commentators to the danger of unregulated female sexuality. Henry Mayhew's determination to expose (and, by extension, control) the "prostitution" he identified among needlewomen in 1849 expresses the same concern to curtail female promiscuity that Lord Ashley voiced in the 1844 parliamentary debate about factory conditions.[17] For both Mayhew and Lord Ashley, the relevant issue was any extramarital sexuality, not just sex for hire; Mayhew's interviews make it clear that for him any woman who lived or had sexual relations with a man outside of marriage was a prostitute.

Representations of the governess in the 1840s brought to her contemporaries' minds not just the middle-class ideal she was meant to reproduce but the sexualized, often working-class women against whom she was expected to defend, revealing the mid-Victorian fear that the governess could not protect middle-class values because she could not be trusted to regulate her own sexuality. The lunatic's sexuality might have been rhetorically contained by medical categories such as hysteria, after all, but the prostitute's sexual aggression was undisguised; to introduce either such sexuality or such aggression into the middle-class home would have been tantamount to fomenting revolution, especially in a period in which both were imaginatively linked to the discontent expressed by disgruntled members of the working class and by the "strong-minded women" who were just beginning to demand reform. The conjunction of economic, moral, and political anxieties that could be mobilized by the image of an army of aggressive, impoverished governesses emerges in the warning advanced by the author of "Hints": if someone does not remedy the current injustices, "the miseries of the governess may even swell that sickening clamour about the 'rights of women' which would never have been raised had women been true to themselves" (H 573).

This author's wishful plea that women be "true to themselves" explicitly enjoins middle-class employers and employees to unite in defense of the domestic ideal the governesses' distress threatens to disturb. Implicitly, however, the plea for women to unite has more subversive implications, because it calls attention to the fact that middle-class women have something in common, which is epitomized in the governesses' plight. This more controversial reading of the governesses' situation was made explicit in 1847 by Elizabeth Rigby, later Lady Eastlake, in her review of *Vanity Fair, Jane Eyre,* and the 1847

[17]See Mayhew, "Second Test—Meeting of Needlewomen Forced to Take to the Streets," in *The Unknown Mayhew,* 200–16; and Anthony Ashley Cooper (Lord Ashley, later the seventh earl of Shaftesbury) in *Hansard's Parliamentary Debates,* 3d series, 15 March, 1844, cc. 1088–89, 1091–96, 1099–1100.

Report of the Governesses' Benevolent Institution. Like many other essayists, Lady Eastlake's express concern was the fate of governesses who could no longer find work, for as she phrases it, their situation more "painfully expresses the peculiar tyranny of our present state of civilization" than any other social ill (*VF* 181). Lady Eastlake, along with many male commentators, found the governess so affecting because she epitomized the helplessness unfortunate individuals experienced not just from ordinary poverty but from the volatile fluctuations of the modern, industrializing economy; the toll these fluctuations exacted had become starkly visible in the depression of the 1840s, and contemporaries feared such hardship lay behind working-class discontent. But to Lady Eastlake, the governess seemed a special kind of victim, for unlike lower-class men, she was born neither to discomfort nor to labor. "The case of the governess," she explains, "is so much the harder than that of any other class of the community, in that they are not only quite as liable to all the vicissitudes of life, but are absolutely supplied by them." What was distressing to Lady Eastlake was that the governess's plight could be many middle-class woman's fate. Lady Eastlake recognized, however reluctantly, that the governess revealed the price of dependence on men. "Take a lady, in every meaning of the word, born and bred, and let her father pass through the gazette, and she wants nothing more to suit our highest *beau ideal* of a guide and instructress to our children. We need the imprudencies, extravagancies, mistakes, or crimes of a certain number of fathers, to sow that seed from which we reap the harvest of governesses" (*VF* 176).

Such a recognition could have led Lady Eastlake to identify fully with the "lady" whose imprudent, extravagant, or criminal father has squandered her security; it could have led her, as it did Barbara Bodichon, to urge women to unite against the dependence that tied them to their fathers' luck and business sense. Instead, however, Lady Eastlake explicitly rejects such a conclusion; she defends against her identification with the governess by simply asserting the necessity of women's dependence, which she bases on the natural difference between men's work and the "precious" work of women. "Workmen may rebel," Lady Eastlake writes, "and tradesmen may combine, not to let you have their labour or their wares under a certain rate; but the governess has no refuge—no escape; she is a needy *lady*, whose services are of too precious a kind to have any stated market value, and is therefore left to the mercy, or what they call the *means*, of the family that engages her" (*VF* 179).

In the economy that places the governess's "precious" work above market value but beneath a fair wage, Lady Eastlake sees that moral superintendence is simultaneously being devalued and exploited. Still, she insists that things must be this way: after all, the difference between work whose value can be judged and work that is too "precious" to be subjected to market valuation is what saves ladies from being like men. But if the difference between working men and leisured ladies is obvious to Lady Eastlake, the definition of ladies becomes problematic when one must establish some difference *among* them. The problem, as she formulates it, is that the difference among ladies is difficult to see because it is not based on some natural distinction. It

> is not one which will take care of itself, as in the case of a servant. If she [the governess] sits at table she does not shock you—if she opens her mouth she does not distress you—her appearance and manners are likely to be as good as your own—her education rather better; there is nothing upon the face of the thing to stamp her as having been called to a different state of life from that in which it has pleased God to place you; and therefore the distinction has to be kept up by a fictitious barrier which presses with cruel weight upon the mental strength or constitutional vanity of a woman. (*VF* 177)

Because neither sex nor class "stamp[s]" the governess as different from the lady who employs her, Lady Eastlake is once more drawn toward identifying with her. Yet even though she realizes the barrier between them is "fictitious" and "cruel," Lady Eastlake will not lower it for a moment. Instead, she turns away again, this time decisively, by appealing to another kind of nature—"the inherent constitution of English habits, feelings, and prejudices." "We shall ever prefer to place those immediately about our children who have been born and bred with somewhat of the same refinement as ourselves. We must ever keep them in a sort of isolation, for it is the only means for maintaining that distance which the reserve of English manners and the decorum of English families exact" (*VF* 178). Lady Eastlake's appeal to "the inherent constitution" of the English is meant to resolve the paradox whereby two persons identical as to class and sex must nonetheless be treated differently. It does so both by generalizing middle-class "reserve" and "decorum" to "all English families" and by rationalizing a difference among members of the middle class that is otherwise unaccountable: the difference of circumstances or luck.

Lady Eastlake's discussion of governesses follows her reviews of two recently published governess novels, *Vanity Fair* and *Jane Eyre*.[18] The

---

[18]Other early reviews of *Jane Eyre* include George Henry Lewes's review in *Fraser's Magazine* (December 1847), 690–63; John Eagles's essay in *Blackwood's Magazine* (Octo-

substance of these reviews highlights both the conservatism and the potential subversiveness of Eastlake's position. In general, Lady Eastlake approves of Thackeray's novel, despite the immorality of Becky Sharp, but she declares the heroine of *Jane Eyre* to be "vulgar-minded," a woman "whom we should not care for as an acquaintance, whom we should not seek as a friend, whom we should not desire for a relation, and whom we should scrupulously avoid for a governess" (*VF* 176, 174). Eastlake formulates her objections in religious language, but she focuses specifically on the threat this heroine poses to the barrier she will soon admit is "fictitious"—the barrier between one wellborn (if penniless) lady and another. "It is true Jane does right" when she decides to leave Rochester, Lady Eastlake grudgingly admits,

> and [she] exerts great moral strength, but it is the strength of a mere heathen mind which is a law unto itself. . . . Jane Eyre is proud, and therefore she is ungrateful too. It pleased God to make her an orphan, friendless, and penniless—yet she thanks nobody, and least of all Him, for the food and raiment, the friends, companions, and instructions of her helpless youth. . . . The doctrine of humility is not more foreign to her mind than it is repudiated by her heart. It is by her own talents, virtues, and courage that she is made to attain the summit of human happiness, and, as far as Jane Eyre's own statement is concerned, no one would think that she owed anything either to God above or to man below. (*VF* 173)

As Lady Eastlake continues, her religious argument becomes an explicit warning against the political upheavals threatened by working-class discontent. What has happened here is that the difference of circumstance that Lady Eastlake acknowledges to be a matter of chance has become a matter of class, and this difference she assumes to be authoritative because it is appointed by God. "Altogether the auto-biography of Jane Eyre is preeminently an anti-Christian composition," she asserts. "There is throughout it a murmuring against the comforts of the rich and against the privations of the poor, which, as far as each individual is concerned, is a murmuring against God's appointment. . . . There is a proud and perpetual assertion of the rights of man . . . a pervading tone of ungodly discontent which is at once the most prominent and the most subtle evil which the law and the pulpit, which all civilized society in fact has at the present day to contend with. We do not

ber 1848), 473–74; [H. R. Bagshawe], "*Jane Eyre, Shirley,*" *Dublin Review* 28 (March 1850), 209–33; [G. H. Lewes], "The Lady Novelists," *Fraser's Magazine,* 58 o.s., 2 n.s. (July 1852), 129–41; and [E. S. Dallas], "Currer Bell," *Blackwood's Magazine,* 82 (July 1857), 77–94.

hesitate to say that the tone of mind and thought which has overthrown authority and violated every code human and divine abroad, and fostered Chartism and rebellion at home, is the same which has also written Jane Eyre" (*VF* 173–74).

If this objection targets the class issues contemporaries associated with the governess, then Lady Eastlake's other complaint about *Jane Eyre* centers on the second anxiety this figure aroused. The protagonist's "language and manners . . . offend you in every particular," she asserts, especially when Rochester "pours into [Jane's] ears disgraceful tales of his past life, connected with the birth of little Adele" and the governess "listens as if it were nothing new, and certainly nothing distasteful" (*VF* 167, 164). What offends Lady Eastlake here is the "perpetual disparity between the account [Jane Eyre] herself gives of the effect she produces, and the means shown us by which she brings that about"—the gap between Jane's professed innocence and the sexual knowledge the author insinuates in the language and action of the novel. The implication is that the author of the novel knows more about sexual matters than the character admits and that the novel is "vulgar" because it makes the hypocrisy of women's professed innocence legible.

Even though Lady Eastlake complains so strenuously about *Jane Eyre*'s "gross vulgarity"—or rather, precisely because of this complaint—she draws out the similarities rather than the differences between herself and the author of the novel. If Lady Eastlake sees sexuality in Jane's "restlessness," after all, there is little to distinguish her from the writer who created this sexuality in the first place. Just as Lady Eastlake inadvertently exposes her likeness to the governess, so she betrays her resemblance to the author she disdains. If we turn for a moment to Brontë's novel, we can begin to identify some of the implications of this similarity and some of the reasons why discussions of the governesses' plight sparked other controversies that eventually challenged the domestic ideal.

Jane Eyre may not be either a lunatic or a fallen woman, but when she refuses Rochester's proposal that she become his mistress in chapter 27, her language specifically calls to mind the figures to whom the governess was so frequently linked by her contemporaries. Despite her passion, Jane says, she is not "mad," like a lunatic; her principles are "worth" more than the pleasure that becoming Rochester's mistress would yield.[19] The two women metaphorically invoked here are also

---

[19]Charlotte Brontë, *Jane Eyre*, ed. Q. D. Leavis (Harmondsworth, Eng.: Penguin Books, 1966), 344, hereafter cited in the text. *Jane Eyre* was initially published by Smith, Elder.

literally dramatized in the two characters that precede Jane Eyre as Rochester's lovers—the lunatic Bertha and the mistress Céline Varens. But if the juxtaposition of these characters calls attention to the problematic sexuality that connects them, the way that Brontë works through Jane's position as governess seems to sever the links among them. Read one way, Brontë's novel repeats conservative resolutions of the governesses' plight such as Lady Eastlake's, for Jane's departure from Rochester's house dismisses the sexual and class instabilities the governess introduces in such a way as to make Jane the guardian of sexual and class order rather than its weakest point. When considered in terms of the entire novel, however, Brontë's treatment of the governess problem does not seem so conservative. In introducing the possibility that women may be fundamentally alike, Brontë raises the subversive suggestions adumbrated by Lady Eastlake in a more systematically critical way.

The issues of sexual susceptibility and social incongruity that contemporaries associated with the governess are inextricably bound up with each other in Jane's situation at Thornfield Hall. Jane is vulnerable to Rochester's advances because, as his employee, she lacks both social peers and the means to defend herself against her attractive, aggressive employer. But Brontë symbolically neutralizes both of these problems by revising the origin, the terms, and the conditions of Jane's employment. While Jane does seek employment because she has no one to support her, Brontë makes it clear that the social incongruity others might attribute to her position as governess precedes Jane's acceptance of this work. It is, in part, a family matter; Jane is "less than a servant," as her cousin John Reed sneers, because she is an orphan and a dependent ward (44). In part, Jane's "heterogeneity" comes from her personality; she is called "a discord" and "a noxious thing," and she thinks her temperament makes her deserve these names (47).

The effect of making Jane's dependence a function of family and personality is to individualize her problems so as to detach them from her position as governess. Brontë further downplays the importance of Jane's position by idealizing her work. Not only is there no mother to satisfy at Thornfield and initially no company from which Jane is excluded, but Adele is a tractable, if untaught child, and Jane's actual duties are barely characterized at all. Beside the physical and psychological deprivations so extensively detailed in the Lowood section of the novel, in fact, what Jane terms her "new servitude" seems luxurious; the only hardship she suffers as a governess is an unsatisfied craving for something she cannot name—something that is represented as romantic love.

When Rochester finally appears at Thornfield, Brontë completes what seems to be a dismissal of Jane's employment by subsuming the economic necessity that drove Jane to work into the narrative of an elaborate courtship. Rochester's temperamental "peculiarities," for which Mrs. Fairfax has prepared us, lead him to forget Jane's salary at one point, to double, then halve it, at another. By the time Blanche Ingram and her companions ridicule the "anathematized race" of governesses in front of Jane, Brontë has already elevated her heroine above this "race" by subordinating her poverty to her personality and to the place it has earned her in Rochester's affections. "Your station," Rochester exclaims, "is in my heart." The individualistic and psychological vocabulary Rochester uses here pervades Brontë's characterization of their relationship: "You are my sympathy," Rochester cries to Jane at one point (342); "I have something in my brain and heart," Jane tells the reader, "that assimilates me mentally to him" (204).

When Rochester proposes marriage to Jane, the problems of sexual susceptibility and class incongruity that intersect in the governess's role ought theoretically to be solved. In this context, Mrs. Fairfax's warning that "gentlemen in [Rochester's] station are not accustomed to marry their governesses" (287), Blanche Ingram's admonitory example of the governess dismissed for falling in love (206–7), and Jane's insistence that she be treated as a "plain, Quakerish governess" (287) all underscore the alternative logic behind Jane's situation—a logic that eroticizes economics so that class and financial difficulties are overcome by the irresistible (and inexplicable) "sympathy" of romantic love. But if translating the class and economic issues raised by the governess resembles the psychologizing gesture prominent in some other Victorian novels, Brontë's novel here takes a different turn. For the very issues that foregrounding personality and love should lay to rest come back to haunt the novel in the most fully psychologized episodes of *Jane Eyre:* Jane's dreams of children.[20]

According to Jane's exposition in chapter 21, emotional affinity, or "sympathy," is a sign of a mysterious but undeniable kinship, "the unity of the source to which each traces his origin" (249). But Jane's discussion of sympathy here focuses not on the bond of kinship, which she claims to be explaining, but on some *disturbance* within a family

[20]Other essays on these dreams include Margaret Homans, "Dreaming of Children: Literalization in *Jane Eyre* and *Wuthering Heights*," in *The Female Gothic*, ed. Juliann E. Fleenor (Montreal: Eden Press, 1983), 257–79; and Maurianne Adams, "Family Disintegration and Creative Integration: The Case of Charlotte Brontë and *Jane Eyre*," in *The Victorian Family: Structure and Stresses*, ed. Anthony S. Wohl (London: Croom Helm, 1978), 148–79.

relationship. Specifically, Jane is recalling her old nursemaid Bessie's telling her "that to dream of children was a sure sign of trouble, either to oneself or to one's kin" (249). Jane then reveals that Bessie's superstition has come back to her because every night for a week she has dreamed of an infant, "which I sometimes hushed in my arms, sometimes dandled on my knee, sometimes watched playing with daisies on a lawn. . . . It was a wailing child this night, and a laughing one the next: now it nestled close to me, and now it ran from me" (249). This revelation is immediately followed by Jane's discovery that the obvious "trouble" presaged by her dream is at her childhood home, Gateshead: John has gambled the Reed family into debt and is now dead, probably by his own hand, and Mrs. Reed, broken in spirit and health, lies near death asking for Jane.

The implications of this "trouble" surface when this reference is read against the other episodes adjacent to the dream. Her journey to Gateshead follows two scenes in which Rochester wantonly taunts Jane with his power: in chapter 20 he teases her that he will marry Blanche Ingram, and in chapter 21 he refuses to pay her her wages, thereby underscoring her emotional and financial dependence on him. At Gateshead, Jane discovers that Mrs. Reed has also been dreaming of a child—of Jane Eyre, in fact, that "mad," "fiend"-like child who was so much "trouble" that Mrs. Reed has withheld for three years the knowledge that Jane does have other kin, and that her uncle, John Eyre, wants to support her (260, 266–67). Mrs. Reed's malice has thereby prolonged Jane's economic dependence and deprived her of the kinship for which she has yearned. Jane explicitly denies feeling any "vengeance . . . rage . . . [or] aversion" toward Mrs. Reed, but her very denial calls attention to the rage she did express when she was similarly helpless at Lowood. The structural similarities among the scenes convey the impression that John Reed's suicide and the stroke that soon kills Mrs. Reed are displaced expressions of Jane's anger at them for the dependence and humiliation they have inflicted upon her. These symbolic murders, which the character denies, can also be seen as displacements of the rage at the other figure who now stands in the same relation of superiority to Jane as the Reeds once did: Rochester. The fact that both the character and the plot of the novel deny this anger, however, leads us to the other "trouble" adjacent to this dream of a child: Bertha's attack upon her brother, Richard Mason.

As soon as Mason enters the narrative, he is rhetorically linked to Rochester: he appears when and where Rochester was expected to appear, and in her description of him Jane explicitly compares him to Rochester (218, 219). Like the sequence I have just examined, Mason's arrival punctuates a series of painful reminders of Jane's dependence and marginality; he interrupts the engagement party (when Jane, obsessed with watching Rochester and Blanche, specifically denies that she is jealous [215]) and his arrival is immediately followed by the gypsy scene, in which Rochester so completely invades Jane's thoughts that she wonders "what unseen spirit" has taken up residence in her heart (228). When the gypsy reveals that s/he is Rochester, Jane voices more rage towards her "master" than at any other time: "It is scarcely fair, sir," Jane says; "it was not right" (231). Jane's hurt is soon repaid, however, even if what happens is not acknowledged as revenge. Jane suddenly, and with a marked carelessness, remembers Mason's presence. The effect upon Rochester is dramatic. Leaning on Jane as he did once before (and will do again), Rochester "staggers" and exclaims, "Jane, I've got a blow—I've got a blow, Jane!" (232). The "blow" Jane's announcement delivers is then graphically acted out when Bertha, who is Jane's surrogate by virtue of her relation to Rochester, attacks Mason, whose textual connection to Rochester has already been established. As before, anger and violence are transferred from one set of characters to another, revenge is displaced from Jane's character, and agency is dispersed into the text.

The text—not as agent but as effect—turns out to be precisely what is at stake in these series, for in each of them Rochester's most serious transgression has been to usurp Jane's control over what is, after all, primarily her story. In the gypsy scene he has told her what she feels in words as "familiar . . . as the speech of my own tongue" (231), and in the scene immediately following Bertha's assault upon Mason, he has usurped her authority even more, first commanding her not to speak (239), then asking her to imagine herself "no longer a girl . . . but a wild boy"—to imagine she is Rochester, in other words—while he tells *his* story to her as if she were telling her own story to herself (246–47). The precarious independence Jane earned by leaving Gateshead has been figured in the ability to tell (if not to direct) her own story; thus, the measure of autonomy gained by translating Jane's economic dependence into a story of love is undercut by Rochester's imperious demand that she listen to him tell his story and hers, that she be dependent—seen and not heard—as women (particularly governesses) should be.

Jane's second reference to dreaming of children extends and elaborates this pattern of enforced dependence and indirect revenge. Once more, Jane's narration of the dream is temporally displaced from the moment of her dreaming. When she does disclose to Rochester and the reader what frightened her, Jane also reveals that she had twice been dreaming of a child when Bertha awakened her. In the first dream, "some barrier" divided her from Rochester. "I was following the windings of an unknown road," Jane explains; "total obscurity environed me; rain pelted me; I was burdened with the charge of a little child. . . . [M]y movements were fettered, and my voice still died away inarticulate; while you, I felt, withdrew farther and farther every moment" (309). In the next dream, of Thornfield Hall in ruins, the child still encumbers Jane. "Wrapped up in a shawl," she says,

> I still carried the unknown little child: I might not lay it down anywhere, however tired were my arms—however much its weight impeded my progress, I must retain it. I heard the gallop of a horse. . . . I was sure it was you; and you were departing for many years, and for a distant country. I climbed the thin wall with frantic, perilous haste. . . . The stones rolled from under my feet, the ivy branches I grasped gave way, the child clung round my neck in terror, and almost strangled me. . . . I saw you like a speck on a white track, lessening every moment. . . . The wall crumbled; I was shaken; the child rolled from my knee, I lost my balance, fell, and woke. (310)

To this "preface" Jane then appends the story of the "trouble" that followed: Bertha's rending of Jane's wedding veil. This is immediately followed by the much more devastating "trouble" of Mason's denunciation in the church, Rochester's revelation that he is already married, and the obliteration of Jane's hopes to formalize her "kinship" with Rochester.

Alone in her bedroom, Jane surveys her ruined love, which she likens to "a suffering child in a cold cradle"; once more she denies that she is angry at Rochester ("I would not ascribe vice to him; I would not say he had betrayed me" [324]) but even more explicitly than before the plot suggests that the person who has hurt Jane is now indirectly suffering the effects of the rage that follows from such hurt: Jane's letter to John Eyre, after all, led her uncle to expose to Mason her planned marriage, and Jane's desire for some independence from Rochester led her to write her uncle in the first place. In this instance, of course, Jane initially suffers as much as—if not more than—Rochester does: not only is she subjected to the humiliating offer of his adulterous love but she also forces herself to leave Thornfield and almost dies as a consequence. Jane's suffering, however, turns out to be only the first stage in her gradual recovery of kinship, independence, money, and enough mastery to write both her story and Rochester's. By contrast, Rochester is further reduced by the novel's subsequent action; when he is blinded and maimed in the fire Bertha sets, the pattern of displaced anger is complete again.[21]

Why does dreaming of children signify "trouble" in these sequences and why does the trouble take this form? When Jane dreams of children, there follows some disaster that is a displaced expression of the anger against kin which the character denies. In the sense that narrative effect is split off from psychological cause, *Jane Eyre* becomes at these moments what we might call a hysterical text, in which the body of the text symptomatically acts out what cannot make its way into the psychologically realistic narrative. Because there was no permissible plot in the nineteenth century for a woman's anger, whenever Brontë explores this form of self-assertion the text splinters hysterically, provoked by and provoking images of dependence and frustration.

Dreaming of children, then, is metonymically linked to a rage that remains implicit at the level of character but materializes at the level of plot. And *this* displacement signifies "trouble" both because the children that appear in these dreams metaphorically represent the dependence that defined women's place in bourgeois ideology (and was epitomized in the governess) *and* because the disjunction characteristic of these narrative episodes shows that hysteria is produced as the condition in which a lady's impermissible emotions are expressed. What Jane's dreams of children reveal, then, in their content, their placement, and their form, is that the helplessness enforced by the governess's dependent position—along with the frustration, self-denial, and maddened, thwarted rage that accompanies it—marks every middle-class woman's life because she is not allowed to express (or possess) the emotions her dependence provokes. The structural paradigm underlying the governess's sexual vulnerability and her social incongruity—her lunacy and her class ambiguity—is dependence, and this is the condition all middle-class women share.

From one perspective, Brontë seems to neutralize the effects of this revelation and to minimize its subversive implications. By having Jane leave Thornfield, Brontë seems to reformulate her dilemma, making it once more an individual, moral, emotional problem and not a function of social position or occupation. As soon as Jane stops being a governess, she is "free" to earn her happiness according to the paradoxical terms of the domestic ideal: even the skeptical Lady Eastlake concedes that the

[21]See Sandra M. Gilbert and Susan Gubar, *The Madwoman in the Attic: The Woman Writer and the Nineteenth-Century Literary Imagination* (New Haven: Yale University Press, 1979), 336–71.

self-denial Jane expresses in renouncing Rochester's love and nearly starving on the heath gives her a right to earthly happiness. When Jane discovers she has both money and kin, then, the dependence epitomized by the governess's position seems no longer to be an issue—a point made clear by the end to which Jane puts her newfound wealth: she liberates Diana and Mary from the life of the governess and so frees them to a woman's "natural" fate—marriage.

From another perspective, however, Brontë's "resolution" of the governess's dilemma can be seen to underscore—not dismiss—the problem of women's dependence. After all, it is only the coincidence of a rich uncle's death that can confer autonomy and power upon a single woman, suggesting just how intractable her dependence really was in the 1840s. Brontë also calls attention to the pervasiveness of this dependence in the very episode in which Jane ceases to be a governess, the episode at Whitcross. As soon as Jane is not a governess, her irreducible likeness to other women returns with stark clarity—and in the very form that relieving Jane of her economic dependence should theoretically have displaced: the sexual vulnerability and class uncertainty epitomized in the lunatic and the fallen woman. "Absolutely destitute," "objectless and lost," Jane is mistaken for an "eccentric sort of lady," a thief, and a figure too "sinister" to be named: "You are not what you ought to be," sneers the Riverses' wary servant (349, 355, 361).

The return of these other women at the very moment at which Jane is least of all a governess functions to reinscribe the similarity between the governess and these sexualized women. At the same time, it lets us glimpse both why it was so important for contemporaries like Lady Eastlake to insist that the governess was different from other women and why it was so difficult to defend this assertion. That the associations return even though Jane is *not* a governess suggests the instability of the boundary all the nonfiction accounts of the governess simultaneously took for granted and fiercely upheld—the boundary between such aberrant women as lunatic, prostitute, and governess and the "normal" woman, the woman who is a wife and mother.

That the governess was somehow a threat to the "natural" order superintended by the middle-class wife is clear from essayists' insistence that the governess's availability kept mothers from performing their God-given tasks. This interruption of nature, in turn, was held responsible for the "restless rage to push on" that was feeding class discontent (H 572). If "ladies of the middle rank resume[d] the instruction of their own children, as God ordained they should," the author of "Hints" asserted, "if mothers would obey their highest calling, many who now fill their places would be safer and happier in their lower vocation" (H 581). At stake, according to this writer, is not only the happiness of those "daughters of poor men" who are now "crammed by a hireling" instead of being taught domestic skills but also the "depth and breadth of character" all women should display. "Surely it must be acknowledged that women whose lesson of life has been learned at mothers' knees, over infant's cradles, will be more earnest and genuine than those taught by a stranger, however well qualified" (H 581).

This intricate weave of assumptions about class relations and female nature reproduces the ideological equation to which I have already alluded: that morality and class stability will follow the expression of maternal instinct, a force that is grounded in God's order and the (middle-class) female body. In this representation, maternal instinct is paradoxically both what distinguishes the mother from the governess and what naturally qualifies the former to perform the services the latter must be trained to provide.

> New difficulties and responsibilities meet [the governess] every day; she is hourly tried by all those childish follies and perversities which need a mother's instinctive love to make them tolerable; yet a forbearance and spring of spirits is claimed from the stranger, in spite of the frets she endures, which He who made the heart knew that maternal affection only could supply, under the perpetual contradictions of wilful childhood. This strength of instinct has been given to every mother. It enables her to walk lightly under a load which, without it, she could not sustain. (H 574)

Positioning the governess against a normative definition of woman as wife and mother reinforced the complex ideological system that dominated mid-Victorian Britain. This juxtaposition shored up the distinction between (abnormal) women who performed domestic (in this case maternal) labor for wages and those who did the same work for free, as an expression of a love that was generous, noncompetitive, and guaranteed by the natural force of maternal "instinct." The image of an arena of "freedom" for women was, in turn, central to the representation of domesticity as desirable, and this representation, along with the disincentive to work outside the home that it enforced, was instrumental to the image of women as moral and not economic agents, antidotes to the evils of competition, not competitors themselves. Finally, the picture of a sphere of relative freedom was crucial to establishing some boundary to the market economy; the wife, protected and fulfilled by maternal instinct, was living proof that the commodification of labor, the alienation of human relations, the frustrations and disappointments inflicted by economic vicissitudes stopped at the door of the home.

From this complex ideological role, we can see that laments about the governess's plight in the 1840s belonged primarily to a discourse about domestic relations, which was necessarily a discourse about gender, class, and the nature of labor as well.

The problem was that governesses—especially in such numbers and in such visibly desperate straits—gave the lie to the complex of economic and domestic representations that underwrote this ideology. Not only did the governess's "plight" bring the economic vicissitudes of the market economy into the middle-class home, thereby collapsing the separation of spheres, but the very existence of so many governesses was proof that, whatever middle-class women might want, not all of them could be (legitimate) mothers because they couldn't all be wives. As the 1851 Census made absolutely clear, there simply weren't enough men to go around. Moreover, there was something dangerously unstable about even the putatively reliable force of maternal love. Moralists admitted that "love" was a notoriously difficult emotion to define and that the distinction between one kind of love and another required constant defense. What, they worried, could prevent "the key-stone of the stupendous arch which unites heaven to earth, and man to heaven" from becoming *"morbid sentimentality—an ungovernable, tumultuous passion"*—especially if the person who should incarnate the former was distinguished from the victim of the latter only by maternal instinct, which even the most optimistic moralists admitted was unstable.[22] According to the logic of these fears, the governess not only revealed what the mother might otherwise have been; she also actively freed mothers to display desires that were distinctly *not* maternal, thus setting up the unsettling possibility that a mother's "jealousy" and her energies might find an object other than the one "nature" had decreed. "If more governesses find a penurious maintenance by these means," Lady Eastlake warned, "more mothers are encouraged to neglect those duties, which, one would have thought, they would have been as jealous of as of that first duty of all that infancy requires of them" (*VF* 180).

These warnings suggest that even though the unemployed mother

---

[22]"Love," *The Governess: A Repertory of Female Education* 2. 3 (1855), 94. This periodical was founded in 1854 and continued publication at least until 1856. In addition to essays on educational theory, it included both practical help for governesses (directions and patterns for "fancy needle work," sample lesson plans, and quizzes for periods of English history) and a correspondence section that elicited extremely pragmatic complaints and suggestions from governesses (as to the poisonous properties of the coloring agent in modeling wax, for example). In 1855 the editors of the periodical described it as Christian but nonsectarian and as "the *first*—and for twelve months . . . the *only* periodical on the subject of Female Education" (*The Governess* [London: Darton, 1855], iii).

Mary Poovey

functions as the norm in the essays I have been examining and in the symbolic economy of which they are a part, motherhood had to be rhetorically constructed *as* the norm in defiance of real economic conditions and as a denial of whatever additional desires a woman (even a mother) might have. My reading of *Jane Eyre* suggests that pegging the "problem" of female sexuality to class difference (as some writers did) was not always sufficient to repress the contradiction written into the domestic ideal. Brontë's novel reveals that the figure from whom the mother had to be distinguished was not just the lower-class prostitute but the middle-class governess as well, for the governess was both what a woman who should be a mother might actually become and the woman who had to be paid for doing what the mother should want to do for free. If the fallen woman was the middle-class mother's opposite, the middle-class governess was her next of kin, the figure who ought to ensure that a boundary existed between classes of women but who could not, precisely because her sexuality made her resemble the women from whom she ought to differ.[23]

This is the ideological economy whose instabilities Brontë exposes when she "resolves" the problem of the governess by having Jane marry Rochester. Jane's marriage imperils this symbolic economy in two ways. First, despite her explicit disavowal of kinship, Jane has effectively been inscribed in a series that includes not just a lunatic and a mistress but also a veritable united nations of women. In telling Jane about these other lovers, Rochester's design is to insist upon difference, to draw an absolute distinction between some kinds of women, who cannot be legitimate wives, and Jane, who can. This distinction is reinforced by both racism and nationalist prejudice: Bertha's West Indian origin "explains" her madness, just as Céline's French birth "accounts for" her moral laxity. But Jane immediately sees that if she assents to Rochester's proposal, she will become simply "the successor of these poor girls" (339). She sees, in other words, the likeness that Rochester denies: *any* woman who is not a wife is automatically like a governess in being dependent, like a fallen woman in being "kept."

Emphasizing the likeness among women is subversive not merely because doing so highlights all women's dependence—although this is, of course, part of the point. Beyond this, the fact that the likeness Brontë stresses is not women's selflessness or self-control but some

[23]Nancy Armstrong discusses the problematic position of the governess in *Desire and Domestic Fiction: A Political History of the Novel* (New York: Oxford University Press, 1987), 79. The unstable boundary between the governess and the mother was explicitly explored by Mrs. Henry Wood in *East Lynne* when the (disfigured) mother returns home as the governess for her own children.

internal difference suggests that the contradiction repressed by the domestic ideal is precisely what makes a woman womanly. This internal difference is figured variously as madness and sexuality. Jane's own descriptions of herself show her growing from the "insanity" of childhood rebellion to the "restlessness" of unspecified desire: "I desired more . . . than I possessed," she says (141). In the passage in chapter 12 in which Jane describes this "restlessness," she specifically compares it to the "ferment" that feeds "political rebellions," and she explicitly opposes it to the self-denial that caring for children requires. This passage returns us once more to Jane's dreams of children, for the manifest content of the majority of those dreams reveals how carrying a child burdens the dreamer, impeding her efforts to reach her lover or to voice her frustrated love. "Anybody may blame me who likes," Jane says of the "cool language" with which she describes her feelings for Adele, but caring for the child is not enough; "I believed in the existence of other and more vivid kinds of goodness, and what I believed in I wished to behold" (140, 141). Even when Jane has her own child at the end of the novel, her only reference to him subordinates maternal love to the sexual passion that Rochester's eyes have consistently represented.[24]

Positioning Jane within a series of women and characterizing her as "restless" and passionate transform the differences among women, invoked by some other writers to "cure" the problematic sexuality written into the domestic ideal, into a difference within all women—the "difference" of sexual desire. This similarity thus subverts the putative difference between the governess and the lunatic or mistress, just as it obliterates the difference between the governess and the wife. Having Jane marry Rochester—transforming the governess into a wife—extends the series of aberrant women to include the figure who ought to be exempt, who ought to be the norm. The point is that as boundary between these two groups of women the governess belongs to both sides of the opposition: in her, the very possibility of an opposition collapses.

The second sense in which Jane's marriage is subversive follows directly from this relocation of difference. If all women are alike in being "restless," then they are also like—not different from—men. Charlotte Brontë makes this point explicitly in chapter 12, in the passage I have been quoting. "Women are supposed to be very calm generally," Jane notes, "but women feel just as men feel; they need exercise

---

[24]The only reference to Jane's child is this sentence: "When his first-born was put into his arms, he could see that the boy had inherited his own eyes, as they once were—large, brilliant, and black" (*Jane Eyre*, 476).

Mary Poovey

for their faculties, and a field for their efforts as much as their brothers do; they suffer from too rigid a restraint, too absolute a stagnation, precisely as men would suffer; and it is . . . thoughtless to condemn them, or laugh at them, if they seek to do more or learn more than custom has pronounced necessary for their sex" (141). The implications of this statement may not be consistently drawn out in this novel, but merely to assert that the most salient difference was located within every individual and not between men and women was to raise the possibilities that women's dependence was customary, not natural, that their sphere was kept separate only by artificial means, and that women, like men, could grow through work outside the home. Even though Jane marries Rochester, then, she does so as an expression of her desire, not as the self-sacrifice St. John advocates; and the image with which she represents her marriage fuses man and woman instead of respecting their separate bodies, much less their separate spheres. "Ever more absolutely bone of his bone and flesh of his flesh," Jane represents herself as taking the law of coverture to its logical extreme.

What Lady Eastlake objected to in *Jane Eyre* is exactly this subversive tendency. But despite her objection, Eastlake's intermittent—and irrepressible—recognition that the governess's plight is, theoretically at least, that of every middle-class woman repeats Brontë's subversive move. Moreover, Eastlake's charge that the "crimes of fathers" sow the crop of governesses fingers men as the villains behind women's dependence even more specifically than Brontë was willing to do.[25] This charge—that men are responsible for the fetters women wear—also appears in the bitter myth recounted in "Hints on the Modern Governess System." " 'Twas a stroke of policy in those ranty-pole barons of old to make their lady-loves idols, and curb their wives with silken idleness. Woman was raised on a pinnacle to keep her in safety. Our chivalrous northern knights had a religious horror of the Paynim harems. They never heard of Chinese shoes in those days, so they devised a new chain for the weaker sex. They made feminine labour disgraceful" (H 576). Implied here is that women had to be idolized and immobilized in order for some men to think them safe from other men's rapacious sexual desire and from their own susceptibility. Just as some medical men attempted to regulate medical practice so as to control fears about sexuality, so our "chivalrous northern knights" curtail women's honor-

[25]Jane's father is only obliquely held responsible for her situation—but her maternal grandfather is more directly to blame. Jane's father, a poor clergyman, wooed her mother into marriage against her father's wishes, and it was the old man's inexorable anger that caused him to leave all his money to Jane's uncle, thus leaving her penniless and dependent when her parents died.

able labor to protect men from the appetite they represent as uncontrollable and destructive.

Neither Lady Eastlake nor the author of "Hints on the Modern Governess System" developed this indictment of men into an extended argument; instead, they continued to see the problem in terms of a natural difference between the sexes which made women's dependence inevitable. So fixed did these writers imagine women's dependence to be, in fact, that the only solution they could devise was to defer their criticism of men, to make women responsible for remedying the trouble they identified: Lady Eastlake yokes her plea that upper-class employers pay their governesses higher wages to an exhortation to middle-class women—not to mention those in lesser ranks—to resume their maternal duties; and the author of "Hints" explicitly states that "the modern governess system is a case between woman and woman. Before one sex demands its due from the other, let it be just to itself" (H 573).

I want to end this discussion of *Jane Eyre* and governesses with a few reflections on the implications—and limitations—of the methodology I have been using. Implicitly, I have been arguing that the kinds of associations a psychoanalyst elicits in an analytic session are neither free nor personal (nor even solely linguistic). Instead, the associations between, for example, governess and lunatic, governess and prostitute, governess and wife, are, in the last instance, cultural; both the links between images and the strategies with which a text like *Jane Eyre* works through the anxieties they provoke are historically specific and culturally determined. These associations, in turn, are part of a complex system of representation that constructs and reinforces sexual difference and the differences within sexual identity, thereby supporting economic and political relations that seem, on the surface, to have little to do with governesses, prostitutes, or wives. That female nature was defined by maternal instinct emerges obliquely in discussions of the woman whose "plight" was a function of having to do a mother's work without this saving instinct. That this definition of female nature was based not in biology but in a sexed division of labor becomes clear when the novel that symbolically addresses this issue betrays the contradictions inherent in the condition it displaces because it cannot solve.

Now obviously, such fields of cultural association are multiple, overlapping, and heterogeneous, and just as obviously, they can be constructed and read in different ways. In that sense, these clusters of cultural associations present versions of the same dilemma any text presents to any reader. Knowing all too well that historical materials are virtually limitless and that all texts can be read another way, I have nevertheless privileged one set of associations so as to produce one, more or less stable interpretation of this representational system. But the dilemma I have masked in my reading and now return to light is no more personal than the associations I have been discussing. Instead, it seems to me emblematic of the cultural and intellectual position Western academics (particularly feminist critics) currently share: like the governess, we are in a position between—between the powerful guardians of culture, among whom we do and do not belong, and a vast, heterogeneous majority who feel excluded from what we say, and between an outdated ideology of individualism and an ideology of decentered subjects whose hour is not yet here. Whatever our attitude toward this position, I think that the kind of structural psychoanalysis I have been using here gives feminists a vocabulary with which to articulate this in-between position (and this seems to me one explanation of its current popularity, of the fact of this conference). The tropes of displacement, transference, and the unconscious construct meaning and the subject in the image of this split because they acknowledge the longing for unity at the same time that they construct the subject and meaning as heterogeneity and loss.

I am not saying that psychoanalytic paradigms of the nature and production of the subject or meaning are "true," that is, outside of history. On the contrary, I believe that these paradigms are precisely historical, that this language is the best we have right now for discussing the cultural and textual production of meaning because it articulates—and lets us manage—the dis-ease of our historical position. While there is no more absolute ground for emphasizing history than penis envy or absent mothers, the practical implications of this choice are real: it makes a difference if we keep the historicity of psychoanalysis in mind, if we notice how it positions us as subjects, even as it positions the texts we read. For if one accepts the idea that there are universal psychological configurations and universal paradigms of meaning—no matter what they are—then one's place as a woman in a system of sexual difference is given; there is no basis for politics because there is no hope for change. Only if we historicize the psychoanalytic tools we use can we see how sexual difference is socially produced, how woman is a position within a history and economy of classed and gendered representation, and how, recognizing that position, women (and men) can resist this construction and this place. Only such a move—within but also against psychoanalysis—enables a feminist practice that goes beyond poststructuralist theory, that lets us imagine the possibility—even the terms—for change.

Is Female to Male
as Ground Is to Figure?

Barbara Johnson

> No women, then, if I have read correctly. With the notable exception of
> the mother, of course. But this makes up part of the system, for the
> mother is the faceless, unfigurable figure of a *figurante*. She creates a
> place for all the figures by losing herself in the background.
>
> Jacques Derrida, "All Ears: Nietzsche's Otobiography"

> We must be cured of it by a cure of the ground . . .
> New senses in the engenderings of sense.
>
> Wallace Stevens, "The Rock"

As a way of discussing the relations between feminism and
psychoanalysis, I would like to bring together three well-
known texts, each of which tells the story of a failed cure: Nathaniel
Hawthorne's "Birthmark," Charlotte Perkins Gilman's "Yellow Wall-
paper," and Sigmund Freud's "Fragment of an Analysis of a Case of
Hysteria."[1] While the three cases fail in very different ways, they are
alike in presenting a female patient subject to the therapeutic ambi-
tions of a male doctor. In all three cases, in fact, the initiative toward
therapy comes not from the patient herself but from a man she has in

[1] Page references, given in the text, are to Nathaniel Hawthorne, *The Celestial Railroad and Other Stories* (New York: Signet, 1963); *The Charlotte Perkins Gilman Reader*, ed. Ann J. Lane (New York: Pantheon, 1980); and Sigmund Freud, *Dora: An Analysis of a Case of Hysteria* (New York: Collier, 1963), abbreviated, where necessary, as *Dora*. See also *The Standard Edition of the Complete Psychological Works*, ed. and trans. James Strachey (London: Hogarth, 1953–74), vol. 7. My reading of *Dora* has been greatly illuminated by Charles Bernheimer and Claire Kahane's anthology *In Dora's Case: Freud, Hysteria, Feminism* (New York: Columbia University Press, 1985).

Barbara Johnson

some sense discommoded—which is not to say the woman does not suffer.

The question asked by my title is a rephrasing of Sherry Ortner's famous title "Is Female to Male as Nature Is to Culture?"[2] The terms *figure* and *ground*, which refer to a certain distribution of outline and attention, are of course drawn from the visual arts.[3] That origin is not irrelevant here, since the question of the woman in the texts I will discuss is as much aesthetic as it is medical—or, rather, since the texts reveal a profound complicity between aesthetics and medicine.

For a preliminary description of the figure-ground relationship, I turn to a quotation from Douglas Hofstadter's *Gödel, Escher, Bach*, which I inflect in terms of psychoanalysis and sexual difference:

> When a figure or "positive space" [call this "the male child" or simply "the child" or "Oedipus"] is drawn inside a frame [call this frame "psychoanalytic theory"], an unavoidable consequence is that its complementary shape—also called the "ground," or "background," or "negative space" [call this the "girl" or the "other"]—has also been drawn. In most drawings, however, this figure-ground relationship plays little role. The artist is much less interested in the ground than in the figure. But sometimes an artist will take interest in the ground as well.
>
> Let us now officially distinguish between two kinds of figures: *cursively drawable* ones, and *recursive* ones. . . . A *cursively drawable* figure is one whose ground is merely an accidental by-product of the drawing act. [Later, Hofstadter refers to this as a "recognizable form whose negative space is not any recognizable form."] A *recursive* figure is one whose ground can be seen as a figure in its own right. . . . The "re" in "recursive" represents the fact that both foreground *and* background are cursively drawable—the figure is "twice-cursive." Each figure-ground boundary in a recursive figure is a double-edged sword.[4]

[2]Sherry Ortner, "Is Female to Male as Nature Is to Culture?" in *Woman, Culture, and Society*, ed. Michelle Zimbalist Rosaldo and Louise Lamphere (Stanford: Stanford University Press, 1974).

[3]It might at first sight appear that my question ought to be asked the other way around, particularly with regard to the visual arts, where the "figure" of the woman is often at the center of a representation as the very image of beauty. I would say that the centrality of the female figure in such cases is not an indication of true gynocentrism but is, rather, structured like a fetish, i.e., the woman as idealized *object* is really a substitute for the phallus. See Susan Gubar, " 'The Blank Page' and the Issues of Female Creativity," in *Writing and Sexual Difference*, ed. Elizabeth Abel (Chicago: University of Chicago Press, 1982). Whether woman is seen as ground—the place upon or within which what is interesting stands out—or as figure—a detachable object of degradation or desire—the relations between the sexes seem commonly to have found figuration, at any rate, in various versions of the figure-ground relationship.

[4]Douglas Hofstadter, *Gödel, Escher, Bach* (New York: Vintage Books, 1980), 67.

256

The dream of psychoanalysis is of course to represent sexual difference as a recursive figure, a figure in which both figure and ground, male and female, are recognizable, complementary forms. This dream articulates itself through the geometry of castration in Freud, in which the penis is the figure, or positive space, and the vagina the ground, or negative space. But there are limits to how recursive Freud wishes this figure to be: he wants to stop short of something analogous to M. C. Escher's drawing hands, with male and female each drawing the other. Indeed, the expression "double-edged sword" occurs in the form of a "knife that cuts both ways," which Freud, in a footnote to his essay "Female Sexuality," uses to dismiss the undecidability of his own psychoanalytic authority when the drawing of the male-female relationship threatens to become truly recursive. Having just discussed the difficulties experienced by the woman in accepting "the fact of her castration," Freud notes:

> It is to be anticipated that male analysts with feminist sympathies, and our woman analysts also, will disagree with what I have said here. They will hardly fail to object that such notions have their origins in the man's "masculinity complex," and are meant to justify theoretically his innate propensity to disparage and suppress women. But this sort of psychoanalytic argument reminds us here, as it so often does, of Dostoevsky's famous "knife that cuts both ways." The opponents of those who reason thus will for their part think it quite comprehensible that members of the female sex should refuse to accept a notion that appears to gainsay their eagerly coveted equality with men. The use of analysis as a weapon of controversy obviously leads to no decision.[5]

In a footnote to Joel Fineman's response to Neil Hertz's discussion of male hysteria, which is where I came across Freud's footnote, an additional note is cited: "The editor [of the *Standard Edition*] notes that 'The actual simile used by Freud and in the Russian original is "a stick with two ends."'"[6] Out of this regression of footnotes, the basic question is clear: is the figure of sexual difference in psychoanalytic theory cursive or recursive?

The literary equivalent of the visual image of woman as ground has been richly evoked by Susan Gubar in the form of the blank page, the raw material on which the pen-penis of male creativity inscribes its

[5]Sigmund Freud, "Female Sexuality," in *Sexuality and the Psychology of Love* (New York: Collier, 1963), 199, henceforth abbreviated as FS.
[6]Joel Fineman, *Representations* 4 (Fall 1983), 70. Neil Hertz's essay is titled "Medusa's Head: Male Hysteria under Political Pressure." It appeared in the same issue as Fineman's reply.

figures, the negative space surrounding what is presented as truly inter-esting.[7] When woman does appear as a figure in a text, notes Gubar, she is generally mute, passive, or inert, an idealized object of male desire.

The Isak Dinesen story from which Gubar takes the title of her essay offers one displacement of this figure-ground relationship. The story involves a museum of fine white sheets hung up to display the blood stains produced on the wedding night of royal brides. One of these sheets is blank. Gubar sees both the blood and the blank as figures for female writing—females as the subjects of writing, not merely as its objects. Both figure and ground become figure here, but the blank sheet is more recursive than the stained because it proclaims both ground and figure to be open to interpretation, whereas the stained sheets are produced with the proclamation, "We declare her to have been a vir-gin."

With these considerations in mind, I will now pursue the conjunction between the aesthetics of the figure-ground relationship and the thera-peutics of the male-female relationship by juxtaposing "The Birth-mark" and "The Yellow Wallpaper." In the Hawthorne story, a passion-ate scientist, Aylmer, attempts to remove a crimson birthmark from the white cheek of his wife Georgiana, in order "that the world might possess one living specimen of ideal loveliness without the semblance of a flaw" (205). He succeeds in removing the mark but, in the process, kills Georgiana. In the Gilman story, a woman is confined by her husband, a doctor, to a country house for a rest cure. She begins to focus obsessively on the ugliness of the wallpaper until, in the end, she seems to have become a part of it. The superficial symmetry between the two stories is obvious and suggestive. In both, the therapeutic is underwrit-ten by a strong aesthetic investment. In the male writer's story, the birthmark is an overinvested *figure* inscribed on a page that should be blank. In the female writer's story, the wallpaper is an overinvested *ground*. In the first, the figure *on* the woman-ground is erased; in the second, the woman-figure merges *into* the ground. In both cases, the lady vanishes.

To what extent can these stories be read as allegories of psycho-analysis? At first sight, they seem to be examples not of a talking cure but of a silencing cure. Yet if we take as a subtext the third failed treatment of a female patient, Freud's case of Dora, we find that Dora, too, has recourse to silence, not only in breaking off treatment but in ceasing her denial: "And Dora disputed the fact no longer" (125). In all three stories, it is the male observer who identifies something about the woman as a symptom and who determines the nature of the treatment:

[7]Gubar, " 'The Blank Page' and the Issues of Female Creativity."

Aylmer calls Georgiana's birthmark a defect, John calls Gilman's narrator "slightly hysterical," and Dora's father hands his daughter over to Freud, hoping that she will adjust to *his* version of reality. She adjusts neither to his nor to Freud's.

Let us look, then, at the shifting relations between ground and figure in Hawthorne and Gilman, beginning with Hawthorne's first description of Georgiana's mark:

> In the center of Georgiana's left cheek there was a singular mark, deeply interwoven, as it were, with the texture and substance of her face. In the usual state of her complexion—a healthy though delicate bloom—the mark wore a tint of deeper crimson, which imperfectly defined its shape amid the surrounding rosiness. When she blushed, it gradually became more indistinct, and finally vanished amid the triumphant rush of blood that bathed the whole cheek with its brilliant glow. But if any shifting motion caused her to turn pale, there was the mark again, a crimson stain upon the snow, in what Aylmer sometimes deemed an almost fearful distinctness. Its shape bore not a little similarity to the human hand, though of the smallest pygmy size. Georgiana's lovers were wont to say that some fairy at her birth hour had laid her tiny hand upon the infant's cheek, and left this impress there in token of the magic endowments that were to give her such sway over all hearts. Many a desperate swain would have risked life for the privilege of pressing his lips to the mysterious hand. It must not be concealed, however, that the impression wrought by this fairy sign manual varied exceedingly, according to the difference of temperament in the beholders. (204–5)

The mark on Georgiana's cheek is a mark of intersubjectivity: it is interpreted differently by different beholders, and it interprets *them* in response. This "fairy sign manual" is what Lacan might call "a signifier that represents a subject for another signifier." It is the *relation* between figure and ground that shifts in response to another, but the ground is what responds while the figure remains constant. It is perhaps this point of autonomy that does not *simply* reflect (the woman as "pas toute") which makes the mark so irritating to Aylmer. If the cheek is ground and the birthmark figure (figure of being born a woman as well as being of woman born), then what Aylmer wishes to do in erasing the mark is to erase the difference—to erase sexual difference—by reducing woman to "all," to ground, to blankness.[8] And he does indeed succeed in consigning this woman to the ground.

[8]Many readers have seen Aylmer's response to the birthmark as a response to female sexuality. It is instructive, however, to see the terms in which they gloss this. Simon O. Lesser, for instance, suggests that the mark "may represent female sexuality—that is, be a castration symbol." *Fiction and the Unconscious* (Boston: Beacon Press, 1957), 88. If the figure is not read as recursive, female sexuality can only be read as castration.

Barbara Johnson

In Gilman's "Yellow Wallpaper," the female narrator has been confined for treatment by her physician husband, a man of science like Aylmer, a man who "scoffs openly at any talk of things not to be felt and seen and put down in figures." As has often been noted, the first use of the word *paper* refers to the paper (called the "dead paper") on which the narrator is writing her journal (which at first coincides with the story we are reading), even though her husband has forbidden her to write.[9] It is clear, therefore, that the paper that comes alive on the walls is related to the dead paper on which the narrator is forbidden to write. The following passages demonstrate the gradual animation of the paper through a shift in the figure-ground relationship.

At first, the design is unified:

> I never saw a worse paper in my life. One of those sprawling, flamboyant patterns committing every artistic sin. (5)

Then a figure begins to take shape *in the ground:*

> This wallpaper has a kind of sub-pattern in a different shade, a particularly irritating one, for you can only see it in certain lights, and not clearly then.
> But in the places where it isn't faded and where the sun is just so—I can see a strange, provoking, formless sort of figure that seems to skulk about behind that silly and conspicuous front design. (8)

The figure in the ground begins to look like a woman:

> Behind that outside pattern the dim shapes get clearer every day.
> It is always the same shape, only very numerous.
> And it is like a woman stooping down and creeping about behind that pattern. (11)

The ground begins to rebel against the dominant figure:

> The faint figure behind seemed to shake the pattern, just as if she wanted to get out. (11)

> I lay there for hours trying to decide whether that front pattern and the back pattern really did move together or separately. (12)

Suddenly, we are not sure which side of the paper the narrator is on:

[9]See, for example, Annette Kolodny, "A Map for Rereading," in *The New Feminist Criticism*, ed. Elaine Showalter (New York: Pantheon, 1985); and Paula Treichler, "Escaping the Sentence," *Tulsa Studies in Women's Literature* 3 (Spring/Fall 1984).

By daylight she is subdued, quiet. I fancy it is the pattern that keeps her
so still. It is so puzzling.
It keeps me quiet by the hour. (13)

I think that woman gets out in the daytime! (15)

Finally, the crossing is complete:

I don't like to look out of the windows even—there are so many of those
creeping women, and they creep so fast.
I wonder if they all came out of that wallpaper as I did?
I don't want to go outside.
For outside you have to creep on the ground. (18)

If at first it seems that the woman projected into the paper is trying to
move from ground to figure, by the end of the story the narrator has
moved *herself* past the outside, upper figure into a ground that cannot
be located in real space. To escape figuration in the patriarchal conception of the real (the upper pattern), she has relocated elsewhere. But this
alternative real can be figured only as madness, the erasure of the
figure/ground distinction. The cursively drawable figure becomes recursive with a vengeance, turning the narration itself into a double-
edged sword. In the end we don't know which side of the paper she is on,
and hence, we no longer know quite where to locate *ourselves*. Hawthorne's story, too, becomes recursive—"twice told"—with even more
catastrophic results. The moment the figure/ground distinction is
erased, it self-destructs. This can be read as a story of "failed idealism"
only by readers who cannot see its recursiveness.[10]

Freud's attempt to draw the geometry of castration into a narrative of
female development offers a similar set of complexities. Freud knows
where the story starts (the mother) and where the story "must" end
(Freud's "must"), but the narrative of how the woman converts the
"fact of her castration" into something desirable is a real challenge,
even to a storyteller as gifted as Freud.

He begins with the known figure—the male—and seeks the specificity of the female by comparison.

There is another, far more specific motive for the turning away from the
mother, arising out of the effect of the castration-complex on the little
creature without a penis. Some time or other the little girl makes the

---

[10]For a truly recursive ("resisting") reading of "The Birthmark," see Judith Fetterley,
The Resisting Reader (Bloomington: Indiana University Press, 1978), 22–33.

Barbara Johnson

discovery of her organic inferiority, of course earlier and more easily if she has brothers or other boy companions. We have already noted the three paths which diverge from this point: (a) that which leads to the suspension of the whole sexual life, (b) that which leads to the defiant over-emphasis of her own masculinity, and (c) the first steps towards definitive femininity. (FS 200–1)

The turning-away from the mother is a most important step in the little girl's development: it is more than a mere change of object. We have already described what takes place and what a number of motives are alleged for it; we must now add that we observe, hand in hand with it, a marked diminution in the active and an augmentation of the passive sexual impulses. . . . The transition to the father-object is accomplished with the assistance of the passive tendencies so far as these have escaped overthrow. (FS 207–8)

What the Hawthorne and Gilman stories show is the *cost* of adopting the third choice, the choice of "definitive femininity." These stories are stories of an education in passivity: Georgiana is an excellent student; Gilman flunks. It is her teacher who lies motionless on the floor at the end of the story.

Yet both stories are narratives of the woman's growing complicity in her own destruction. Georgiana learns suicide as masochistic self-effacement, while Gilman's narrator learns madness as masochistic self-assertion. How does the complicity work? The stories point to a number of answers.

In both cases, the husband seems to have organized the world around his love for his wife and his concern for her problem. Aylmer stakes his scientific pride on success at removing the birthmark; John rents a house in the country and organizes family life around his wife's illness. This concern makes it impossible for the woman to protest, since she cannot do so without seeming ungrateful or at least without losing her centrality in her husband's world. Both Georgiana and Gilman's narrator are prisoners of an idealization. The cost of their attaining a valued status in the world is to become an object in someone else's reality and, hence, to have, in fact, *no* status in the world. If woman's value is only assured by the place assigned to her by patriarchy, then the alternatives can only be u-topian. The symptom that both Aylmer and John are trying to remove is the mark of femininity itself as both more and less than what is required of women by patriarchal structures. Femininity, in other words, is by nature a "normal ill."[11]

[11]It is hardly necessary to recall that the conference for which this essay was written took place in Normal, Ill.

Both the "mark" and the "paper" can be seen as figures for women's writing. Georgiana's "bloody hand," a kind of *écriture féminine* that is both corporal and cheeky, throbs to its own rhythms in response to the world until she is taught to feel so ashamed of it that she is ready to die rather than live with her horrible deformity. Gilman's narrator, too, learns to renounce her writing: "I did write for a while in spite of them; but it *does* exhaust me a good deal—having to be so sly about it, or else meet with heavy opposition" (4). Both women, in other words, internalize the rejection of their writerly self.

What this internalization indicates is that the repression of writing is related to a repression of ambivalence. The woman is not allowed to have mixed feelings, to be "composite" or "interwoven." She must renounce everything about which she has negative feelings, even when those feelings are internalized from the opinions of others. Ultimately, the thing about which she feels ambivalent, and which she renounces, is herself.

In Freud, too, the "composite" nature of the woman is what is not allowed to stand. Frustrated in what Luce Irigaray has called the "dream of symmetry,"[12] Freud discovers not that woman *is* the second sex, but that she *has* a second sex:

> It will help our exposition if, as we go along, we compare the course of female development with that of the male.
>
> First of all, there can be no doubt that the bisexual disposition which we maintain to be characteristic of human beings manifests itself much more plainly in the female than in the male. The latter has only one principal sexual zone—only one sexual organ—whereas the former has two: the vagina, the true female organ, and the clitoris, which is analogous to the male organ. . . . The sexual life of the woman is regularly split up into two phases, the first of which is of a masculine character, whilst only the second is specifically feminine. Thus in female development there is a process of transition from the one phase to the other, to which there is nothing analogous in males. A further complication arises from the fact that the clitoris, with its masculine character, continues to function in later female sexual life in a very variable manner, which we certainly do not as yet fully understand. (FS 197)

The irritation Freud feels at this excess organ comes out in his triumphant revelation of Dora's supposed secret: her masturbation.

> When I set myself the task of bringing to light what human beings keep hidden within them . . . by observing what they say and what they show, I

[12]Luce Irigaray, *Speculum* (Paris: Minuit, 1974).

thought the task was a harder one than it really is. He that has eyes to see and ears to hear may convince himself that no mortal can keep a secret. If his lips are silent, he chatters with his finger-tips; betrayal oozes out of him at every pore. . . .

The reproaches against her father for having made her ill, together with the self-reproach underlying them, the leucorrhoea, the playing with the reticule, the bed-wetting after her sixth year, the secret which she would not allow the physicians to tear from her—the circumstantial evidence of her having masturbated in childhood seems to me complete and without a flaw. (*Dora* 96–97)

In this notoriously fragmented and incomplete case history, Freud's pleasure at an interpretation that is "complete and without a flaw" is striking. Also striking is the parallel between Freud's scientific jubilation and the triumph anticipated by Aylmer as he prepares to render his wife "complete and without a flaw." Indeed, that throbbing birthmark, that hand already upon Georgiana's body, that "little mark," as Georgiana describes it, "which I cover with the tips of two small fingers," may perhaps be read as the displacement upward precisely of that troublingly excessive female organ. Precedent for such a displacement can be found in the continuation of the passage I have just quoted from *Dora*:

In the present case I had begun to suspect the masturbation when she had told me of her cousin's gastric pains . . . and had then identified herself with her by complaining for days together of similar painful sensations. It is well known that gastric pains occur especially often in those who masturbate. According to a personal communication made to me by W. Fliess, it is precisely gastralgias of this character which can be interpreted by an application of cocaine to the "gastric spot" discovered by him in the nose, and which can be cured by the cauterization of the same spot. (97)

It is hard not to see the scientific energies deployed by Aylmer, Freud, and Fliess in the face of this wandering spot as a sign of patriarchal befuddlement at the multiformity of female sexuality. "The Birthmark," indeed, can be read as a story of fatal clitoridectomy.

This is not to substitute a clitorocentric universe for a phallocentric one but rather to take the clitoris, as Gayatri Spivak and Naomi Schor have both suggested, as a synecdoche for the possibility that the world could be articulated differently, that resistance is always the sign of a counterstory, that the "knife that cuts both ways" does so not because the stories are symmetrical but because each of them is differently situated, serves different ends, and accounts for different things.[13] There is no guarantee that the figures in a *truly* recursive figure would fit together at all.

Freud's story of female sexuality, like Hawthorne's, is a story of renunciation required by the needs of symmetry: "In women the development of sexuality is complicated by the task of *renouncing* that genital zone which was originally the principal one, namely, the clitoris, in favor of a new zone—the vagina" (FS 194). But as Freud's own repeated analysis shows, this renunciation is never any more "complete and without a flaw" than another renunciation Freud considers equally necessary: "We have, after all, long since *given up* any expectation of a neat parallelism between male and female sexual development." (FS 195) What is at stake in the relationship between psychoanalysis and feminism can indeed be summed up in this relationship between renunciation *for* symmetry and renunciation *of* symmetry.

Having now reached a point of closure in my argument, I would like to end by examining how closure is marked in each of the three texts I have been discussing. I find such a gesture most emphatically inscribed in "The Birthmark." Early in the text, we are promised a "deeply inpressive moral." Hawthorne does not fail to deliver what bears all the stylistic marks of an authoritative conclusion. Yet in attempting to capitalize morally upon the failed hubris of science, the narrator actually repeats the error he has just documented. The plea for interwovenness and incompletion is couched in a language that attempts to achieve the same type of objective mastery its message is designed to demystify.

> As the last crimson tint of the birthmark—that sole token of human imperfection—faded from her cheek, the parting breath of the now perfect woman passed into the atmosphere, and her soul, lingering a moment near her husband, took its heavenward flight. Then a hoarse, chuckling laugh was heard again! Thus ever does the gross fatality of earth exult in its invariable triumph over the immortal essence which, in this dim sphere of half development, demands the completeness of a higher state. Yet, had Aylmer reached a profounder wisdom, he need not thus have flung away the happiness which would have woven his mortal life of the selfsame texture with the celestial. The momentary circumstance was too strong for him; he failed to look beyond the shadowy scope of time, and, living once for all in eternity, to find the perfect future in the present.

[13]See Gayatri Chakravorty Spivak, "French Feminism in an International Frame," and Naomi Schor, "Female Paranoia," both in *Feminist Readings: French Texts/American Contexts, Yale French Studies* 62 (1981).

Barbara Johnson

What is astonishing about this passage is that it wants to have its interwovenness and deny it, too. The multiplication of contradictory categories is contained within a grammar of moral certainty. The meaning of these assertions is open to doubt; their claim-to-mean is not.

"I did not succeed in mastering the transference in good time," writes Freud at a similar point in his story. These descriptions of failure are couched in the language of *narrative* control. From whose perspective does one say "Thus ever . . ."? Georgiana is dead, Dora is still somatizing along, and Hawthorne and Freud have gone into high oratorical gear. Whatever the damage done by their finished or unfinished business, the story must have its proper ending, its concluding scientific postscript:

> Years have gone by since her visit. In the meantime the girl has married, and indeed—unless all the signs mislead me—she has married the young man who came into her associations at the beginning of the analysis of the second dream. Just as the first dream represented her turning away from the man she loved to her father—that is to say, her flight from life into disease—so the second dream announced that she was about to tear herself free from her father and had been reclaimed once more by the realities of life. (144)

"The perfect future in the present," "the realities of life": each story ends by pledging its allegiance to a larger story, a larger sense of coherence, a larger set of myths. In contrast, Gilman ends with the very voice of inconclusiveness:

> "I've got out at last," said I, "in spite of you and Jane. And I've pulled off most of the paper, so you can't put me back!"
> Now why should that man have fainted? But he did, and right across my path by the wall, so that I had to creep over him every time! (20)

While the figure of the patriarchal story lies senseless on the floor, the escaped story creeps wildly around in circles. Gilman's ending could not be more different from Freud's or Hawthorne's. Or could it? Twenty years later, Gilman published a sequel titled "Why I Wrote 'The Yellow Wallpaper,'" which documents the therapeutic effects of the story on other women suffering from the rest cure and concludes, "It was not intended to drive people crazy, but to save people from being driven crazy, and it worked" (20). The impulse to put the story to work therapeutically is equally irresistible to all three authors, as it has, no doubt, been to me. Feminism is structured no less therapeutically than the normalizing patriarchal therapies it is designed to combat. The suspicion arises, however, that it is precisely the therapeutic haste toward closure that works in a countertherapeutic way.

266

In all three cases, then, the text concludes with a coda that takes the story itself as its object. Each author stands back from the story as *its reader*, salvaging from the wreckage of its characters the therapeutic coherence of a moral. Transference here is transference onto the story itself as value-object. A quotation from Dinesen's "Blank Page" can perhaps serve to underscore this transference onto story as the moral of *our* transference onto all three tales: "Where the story-teller is loyal, eternally and unswervingly loyal to the story, there, in the end, silence will speak. Where the story has been betrayed, silence is but emptiness. But we, the faithful, when we have spoken our last word, will hear the voice of silence."[14]

Loyalty to the story does not, however, guarantee an unproblematic relation to silence. I would like to conclude by sounding a dimension of silence that may have been going unheard in my remarks. Freud, Hawthorne, and Gilman all write about middle-class white men and women. The very equation of the woman's body with the blank page implies that the woman's body is white (indeed, of a whiteness no actual bodies possess). And the concept of femininity as passivity is applicable only to a certain class of women, even within the texts we have been reading. Are there, perhaps, other figures trapped in the ground of these literary carpets?

In the Gilman and Hawthorne stories, several figures are standing in the background—Mary, who cares for the children; Jennie, the house-keeper; and Aminadab, the personification of matter and physical work, placed beside the sorcerer Aylmer as Caliban is beside Prospero. This background role is often played, in white Western literature, by non-white characters. (In pointing this out, I am, of course, prolonging the colonial gesture of *equating* race and class.) The two most-cited capsule descriptions of black characters in white American fiction, I think, are that of Topsy, who "just grew," and of Dilsey, who "endured." This is another way of denying a character the status of figure and confining him or her to ground. Topsy has no origin; Dilsey has no end; they have no story, no history, nothing to put into figure. Anne Tyler, in her novel *Searching for Caleb*, plays upon the invisibility—the purloined-letter status—of the black characters that occupy the ground of much white American literature. In that novel, a white family, searching for a son who has disappeared, is never able to trace him until someone finally thinks to ask the black couple working for the family, who knew all along but were never asked.

[14]Isak Dinesen, "The Blank Page," *The Norton Anthology of Literature by Women* ed. Sandra Gilbert and Susan Gubar (New York: Norton, 1985), 1419.

In short, there are many other invisible men and women trapped in the wallpaper of the Western canon or caught in the divisions of labor that neither psychoanalytic nor feminist theory has taken sufficiently into account—figures that have often remained consigned to the background of discussions of feminism and psychoanalysis. Could some of these figures be discerned through a reading of another birthmark, the birthmark imprinted on the face of Toni Morrison's Sula? Perhaps, but that would have to be the subject of another essay.

13

Reader, Text, and Ambiguous Referentiality in "The Yellow Wall-Paper"

Richard Feldstein

A Critical Consensus

Critics who have written on "The Yellow Wall-Paper" disagree on the most basic issues pertaining to the text. Is it a short story or a novella; should we underline its title or place it in quotation marks? The 1899 edition presents a novella format, but, in fact, "The Yellow Wall-Paper" first appeared as a short story in 1892.[1] There is also disagreement among critics about the writer's name: is it Charlotte Perkins, Charlotte Stetson, Charlotte Perkins Stetson, Charlotte Gilman, Charlotte Perkins Gilman, or Charlotte Perkins Stetson Gilman? Although each name relates to a phase in the writer's life, many commentators have arbitrarily chosen one designation to use normatively when discussing the writer's life and work. Ironically, this confusion over text's and writer's names was in part generated by Charlotte Perkins Gilman herself, who was anything but consistent in the names she used or the way she spelled *wall-paper*. If Gilman had the advantage of our perspective, she might have been pleased by this confusion of textual identity (is *wall-paper* one word or two) and amused by the critics' befuddlement over her name. Even without a historical perspective, however, she might have predicted such bafflement, possibly foresaw the manipulation of the names of the fathers—Perkins, Stetson, Gilman—as a means of destabilizing the process of signification by presenting a proliferation of signifiers that ironically generate a paucity of signifieds.

[1] Charlotte Perkins Gilman, *The Yellow Wall Paper* (Boston: Small, Maynard, 1899); Gilman, "The Yellow Wall-Paper," *New England Magazine* 5 (1891–92), 647–56.

Richard Feldstein

Meanwhile, Gilman's editors have repeatedly altered the spelling of *wall-paper*, the overdetermined signifier that refers to both the title and the image of protean change featured in the story. The Feminist Press edition would have us believe that Gilman hyphenated the compound in the narrative but gave it in the title of the short story as *Wallpaper*.[2] But the original manuscript presents a different configuration: the use of *wall-paper* shifts arbitrarily, in defiance of any unvarying pattern of logic. The initial five references are *wallpaper, wall paper, wall-paper, wall paper, wall-paper*; its spelling then becomes more ambiguous because *wall-paper* then appears twice, hyphenated at the end of both lines; the final five references construct the indeterminate pattern of *wall-paper, wall paper, wall-paper, paper*, and *wall paper*.[3] Editors of the *New England Magazine*, where the story first appeared, could not abide such "confusion," so they altered the spelling to impose uniformity of textual reference. The title remained "The Yellow Wall-Paper," and the narrative reference still provided the ambiguous alteration of *wall-paper* and *wall paper*, but now there was a perceptible, though random, pattern of word usage: initially, there are three references to *wall-paper*; then, inexplicably, *wallpaper* appears five times before the pattern reverses itself and *wall-paper* is used four times. The next time the story was published, in 1899, Small, Maynard & Company consistently presented the compound as *wall paper*. Today, the version in *The Norton Anthology of Literature by Women* imposes the counterconsistency of *wallpaper*.[4] From Gilman's original manuscript, however, it is apparent that the word(s) *wall(-)paper* were conceived as a shifter calculated to create ambiguity about a referent that resists analysis, even as the narrator resists her husband's diagnosis and prescription for cure.

Despite such confusion, a critical consensus has developed on two issues central to "The Yellow Wall-Paper": John is the story's antagonist and the narrator/protagonist succumbs to a progressive form of madness. There is almost universal agreement that John is a turn-of-the-century patriarchal physician whose diagnosis of "a slight hysterical tendency" imprisons his wife within the prescription for her cure (10). Colluding with his brother and the likes of Weir Mitchell, John prescribes the placebolike "rest cure," which discourages work and isolates the patient from society. But the doctor who hypocritically

[2]Gilman, *The Yellow Wallpaper* (Old Westbury, N.Y.: Feminist Press, 1973). For ease of referral, all subsequent references, unless otherwise noted, are to this edition of the text.
    [3]Gilman, "The Yellow Wall-Paper," Schlesinger Library, Radcliffe College, Charlotte Perkins Gilman Collection, Folder 221.
    [4]Gilman, *The Yellow Wallpaper*, in *The Norton Anthology of Literature by Women*, ed. Sandra M. Gilbert and Susan Gubar (New York: Norton, 1985), 1148–61.

pretends to be a neutral observer is emotionally implicated in the transference between husband and wife. Thus compromised, he relies on a realistic credo, openly scoffing "at any talk of things not to be felt and seen and put down in figures," a position he authorizes while policing his wife, making certain that her behavior complies with the regime suggested by his diagnosis (9). To counter these tactics, the narrator constructs representational strategies that privilege the spatial image over its analysis, modernist strategies that inform the imagist anthologies of the early twentieth century. Implementing this aesthetic through her writing and later through a purposeful acting out, the narrator produces a feminist counterdiscourse that opposes John's dualistic nineteenth-century empiricism with its dyads of good/evil, right/wrong, and, most relevant to this story, rational/irrational.

We can measure John's success in subjugating the narrator by the number of critics who direct our attention to the question of woman's madness as a central issue of the text. Critics generally agree that the narrator's condition deteriorates after she stops writing in her journal and becomes obsessed with the wall-paper. After the narrator substitutes a fixation with the wall-paper for her previous interests, she becomes protective toward the paper and the fantasized double(s) who inhabit it, eventually going so far as to threaten that "no person touches this paper but me,—not *alive*" (33). Because she recognizes these double(s) as fellow victims of a phallic system that resembles the wallpaper's restrictive outside pattern, the narrator believes that her projections might share a common psychogenesis with her: "I wonder if they all come out of the wall-paper as I did?" (35). Commentators who assert that the narrator's madness is genuine not only point to this quotation but to a list of other disconcerting facts to make their case—the narrator gnaws on her bedstead, crawls around the room with her shoulder against a long smooch in the paper, thinks about throwing herself out of a window, and determines that a rope is necessary to apprehend her double(s), who have escaped the wall-paper to creep over the lawn. Commentators who consider these actions conclusive evidence of madness find it difficult to accept Gilman's protagonist as a feminist, especially since she seems incapable of fending off insidious forms of surveillance.

In a recent issue of *Tulsa Studies in Women's Literature* there is a debate among three feminist critics—Paula Treichler, Karen Ford, and Carol Neely—which provides a representative sampling of critical opinion. Declaring that the narrator's final "confinement, infantilization, trivialization, banishment from discourse, [and] madness" are a triumph for patriarchy rather than a statement of feminism, Carol

Richard Feldstein

Neely argues that we should view that act of crawling at the end of the story not as "a victory for the narrator but as her defeat." As for the wallpaper itself, Neely considers that important symbol to be representative of patriarchal discourse "as perceived by women who look at it close up for [too] long."[5] Karen Ford also wonders what value the wall-paper holds for feminists; if it is "a new vision of women," she asks, "why is the narrator tearing it down?" Like Neely, Ford criticizes the narrator for "creeping as though she, like its [the wallpaper's] designs, is lame." On the question of madness, she concurs with Neely that no matter how "dignified and victorious these resolutions into madness and death may seem in relation to the compromised life of marriage and motherhood, they are not ultimately acceptable because suicide is not a viable alternative to a fulfilling life."[6] If one reads the short list of critical articles on "The Yellow Wall-Paper," it becomes apparent that on such issues Neely and Ford speak for the majority of critics who have analyzed the story.

In this issue of *Tulsa Studies*, Neely and Ford were responding to an essay written by Paula Treichler, "Escaping the Sentence: Diagnosis and Discourse in 'The Yellow Wallpaper,'" which appeared a year before.[7] Neely's and Ford's essays are followed by Treichler's rebuttal, "The Wall behind the Yellow Wallpaper: Response to Carol Neely and Karen Ford." Although Treichler concedes that both scholars' "interpretations of the yellow wallpaper metaphor are logical and persuasive," in an adept display of counterlogic, she notes that the text remains "an open and contested terrain" of language "which different people and groups inhabit, and 'work over' in many different ways." Treichler believes in an overdetermined conceptual space, in "multiple discourses," evolved in "multiple contexts," and thus she warns against an either-or reductionism, claiming that "women's discourse is never truly 'alternative' but rather inhabits the same terrain as the 'patriarchal discourse' it challenges." According to her reading, regression from linguistic expression to visual captation is not solely an act of compliance because it allows for the establishment of a counterdiscourse on "a highly policed terrain in which attempts at counterdiscourse are discouraged or forbidden."[8] This politicized regression through which

[5]Carol Thomas Neely, "Alternative Women's Discourse," *Tulsa Studies in Women's Literature* 4 (1985), 316.

[6]Karen Ford, "'The Yellow Wallpaper' and Women's Discourse," *Tulsa Studies in Women's Literature* 4 (1985), 310, 311, 313.

[7]Paula A. Treichler, "Escaping the Sentence: Diagnosis and Discourse in 'The Yellow Wallpaper,'" *Tulsa Studies in Women's Literature* 3 (1984), 61–77.

[8]Paula A. Treichler, "The Wall behind the Yellow Wallpaper: Response to Carol Neely and Karen Ford," *Tulsa Studies in Women's Literature* 4 (1985), 324, 325, 327.

the narrator endeavors to liberate the women of the wall-paper allows her to work through a conflict not previously visualized because of its unacceptability to consciousness. If we consider this important political dimension of the narrator's acting out, her "regression" can be framed by quotation marks to indicate the possibility of an ironic interpretation.

An Ironic Reading of the Wall(-)Paper

If we read "The Yellow Wall-Paper" ironically and not simply as a case history of one woman's mental derangement, the narrator's madness becomes questionable, and the question of madness itself, an issue raised as a means of problematizing such a reading. Reconfigured, the text becomes an allegorical statement of difference, pitting John, an antagonist and a proponent of realism who condemns his wife as a stricken romantic, against a nameless protagonist whose ironic discourse opposes the empirical gaze of the nineteenth-century American realist to a modern, not romantic, configuration—the wall-paper as gestalt—with its shifting significations born of the intermixture of figure and ground. The wall-paper is given to protean changes of shape from the sun- or moonlight reflecting on it. Combine this mutability with another variable: the wall-paper is a mirroring screen for the protagonist's projections, and the paper becomes an overdetermined construct destabilizing signification. Like the wall-paper, the text itself shifts, a signifier generating possibilities of interpretation while providing for a metacritique of its textuality.

From the standpoint of American realism, the narrator's obsession with the wall-paper constitutes a regression from a linguistic presentation, the one she would write if John would allow her "work," to an imaginary reconfiguration, an identification with mirror images in the paper as gestalt. From John's perspective, the narrator is a hapless romantic, a "little girl," a "blessed little goose," in other words, a regressed creature (23). Read ironically, however, her "regression" becomes purposeful—a cunning craziness, a militant, politicized madness by which the narrator resists the interiorization of authority. Through gestural comment, in a pantomime of subversion, the protagonist carefully enacts a series of reversals by exerting what little control she can as the madwoman in the nursery: she feigns sleep at night, sleeps during the day; she refuses to eat when eating is prescribed; she pretends not to write while writing a stratified discourse, literally a "writing" of the body, the sinuous crawl of an Eve/Satan composite

Richard Feldstein

commenting on the androcentric myth of the Fall. All the while the protagonist, though appearing to regress, maintains a level of ironic distance from her object of commentary.

From this point of view, the conclusion that the narrator of "The Yellow Wall-Paper" has a nervous breakdown, an oft-given answer to the difficulties posed by the text, becomes suspect. Although Gilman herself in *The Living of Charlotte Perkins Gilman* states that "The Yellow Wall-Paper" is a story about a woman's "nervous breakdown," later in her autobiography, she asserts another, more didactic purpose for having written the story: to prevent medical practitioners from prescribing "the rest cure" for "hysterical" patients.[9] In other words, Gilman consciously conceived "The Yellow Wall-Paper" from conflicting impulses; one accepted the narrator as simply "mad" and the other politicized the question of woman's madness and its "cure." Born of this conflict is a feminist text using modernist strategies in opposition to the prevailing literary theory of the period, American realism, which foreclosed examination of the complexities and inconsistencies posed by not only Gilman herself but a multilevel textuality that enunciates ambiguity. From this ironic perspective, to read "The Yellow Wall-Paper" as simply a flat representation of one woman's progressive descent into insanity is to diagnose the protagonist's case by means of the empirical ontology championed by the protagonist's doctor husband John, her doctor brother, and the *sujet supposé savoir*, Doctor Weir Mitchell.

Within the time frame of the story the protagonist comes to a modernist realization, that the field of representation is as important as that which is represented. This lesson is learned only after she pleads with John to acknowledge her illness as serious, but he dismisses her symptoms as the product of an overactive imagination. As physician and husband, John consolidates his authority to undermine the protagonist's confidence in her intuitive understanding of her illness. No matter how often she pleads for John's sympathy, once he claims that "she shall be as sick as she pleases," her case history is judged on the basis of his opinion and that of a consulting physician, if John decides that step is necessary (24). Once she understands this patriarchal logic, the nameless protagonist rechannels her effort into the symbolic sphere to counter John's simplistic notion of transparent reality.

We are then left asking if there is a therapeutic value in such acting out. More specifically, is there therapeutic value in the narrator's crawl-

[9]Gilman, *The Living of Charlotte Perkins Gilman* (New York: Arno-Hawthorne Books, 1972), 118–21.

ing as a means to shock her husband? To answer these questions, we need to consider the context. In most cases, patients who distrust their analysts terminate analysis. Unsatisfied Dora dumps Freud, who found it difficult to analyze the countertransference. But the protagonist in "The Yellow Wall-Paper" remains a captive to her husband, secluded in a room with barred windows, beyond a "gate at the head of the stairs," under the watchful eyes of John and Jennie (14). While other patients simply withdraw from analysis, the nameless protagonist must either file for divorce (as Gilman did in her lifetime) or find another effective means to register her dissatisfaction with the inequity of their relationship. Mindful of John's desire to misread her symptoms, the narrator chooses to act out, visualizing her experience, highlighting the common predicament she shares with other women victimized by patriarchy. She thus stages herself in the field of representation.

Within this context we observe the narrator creeping. Round a circle she goes, brushing against the paper that stains all who touch it. Prohibited from writing in her journal, the narrator embodies herself as a stylus writing the line, her body being written in the process. Round she goes, drawing the circle of certainty, diagrammatically constructing the binding process of obsession. When John discovers this activity, he faints. After he is revived, would he characterize her ritual as one of the narrator's many fixations with the wall-paper or with the women in it? If he did so, John's condemnation would not dissuade the narrator from recognizing that he exhibits his own fixations, especially the claim to a definitive diagnosis of her case, articulated with a fixed certainty that feigns objectivity while denying the countertransference. He thus constitutes an incontrovertible truth, a facet of the real he withholds from the symbolic order, dialectical transformation, and the network of free association.

The act of creeping is also a culminating illustration of the protagonist's disaffection with her husband. By the end of the story, she demonstrates the power to "see through" John when he pretends "to be loving and kind" (34). Her dissatisfaction with him becomes such that she wishes he "would take another room!" (31). Kept secluded for weeks on end in their country estate and banished for protracted periods to her bedroom, the protagonist decides to seek like revenge, if only for an instant, by locking John out of their bedroom. After fetching the key from under the plantain leaf, John goes to their bedchamber and enters an unidealized, contested space of intersubjectivity he finds confronting. John is confronted with the narrator's invocation of the Fall, in which woman works in tandem with Satan to violate knowledge. According to this myth, the fallen Eve/Satan composite combines to oust humanity from the garden, sentencing it, in Lacanian parlance, to a confrontation with its limitations as barred subjects ($) forever separated from the Other. In the narrator's enactment of the Fall, woman is yet again blamed for the interpenetration of desire and knowledge. By creeping, the narrator draws attention to the misogynist nature of this condemnation, which presupposes that knowledge maintains a safe haven or conceptual space not permeated with desire.

An Attendant Inclusiveness

It is of less consequence whether an interpretation is ironic if we conflate the identity of the narrator with that of the protagonist in the story. Until recently, critics have not distinguished between the protagonist who stops writing in her journal and the narrator who produces that journal, which becomes our narrative, an effective example of counterdiscourse with political implications for feminists. If the protagonist and the narrator are one character, the narrator's journal poses a contradiction to the theory that the protagonist stopped writing when she regressed from the linguistic to the imaginary level of articulation. This problem, however, has been brushed over while critics place the narrator at an impossible interface: as an extension of the protagonist in the narrative and/or as a representation of the biological author, Charlotte Perkins Gilman. To accept the later conflation is to misread the symbolic for the real, a dimension that cannot be grasped through a dramatico-thematic explication.

An equation is made between the narrator and the protagonist early in "The Yellow Wall-Paper." At the end of the first segment the narrator writes, "We have been here two weeks, and I haven't felt like writing before, since that first day" (13). From this statement and others we are led to believe that we now read what she once wrote. Later in the story the narrator reinforces the impression that she is identical to the protagonist, explaining, "I am sitting by the window now, up in this atrocious nursery, and there is nothing to hinder my writing as much as I please, save lack of strength" (13). This set of quotations indicates that Gilman expended some effort to establish the link between the narrator/journalist and the protagonist in the story. As events unfold, however, John continues to debunk his wife's "imaginative power and habit of story-making" (15) so that she decides the effort needed to oppose her husband is "greater than the relief" she gets from writing (21). About two-thirds of the way through, the narrative records that the protagonist becomes too absorbed in her contemplation of the wall-paper to make reference to her need to write. It is this redirection of interest which leaves us with the seemingly irreconcilable contradiction I have described: if the protagonist stops writing, how do we explain the completion of her journal? To ask Paula Treichler's question: how do we understand a narrative that "is unfolding in an impossible form?"[10]

We could invent many conclusions to explain the radical disjuncture created by the characterological splitting of narrator/narrated. For instance, we could deny the split by concluding that after the protagonist creeps over her husband and the story ends, she writes her recollection of the final scene in her journal. We could also deny the narrator/ narrated division by arguing for a chronological transposition in which the protagonist writes the second segment of her narrative after the fact, in effect providing us with documentation of her recovery. The last scenario most obviously parallels the accounts we have of Gilman's own life, how she divorced her husband, left her child with him, and then wrote "The Yellow Wall-Paper." If we reject a psychobiographical reading, however, and insist instead that the text be treated as a linguistic artifact, we are free to reconstruct traces of an ever-changing, inconsistent narrative in the same way that the protagonist grafts onto the wall-paper a gestalt with fluid boundaries.

The account the narrator provides is a written transcription inexplicably interrupted and succeeded by a spoken account in which she relates details of her life to a hypothetical audience of confidants. For as the story concludes, we confront yet another contradiction when the narrator asserts she is speaking to us, not writing in her journal, as she had previously explained: "I have found out a funny thing, but I shan't *tell* it this time!" (31, my emphasis). This statement, which equates narrative technique with a verbal recounting of events, is like a question asking how it should be read. It is especially significant because of the protagonist's previously stated concern for being allowed to write, a point of pique in the first half of the story, a mute issue in the second. No matter how we choose to read this contradiction, however, it will remain unassimilable to an interpretation of the text. Whichever reading we choose to affix univocal meaning onto a purposely ambiguous text will impose a thematic reduction that should be resisted, just as Gilman resisted Weir Mitchell's diagnosis and her protagonist resisted John's phallocentric assessment of her situation.

The aim of this essay is to raise a feminist question cast in postmodernist terms: did Charlotte Perkins Gilman, grounding her critique in gender difference, use modernist techniques to form a disjunctive text

[10]Treichler, "Escaping the Sentence," 73.

that plays on the question of identity when emphasizing the narrator/ narrated split that presents one entity as two? Could it be possible that Gilman intended the narrator to be both the same as and different from the protagonist, just as she believes the protagonist to be the same as and different from her double(s), the imprisoned other(s) in the wall-paper? From this perspective one slides into two with the shifting of signification. If we look back to the original manuscript of "The Yellow Wall-Paper," we are reminded that Gilman confused the issue of whether wall-paper was one word, two conjoined by a hyphen, or two separate words, whether this central referent—the paper—already a screen for the protagonist's projections, could become more ambiguous, a lure for transposition by critics and anthologists alike.

Besides foregrounding the modernist concern with self-reflexivity, Gilman's presentation of the wall-paper as mirror depicts the intrapsychic splitting and the consequent objectification of fantasy which produces what Lacan calls *méconnaissance*.[11] Lacan explains that in the mirror stage the child develops the ability to differentiate itself from its projective image, a developmental achievement of zero to one (awareness of "self") and one to two (distinction between subject and other). Like Lacan's infant, the creeping narrator is faced with overcoming a motor incapacity when she peers into the looking glass (actual or not), and like this infant, the reader faces a text that reflects itself as a literary artifact through the differentiation of the text's spelling from the wall(?)paper cited in the narrative. Like the infant and the narrator, we reassemble bits and pieces of perception into a unified configuration that fictionalizes analysis even as it calls attention to the stage where the first fictions were formed. Thus, we are left to *identify* with the object of our choice: with the protagonist, whose loss of boundaries causes us to experience a similar loss of identity, with the narrator, whose prose writes itself as a presence absent from most critics' deliberations, with both or neither of these narrative constructs. We configure our own fictions.

The use of text as mirror problematizes interpretation because it produces a doubling that, like the reductio ad absurdum of irony, resists the easy answer or definitive diagnosis. "The Yellow Wall-Paper," however, does not merely present a text that mirrors itself, since the story/ novella also insists on its status as a question, a hesitation that replicates the narrative it recounts. In this way the text maintains a differ-

---

[11]See Jacques Lacan, "The Mirror Stage as Formative of the Function of the I as Revealed in Psychoanalytic Experience," in *Ecrits: A Selection*, trans. Alan Sheridan (New York: Norton, 1977), 1–7.

ence that remains unassimilable to a theoretical perspective that would reassemble it for its own advantage. This strategy of resistance is similar to the one Todorov describes as *fantastic* in a book by the same name.[12] The fantastic presents a textual resistance that induces us to suspend our judgment when interpreting an event as representative of either the supernatural (the women in the wall-paper are ghosts) or the uncanny (the protagonist projects self-aspects to form her double[s]). The fantastic exists, then, suspended between these dimensions, a contradiction to both, a pause or hesitation that, through its inconclusiveness, questions the validity of our assertions. If we apply Todorov's theory of the fantastic to "The Yellow Wall-Paper," we have yet another reason to suspend our judgment, especially since the protagonist acknowledges, as early as the second paragraph, the possibility of a supernatural interpretation—these "secure ancestral halls" are haunted (9). Such a conservative interpretation, which privileges the supernatural manifestation of gothic romanticism while discarding historical and cultural analysis, should not be confused with Todorov's notion of the fantastic, which delights in the ambiguity articulated in expressed difference.

Stated another way, "The Yellow Wall-Paper" is more a writerly than a readerly text, which Gilman designed to challenge her readers to produce, not merely consume. Gilman's protagonist, who configures a text from her vision of the wall-paper, illustrates a means of reading that allows for a play of difference, just as her protagonist allows for the play of sun and moon off the wall-paper's surface. This is how Gilman's text presents itself to us, an ambiguous, doubled referent, cast in the interrogative mode, a gestalt of changing patterns. Text as question formulates an inconclusiveness that attends enigma generated in part by the hyphen between wall and paper—a sign of difference and reminder of text as Other to which we look for closure, a means of satisfying unsatisfiable desires.

[12]Tzvetan Todorov, *The Fantastic: A Structural Approach to a Literary Genre*, trans. Richard Howard (Ithaca: Cornell University Press, 1975).

14

Hysteria, Feminism, and the Case of *The Bostonians*

Claire Kahane

> "Wherever the hysteric goes, she brings war with her."
> Moustapha Safouan, "In Praise of Hysteria"

The second half of the nineteenth century was marked by two related developments: one was the clinical description of hysteria, a disease primarily affecting women and characterized by such physical symptoms as loss of voice and local paralysis with no apparent somatic etiology. The other was the women's movement, which challenged the nineteenth-century conception of the female subject and its place in culture by demanding suffrage. Although one was a psychopathology and the other a political movement, these historical developments intersected in their inverse relation to the speaking woman. Indeed feminism, in its commitment to giving women public voice not only through suffrage but also through its use of the woman orator, seemed the mirror image of hysteria, in which the body spoke what the voice could not. If hysteria raised the issue of the silencing of women's desire, feminism insisted on speaking it. It is the relationship among hysteria, feminism, and the figure of the speaking woman that I want to address by looking first at the etiology of hysteria as developed by Freud and then at its representation in *The Bostonians*, by Henry James.

Psychoanalysis and Hysteria

It was Freud who first insisted that hysteria should be read, that it was, in his terms, "a malady through representation."[1] What Freud first

[1] This is a quotation from Freud, but I cannot find the citation.

reported of hysteria is now familiar to most of us: hysterics suffered from reminiscences, first conceived as traumatic memories of seduction by paternal figures which, unacceptable to consciousness, were repressed but continued to manifest their effects in symptoms that enacted the content of the repression. This first formulation, the basis of Freud's early seduction theory, was later reconceived: hysterics were "remembering" not actual seductions but unacceptable fantasies of seduction, fantasies of a desire for the father and the repudiation of that desire which were written across the body, rather than articulated in language.

Moreover, Freud took note of an aural source of hysterical fantasy, of voices heard in preoedipal infancy, articulations whose meaning was deferred. "The point that escaped me in the solution of hysteria lies in the discovery of a new source from which a new element of unconscious production arises. What I have in mind are hysterical phantasies, which regularly, as it seems to me, *go back to things heard* by children at an early age and only understood later. The age at which they take in information of this kind is very remarkable—from the age of six to seven months onwards."[2] These "things," heard before the child understands language, leave a memory trace, which is activated at a later moment, when voiced sound "means," by a repetition that strikes a chord over the interval. This resonance when experienced as dissonance can provoke hysterical conflict as well as the auditory hallucinations that typically accompany psychosis.[3] Although, as Juliet Mitchell points out, Freud's subsequent work emphasized the primacy of vision in the etiology of neurosis, the trace of the voice and the importance of auditory phenomena in hysterical case histories suggest that hysterics, as Mitchell remarks, have "heard something that . . . made them ill."[4] If the illness of hysteria took the form of a silencing, Freud's cure would make them talk.

I think it significant that psychoanalysis begins as the talking cure; what seems specific to the talking cure is the embodied presence of two subjects, who are connected by the voice, which vanishes, leaving only the trace of its effect. Lacan noted, "What happens in an analysis is that the subject is, strictly speaking, constituted through a discourse, to which the mere presence of the psychoanalyst brings, before any intervention, the dimension of dialogue."[5] The mere presence of the ana-

---

[2]Sigmund Freud, "Letter 59," in *The Standard Edition of the Complete Psychological Works,* ed. and trans. James Strachey (London: Hogarth, 1953–74), 1:244–45.

[3]Jerome Oremland, a San Francisco psychoanalyst, informs me that psychosis is characterized by auditory hallucinations, not visual ones.

[4]Juliet Mitchell, *Women: The Longest Revolution* (New York: Pantheon, 1984), 298.

[5]Jacques Lacan, "Intervention on Transference," rpt. in *In Dora's Case: Freud, Hys-*

Claire Kahane

lyst: the body before intervention is theoretically associated with the mother, with plenitude, but the body of the analyst, which assumes to itself the symbolic function of the father, compels dialogue, compels the subject to speak itself into being while the analyst listens. The talking cure moves the subject away from the body and into language by means of the voice, which participates in both.

Most present to the senses and yet evanescent, both there and not there, the voice is uncanny in its effects. As articulated sound, the voice makes most flagrant what Julia Kristeva calls the semiotic register of discourse: tone, rhythm, music—the body speaking, which is the privileged register of the mother in patriarchy. Yet the voice speaks language, the signifiers of maternal absence. The speaking voice stands somewhere between the body and the symbolic system; like a transitional object, it binds the speaker to the listener at the same time that it allows for separation, revealing to the listening ear, through a tone and timbre that are not always under the speaker's control, the state of the speaker's interiority. It also invades the open ear of the listener, who is thus put into a passive position that he or she cannot control.[6] Perhaps most significant, the speaking voice marks the gender of the speaker, marks a difference in register and pitch, a difference in the speaking body of which the listener is always aware.

Psychoanalysis did not begin as only a talking cure, however; in its earliest stages it used not only the voice but also the hand. Freud began his sessions with the pressure of his hand on the head of the hysteric, who was thus induced to speak. The image—a familiar one to the nineteenth century—is that of the healer, the mesmerist. It is a less than respectable image that Henry James called upon in *The Bostonians*, in which the father's laying on of hands evokes the daughter's eloquent tongue. This laying on of hands had its respectable counterpart in the activities of male physicians, patriarchal experts of the body whose practices often depended upon those "nervous" women who

teria, Feminism, ed. Charles Bernheimer and Claire Kahane (New York: Columbia University Press, 1985), 93.

[6]There is a good deal of literature on the place of the ear in fantasy; see, for example, Ernest Jones's essay on the fantasy of insemination through the ear of the virgin in *Essays in Applied Psycho-Analysis*, 2 vols. (New York: International Universities Press, 1964), 2:266–357; also *The Ear of the Other*, a collection of discussions with Jacques Derrida, ed. Christie V. McDonald, trans. Peggy Kamuf (New York: Schocken Books, 1985); Thomas G. Pavel, "In Praise of the Ear (Gloss's Glosses)," in *The Female Body in Western Culture*, ed. Susan Rubin Suleiman (Cambridge, Mass.: Harvard University Press, 1986). Julia Kristeva notes, "That the female sexual organ has been transformed into an innocent shell which serves only to receive sound may ultimately contribute to an eroticisation of hearing and the voice, not to say of understanding." "Stabat Mater," in *The Female Body in Western Culture*, 108.

were afflicted with headaches, stomachaches, paralysis, and a host of bodily effects of mysterious origin. For many of these women the only hands ever laid upon them in their adult lives were the hands of the physician. Not surprisingly, then, the doctor-patient relationship often provoked complications that Freud would later describe as transference, an eroticization along lines already established in the past, primarily, as Freud conceived it, the father-daughter relationship—although he later acknowledged that the mother-daughter relationship was operative as well. Indeed, the doctor subsumes both maternal and paternal functions in an intimacy that is forbidden elsewhere, an intimacy that provided the homeopathic ground for treating hysteria.

Although Freud initially used the suspect mesmerist method to evoke the secret of the hysteric, since he believed hysterics' stories of the father's seductions, by the time of the Dora case, Freud kept his hands off and relied on the technique of free association. Yet the liberated tongue of the hysteric and the listening ear of the analyst did not constitute a neutral intercourse. Although Freud defensively insisted on keeping his aural/oral technique dry,[7] he realized that often the fantasies were themselves a production of the talking cure, of the embodied relationship between doctor and patient: "I was at last obliged to recognize that these scenes of seduction had never taken place, and that they were only phantasies which my patients had made up or *which I myself had perhaps forced on them.*"[8] That is, Freud's own vocal interventions could constitute the fantasy of seduction and contribute to the silencing of the hysteric; his voice could seduce or overwhelm hers, if she listened. But hers could also seduce him, if she talked.

Whether Freud forced his own fantasies upon his patients by his seductive interventions or evoked them by his mere presence as the father-healer, both in the early *Studies in Hysteria* and in the more elaborated case history of Dora, one can see Freud's own role in constructing the hysteric's story. Freud's plot, however, was not original; taking the plot of Oedipus, the story of masculine desire, he reversed it for women; turning Oedipus into Oedipa, he tried to write the hysteric's story as the daughter's fated desire for the father and repudiation of the mother.

To recall the principal facts of the Dora case as Freud discloses them, Dora's father, engaged in an affair with Frau K., had handed Dora over to

[7]The erotic play of the signifiers *dry* and *wet* is very pronounced in Freud's case of Dora, and has been commented upon before. See, for example, Neil Hertz, "Dora's Secrets, Freud's Techniques," in *In Dora's Case*, 229.

[8]Freud, *On the History of the Psycho-Analytic Movement*, (1914), *Standard Edition*, 14:34, my italics.

Claire Kahane

Herr K. in return for his complicity, and Dora herself had raised no objections to this arrangement, even suppressing information about a sexual advance by Herr K. when she was fourteen. But in a crucial scene Herr K. propositions her in words that repeat a phrase that Dora had heard before—"I get nothing out of my wife"—the phrase used to seduce the governess before her, and it is this repetition that triggers her slap in his face, and her flight. Although Dora refuses to continue her role in this sordid melodrama, she is left with symptoms—loss of voice, fainting fits, a mysterious limp—which, according to Freud's theory, are compromise formations that express repressed sexual wishes. In this logic, Dora must have a secret desire as well as a conscious repudiation. Thus, while Freud confirms Dora's perceptions of her situation as a manipulated object of exchange, he goes further and determines that rather than being merely repulsed by Herr K.'s actions, Dora unconsciously desires the virile—and in Freud's eyes entirely "prepossessing"—Herr K. Freud here reveals his own attraction to the object he desires *for* her. Through a series of brilliantly compelling interpretations, Freud presses Dora to recognize this desire, and, in a perverse confusion of fantasy and reality, even to consider *marrying* Herr K.

But Freud's failure with Dora compelled him both to modify his understanding of hysteria and to rewrite in a series of footnotes the conventional heterosexual plot on which it had been based. Dora revealed that the secret of the hysteric was not only an unacknowledged desire for the father—the core fantasy for the conventional female oedipal complex and the determining factor in the assumption of femininity—but also an unacknowledged *identification* with him; Dora felt not only rivalry with the woman who was her father's love object and Herr K.'s wife but sexual desire as well. As Freud himself concluded in a digression, her love for Frau K. was "the deepest unconscious current in her psychic life."[9] By leading Freud to infer the essential bisexuality of hysteria—"The hysterical symptom is the expression of both a masculine and a feminine unconscious phantasy"[10]—Dora problematized the conventional oedipal narrative, with its fixed heterosexual scenario, and revealed instead an essential instability of gender, a fluidity of aim and object in the erotic life of men and women.

What I find most striking, however, is that Freud constituted the intimacy of their relations as a series of conversations on sexual matters, conversations that mimicked the very nature of the talking cure in

[9]Freud, *Dora: An Analysis of a Case of Hysteria* (New York: Collier Books, 1963), 142 n. 2, and see *Standard Edition*, 7:120 n. 2.
[10]Freud, "Hysterical Phantasies," *Dora*, Collier edition, 151.

which he was engaged and in which he occupied the transference position of Frau K. While he attributed Dora's aphonia to the absence of Herr K., was it not more a consequence of her being left alone to talk with Frau K.? Precisely because feminine sexuality was Freud's dark continent, he could not acknowledge the transference implications of Dora's relationship to Frau K., which would have placed him in the position of a woman. Nor could he openly admit his identification with Dora, the vulnerable hysteric, although his text shows him caught up in his fantasy of the daughter's desire.[11]

"Hysteria is the daughter's dis-ease," Juliet Mitchell writes, whether it occurs in men or women.[12] What does it mean to be a daughter in the narrative of psychoanalysis? Why is it so problematic? The daughter signifies the oedipal child who not only desires the father but more specifically desires to be the *object* of the desire of the father; to be the feminine oedipal child is to desire to yield to the other, a desire psychoanalysis terms "passive." It was a scene of passive sexuality that Freud had first pointed to as the traumatic experience in the etiology of hysteria, and although he moved from the seduction theory to the theory of infantile fantasy, even in fantasy the pleasure of passive sexuality remained problematic for Freud. Desire in this form, as an eroticized submission as object rather than subject of desire, is the desire that Freud ultimately located in the death drive, in a primary masochism in which the subject seeks pleasure in a return to nonbeing, to nondifferentiation, to silence.[13] In conflict with that pleasure, the hysteric simultaneously struggles to assume the position of subject, to speak—in Freud's terms, to express a masculine unconscious fantasy. Thus Dora, who represents through her symptoms—her aphonia, her coughing fits, her limp—the desire of the object, objectifies in her body the dilemma of the object cut off from the control of speech: the object without tongue.

Significantly, in the discourse of psychoanalysis the object without a tongue is a figure of castration, castration being the privileged metaphor of a primary loss in psychoanalytic discourse—a discourse pointedly phallocentric, as the term makes clear. In contemporary feminist discourse, however, when women give voice to what has been repressed, it is the figure of rape that carries the emotional valence of primary

---

[11]Both Madelon Sprengnether, in "Enforcing Oedipus: Freud and Dora," and Neil Hertz, in "Dora's Secrets, Freud's Techniques," make the point that Freud unconsciously identifies with Dora and defends against that feminine identification. See *In Dora's Case.*

[12]Mitchell, *Women*, 308.

[13]See *Beyond the Pleasure Principle* (1920), *Standard Edition*, vol. 13, for Freud's discussion of primary masochism.

Claire Kahane

violation and loss. But there is an essential difference in such discourse between the masculine and feminine metaphors: castration remains a trope, a figure of discourse rather than an actual physical danger the ego must avoid; rape is both a figure and a threatening actual possibility. The difference obviously must have some bearing on the affective life of the sexes, undermining the safe space of fantasy in the erotic life of women. Perhaps this is one reason that women more often than men are prone to hystericize the body that is threatened, while men more readily hystericize discourse. When hysterical fantasies are articulated through language, both castration and rape, the masculine and feminine figures of absolute loss, alternate in an elusive bisexual interplay of fear and desire which shadows their texts.

The Text and the Speaking Woman

Dora's case history was Freud's most elaborate translation of the speaking body. Written up in 1900, although published in 1905, the text is particularly well situated to represent the sexual problematics of the turn of the century. That turn, moreover, put the screws to representation of all sorts. As Steven Marcus notes, Freud assumed that a coherent life story was a sign of mental health and interpreted "the patient's inability to give an ordered history of his life" as the sign of repression. Hysterical discourse was fragmentary, digressive, and full of gaps. Pointing to the disingenuousness, gaps in memory, shifting chronologies of Freud's own fragmentary narrative, hysterical by his own definition, Marcus shows that Freud was a great modernist writer, and the Dora case an exemplary modernist novel precisely because of these hysterical symptoms.[14] Because of his own hysterical proclivity and powerfully ambivalent countertransference, Freud was compelled to write the kind of narrative—multidimensional, digressive, fragmentary—that in the next two decades became formalized as literary modernism. Reversing and extending Marcus's analogy, I would suggest that a good many late nineteenth-century texts can profitably be called premodernist and hysterical, that as symptomatic narratives, they articulate the problematics of sexual difference, a difference challenged in great part by nineteenth-century feminism. In this connection the Dora case provides a useful analogy for reading not only characters, as they enact hysterical scenes and symptoms, but also the performance of

[14]Steven Marcus, "Freud and Dora: Story, History, Case History," reprinted in *In Dora's Case*, 56–91.

texts, as they embody their phantasms, struggle with the meaning of difference and resist the compulsion toward a linear oedipal plot.

The nineteenth-century faith in difference, in separate spheres of mind and action for men and women, had been almost absolute, indeed not just as faith but as science. Darwin's *Descent of Man*, which argued that women had evolved differently from men, that their nurturant domestic capabilities fitted them for home and hearth, while men had evolved aggressive, competitive abilities that were meant to be exercised in the public arena, re-presented Victorian scripture on gender difference. From this "truth" Victorian writers had produced a great tradition of narrative controlled by difference, by the discrete separation of subject and object, public and private, active and passive—categories intimately linked to the radical dualism of masculine and feminine. But by the end of the nineteenth century, categories of difference were being undermined, in America especially, by the increasingly vociferous women orators who demanded a different cultural position for women. No longer required to raise their voices in the cause of abolition, in the decades following the Civil War the "herd of vociferating women," as James's protagonist calls the feminists in *The Bostonians*, transferred their newly developed oratorical skills to the cause of women's rights. By the turn of the century, their voices were heard on the Continent as well. In calling for women to act in the public arena—the height of immodesty and itself an assault on chastity—and in creating that infamous figure, the new woman, who acted just like a man, the feminist movement figured to the patriarchal mind a threat to the entire symbolic structure of binary oppositions. (The 1867 New York Constitutional Convention expressed this fear by rejecting suffrage as an innovation "so revolutionary and sweeping, so openly at war with a distribution of duties and functions between the sexes as venerable and pervading as government itself, and involving transformations so radical in social and domestic life.")[15] Menaced by a vision of cultural apocalypse and yet also exhilarated by the possibilities, turn-of-the-century writers, both male and female, represented their ambivalence in fictional forms that begin as hysterical articulations of their

---

[15]Quoted in Ellen DuBois, "The Radicalism of the Woman Suffrage Movement: Notes toward the Reconstruction of Nineteenth-Century Feminism," *Feminist Studies* 3 (Fall 1975), 68. Also see Juliet Mitchell's excellent discussion of the relation between nineteenth-century feminism and hysteria, "Feminism and the Question of Women," in *Women: the Longest Revolution*. Although my argument was developed before I read Mitchell's chapter, our discussions overlap considerably. Our primary difference is that Mitchell conflates feminism and hysteria, while I contrast them, a difference which takes us on divergent paths.

own labile sexuality and become formalized later as the tenets of literary modernism.

It is especially significant for my argument that the women's movement was characterized by giving women voice, not only metaphorically through suffrage but literally in the pervasive speechifying by women on platforms around the world. The woman speaking was experienced as a particularly radical gesture. In the histories of the feminist movement, the item always mentioned first to illustrate its revolutionary impact is the appearance of the woman speaker before a mixed audience.[16] Not only did the woman orator appropriate a male province, but the figure of the woman on the platform, both exhibiting herself and speaking with the voice of authority, seems to have been particularly unsettling to male consciousness, judging from the heap of ridicule she elicited. If language is predicated upon maternal absence, the woman with a voice represented the power of the maternal body as a figure of presence, as well as the power of the father's language. An avatar of the Medusa, the speaking woman confronted the male listener with his own passivity, and more often than not he responded by stiffening his neck against her insinuations.

The Bostonians, a novel about the feminist subversion of difference through the figure of the speaking woman, is an exemplary text in this regard, for although it preceded the modernist period by several decades, like the Dora case, it exhibits many of the textual characteristics of modernist form. With its unreliable narrator, its shifting identifications, its digressions and contradictions, James's hysterical narrative, like Freud's narrative of Dora, manifests in symptoms an anxiety about gender that it cannot speak directly.

The ostensible plot of *The Bostonians* concerns the struggle between Olive Chancellor, a New England feminist, and Basil Ransom, her conservative southern cousin, for the love and possession of Verena Tarrant, an ingenue gifted with inspired speech, for which, significantly, she assumes no agency. Olive, painfully shy and unable to speak in public, wants Verena and her voice for the public cause of women's rights; Basil, whom James calls "a representative of his sex" and his most important character, desires her for private pleasure. James represents their conflict as the ultimate civil war, the battle between male and female—between patriarchy and matriarchy more generally—for the possession of the daughter and the right to inscribe her in the narrative of culture.

But the more hysterically charged issue of *The Bostonians* is the

---

[16]This observation was made by historian Ellen DuBois in conversation.

imperiled future of sexual desire and the difference on which it is based, which James saw as threatened by the women's movement. In a revealing early comment about his prospective novel James calls it an "episode connected with the *so called 'woman's movement'* " and tells us that wanting to write "a very American tale . . . characteristic of our social conditions," he found the most salient and peculiar point in our social life "the situation of women, the decline of the sentiment of sex, the agitation on their behalf."[17] The bracketing of "the decline of the sentiment of sex" by "the situation of women" and "the agitation on their behalf" is precisely what James fears: he envisions a kind of impending doom of aphanisis, to use Ernest Jones's term, a loss of desire which, since desire depends on difference, is a consequence of women's "agitation" for equality.

The subject of difference pervades the novel; North and South, freedom and slavery, speech and writing, the tongue and the touch, public and private—the novel continually sets up these oppositions, binds them to the difference between masculine and feminine, and then flirts with their collapse. Indeed, the discourse of *The Bostonians* supports the vision of Margaret Fuller, in *Woman in the Nineteenth Century* that "male and female represented two sides of a great radical dualism. But in fact they are perpetually passing into one another. Fluid hardens to solid, solid rushes to fluid, there is no wholly masculine man, no purely feminine woman."[18] Like Fuller, James maintains a radically dualistic structure while showing its boundaries to be permeable. But unlike Fuller's, James's text presents hysterical moments when difference collapses, and that collapse is experienced as a feminization. Listen for a moment to the sound of this passage in which Basil Ransom reveals his desire to save his own sex; when asked, "To save it from what," he replies:

> From the most damnable feminization! I am so far from thinking, as you set forth the other night, that there is not enough woman in our general life, that it has long been pressed home to me that there is a great deal too much. The whole generation is womanized; the masculine tone is passing out of the world; it's a feminine, a nervous, hysterical, chattering, canting age, an age of hollow phrases and false delicacy and exaggerated solicitudes

[17]*The Notebooks of Henry James*, ed. F. O. Matthiessen and Kenneth B. Murdock (London: Oxford University Press, 1947), 46–47, cited in the Appendix to *The Bostonians*, ed. Alfred Habegger (Indianapolis: Bobbs-Merrill, 1976), 429, my italics. All quotations from *The Bostonians* are from this edition.

[18]Margaret Fuller, *Woman in the Nineteenth Century*, quoted in *The Norton Anthology of Literature by Women*, ed. Sandra Gilbert and Susan Gubar (New York: Norton, 1985), 301–2.

Claire Kahane

and coddled sensibilities, which if we don't soon look out, will usher in the reign of mediocrity of the feeblest and flattest and the most pretentious that has ever been. The masculine character, the ability to dare and endure, to know and yet not fear reality, to look the world in the face and take it for what it is—a very queer and partly very base mixture—that is what I want to preserve, or rather as I may say, to recover; and I must tell you that I don't the least care what becomes of you ladies while I make the attempt! (318)

Note the exclamation points, the syntax of disruption, of breathless, pauseless sentences that accumulate signifiers of anger: this ranting utterance is coded for vehemence and is, in the colloquial sense of the term, a hysterical harangue. Yet James's narrator tells us that "the poor fellow delivered himself of these narrow notions with low, soft earnestness . . . that it was articulated in [a] calm, severe way, in which no allowance was to be made for hyperbole." It is impossible to articulate that passage calmly. In what is arguably the most hysterical eruption in the narrative, this disjunction between the textual effect of Ransom's voice and the narrative commentary on it points to the narrator's lack of distance from Ransom, to a sympathy based upon their mutual apprehension of women's power to "feminize." Although at various points in the novel James's narrator intervenes to dissociate his opinions from Ransom's, as when he alludes to the brutal impulses underlying Ransom's male code of chivalry and his sadistically toned relation to women or when he ridicules Ransom's reactionary views about women, those very interventions are made to relieve the textual confusion between Ransom and the narrator. Like Freud with Herr K., James seems to think Ransom extremely prepossessing, for only Olive Chancellor actively dislikes him, and that dislike is represented as hysterical, that is, a consequence of her fear of men and her desire to possess Verena.

The most blatant similarity between Ransom and the narrator is their use of ridicule (*The Bostonians* is the only James novel considered a satire). I find it interesting that the figure subject to the greatest ridicule also elicits the only other blatantly hysterical rupture in the narrative surface: Miss Birdseye, the pathetically ineffectual feminist who so much resembled Elizabeth Peabody that William James cautioned his brother about causing embarrassment by his ridicule of her. In an interpolation comparable in its outrage only to Basil Ransom's outburst, the narrator, having said she belongs to the Short Skirts league, suddenly erupts venomously: "This did not prevent her being a confused, entangled, inconsequent, discursive old woman whose charity began at home and ended nowhere, whose credulity kept pace with it, and who knew less about her fellow-creatures, if possible, after fifty years of humanitary zeal, than on the day she had gone into the field to testify against the iniquity of most arrangements" (26). Why is the narrator so angry? Described as totally lacking in knowledge of the real by both Olive and Ransom, Miss Birdseye, a representation of transcendental excess, opens her house to everyone, gives succor indiscrimately to Negroes and refugees—and James fumes,[19] as in this shrill and at times incoherent passage that begins, significantly, with a reference to her ineffectual talk:

> She talked continually, in a voice of which the spring seemed broken, like that of an over-worked bell-wire; and when Miss Chancellor explained that she had brought Mr. Ransom because he was so anxious to meet Mrs. Farrinder, she gave the young man a delicate, dirty, democratic little hand, looking at him kindly, as she could not help doing, but without the smallest discrimination as against others who might not have the good fortune (which involved, possibly, an injustice) to be present on such an interesting occasion. (26)

The narrator's irritation with her impotent talk is joined to an insidious little trio of signifiers—delicate, dirty, democratic—to give us James's moral sensibility at its crudest. A precursor to the xenophobia of such modernist writers as Eliot and Pound, who seemed especially to fear contamination by the immigrant hordes, it marks the novel's recurrent concern with difference and the violation of boundaries. Through the image of the delicate, dirty, democratic hand, James transforms a political threat into a physical and sexual one in the kind of hysterical slippage that pervades the novel.

The novel is full of images of hands that are symptomatically eroticized: the hands of the feminist are "cold and limp"; their judgment is "like a soft hand"; the hands of the father, notably Selah Tarrant, are presented as outrageous in their manipulation of women. But the primary physical image fetishized in the novel is the speaking voice. Each of the characters is marked by a relation to the speaking voice. Thus the feminization Basil fears is initially figured by his voice. The narrator describes Ransom in flagrantly phallic terms as "very long, hard, like a column of figures," with a leonine head "to be seen above the level of a crowd on some judicial bench." After accumulating such masculine signifiers, however, the narrator remarks that "if we are readers who like a complete image, who read with the senses as well as with the

---

[19]See Neil Schmitz, "Mark Twain, Henry James, and Jacksonian Dreaming," *Criticism* 27 (1985), 155–73, on James's attitudes.

reason"—and here this opposition is clearly gendered—then we must not forget the feminine components of this phallic figure, namely that Ransom "prolonged his consonants and swallowed his vowels, that he was guilty of elisions and interpolations which were equally unexpected, and that his discourse was pervaded by something sultry and vast, something almost African in its rich, basking tone, something that suggested the teeming expanse of the cotton field" (5). Playing on the same geopsychological dichotomy that Henry Adams exploits in the *Education*—the South is warm, earthly, sensual, i.e., feminine, while the North is judicial and cold, i.e., masculine—James shows the integrity of Basil's judicial erectness riven by a guilty voice. Indeed, the southern discourse reveals itself as *guilty* through the voice, its guilt signified by the gaps (elisions) and discursive ruptures (interpolations) that are the textual signs of repression. What is it guilty of? James remarks on the "African" sensuality that has infused the voice of the South through a guilty intercourse and also marks this voice as feminine by noting the "curious feminine softness with which Southern gentlemen enunciate." Thus the drawl, the voice of the South, reveals in its physical being the oppression and repression of blacks and women, both of whom signify sexuality, at the same time that it is seductive for that very incorporation. Although James had originally thought to make his hero a westerner, by writing Ransom as a southerner, he could use the drawl—the voice of an already violated South—to subvert the grim and hard signifiers of Ransom's masculinity.

Just as Basil's feminization is marked by a relation to speech, so James uses speech to mark the feminization of all the male characters. Mrs. Tarrant, Verena's mother, descended from a line of public speakers, is humiliated by her husband's inability to speak, and although he has proved his "eloquence of the hand," her family "had never set much store on manual activity; they believed in the influence of the lips" (70). The unctuous journalist Matthew Pardon's sentences are "imperfectly formed" and punctuated by such effete ejaculations as "Goodness gracious" (116) and "Mercy on us." As James parodies the flatulence of the speech of his contemporaries, it seems clear that he is concerned with his own potency as a writer, a concern perhaps exacerbated by the fact that his own style could be characterized—and essentially was by his brother—as feminine in its circumlocutions, its deferral of the point, and its frequent use of a female consciousness to explore his interests.

Of course it is Olive, Ransom's antagonist, the feminist reformer, about whose psychology James was most curious, who is most marked by a neurotic relation to speech. Articulate in private but voiceless in public, Olive is described as morbid, obsessed with bodily images of the unhappiness of women—"The voice of their silent suffering was always in her ears, the ocean of tears that they had shed from the beginning of time seemed to pour through her own eyes"—and in need of a physical means of representing it. "A voice, a human voice is what we want" (54), Olive cries, and her response after hearing Verena speak, "what a power, what a power" (76), her vision of their partnership as an "organic whole" (144) show how fetishistically the voice functions in this novel. Just as the fetish wards off anxieties about difference by displacing absence with presence, so the issue of the novel comes to rest in questions associated with the voice as fetish: who possesses its power, what does it veil or reveal?

We know what Olive wants to use the fetishized voice for: to expose the silent suffering of women. Ransom, on the other hand, wants to keep the secret, to hold his tongue, for as James tells us, again using the image of an unhappy woman, Ransom's "heart's desire" is "to be quiet about the Southern land, not to touch her with vulgar hands, to leave her alone with her wounds and her memories, not prating in the market-place either of her troubles or her hopes" (48). To be quiet and not to touch—these prohibitions on the voice and the hand are repeatedly voiced by Ransom and transgressed by the feminists.

If Ransom wants his women quiet, his desire, paradoxically, is aroused not by Verena's image—"her exhibition is not exciting" (57)—but by her voice, a voice whose power is elicited by her father's touch. Ransom especially resents "Tarrant's grotesque manipulations . . . as much as if he himself had felt their touch. . . . They made him nervous, they made him angry" (57). In this revealing textual moment, James points to Ransom's identification with Verena and flirts with the pleasure as well as the fear of being handled, being manipulated, being objectified. Although Ransom and the narrator quickly cover over this moment, Ransom as listener remains vulnerable and therefore defensively derisive about Verena's speech, which, as we are given it in the text, is very seductive: Verena "pours into the ears of those who still hold out, who stiffen their necks and repeat hard, empty formulas, which are as dry as a broken gourd" a feminist vision of enlightened self-interest, of relations based on "generosity, tenderness, sympathy where there is now only brute force and sordid rivalry" (255). But Basil asserts his masculinity by obliterating the words as signifiers and hearing only the music of her voice, the erotics of the voice, the voice of the nightingale. She can sing but not signify; she can give pleasure but not "mean." Thinking that "she speechifies as a bird sings," he tells her, "I don't listen to your ideas, I listen to your voice" (216). Like Philomela, who was raped and whose tongue was cut out so that she could not tell

Claire Kahane

the tale, Verena will ultimately be silenced in the presence of Ransom, will be abducted by Ransom in a climax that resonates both etymologically and psychologically as a rape and a castration, and substantiates the subtextual image of the unhappy woman.

Once one begins to listen to the speaking body of the text the figure of rape is ubiquitous; listen to James's description of Tarrant's relation to the newspaper offices and vestibules of hotels, the centers of worldly power: "He . . . had a general sense that such places were national nerve-centres, and that the more one looked in, the more one was 'on the spot'. The *penetralia* of the daily press, were however, still more fascinating, and the fact that they were less accessible, that here he found barriers in his path, only added to the zest of forcing an entrance. . . . He was always trying to find out what was 'going in'; he would have liked to go in himself, bodily, and failing in this, he hoped to get advertisements inserted gratis. . . . He expected his revenge for this the day after Verena should have burst forth; he saw the attitude in which he should receive the emissaries who would come after his daughter" (99). In this image of the father who is impotent to go in himself, who thus needs a substitute phallic object, Verena is not only the daughter but the father's phallus, so that her silencing is also a castration. A rape and a castration—both the feminine and the masculine signifier of loss are manipulated in the text's hysterical bisexuality; both figures are implicated in the pervasive textual fetishizing of the laying on of hands and the eloquent tongue.

As if nature herself demands only the oedipal plot, requires the ransom of heterosexuality to maintain human culture, the narrative moves inexorably to take Verena from the woman and give her to the man by reversing in a series of confrontations the place of the voice. To justify this reversal, James gives us a revealing little scenario: while Ransom insinuates himself into the ear of Verena, Olive wanders around Washington Square contemplating Verena's future as a feminist; the foreshadowing is unmistakable:

The trees and grass-plats had begun to bud and sprout, the fountains plashed in the sunshine, the children of the quarter, both the dingier types from the south side, who played games that required much chalking of the paved walks, and much sprawling and crouching there, under the feet of passers, and the little curled and feathered people who drove their hoops under the eyes of French nursemaids—all the infant population filled the vernal air with small sounds which had a crude, tender quality, like the leaves and the thin herbage. (300)

This representation of the sounds of the children is meant to signify the voice of nature, a nature that thus requires Verena's complicity in her abduction for the sake of the race. And it is meant to be a sharp contrast to the topography of the southern cape, the feminist enclave to which Olive takes Verena in an effort to elude Ransom: "The ripeness of summer lay upon the land, and yet there was nothing in the country Basil Ransom traversed that seemed susceptible of maturity; nothing but the apples in the little tough, dense orchards, which gave a suggestion of sour fruition here and there, and the tall, bright goldenrod at the bottom of the bare stone dykes" (329). In the midst of this highly allusive suggestion of "sour fruition" and "bare stone dykes" at Marmion, Ransom and Verena have the conversation Olive has tried to prevent. Empowered by having had a piece of writing accepted for publication, Ransom proposes their marriage and her silence. Although he tells her, "It's not to make you suffer, . . . I don't want to say anything that will hurt you," as she entreats him "to spare her," to allow her to continue speaking for women, James points to his aggressive desire: "A quick sense of elation and success began to throb in his heart, for it told him . . . that she was afraid of him, that she had ceased to trust herself, that the way he had read her nature was the right way (she was tremendously open to attack, she was meant for love, she was meant for him)" (349). And Ransom does attack through the vulnerable and open ear:

> The words he had spoken to her . . . about her genuine vocation, as distinguished from the hollow and factitious ideal with which her family and her association with Olive Chancellor had saddled her—these words the most effective and penetrating he had uttered, had sunk into her soul and worked and fermented there. . . . the truth had changed sides; the radiant image began to look at her from Basil Ransom's expressive eyes: it was always passion, but now the object was other. (349)

From this point to the climax of the novel, Ransom's actual abduction of Verena, Ransom's words are supported by the narrator's acts of violent manipulation, which move the novel toward its inevitable oedipal resolution; Verena's voice, previously a gift from her father, which she and Olive had appropriated, will now be made to "lubricate" her private life with Ransom, rather than "gushing out at a fixed public time and place." In an increasingly contradictory sequence, the narrator redefines her relationship to Olive and feminism as "a desire to please others" and her relationship to Ransom as "a push to please herself." But this masculine redefinition of feminine desire is precisely not what James shows Verena's fate to be; rather, as Verena, unable to resist the languor of objectification, is tempted into passivity, she becomes Ransom's possession, as the narrator ultimately suggests.

Claire Kahane

In a final scene, almost surreal in its representation of tensions and contradictions, Verena shrieks for Olive as Ransom wrenches her away "by muscular force" but is also glad to be taken. But as Ransom leads the weeping girl away, the narrator remarks in perhaps the most subversive ending to a heterosexual marriage plot: "It is to be feared that with the union, so far from brilliant into which she was about to enter, these [tears] were not the last she was destined to shed."

Thus at the same time that James takes Verena from the woman and gives her to the man, Ransom is undermined, and Olive emerges as an increasingly sympathetic figure, tragic and heroic. Indeed, Olive, by this point the most complex character in the novel, is finally the real interest of the book. The character who will never marry, whose most passionate relationships are with her own sex, Olive ultimately figures James's own problematic sexuality most closely. Like Freud with Dora, James had to identify with his subject to constitute her in language, and that identification proved extremely disturbing. Investigating what he called her typical morbidity, James came to represent its source in a hysterical fantasy of violation, a fantasy that equates speaking with potency and silencing with being raped and castrated, a fantasy I suggest James shared, given its dispersion throughout the text and its emergence at the climax. Thus the novel bears out Olive's assessment of the "unhappiness of women" as "inevitable"; *The Bostonians* reveals the secret of the hysteric to be the same as the secret of sexuality based on conventional patriarchal gender positions, reveals the inevitable unhappiness of women who assume the feminine position of silence and passive desire. While James the gentleman identifies with Ransom's prohibition against the exposure of secrets, James also, like Olive, exposes the lie of the conventional happy marriage plot of the nineteenth century and confirms Olive's "morbid" vision in his unsettling last line.

There is another final scene, a scene we can only hear, since it takes place on stage in the novel, while the reader is behind the scenes. At the same time that Verena is being abducted, Olive, "seeing fierce expiation in exposure to the mob" (425), goes on stage to confront the angry audience waiting for Verena to speak, expecting to be hooted and insulted. James juxtaposes her "morbid" desire for martyrdom to Verena's complicitous abduction to make them analogous, both an expression of the same masochistic desire. But at the same time he likens Olive to "a feminine firebrand of Paris revolutions, erect on a barricade or even the sacrificial figure of Hypatia, whirled through the furious mob of Alexandria" (425). This association of Olive with revolutionary violence recalls Neil Hertz's remark that "a confrontation with a woman is an emblem of what revolutionary violence is about," that behind this frequent representation of revolutionary violence as a fierce woman "manning" the barricades is an anxiety that conflates sexual, social, and economic upheavals of male privilege with castration.[20] Olive as feminist firebrand becomes a potential phallic woman, arousing the narrator's apprehension. Thus her ambiguous position at the end, out of sight but within voice range, allows James to play out his ambivalence without resolving it. At the end of *The Bostonians*, we hear the crowd, which Olive had presumed would hoot and jeer, fall silent at her appearance, and we are left wondering if she will be able to speak, if she can voice herself into agency. James must have wondered also.

[20]See Neil Hertz, "Medusa's Head: Male Hysteria under Political Pressure," *Representations* (Fall 1983), 27–54.

15

(M)other Eve: Some Revisions of the Fall in Fiction by Contemporary Women Writers

Madelon Sprengnether

> The loss of the daughter to the mother, the mother to the daughter, is the essential female tragedy. We acknowledge Lear (father-daughter split), Hamlet (son and mother), and Oedipus (son and mother) as great embodiments of the human tragedy; but there is no presently enduring recognition of mother-daughter passion and rapture.
>
> Adrienne Rich, *Of Woman Born*

One winter several years ago, when I was living in Los Angeles, I haunted the local secondhand bookstores looking for fiction by women writers. I discovered in this random and musing way a small book about a young girl's passage from childhood to adolescence called *The Greengage Summer*.[1] It begins like this:

> On and off, all that hot French August, we made ourselves ill from eating the greengages. Joss and I felt guilty; we were still at the age when we thought being greedy was a childish fault and this gave our guilt a tinge of hopelessness because, up to then, we had believed that as we grew older our faults would disappear, and none of them did. Hester of course was quite unabashed; Will—though he was called Willmouse then—Willmouse and Vicky were too small to reach any but the lowest branches, but they found fruit fallen in the grass; we were all strictly forbidden to climb the trees. (3)

I recognized a familiar pattern (the eating of fruit followed by guilt) in a somewhat unfamiliar setting. The narrator is female, and her story,

---

[1]Rumer Godden, *The Greengage Summer* (1958; rpt. New York: Viking Penguin, 1986). All quotations of *The Greengage Summer* in this essay refer to this edition.

though it embraces her younger siblings, primarily concerns herself and her sixteen-year-old sister. As I read further I became convinced that the novel couches its own drama of coming of age in terms of one of the oldest stories of all: the Fall.

I became particularly sensitive at this time to the use of garden imagery by women writers and began slowly to perceive an interesting pattern in some of the fiction I was reading. In the middle of one sleepless night, I jotted down the following notes.

> I woke up thinking about *The Greengage Summer* and other books by women I have read that deal with the myth of the Fall, through garden imagery or otherwise. What struck me is that women writers' versions of the Fall are different from men's in that for women it is a mother/daughter story, and the Fall is portrayed in terms of the loss of the mother.[2] This shift is not perhaps immediately apparent because women read through the Genesis story as well as men, but these fictions have a different twist.

I have chosen to describe the development of my interest in the topic of this essay because I want to emphasize the tentative, speculative, and evolutionary nature of the argument that follows. I suggest that by making a series of related interpretive gestures, we may discover an unexpected text in the guise of a familiar story, one that is capable, in turn, of altering our cultural awareness. The effort required to make these interpretive gestures and to perceive this unexpected text, however, involves a kind of inner displacement as well, in this case a psychic disengagement from the biblical master plot that provides an aura of familiarity and from the oedipal master plot that sustains it. In my reading of women writers' treatment of the Fall, I see a group of fictions that challenge some of our most cherished stories of cultural

---

[2]Jane Lilienfeld touches on this theme when she discusses Colette's portrayal of her mother in "Reentering Paradise: Cather, Colette, Woolf and Their Mothers," *The Lost Tradition: Mothers and Daughters in Literature*, ed. Cathy N. Davidson and E. M. Broner (New York: Frederick Ungar, 1980), 160–75. Jeffrey Andreson argues from a psychoanalytic standpoint that the motif of falling in dreams and other clinical material supplied by patients generally signifies the loss of the mother. See "The Motif of Falling: Falling and the Loss of the Mother," *Psychoanalytic Review* 72 (Fall 1985), 403–19. In "Narrative Structure(s) and Female Development: The Case of *Mrs. Dalloway*," Elizabeth Abel describes the submerged narrative of *Mrs. Dalloway* "as a story of pre-Oedipal attachment and loss." See *The Voyage In: Fictions of Female Development*, ed. Elizabeth Abel, Marianne Hirsch, and Elizabeth Langland (Hanover, N.H.: University Press of New England, 1983), 161–85, 164. Woolf, says Abel, represents female development in terms of the daughter's loss of a "prelapsarian" world of female-centered relationships and her movement into the oedipalized realm of heterosexual bonds. Though my own analysis of the daughter's separation from her mother in the novels I discuss differs from Abel's in important respects, I am indebted to her rich and evocative reading of Woolf.

and personal development, calling into question some of the ways woman has been represented in psychoanalytic theory as well as literature.[3] By describing these rival fictions, I hope to set others in motion, to create a field of reverberation that will continue to generate new ways of interpreting and imagining.

I have chosen to discuss four novels, *The Greengage Summer, Annie John, During the Reign of the Queen of Persia,* and *Housekeeping* in terms of the following features: a garden setting and a more or less conscious allusion to the Fall; a focus on the mother-daughter relationship and the process of separation and loss; an adolescent crisis involving a confrontation with death.[4] These novels, with individual variations and emphases, tell similar stories of the daughter's separation from her mother, a transformation of her awareness of mother into (m)other, and an incorporation of (m)other into her own self-image. Whereas "mother" in this essay represents a fantasy of plenitude, an Edenic state of oneness with the body of the mother, "(m)other" represents that which cannot be appropriated by the child's or infant's desire and hence signals a condition of division or loss.[5]

That which cannot be appropriated, in my view, is also what precipitates the organization of a self, which in turn enfolds an awareness of absence, or, in Lacan's terms, "lack."[6] The novels I discuss treat the process of self-construction through that of mourning, or the decon-

---

[3]In *Alice Doesn't: Feminism, Semiotics, Cinema* (Bloomington: Indiana University Press, 1984), Teresa de Lauretis distinguishes between "woman," a product of Western patriarchal discourse, and "women," the historical beings whose subjectivity has yet to be defined and the terms of whose material existence remain largely undocumented. Although the novels I discuss in this essay cannot have escaped the discursive traditions that have shaped our conceptions of "woman," they modify them in the direction of representing "women."

[4]Joan Chase, *During the Reign of the Queen of Persia* (New York: Random House, 1984). Jamaica Kincaid, *Annie John* (New York: Farrar, Straus, Giroux, 1983). Marilynne Robinson *Housekeeping* (New York: Bantam Books, 1982). Subsequent references to these works within this essay are to these editions.

[5]I have borrowed this term, which signals the otherness contained in the figure of mother and, hence, her separateness or autonomy from her offspring, from the title *The (M)other Tongue: Essays in Feminist Psychoanalytic Interpretation*, ed. Shirley Nelson Garner, Claire Kahane, and Madelon Sprengnether (Ithaca: Cornell University Press, 1985). For a summary and analysis of the concept of mother-infant symbiosis which informs object-relations theory, see Nancy Chodorow, *The Reproduction of Mothering* (Berkeley: University of California Press, 1978).

[6]For a lucid exposition of Lacan's position on the construction of the ego, see Jacqueline Rose, "Introduction II," to *Feminine Sexuality: Jacques Lacan and the Ecole Freudienne*, ed. Juliet Mitchell and Jacqueline Rose (New York: Norton and Pantheon, 1985), 27–57. Mitchell, in the same volume, states succinctly, "A primordially split subject necessitates an originally lost object" (25). That the originally lost object is the mother seems clear in Freud's accounts, less so in Lacan's.

struction of "mother" into "(m)other." This process does not depend, as it does in Freud's and Lacan's accounts, on the intervention of the father, although it may include references to heterosexual relationships.[7] Rather, these novels, in rewriting the story of the Fall, present a revised account of the origins of consciousness and subjectivity, one that does not inevitably support a patriarchal definition of culture or the symbolic order. To elucidate these claims, I want first to consider some aspects of Freudian theory that threaten to undermine the phallocentrism of his enterprise at the same time that they act powerfully to sustain it.

The Son's Story

Freud's account of femininity leads him to a formulation of the mother's desire as a perfect complement to that of her son: "A mother is only brought unlimited satisfaction by her relation to a son; this is altogether the most perfect, the most free from ambivalence of all human relationships."[8] The oedipal boy's love for his mother, in this description, is returned in full, even unlimited measure. By sublimating her desire for a penis in her pleasure at having produced a son, moreover, the mother provides a gratifying reflection of infant male narcissism, creating a self-sufficient (and incestuous) unit that only the father appears to threaten. Absent the castration complex, the mother-son relationship offers an image of blissful union free of internal conflict or disruption. Stated thus, and removed from the context of Freud's troubled narration of female development, this construction reveals the mother's desire as wish fulfillment. What the mother desires is what the son needs from her, a love that revolves around his infant subjectivity, unconditional and presumably also immutable.

Viewed as a fantasy construction, Freud's statement that the mother

[7]Lacan, following Freud, postulates the paternal function in terms of a disruption of the mother-child dyad. The "name of the father" simultaneously oedipalizes the child and introduces him/her into the realm of cultural production. I am suggesting, rather, that the disruption of the mother-infant bond is internal to its dynamics and not dependent on the "interference," literal or symbolic, of the father. I have limited my own discussion here to the figurations of the novels under question. Needless to say, in my emphasis on the mother-daughter bond, I have neglected the various ways in which these novels represent paternity and heterosexual relations. I do not wish to suggest a consensus among these novels on these subjects, only to direct attention to the priority of the mother-daughter relationship and the independence of its workings.

[8]See Sigmund Freud, *New Introductory Lectures on Psycho-Analysis*, in *The Standard Edition of the Complete Psychological Works*, ed. and trans. James Strachey (London: Hogarth, 1953–74), 22:112–35.

finds "unlimited satisfaction" in her relationship with her son appears to function as a defense against the infant's anxiety regarding maternal loss. The prohibition against incest, then, by locating the condition of frustration in the agency of the father, protects a fantasy of maternal plenitude at the same time as it drives a wedge between the son and the object of his desire. The mother, in this construction, does not betray her son's infantile love. Rather, she acquiesces in the father's enactment of the oedipal drama, submitting to *his* law. As a result of the father's intervention, moreover, the son learns to separate the figure of woman into mother and object of desire.

This story has a twofold effect, I believe. It preserves an image of mother as a source of unambivalent, albeit asexual love, at the same time as it engenders a dark female double, the woman who is object of desire, unstable and often degraded. While the separation between these two figures may prevent one kind of patriarchal violence (the tragedy of Oedipus), it performs another on female subjectivity. Freud generally attributes this outcome to the workings of the castration complex, but some of his own writings suggest that his formulation of the oedipal drama acts as a screen for a deeper dread elicited in reaction to the preoedipal (m)other.[9]

In his essay "The Theme of the Three Caskets," Freud gives mythological priority to the figure of the mother. Arguing a structural resemblance between the choice presented to Bassanio in Shakespeare's *Merchant of Venice* and King Lear's confrontation of his three daughters, Freud maintains that the symbolism of three refers to the Fates of classical mythology. Pushing this analogy farther, he relates it to the judgment of Paris, claiming that Aphrodite, the goddess of love, once represented her seeming opposite, the goddess of death. He finds a source for this startling transposition in the ancient mother goddess

[9]Reviewing Freud's case histories, Iza Erlich concludes that Freud "could not bring himself to look closely at the mother." See "What Happened to Jocasta," *Bulletin of the Menninger Clinic* 41 (May 1977), 280–84, 284. Coppélia Kahn, in "The Hand That Rocks the Cradle: Recent Gender Theories and Their Implications," in *The (M)other Tongue*, 72–88, attributes this failure to the patriarchal construction of masculinity, which "depends on denying, in myriad ways, the powerful ambivalence that the mother inspires" (88). Similarly, E. Ann Kaplan in *Women and Film: Both Sides of the Camera* (New York: Methuen, 1983), says that "the domination of women by the male gaze is part of the patriarchal strategy to contain the threat that the mother embodies" (205). The most extensive (and philosophical) treatment of the repression of motherhood and mothering from Western patriarchal discourse appears in Luce Irigaray's *Speculum of the Other Woman*, trans. Gillian C. Gill (Ithaca: Cornell University Press, 1985). Irigaray reads Plato's fable of the cave as a fantasy of male self-authorship and, correspondingly, as a defeat of the womb.

worship of the East.[10] At the end of this essay, Freud makes explicit the connection between his reading of the triple goddess of antiquity and the infolded image of the preoedipal mother:

> We might argue that what is represented here are the three inevitable relations that a man has with a woman—the woman who bears him, the woman who is his mate, and the woman who destroys him; or that they are the three forms taken by the figure of the mother in the course of a man's life—the mother herself, the beloved one who is chosen after her pattern, and lastly the Mother Earth who receives him once more. But it is in vain that an old man yearns for the love of woman as he had it first from his mother; the third of the Fates alone, the silent Goddess of Death, will take him into her arms.[11]

It is not surprising that Freud should speak in the same breath of mother and beloved, who, after all, are divorced in imagination only by virtue of the castration complex. In the light of his idealization of the mother-son relationship, it is almost shocking, however, that he should reveal the hidden face of the mother as death. If the male subject typically splits his erotic impulses toward women on the basis of an earlier division between mother and object of desire, he almost entirely suppresses this third aspect of his responses to the woman who bears him. I suggest that the castration complex functions theoretically in Freud's system to shield the son from a direct apprehension of the radical otherness of mother, who not only does not simply mirror her infant's infatuation but whose power to withhold love appears to threaten his annihilation.[12] By neatly separating the aspects of the

[10]Freud was familiar with the work of Bachofen and Frazer. Here he seems to conflate the notion of a triple goddess with that of the goddesses of the fertility cults. It would not be surprising in this context that he would also associate the death of the goddess's son/lover with castration. If, in fact, this is the case, Freud's inability in *Totem and Taboo* to provide an adequate account of the place of goddess worship in his mythology of human development would seem to result from repression. What is significant here for my purpose is Freud's fleeting analogy between the figure of a triple goddess and the preoedipal mother, an analogy that he was not able to build on for reasons that I suggest in this essay. In my own reading of contemporary women's fiction, I adopt the analogy of the triple goddess because of its usefulness in describing the power inherent in the position of mother, a power that is for the most part contained or suppressed in patriarchal culture. My argument does not depend on a particular historical understanding of the relationship of matriarchy to patriarchy, nor does it rely for validation on the actual status of goddess worship in prehistoric societies.

[11]Freud, "The Theme of the Three Caskets," *Standard Edition*, 12:301.

[12]See, for instance, Dorothy Dinnerstein, *The Mermaid and the Minotaur* (New York: Harper and Row, 1976), which maintains that patriarchal social organization functions in part to defend against the fears aroused in the child by the awesome power of the preoedipal mother.

"triple goddess" and repressing the intimations of mortality contained in the memory of her flesh, Freud's oedipal theory effectively divides and conquers the preoedipal (m)other. Tamed and appropriated, she then serves the patriarchal order that declares her reproductive powers irrelevant to the production of culture.[13]

Freud's bad faith in regard to the preoedipal (m)other, however, betrays itself repeatedly in asides, footnotes, and occasional expressions of ignorance on the subject of femininity. It surfaces tellingly in his essay on the uncanny. Arguing that the perception of the *Unheimlich* refers to something familiar that has undergone a process of repression, Freud offers the following example:

> It often happens that neurotic men declare that they feel there is something uncanny about the female genital organs. This *unheimlich* place, however, is the entrance to the former *Heim* [home] of all human beings, to the place where each one of us lived once upon a time and in the beginning. There is a joking saying that "Love is home-sickness"; and whenever a man dreams of a place or a country and says to himself, while he is still dreaming: "this place is familiar to me, I've been here before", we may interpret the place as being his mother's genitals or her body. In this case, too, the *unheimlich* is what was once *heimisch*, familiar; the prefix *"un"* ['un-'] is the token of repression.[14]

Freud maintains in this instance that women's genitals appear uncanny or unhomelike because of repression. Earlier, however, he says that the word *heimlich*, like other primal words that contain antithetical meanings, designates not only what is familiar and known but also what is secret or concealed. *Unheimlich* thus appears as a split off meaning of *heimlich*. The process of "repression" involves the removal of ambiguity from the word, a failure to acknowledge its inherent double nature. The estrangement Freud speaks of in relation to the female genitals is thus not a secondary condition (as in the adding of a prefix) but an originary one. The body of the (m)other, both known and unknown, secret and familiar, provides the prototype of the uncanny.

Had Freud pursued his interest in the triple goddess of antiquity and his intuitions regarding the uncanny he might have arrived at some startling conclusions concerning the preoedipal (m)other as a figure who represents both home and not home, whose body is the site of both presence and absence, plenitude and loss. Instead, he circles around this

---

[13]Adrienne Rich lucidly details this process in her analysis of the "institution" of motherhood in *Of Woman Born* (New York: Norton, 1976). See also Irigaray's *Speculum*.
[14]Freud, "The 'Uncanny,'" *Standard Edition*, 17:245.

perception, preferring finally to preserve the fantasy of mother as the source of unconditional love and a focus of nostalgic longing. This choice, however disappointing, is not surprising, given the preexisting level of cultural support for it. Woman in the patriarchal imagination is typically divided according to the functions she is perceived to represent and in such a way as to idealize maternity. Despite Freud's own position as an agnostic Jew, his account of the vicissitudes of desire via the Oedipus and castration complexes parallels and reinforces the split encoded in Western Christianity between woman as asexual mother (Mary) and as erotic object (Eve).[15] The third and most terrifying aspect of the preoedipal (m)other, the autonomy of her desire, perceived by the infant as the threat of death, is frequently marginalized and scapegoated in the figure of woman as witch.[16] If I am correct in my reading of the son's story as one that acts to divide the image of the preoedipal (m)other in order to preserve a fantasy of maternal plenitude, then the story of the daughter, who stands to inherit her mother's position (culturally if not biologically) would seem to involve a different range of possibilities.

[15]Marina Warner traces the theological path that led to the Marian mythology of asexual motherhood and the concomitant opposition between the images of woman as either virgin or whore. See *Alone of All Her Sex: The Myth and Cult of the Virgin Mary* (New York: Vintage Books, 1983). Elizabeth Judd examines this opposition, which she terms "fair maiden and dark lady," in the development of courtly love rhetoric and in associated linguistic changes in Middle English in "Fair Maiden and Dark Lady: The Impact of Sexual Stereotypes in Modern English," in *Sprachwandel und feministische Sprachpolitik: Internationale Perspektiven,* ed. Marlis Hellinger (Opladen: Westdeutscher, 1985), 148–68. In an essay on Greek myth Ada Farber discusses the division of female functions into the categories of eroticism, nurturance, and mature capability. She regards this "segmentation of the mother" as a process that protects the male ego from castration anxiety. See "Segmentation of the Mother: Women in Greek Myth," *Psychoanalytic Review* 62 (1975), 29–47. The absence commented on here certainly extends beyond the realm of Greek myth. Jim Swan, in "*Mater* and Nannie: Freud's Two Mothers and the Discovery of the Oedipus Complex," *American Imago* 31 (1974), 1–64, describes the evolution of Freud's concept of the Oedipus complex as the outcome of his split image of mother into *mater,* his idealized and "pure" biological mother, and "nannie," the nurse whom he regards as the agent of his first sexual arousal and humiliation. By dissociating *mater* from nannie, Swan maintains, Freud not only preserves an image of asexual motherhood, he also avoids an acknowledgement of his own dependency in relation to a mother who has the power both to elicit his desire and to shame him. Finally, Susan (Contratto) Weisskopf, in "Maternal Sexuality and Asexual Motherhood," *Signs* 5 (1980), 766–92, describes some of the consequences for women of this cultural heritage, which encourages an internal split in the female personality.

[16]Barbara Walker is correct, I think, in her reading of the old woman as one who reminds us (in part) of death. See *The Crone: Woman of Age, Wisdom and Power* (New York: Harper and Row, 1985). In a patriarchal culture constructed on the denial of the mortality implicit in the condition of being born of woman, this figure will be subject to excoriation or ostracism.

Madelon Sprengnether

The Daughter's Story

Of the four novels I want to consider, *The Greengage Summer*, by Rumer Godden, is the earliest (1958) and in many ways the most conventional. The biblical structure, for instance, is most clearly articulated in this book, which portrays the understanding of good and evil as the outcome of a young girl's first awareness of the complexity (and, in this case, violence) of heterosexual relations. This general framework, however, only partially obscures a preoedipal counterplot, which involves a prior fall in the girl's separation from her mother, an event that contributes to an awareness of death.

In the beginning of the novel, the children of the Grey family function more or less as a group, united in their discontent with the quiet and uneventful character of their life. Irritated with what she perceives as the selfishness of her children, which she attributes to their lack of awareness of history, Mother (who is so designated throughout the novel) decides to take them from their home in England on an excursion to the battlefields of France. She seeks lodging, in particular, near the cemeteries. The moment they arrive in France, however, Mother is taken seriously ill, and she spends the rest of the novel in the hospital. Liberated from her protection, the children explore their new and (as they discover) dangerous environment.

Among the inhabitants of the hotel, there is an international jewel thief named Eliot, who takes the semiorphaned children under his protection in part to camouflage his secret activities. He is drawn, however, to the eldest girl, Joss, who begins in his presence to discover her powers of sexual attraction. Although he does not actively romance her, their mutual interest ignites sparks of rivalry and jealousy from his mistress Zizi and the servant boy Paul, who has his own designs on Joss. The younger sister, Cecil, narrates the ensuing painful events, involving her own near rape by Paul and Paul's murder by Eliot.

The novel focuses, through Cecil's narration, on her development from child into woman, which is set in motion by her mother's illness. "To wake for the first time in a new place," Cecil comments on her first morning at the hotel Les Oeillets, "can be like another birth" (31). It is also a death. The murder that climaxes the novel is prefigured by references to events of World War II in the carefully exhibited bullet holes that line the stairway, the blood stain (attributed to the death of an American soldier) in one of the bedrooms, and the skull in the garden, ritually dug up by the dogs Rita and Rex, who sniff out the piece of liver that is their reward. Paul himself is a product of the war, an illegitimate child abandoned by his mother during the American occupation. Through him, Cecil's experience of the French garden at the hotel Les Oeillets becomes inseparable from the experience of death.

Almost the first thing Cecil does on her first day at the hotel is to eat fruit from the garden. "Stepping in dew, my head in the sun, I walked into the orchard and, before I knew what I had done, reached up to touch a greengage. It came off, warm and smooth, into my hand. I looked quickly round, but no one came, no voice scolded and, after a moment, I bit into the ripe golden flesh. Then I ate another, and another until, replete with fruit and ecstasy, I went back to my post" (45). Her next observation, on encountering Eliot, makes the biblical allusion explicit. "I do not know, but, as if the first greengage had been an Eden apple, I was suddenly older and wiser and did not try to speak to him" (45). At another point, she refers to the time in England when life revolved around her mother as "our Eden world" (57). She also regards the arrival of her first period as "Eve's curse" (176). Early in the novel, moreover, Cecil makes the symbolic equation between garden and cemetery that emerges fully in the concluding events. When she notes that the battlefields they have come to visit are now covered with flowers, her sister replies: " 'Do the soldiers come up in the corn?' . . . but of course the soldiers were not there, except those who had been blown to pieces or rotted where they fell, 'like the soldier in the garden,' said Hester. . . . 'Mr. Stillbotham says the cemeteries are beautiful, like gardens, . . . Comme les jardins' " (69). Paul's rude reply, "Be a good boy, get killed in the war, Papa and Mama come see you in pretty garden" (69), causes Cecil to reflect on the possibility of her own death. "I could not help thinking of the skull, and the bullet holes; I wondered what it was like to be buried and not to be sitting in this pretty satin-papered dining room, eating the things the visitors ate, hors d'oeuvres and pâté, poulet à l'estragon, veal and steaks, salads and greengages, and I hoped I need never be dead" (70). Cecil's eating of the greengages seems to precipitate her into time and change, into an awareness of the biological processes that will inevitably entail her own death.

Joss's anger with Zizi, who interrupts her relationship not only with Eliot but also with the elderly painter who subsequently takes her under his wing, provokes her to flirt dangerously with Paul. Realizing that he intends to break into her bedroom at night, she appeals to Cecil for help. Cecil, who claims that she is not afraid of Paul, offers to take her place, believing that she can discourage him. Her bravado fails her, however, as she contemplates the depth of Paul's rage and the possible effects of his frustration at not finding Joss. Neither has she reckoned on Eliot's mysterious behavior or his cool capacity for violence. Although Eliot rescues her from a possible rape by pulling Paul from the ladder he

Madelon Sprengnether

has placed against the outside wall, he kills the boy to prevent him from
scotching his own plans involving burglary and escape. It is Cecil who
begins to unravel the skein of lies Eliot has woven to mask his illegal
activities, and it is she who discovers the body of Paul in the garden.
Following Rita and Rex, who are on the scent of something other than a
piece of liver, she first pauses in the orchard to eat some greengages. On
finding Paul's body among the leaves, she throws up. "Too many greengages," comments Madame Corbet, who discovers her somewhat later.
"I did not contradict her. I could not, I could only gasp and moan; and
she was right, it was as if I were trying to fling out Paul, Eliot, Les
Oeillets, all of it; a sudden rising of my stomach to my mouth in the
same way that the orchard had run up into the sky" (195).

Cecil cannot, however, expel her experience as easily as she can
disgorge the greengages. What she has learned has alienated her from the
girl she was and the world she now looks back on with grief and longing.
When Madame Corbet scolds her for being "too big a girl to eat so many
[greengages]" (195), Cecil inwardly protests, "I'm not big. I'm little, too
little," a refrain that runs through the end of the novel, uniting the
children in their desire for Mother. When Vicky bursts into tears,
wailing "I want Mother," Cecil joins her. "Mother. If only Mother were
here for us in this terror! But there was no one, no one for us, and we
quailed like little rabbits, chased and cornered, ready to be snared.
Helplessly we wept" (212–13). Finally even Joss breaks down. "Joss, dignified, aloof, almost grown-up Joss, crumpled like a little girl. 'Mother, I
want Mother,'" (215) she wails.

Summoned by a telegram from Eliot, the children's Uncle William
arrives to rescue them from their distress. Despite Eliot's criminal
behavior, however, the children remain loyal to him, refusing to divulge everything they know about his movements to the local inspec-
tor. Cecil and Joss, as the oldest girls, inherit their mother's world of
mixed emotions and problematic moral understanding. This drama
that separates them from their childhood also divides them from their
now idealized past. More specifically, they have lost Mother and all that
she represents. It is Mother herself who initiates this separation when
she insists that her children give up their insularity by visiting the
battlefields of France. In this respect, she implicitly denies the fantasy
construction of her as a locus of "unlimited satisfaction," as someone
who represents a state of gratification or plenitude.

The Greengage Summer, by couching its drama of mother-daughter
separation explicitly in the context of the Fall, diverts our attention
somewhat from the radical nature of its assumptions regarding female
development. The more recent novel *Annie John* reverses this pattern

308

of emphasis, muting the biblical framework to focus on the relationship between mother and daughter. Like *The Greengage Summer*, this novel represents self-formation as a deconstruction of the Edenic fantasy of mother-child union, at the same time as it problematizes the figure of mother.[17]

Annie John, an autobiographical novel by Jamaica Kincaid, is the story of a young black girl's coming of age on an island in the West Indies. The novel begins with Annie's first awareness of death, which coincides with anxieties and premonitions about abandonment by her mother; it concludes with Annie's departure at age seventeen for England. Annie's separation from her mother takes place in stages that include grief and terror, intense hostility toward her mother, lies and concealment of her activities, and transfer of her affections to other girls. The book culminates with an episode of severe illness in which Annie undergoes a final metamorphosis that gives rise in turn to a decision to leave the island. *Annie John*, like *The Greengage Summer*, moreover, is narrated retrospectively so that there is no time at which separation has not already taken place.

The novel opens with Annie's brief reminiscence of a time when death did not touch her personally. "For a short while during the year I was ten, I thought only people I did not know died" (3). Observing funeral ceremonies in the cemetery that faces their summer house one year, she learns from her mother that children are always buried in the morning. Until then, Annie comments, "I had not known that children died" (4). This sudden realization leads to even more disturbing knowledge, also conveyed to her by her mother. Annie fears the dead because she believes that they can pursue the living, causing them in turn to die. "My mother," she declares, "knew of many people who had died in such a way. My mother knew of many people who had died, including her own brother" (4). This piece of information is followed by the observation that a girl younger than herself had actually died in her mother's arms and that her mother had prepared the body for burial in a coffin built by her carpenter father.

Annie clearly associates knowledge of and rituals surrounding death with her mother, who, as a result, takes on a new and threatening

[17]Susan Suleiman problematizes the concept of mother-infant fusion by focusing on maternal desire in her essay "Writing and Motherhood," in *The (M)other Tongue*, 352–77. Judith Kegan Gardiner concludes a recent essay on psychoanalysis and feminism with the sage reminder that "mothers are all persons who resent being treated only through our needs." See "Mind Mother: Psychoanalysis and Feminism," in *Making a Difference: Feminist Literary Criticism*, ed. Gayle Greene and Coppélia Kahn (London: Methuen, 1985), 113–45, 139.

aspect. One day, Annie's fascination with death leads her to a funeral parlor, where a girl her own age is laid out for viewing by family and friends. When she returns home, having forgotten an errand for her mother, she lies about where she has been. This sequence of events establishes a pattern for the novel as a whole: Annie's growing distance from her mother, whom she perceives as a betrayer, her fears about her own survival, and the shell of privacy she creates through deceit, as a form of self-protection.

Annie's education concerning death is interspersed with anecdotes that describe a state of previous harmony between herself and her mother—a time when she considered her mother entirely beautiful:

> Her head looked as if it should be on a sixpence. What a beautiful long neck, and long plaited hair, which she pinned up around the crown of her head because when her hair hung down it made her too hot. Her nose was the shape of a flower on the brink of opening. Her mouth, moving up and down as she ate and talked at the same time, was such a beautiful mouth I could have looked at it forever if I had to and not mind. (19)

Annie also remembers with pleasure her mother's habit, when cleaning house, of airing the trunk with her baby things and telling her the story of her own life. She summarizes her contentment from that time, saying, "It was in such a paradise that I lived" (25).

Several incidents convey Annie's reactions to the loss of this state of imagined harmony. First, her mother refuses to continue to sew dresses for herself and Annie out of the same cloth; she tells her, "You are getting too old for that. . . . You just cannot go around the rest of your life looking like a little me" (26). Annie comments, "To say that I felt the earth swept away from under me would not be going too far" (26). On another occasion, when her mother refuses to look through the trunk with her, repeating that she is too old for such things, Annie again feels "the ground wash out from under" her (27). It is Annie's mother herself who denies their former intimacy, arousing Annie's suspicion and hostility.

Although Annie shifts the focus of her adulation from her mother to other girls, first Gwen and then the Red Girl, she continues to suffer from her sense of abandonment. A composition she writes for a teacher in her new school reveals the extremity of her feelings. Recalling her trips to the seashore where she would play in the water with her mother, then watch her swim from her place on the shore, Annie relates her terror once on losing sight of her: "A huge black space then opened up in front of me and I fell inside it. I couldn't see what was in front of me and I couldn't hear anything around me. I couldn't think of anything except that my mother was no longer near me" (43). Her mother, when Annie catches sight of her at last, is preoccupied and does not perceive her daughter's distress. It occurs to Annie at this point that she may never be reunited with her, and she retains this feeling despite her mother's later attempts to reassure her. In a recurring nightmare, she sees her mother out at sea sitting on a rock, only "my mother never came back" (44).

As if to confirm the truth of her nightmare, the rift between Annie and her mother, opened by Annie's awareness of death, widens as she moves into adolescence. Although she finds substitutes for her mother's love in the intensity of her friendships with Gwen and the Red Girl, she carries the terror of this first separation with her until it makes her ill. Increasingly, as she approaches this turning point, she imagines her relationship with her mother as a life-or-death struggle. In a dream, Annie finds herself chanting "My mother would kill me if she got the chance. I would kill my mother if I had the courage" (89). She begins to regard her mother as a "serpent" (52) and a "crocodile" (84) for her treachery.

If Annie begins her story fearful of the death of children, her anger with her mother for initiating this terrifying awareness generates wishes for her mother's death. But her sense of identification with her mother, who even bears the same name, inevitably links their fates.[18] Annie sees no escape from this dilemma and the profound ambivalence at its heart. Gradually her misery takes shape in her imagination as "a small black ball, all wrapped up in cobwebs," which, though "no bigger than a thimble," "weighed worlds" (85). Annie grows increasingly listless, until she seems to lose heart completely. Her illness, coinciding with an extended period of rainfall, climaxes the separation from her mother. At the end of it, she observes that the rain has ruined her mother's garden (127), and she resolves to leave her childhood home.

Annie's illness, which has no organic cause, first intensifies her state of conflict, visiting her with hallucinations, and then dissolves it, under the care of her grandmother, the obeah woman Ma Chess. In the early stages of her illness, she appears to regress, as if to recapture thereby the world she has lost. "I was fifteen years old, but the two of them handled me as if I were just born" (113). During this time, she also remembers an occasion when, after a disagreement with her mother, she had wished her dead. This memory causes further disorientation and seemingly bizarre behavior. Deeply alarmed, her mother finally summons her own

---

[18]Kincaid names her heroine after her own mother, Annie, as the dedication of her earlier book of lyric prose, *At the Bottom of the River* (New York: Aventura Vintage Library of Contemporary World Literature, 1985) reveals.

mother, the wise woman Ma Chess. Adept in spiritual matters, as well as the uses of herbal medicine, Ma Chess is the counterpart of Ma Jolie, on whom Annie's mother calls when she fears harm intended to herself or her daughter. "Whatever Ma Jolie knew," however, according to Annie, "my grandmother knew at least ten times more" (123). Annie's grandmother appears opportunely to take the place of her mother, thus relieving the love-hate struggle between them. Remothered by her grandmother, Annie finally emerges from the state of paralyzed conflict that threatens her life.

Ma Chess, who may be viewed as the crone aspect of the triple goddess, relieves Annie's dilemma, I believe, by altering her conception of death. No longer terrorized by the possibility of either her own or her mother's death, Annie reinterprets separation in such a way as to accept and internalize it. Ma Chess, who completes Annie's infantile regression, represents mother not only as origin but also as destiny. Commenting on Annie's father's occupation as a housebuilder, she says, "A house? Why live in a house? All you need is a nice hole in the ground, so you can come and go as you please" (126).

Ma Chess appears, seemingly out of nowhere, to evoke the uncanny, to loosen Annie's death grip on her mother, so that she can regard her simultaneously as home and not home. By problematizing the concept of mother, the fiction releases its heroine into a life of her own. However uncomfortable the awareness that she does not possess her mother's exclusive love, that the mother-daughter unit does not constitute a timeless Eden, Annie's new understanding of her mother is essential to her growing up. What she inherits, then, is something her mother already knows. "So now I, too, have hypocrisy, and breasts (small ones), and hair growing in the appropriate places, and sharp eyes" (133), Annie comments bitterly, momentarily oblivious of the fact that her own mother had arrived at a similar decision to strike out on her own at approximately the same age.

Annie's parting from her island home is balanced between the awareness that "I shall never see this again" (145) and her mother's assurance, "It doesn't matter what you do or where you go, I'll always be your mother and this will always be your home" (147). Both statements are true. The moment encapsulates the antithetical meanings of *heimlich*. Annie's sense of familiarity, finally, is inseparable from that of estrangement, and it is this perception that propels her toward the unfolding of her life.

The relationship between Ma Chess, the obeah woman, and the uncanny opens a space in *Annie John* for Annie's disengagement from her mother. In another recent novel, this function also devolves on an older woman, who, through her age and experience, bears the burden of life's mysteries. Joan Chase's *During the Reign of the Queen of Persia* portrays the gradual dissolution of the female-centered world of four young cousins, who spend summers together on their grandmother's farm in northern Ohio. Their dispersal is perceived as a fall, unequally survived by the four; for one, it is nearly fatal. The almost casual biblical allusion signals the inevitability of this loss, which the novel redefines as mother-daughter separation and mourning.

During the Reign of the Queen of Persia begins with an evocation of pastoral richness and nostalgia, which culminates in the following observation: "When we lived there, on the farm which was right on the edge of the city limits, we thought it the very center of the world, and the green and golden land and wooded hollows which began two blocks over from the railroad loop and then rolled off to obscurity formed a natural barrier to the rest of existence, which we dismissed as the outer darkness" (4). For a time, the four cousins, who luxuriate in this environment, hardly distinguish among themselves as separate personalities. "Uncle Dan treated the four of us the very same and sometimes we thought we were the same—same blood, same rights of inheritance" (5).

During the Reign of the Queen of Persia is remarkable in its use of a plural narrator "we." Although this device suggests a kind of prelapsarian fusion among the four cousins, I believe that the force and focus of the narrative is on division and loss. Like *Annie John*, this novel constructs a retrospective state of "innocence," but the narrative itself is motivated by an awareness of separation—the sine qua non, I would say, of consciousness.

In the first long sequence of the book Celia, the eldest, differentiates herself from the other three through her adolescent conflicts with her mother. Celia's precocious beauty and burgeoning sexuality are a source of alarm to her mother, who vainly tries to restrict her dating. The other cousins, who witness this struggle, regard it as a form of lovers' quarrel, in which both parties fight "for the sake of reconciliation" (36). On another level, however, they perceive that Celia's alteration signals for them as well a moment of irrevocable change.

On one occasion, following a particularly painful confrontation between mother and daughter, the remaining cousins contemplate what is happening to their world: "We were left in the kitchen with the black sea of night awash at the screens. Fireflies like flying phosphorescent fishes sailed through the orchard. Apples fell to their ruin. We could smell them softening in their own brine" (36). Although this passage clearly implies that Celia's movement out of her collective family

313

identity constitutes a fall, later parts of the book, relating an earlier period, locate this moment of schism in the death of Jenny and Anne's mother, Grace.

Grace's death from cancer, which focuses the narrative, also contributes to an essential awareness on the part of the girls about the fallibility and insufficiency of human love. In particular, Grace's death invalidates the vision of her sister Elinor, whose Christian Science evangelism denies the reality of death. At first, Grace, whose illness has already been diagnosed as terminal, responds to her sister's instruction, and the girls, too, hoping for a miracle, fall under her spell. As Grace's illness progresses, however, she begins to reject her sister's attempts at faith healing as misguided, turning against her, finally, in a rage: "Once Aunt Grace sat up and with more strength and fury than we could conceive of, shook off that soothing touch, screamed, 'Goddamn you. How can I ever get you to leave me alone? Just let me die. I'm begging you'" (204). Toward the end, Grace accepts the inevitability of death, as Elinor never can. The girls—torn between Elinor's high-minded and essentially well-meaning passion and the down-to-earth assessment of Gram, who brands Elinor's interference as "pride" and "meddling" (205)—opt finally for the latter, tragic understanding. In opposition to Elinor's categorical statement "love does not fail" (204), they set their own sorrowing conclusion:

> We could see how much she loved us. It was in her face as she gathered us into her arms, welcomed us into the enclosure of the full-flowing black coat with its downy cuffs and collar of ermine. She offered her strength to us, longing to lift us from grief into Life eternal. We could no longer follow her there. We didn't know about divine love, knew only an insufficient human love. But we let her comfort us, her throaty and musical voice, her russet eyes warm in the burrow of her furry coat, starlets of snow blown in her hair. (225)

Grace's death, placed as it is near the end of the book, seems to precipitate the dissolution of the family and the loss of the farm which conclude the narrative. In this way, the loss of mother (for two of the girls) becomes in a larger sense, symbolically, a loss of grace. The focus of the narrative shifts, correspondingly, to Gram, the crone figure, the one whose awareness encompasses the ravages of time and death.

Gram is indifferent to mothering in its conventional and institutionalized forms (not to be confused with lack of feeling for her children). In her minimal attentions to cooking and other household matters and her passion for the racetrack, she is clearly undomestic. At the same time, she is both the pivot and the mainstay of the household, a matriarch. "Gram was the queen bee—that was what Uncle Dan called her. That, or the Queen of Persia, the Empress herself" (5). Her unsentimental perspective on life and death, moreover, gradually achieves ascendancy. In the struggle between Grace and Elinor, she sides with Grace. "All's she wants is to go in peace. And quickly. It's over a year. Why in God's name won't Ellie leave her be? I can hardly stand it" (203). Witness to both her pain and her resignation, the girls perceive her almost as a figure of fate. "Gram stood, horribly aged within the folds of her skin and under the layer of her coat. The time she'd survived was like doom upon her head" (206). It is also Gram's vision that claims them. "So then we knew we were chained to Gram, having nothing more in us than what she was and hoped for" (206).

Gram provides for her wayward and hectic daughters in their living, through her perpetual open house, and in their dying, having bought burial plots for them all in the cemetery at the top of the hill. Her apparent equanimity in the face of the barn burning is characteristic of the long view she adopts. "Ain't no use to cry over spilt milk. It wasn't no good to us anyways. Not anymore" (259). Toward the end of the novel, Gram assumes something of the aura of Della's mother, the old black wise woman whom she consults for fortune telling. To the girls, Della's mother seems both fascinating and frightening, while Grace regards her, significantly, as a witch (255). In the following description, through her association with the uncanny, she appears as (m)other.

> Della's mother was so ancient-looking she might have been mother to the whole world, the burden of it wearing down her pigment to a milky-tea color and blinding her eyes. She was nearly bald except for random cotton bolls that sprouted. Her empty cheeks sucked themselves and we wondered if her clouded eyes even saw the light. We could stay with her only a moment. Just for a glimpse. It was too powerful a place to be; the fogging sweet-smelling smoke from the wood stove, ablaze even in summer, filled the cabin and presences beckoned through that haze, disturbing and suggestive, while the old woman, a worn quilt on her knees, sat expectantly. (255–56)

The girls imagine that Della's mother "had known all that was coming" (256). They attribute the same kind of understanding to Gram when she would eye them "and say significantly although enigmatically, 'Times change'" (257). Although Gram, by selling her land, is the one who literally dismantles the childhood paradise of the four cousins, her actions at this point assume an aspect of impersonality as well as inevitability. In this way, the ruin of the apples that attends Celia's adolescent rebellion, the death of Grace, and the cousins' loss of the "green and golden land" that is for them "the very center of the world," fuse into larger perceptions of mutability.

What is unusual about the Fall as it is reformulated in terms of mother-daughter separation in the novels under discussion, is that it does not scapegoat the woman. The associations that cluster around Eve in the Western patriarchal tradition, which make her responsible for sin and death and condemn her for debased sexuality, do not find expression here. Neither do these novels establish categories of pure and impure women. Instead, they reconceptualize the relationship between mother and daughter around a recognition of the estrangement at its heart, an infiltration of the uncanny that denies the dream of plenitude. Marilynne Robinson's novel *Housekeeping*, a radically revisionary text, reads almost as an allegory of this process.

Housekeeping, a prose poem in the form of a novel, traces the development of two sisters, orphaned by their mother's suicide and raised first by their grandmother Sylvia and subsequently by their aunt Sylvie in a remote town in Idaho called Fingerbone. The tone established from the beginning of this novel emphasizes alterity, as though the entire fiction were narrated from the other side of a looking glass. Ruth describes her grandmother, for instance, as someone who

> had never really wished to feel married to anyone. She sometimes imagined a rather dark man with crude stripes painted on his face and sunken belly, and a hide fastened around his loins, and bones dangling from his ears, and clay and claws and fangs and bones and feathers and sinews and hide ornamenting his arms and waist and throat and ankles, his whole body a boast that he was more alarming than all the death whose trophies he wore. Edmund was like that, a little. (17)

What Sylvia appreciates about her husband is his "otherness," his self-possession. When they would search the woods together for wildflowers, for instance, "he was as forgetful of her as he was of his suspenders and his Methodism, but all the same it was then that she loved him best, as a soul all unaccompanied, like her own" (17). If Sylvia seems strange, it is because she acknowledges an unbridgeable gap between self and other, self and the world. Early in her marriage, she had already concluded "that love was half a longing of a kind that possession did nothing to mitigate" (12).

When their grandmother dies, the two girls, Ruth and Lucille, find themselves in the care of two great aunts, who summon in turn their mother's sister Sylvie. Sylvie's distraction and unworldliness are even more remarkable than her mother's, and her manner of housekeeping decidedly unusual: "Sylvie in a house was more or less like a mermaid in a ship's cabin. She preferred it sunk in the very element it was meant to exclude. We had crickets in the pantry, squirrels in the eaves, sparrows in the attic. Lucille and I stepped through the door from sheer night to sheer night" (99). The two sisters, whom Ruth refers to, in their childhood, as "almost a single consciousness" (98), gradually move apart, divided by their adolescent development and their conflicting responses toward their aunt.

While Lucille mounts an aggressive campaign to conventionalize herself, learning to look and behave like other teenage girls, Ruth adopts Sylvie's unworldly habits and manners. Observing their likeness, Sylvie begins to include Ruth in her hitherto solitary wanderings. One day she takes her across the lake to a remote clearing in the woods and leaves her among the ancient ruins of a house to contemplate her wild surroundings. As the frost on the grass and trees begins to melt, Ruth imagines herself in a garden to which ghost children from the woods are attracted. This fantasy develops into a meditation on motherhood and mourning.

> Lot's wife was salt and barren, because she was full of loss and mourning, and looked back. But here rare flowers would gleam in her hair, and on her breast, and in her hands, and there would be children all around her, to love and marvel at her for her beauty, and to laugh at her extravagant ornaments, as if they had set the flowers in her hair and thrown down all the flowers at her feet, and they would forgive her, eagerly and lavishly, for turning away, though she never asked to be forgiven. Though her hands were ice and did not touch them, she would be more than mother to them, she so calm, so still, and they such wild and orphan things. (153)

This passage seems to recast Ruth's relationship to her own absent mother, as though the fact of loss itself were responsible for its special beauty. For Ruth, desire is born of mourning, and all the pleasure of having, conditional on not having.[19] "To crave and to have are as like as a thing and its shadow. For when does a berry break upon the tongue as sweetly as when one longs to taste it, and when is the taste refracted into so many hues and savors of ripeness and earth, and when do our senses know any thing so utterly as when we lack it?" (152).

Lucille's attempts to be like other girls, which finally precipitate her

[19]Juliet Mitchell formulates this paradox (which she derives from Lacan) in the following way: "The object that is lost only comes into existence *as an object* when it is lost to the baby or infant. Thus any satisfaction that might subsequently be attained will always contain this loss within it. . . . Desire persists as an effect of a primordial absence and it therefore indicates that, in this area, there is something fundamentally impossible about satisfaction itself." See *Feminine Sexuality*, 6.

break with her sister when she leaves to take up residence with a sympathetic schoolteacher in town, appear in Ruth's eyes as evasions of an essential reality. For Ruth, Sylvie's stance as exile expresses her own understanding of the world. Not to confront one's originary loss, in her view, is to condemn oneself to the deeper exile of what the world considers familiar and ordinary. In the wild solitude that Sylvie cultivates, on the other hand, there is another kind of consolation. In this state, Ruth recovers the sense of her lost mother, as she nearly catches sight of the ghost children:

> It is better to have nothing. . . . If I could see my mother, it would not have to be her eyes, her hair. I would not need to touch her sleeve. There was no more the stoop of her high shoulders. The lake had taken that, I knew. It was so very long since the dark had swum her hair, and there was nothing more to dream of, but often she almost slipped through any door I saw from the side of my eye, and it was she, and not changed, and not perished. She was a music I no longer heard, that rang in my mind, itself and nothing else, lost to all sense, but not perished, not perished. (159–60)

The development of Ruth's and Sylvie's points of view in the latter half of the novel is responsible for its radical alterity. As they move toward their decision to put "an end to housekeeping" (209) by setting fire to the house where they had lived, in favor of an openly transient existence, Ruth begins to give shape to her perception of life as necessarily haunted. Casting her meditation within the biblical framework of the expulsion from Eden and the final promised reunion, Ruth imagines the passage of human time as motivated by loss: "The force behind the movement of time is a mourning that will not be comforted. That is why the first event is known to have been an expulsion, and the last is hoped to be a reconciliation and return. So memory pulls us forward, so prophecy is only brilliant memory—there will be a garden where all of us as one child will sleep in our mother Eve, hooped in her ribs and staved by her spine" (192).

Housekeeping, as it deconstructs its title, deconstructs "mother." It is absence, the novel insists, that creates the dream of presence, a dream that must never be taken literally, since its fulfillment lies beyond the limits of human life.[20] The Fall, in this light, is that which is responsible for memory and desire, a moment of separation (like the death of

---

[20]Robinson's formulation of absence as the motivation for the dream of presence corresponds in some respects to Derrida's description of supplementation in *Of Grammatology*, trans. Gayatri Chakravorty Spivak (Baltimore: Johns Hopkins University Press, 1976).

Ruth and Lucille's mother) that precedes the beginning of narrative. "Memory is the sense of loss, and loss pulls us after it. God Himself was pulled after us into the vortex we made when we fell, or so the story goes" (194).

Robinson's use of biblical allusion and analogy expands the context of the novel in such a way as to depersonalize the dilemma of the two orphan sisters. Toward the end, in particular, Ruth embraces the kind of vision attributed to Ma Chess, Gram, or Della's mother. She becomes the voice of the uncanny. Adopting the perspective attributed by Freud to the triple goddess, Ruth surveys her origin and destiny, both of which derive their special character from the fact of her mother's absence. Ruth's otherness, what makes her side with the wild ghost children of the forest, is inherent in the human condition, a separateness that reaches back into the womb, to the beginning of life itself:

> Of my conception I know only what you know of yours. It occurred in darkness and I was unconsenting. I (and that slenderest word is too gross for the rare thing I was then) walked forever through reachless oblivion, in the mood of one smelling night-blooming flowers, and suddenly—My ravishers left their traces in me, male and female, and over the months I rounded, grew heavy, until the scandal could no longer be concealed and oblivion expelled me. But this I have in common with all my kind. By some bleak alchemy what had been mere unbeing becomes death when life is mingled with it. So they seal the door against our returning. (214–15)

Conception itself is responsible for the loss of oblivion which constitutes exile. Being, in this little allegory, is a product of time and memory, both of which weave their substance around absence. Plenitude, in turn, can only be imagined or dreamed by one who has already suffered a fall into human existence. Although the desire for "mother," like the desire for home, will inevitably arise, it is foolish, according to Ruth, to attach resentment to our biological mothers for the failure of such gratification: "Then there is the matter of my mother's abandonment of me. Again, this is the common experience. They walk ahead of us, and walk too fast, and forget us, they are so lost in thoughts of their own, and soon or late they disappear. The only mystery is that we expect it to be otherwise" (215).

Housekeeping is a peculiarly modern Book of Ruth, constructing a fable of the human condition out of the mother-daughter relationship. Rich in biblical allusion, the novel nevertheless refigures the meaning of its sources by dramatically altering their context. *Housekeeping* deals openly with an assumption implicit in the other novels I have discussed—the haunting of existence, which must of necessity divide mother from daughter and the daughter, in turn, from full knowledge of herself. To undo the repression in Freud's thought surrounding the figure of the preoedipal mother is to reveal the body of the (m)other as the site of the uncanny. To suppress what is secret or concealed in her, what is unfamiliar or strange, is, by the same token, to perform an act of psychological violence that falsifies not only the mother's role in relation to culture but also one's own.

On Behalf of the (M)other

If it is true that stories are created out of other stories in the seemingly infinite regress of culture, then it is no surprise that women writers should make use of one of the most powerful among them to deal with their own versions of the origins of consciousness. Because the Fall purports to explain basic facts of the human condition, it offers a convenient point of departure for fiction that seeks to do the same. By recasting this story in terms of mother-daughter separation, however, the writers represented in this essay not only redefine the range of meanings traditionally ascribed to this story, they also suggest some fundamental alterations in the psychic structures it encodes. By reversing the oedipal-preoedipal hierarchy that obscures the figure of the mother at the same time as it privileges the position of the son in Freud's account of sexual difference, these writers open a space for other versions of selfhood.

Though couched specifically in terms of female adolescent development, the fictions I have discussed are equally concerned with the autonomy of the mother's desire—also a matter of significance to the son.[21] For both, the deconstruction of "mother" into "(m)other" involves an awareness of absence, the unavailability of the wish-fulfilling dream of "unlimited satisfaction," and an acknowledgement of one's homelessness in the world. To repress this sense of estrangement, then, by implication infantilizes both partners in the mother-child relationship, contributing, on the one hand, to the domesticated ideal of motherhood that divides women against themselves and, on the other, to the splitting of erotic from tender feelings which plagues the male subject.

[21]Sarah Kofman, in her constitution of woman as enigma by virtue of her indifference to male desire, offers a revisionist interpretation of Freud's concept of female "narcissism." Kofman thus arrives at a formulation of female autonomy that resists the appropriation of the mother's desire in Freud's idealization of the mother-son relationship. See *The Enigma of Woman: Woman in Freud's Writings*, trans. Catherine Porter (Ithaca: Cornell University Press, 1985).

Finally, these novels suggest that such a repression derives its power and attraction from an attempt to avoid the awareness of death which finds metaphoric expression in the crone aspect of the figure of the triple goddess.

What Freud knew intermittently—in *Beyond the Pleasure Principle*, for instance, where he posits the death instinct as the desire of the flesh to return to its inorganic state—these novels express more openly. In the beginnings of life and the body from which we originate, we perceive our ultimate undoing. As Ruth states succinctly, "unbeing becomes death when life is mingled with it" (215). Thus, if we imagine our mothers walking ahead of us too fast and forgetting us, "so lost in thoughts of their own," it is because we know that soon or late they will disappear—as will we ourselves one day.

But this story is finally not so grim. If Freud is correct in his assumption elsewhere that the ego is the "precipitate of abandoned object-cathexes" (as I think he is), then the ego is an elegiac construct, a by-product of mourning, its very existence or presence due to an originary absence.[22] The indwelling of the uncanny which results from our displacement from the dream of plenitude that is "mother" is, in this account, responsible not only for our solitude but also for our very lives. It is loss, according to Ruth, that engenders the extravagance of desire, and desire in turn that leads us on. To embrace this condition, then, as Woolf describes Mrs. Ramsay doing in a moment of stillness when she momentarily sheds her maternal identity to focus on the otherness within, is also perhaps to free oneself for the "strangest adventures."

> For now, she need not think about anybody. She could be herself, by herself. And that was what now she often felt the need of—to think; well not even to think. To be silent; to be alone. All the being and doing,

---

[22]Freud, *The Ego and the Id, Standard Edition*, 19:29. Margaret Mahler, who posits an original state of symbiotic union of the infant with the body of the mother, emphasizes mourning as central to ego development. "The transition from lap-babyhood to toddler-hood goes through gradual steps of a separation-individuation process, greatly facilitated on the one hand by the autonomous development of the ego and, on the other hand, by identificatory mechanisms of different sorts. This growing away process is—as Zetzel, Winnicott and also Sandler and Joffe indicate in their work—a lifelong mourning process." See "On the First Three Subphases of the Separation-Individuation Process," *International Journal of Psycho-Analysis* 53 (1972), 333–38, 333. In a more deconstructive mode, Geoffrey Hartman, writing on mourning and representation in Wordsworth's poetry, suggests that "the psychic role of the lost mother could be . . . a fiction to ground a sense of betrayal arising with consciousness, or self-consciousness." See "A Touching Compulsion: Wordsworth and the Problem of Literary Representation," *Georgia Review* 31 (1977), 345–61, 357–58. From a somewhat different perspective, this statement could be taken to mean that "mother" has always been "(m)other."

expansive, glittering, vocal, evaporated; and one shrunk, with a sense of solemnity, to be oneself, a wedge-shaped core of darkness, something invisible to others. Although she continued to knit, and sat upright, it was thus that she felt herself; and this self having shed its attachments was free for the strangest adventures.[23]

[23]Virginia Woolf, *To the Lighthouse* (New York: Harcourt Brace, 1927), 55.

16

Marguerite Duras and the
Question of a Feminist Theater

Judith Roof

At the beginning of her short essay on theater, "Aller à la
mer," Hélène Cixous asks: "How, as women, can we go to
the theatre without lending our complicity to the sadism directed
against women, or being asked to assume, in the patriarchal family
structure that the theatre reproduces *ad infinitum*, the position of
victim?"[1] Cixous's question focuses on the forced patterns of identification in the endless replication of the oedipal scenario. Woman is
doubly doomed in theater, where the movement of the narrative and
the mechanism of spectacle position her as witness to her own destruction: she must identify with the masculine position or remain alienated, abet the objectification of woman or be victimized in resistance to
it, consume herself as commodity or starve to death. How does woman
watch or write theater in the face of such deeply etched patterns? How
can she avoid a complicity to market, cannibalize, and murder herself?
How does one feminize the theater?

As Cixous's question suggests, the problem of theater is linked to the
"problem" of psychoanalysis: the indelibly oedipal paradigm of theater
is also what Shoshana Felman labels the "specimen story of psychoanalysis."[2] While the oedipal myth provides Freud with the literary
model for the repressed love of mother and fear and hate of father which
he universalizes as a stage in individual development, psychoanalysis
itself is an oedipal quest for the origins of desire, identity, and subjec-

---

[1]Hélène Cixous, "Aller à la mer," trans. Barbara Kerslake, *Modern Drama* 27 (1984),
546.
[2]Shoshana Felman, "Beyond Oedipus: The Specimen Story of Psychoanalysis," in
Lacan and Narration: The Psychoanalytic Difference in Narrative Theory, ed. Robert
Con Davis (Baltimore: Johns Hopkins University Press, 1983), 1021–53.

tivity. The pattern of familial identifications which shapes both theater and psychoanalysis traces the path of theatrical desire in its oedipal quest and is replayed in the analytic situation, where transference and countertransference provide a functional version of these identifications, coupling theater and psychoanalysis in their attempt to reveal— to make spectacular—the ambivalent desire that motivates them. In both cases the woman, the hysteric, is the protagonist/actress whose desire must be brought to light, since it is the truth that generates her performance, her something-to-be-seen. The analyst is her audience, the spectator who looks with his ears, stripping her of a narrative history to bare her repressed desire, finding in the denouement the gaps that reveal the other scene, the unconscious. Seeing and naming the desire releases it; part of woman, it becomes a spectacle and commodity that circulates in gossip, in case histories, on stage, in criticism.

The inseparability of theater and psychoanalysis is based not only on theater's narrative manipulation of the specular but also on the oedipal nature of the mechanisms by which we read and identify with images. As Teresa de Lauretis asserts, "Any imagistic identification and any reading of the image, including its rhetoric, are inflected or overlaid by the Oedipal logic of narrativity; they are implicated with it through the inscription of desire in the very *movement* of narrative, the unfolding of the Oedipal scenario as *drama* (action)."[3] In theater, however, the amalgamation of the oedipal movement of desire and the spectacle provides in the very fact of their confederation the key to their disentanglement. Psychoanalysis provides a model for tracing spectacle through its originating path of desire as the relationship between the two is elucidated in the analytic relationship. By exposing and altering the relationship between desire and image as they are figured in the psychoanalytic analogue, it is possible to manipulate theatrical form so that it subverts the relationship between the movement of narrative desire and the spectacular objectification and commodification of woman. By disclosing the oedipal mechanisms of exchange and desire and by thwarting and interrupting the spectator's identification with the search for the desire of the other, it is possible to break the bond between desire and spectacle temporarily and to reveal it as a gendered project.

In French feminist practice, therefore, the theater, as a resisting, symptomatic form, has become an important genre in the continuing critique of psychoanalysis, and psychoanalysis has become central to feminist attempts to reform theater. As a creative feminist practice that takes account of theoretical analysis, theater has become the scene for a

[3]Teresa de Lauretis, *Alice Doesn't: Feminism, Semiotics, Cinema* (Bloomington: Indiana University Press, 1984), 79.

continued negotiation between feminism and psychoanalysis because of its general investment in spectacle, its community context, its generic resistance to alteration, and its obvious metaphorical connection to psychoanalysis. Even in theoretical explorations of the hysterical figure, theater has been an important "other scene"; the hysterical figure is discussed in overtly theatrical terms by Cixous and Catherine Clément in *The Newly Born Woman*.[4] Theories of the hysteric are retransferred to the theater as proposals for a different play of spectacle and desire in such plays as Cixous's *Portrait de Dora*.

At the nexus of the French feminist struggle to create a woman's theater, Hélène Cixous has actively sought to generate a sympathetic genre through the agency of her own plays, which join theory and praxis in a textual challenge. Asserting in her brief theatrical manifesto that feminist theater should undermine spectacle by ridding stage space of theatricality, privileging the auditory over the visual, ending distanciation, and replacing the text with one of "a body decoding and naming itself in one long, slow push,"[5] Cixous and other French feminist playwrights have begun to transfer to the theater the syntax of a woman's writing as articulated by feminist deconstructive critics. Based on a corporeality of difference (or a difference in corporeality), such a writing attempts to dislodge the primacy of the phallogocentric binary opposition of sameness by breaking down the hierarchy of presence/lack or what Luce Irigaray calls the "old dream of symmetry."[6] The development of a "feminine syntax" based on the body opposes, at least theoretically, a unified, monolithic logos; hence, Cixous's theatrical "body decoding and naming itself" opposes a traditional notion of unified theatrical action, single lines of identification, and individually distinct characters. In such a syntax, as described by Luce Irigaray, "there would no longer be either subject or object, 'oneness' would no longer be privileged, there would no longer be proper meanings, proper names, 'proper' attributes. . . . Instead, that 'syntax' would involve nearness, proximity, but in such an extreme form that it would preclude any distinction of identities, any establishment of ownership, thus any form of appropriation."[7]

The employment of strategies of women's writing has resulted in a theater that expresses simultaneity, as opposed to linearity, and multi-

[4]Hélène Cixous and Catherine Clément, *The Newly Born Woman*, trans. Betsy Wing (Minneapolis: University of Minnesota Press, 1986).

[5]Cixous, "Mer," 547.

[6]Luce Irigaray, "The Blind Spot of an Old Dream of Symmetry," in *Speculum of the Other Woman*, trans. Gillian C. Gill (Ithaca: Cornell University Press, 1985).

[7]Luce Irigaray, "Questions," in *This Sex Which Is Not One*, trans. Catherine Porter with Carolyn Burke (Ithaca: Cornell University Press, 1985), 134.

plicity, fragmentation, and segmentation, instead of unified wholeness, as Josette Féral demonstrates in her examination of the plays of Cixous, Sylvia Plath, Michèle Foucher, and Clare Coss, Sandra Segal, and Roberta Sklar.[8] While this solution typifies many plays by women, it fails to create a distinctly different theater; it flirts with but does not shift the relation between spectacle and narrative. In fact, the practice is not demonstrably different from the writing of many absurdist texts; women's writing *per se* is quickly resubjugated by the exigencies of desire and spectacle attached to the reading and interpretation of images, even though Cixous claims that such writing practices should undermine spectacle itself. Changing the subject matter and style of a piece does not necessarily alter the spectacular movement of desire, which operates separately from (but in collaboration with) style, distance, language, and mechanisms of identification.

For this reason, French feminists began to attack the oedipal shape of narrative itself by revealing the relations among the woman, history, and narrative desire, hoping that by subverting the narrative they could arrest the spectacle and interfere with mechanisms of theatrical identification. As Elin Diamond says in her examination of Marguerite Duras's *India Song*, Caryl Churchill's *Cloud 9*, and Simone Benmussa's *Singular Life of Albert Nobbs*, the "indictment of narrative history" accomplished in each of these plays reveals the nature of theatrical representation as the "recovery of a past narrative replayed for, and narrativized by, spectators in the present." A consciousness of the tactics of representation exposes the source of theatrical spectacle but leaves the "female subject, not transcendent yet not erased."[9] The metaphor of history Diamond employs is one way of assailing the integrity of the narrative, but it tends to neglect the question of spectacular investment except as a correlate to narrative, leaving the woman hanging, still a desired object in an uncertain but insistently spectacular stage space. Though the plays examine and critique narrative, narrative continues to attach inexorably to spectacle; the movement of desire is still a maneuver to see the object of narrative.

Hélène Cixous and Marguerite Duras investigate the relation between spectacle and narrative, introducing different strategies for a transcendent feminist theatrical representation via a theatrical/psychoanalytic analogue. Making use of both feminist syntax and a historical critique of narrative as they inform an overtly psychoanalytic

---

[8]Josette Féral, "Writing and Displacement: Women in Theatre," *Modern Drama* 27 (1984), 549–63.

[9]Elin Diamond, "Refusing the Romanticism of Identity: Narrative Interventions in Churchill, Benmussa, Duras," *Theatre Journal* 37 (1985), 285, 284, 286.

quest, Cixous's *Portrait de Dora* (1976) and Duras's *Véra Baxter* (1980) attempt to break down the link between narrative desire and spectacle. Cixous uses the figure of the hysteric and Freud's terminated case study of Dora as pretext and context for a feminist deconstructive revelation about the nature of theatrical spectatorship in *Portrait de Dora*.[10] Embodying her proposals for a feminist theater, the play splits and doubles characters, voices, and stage space by using a screen, projections, and off-stage voices. Portions of Freud's text are resituated and juxtaposed to fictional episodes, resulting in what Sharon Willis calls "an orchestration, a circulation of voices," created from a splintered narrative. Fragmenting the narrative and the unicity of its source disturbs the connection between narrative desire and spectacle, revealing their collusion with the spectator. As Willis concludes: "This is a *mise en scène* that places us within the scene as well, forces us to find our position mapped there. Disjunction of body and voice, and body and its image, exposes the reciprocal construction of the body as sign on stage and the spectator as subject for that sign, as gendered subject to whom it is addressed."[11] This play, however, still leaves the woman in an uncertain space—hysteria—though the term has been recontextualized. *Portrait de Dora* is feminist theater in active opposition and reference to a traditional theater as well as a still-masterful psychoanalysis. Spectacle and narrative have been scattered, rewoven; the play is a challenge, but a challenge trapped in its relation to the oedipal spectacle.

Marguerite Duras employs the Dora analogy as well, but as a pattern of exchange rather than as a topic. In *Véra Baxter*, subtitled *The Atlantic Beaches* (recalling Cixous's "mer"), Duras's basic strategy is to construct two simultaneous plays: a symptomatic oedipal quest with a shamelessly overt equation of money, desire, and woman, and a play of invisible and indecipherable noise, which remains hidden until the relation of narrative desire and spectacle is severed.[12] The first play acts as a decoy, luring the spectator into an economy of desire which conflates spectacle and analysis and exposes the theatrical commodification of female desire as well as the system of identifications upon which the transference and exchange of that desire is founded. The core of this analytic commerce, Véra does not easily reveal her own desire; rather, her silence and evasions are symptoms of unstable male identities who

[10]Hélène Cixous, *Portrait de Dora*, trans. Sarah Burd, *Diacritics* 13 (Spring 1983), 2–32.

[11]Sharon Willis, "Hélène Cixous's *Portrait de Dora*: The Unseen and the Unscene," *Theatre Journal* 37 (1985), 292, 301.

[12]Marguerite Duras, *Véra Baxter*, in *Dramacontemporary: France*, ed. and trans. Philippa Wehle (New York: PAJ Publications, 1986), 19–41. All subsequent citations will be to this version.

must seek a reassurance of wholeness and affirmation of their own desire as they reflect in her; she is their mirror. The exposition of this commerce is merely a front, which both obscures and enables the construction of Véra's own play within it. Though Véra is posed as the subject, she, too, is a decoy whose presence encourages a traditional investigation of her desire. While appearing to follow the spectators' attempts to plumb the secrets of Véra, the play unravels the circulating and interchangeable currents of exchange which equate Véra's desire and desirability, position this desire as the spectacle, and suggest that theater is the mechanism by which this desire can be seen. A second play, revealed only at the end when Véra's refusal to identify with the Stranger makes visible the metatheatrical machinations of the male characters, is a retrospectively comprehensible play of noise and interference which embodies notions of feminist textual dissonance and subversion while appearing to be a part of the stage environment. The apparently unlocated and shifting noise called "Outside Turbulence" is connected to Véra at the same time as the countertransference is abruptly terminated.

The Oedipal Lure

On the surface *Véra Baxter* seems a traditional search for desire, but even the quest drama reproduces—confesses—its own assumptions and supports. As in earlier plays such as *India Song* and *L'Eden cinéma*, Duras questions the metaphor of history, but here in a distinctly psychoanalytic trope. She situates the confluence of narrative desire and spectacle as an economic system that traps the woman as a commodity in an analytic and theatrical exchange, revealing the investment of narrative in spectacle and the audience's stake in the systems of exchange which make up traditional theater.

The lurid oedipal play in *Véra Baxter* consists of a circulating (psycho)analysis posed as an economic exchange, with Véra's desire at the center of the quest. Véra Baxter, a woman overly faithful to a philanderer, goes to the Atlantic resort town of Thionville in the winter to try to rent a summer villa. Following her there are Michel Cayre, whom Véra's husband, Jean, has paid to have an affair with her, and Monique Combès, formerly Jean's lover. Set in a hotel bar, the first two scenes concentrate on the history of Cayre, Véra Baxter's would-be lover, told first to Monique, then to an eavesdropping Bar Customer. In addition to Cayre's narrative of desire, the first two scenes introduce the unfinished history of the affairs of Jean Baxter, who telephones for Véra every fifteen minutes; a narrative about the failed history of the absent owners of the Colonnades who got a divorce and now must rent out their villa, the house Véra Baxter is trying to rent; the deception of Jean Baxter, who has already rented the Colonnades without his wife's knowledge; and suggestions about the romantic history of Monique and Jean. The Customer is the observer of and potential participant in all the histories; as the final analyst, he is the one who must hear the telling of all of the scenes he has not seen. The last three scenes of the play present Véra at the Colonnades. First Monique, then the Bar Customer, now referred to as the Stranger, meet Véra at the house, where each questions her in an attempt to understand the motives behind her unnatural fidelity, though Monique forces her to admit that she has indeed had an affair with a stranger. In scene 4 Véra recognizes in a telephone conversation with Jean that the marriage to which she has been so faithful is over. In the last scene, the Stranger tries to elicit Véra's desire by identifying with her, but she refuses the identification and she and the Stranger exit to an uncertain future. During the entire play a noise called "Outside Turbulence" has interrupted and played through the conversations.

Two related patterns emerge in this plot: first, a model of psychoanalysis and its transference and countertransference, which implicate the spectator, and, second, an economic model that equates money, desire, and the female object as the commodity of theater and psychoanalysis. The action of the play is much like a psychoanalytic scenario, consisting of the recitation of histories and analyses that function as displaced stages in a narrative quest for the revelation of Véra's desire. The recitation of the many histories situates both the Bar Customer and the theater audience in the place of the analyst, of Freud, who hears of the past exchange, a telling that is retold again by Freud in Dora and seen retold in *Véra Baxter*. The kernel of desire sought by Baxter in his creation of an adulterous scenario reverberates through the layers of seeing and telling which constitute the play, repeating the economy until the narration of personal history becomes the tool by which the characters (and the audience) continue to delve the desire of Véra. The narration of the visual is a way of interpreting, retelling, and recasting the essentially incommensurate phenomena of the spectacle and language when the origin of the perceptible symptom is what is sought by the verbal.

Like psychoanalysis, the dislocation of historical action into narrative in theater makes the narration of history the action by which affairs are revealed and cured. While Freud and the males in Véra's life have their "own view of the material under observation," their archeological

Judith Roof

quest to bring the secrets of their quarry's desire to light is a return to the theatrical process of Oedipus.[13] As Freud says when justifying his narrative methodology in "Fragment of an Analysis," "If it is true that the causes of hysterical disorders are to be found in the intimacies of the patients' psycho-sexual life, and that hysterical symptoms are the expression of their most secret and repressed wishes, then the complete exposition of a case of hysteria is bound to involve the revelation of those intimacies and the betrayal of those secrets."[14] Freud's explication of the "talking cure" embodies the relationship between seeing and telling; hysterical symptoms are visible, even theatrical, and are directly connected to the patients' hidden secrets, which can only be arrived at by "exposition," a word that means both seeing and telling, by which there is a "revelation"—a sight and insight. A narration that is at the same time a seeing is the means by which the theater of hysteria can be translated into a vision of the secret that generates this theater, a secret connected to the desire of the woman, which must be seen in order to certify one's own desirability. The relation of the analytic model to the quest to see is a literal playing out of the less visible impress of oedipal desire upon narrative. Exposing the project of narrative as the subject of theater implicates the stage analysts and the audience and sets the stage for the explosion of the analytic economy so dependent upon the constant deferral of a woman's desire. When the economy is brought into view and the woman is shown to have no desire, the quest becomes hollow, a quest for the sake of desiring, exchanging, controlling.

Caught in the Act

The multiplication of "analytic" audiences, from the Bar to the Stranger to the theater audience itself, dissects the mechanism of watching a play and resituates it as a kind of entrapment in the economy of desire which is intrinsic both to the characters' lives and to the circulation of delayed spectacle inherent in Duras's theater. The play creates and reflects a model of desire which operates like a perverse

---

[13]Sigmund Freud, "Fragment of an Analysis of a Case of Hysteria," *The Standard Edition of the Complete Psychological Works* (London: Hogarth, 1953–74), 7:7–122.

[14]The word *exposition* is taken from *Dora: An Analysis of a Case of Hysteria*, ed. Philip Rieff (New York: Collier, 1963), 22. The translation in the Collier edition is different from the Strachey translation in *The Standard Edition*, which translates the word as "elucidation" (8). This word is revealing, perhaps, in another way, but it does not combine the connotations writing and seeing as the word *exposition* does.

psychoanalytic session in which the analyst characters seek not to cure the patient but to fulfill their own desires by identifying with the scene behind the recital of desire. Replicating in its shifting triangles the relation between audience and stage, *Véra Baxter* exposes spectator identifications with stage characters as instances of metaphorical countertransference, the projection of emotions having to do with the spectator/analyst's past onto characters in the play who are questioned or "analyzed." Revealed by the analysis undertaken by the characters in the play, the interrogator's projections are made evident. From the "superior" vantage point of the theater audience, tricked into an illusion of mastery by the metatheatrical dissection on stage (as the Customer/Stranger is tricked by his own assumed distance from the story he overhears), Véra's case appears to be coherent and unified, though this coherence is a result of the misleading countertransference at play in the audience's desire for narrative integrity and wholeness.

Because the analysis is interrupted and incomplete in the play, the theatrical analyses of Duras's characters catch the audience/analyst in the fantasies of their unrecognized countertransference or unconscious reactions to the elicited narratives of the characters. Like Freud's Dora, the character Véra terminates the questioning, refusing offered identifications and acting as a disruptive agent for the truth of desire as constantly displaced, never fulfilled, and endlessly circulating, like Jean Baxter's money or errant phallus. For the Stranger the question of Dora's desire is a question of her sexuality, of what she wants, but it is simultaneously a question of what he wants. The Stranger wants Véra to transfer her desire to him; in seeking to evoke transference, he reveals his own countertransferred desire to be desired by her, and Véra, in terminating the conversation, leaves him there, exposed. Like Freud, the Stranger can be read in his own gaps as Jacqueline Rose interprets Lacan's reading of Freud:

> The question of feminine sexuality brings with it that of psychoanalytic technique. Thus by insisting to Dora that she was in love with Herr K., Freud was not only defining her in terms of a normative concept of genital heterosexuality, he also failed to see his own place within the analytic relationship, and reduced it to a dual dimension operating on the axes of identification and demand. By asking Dora to realise her "identity" through Herr K., Freud was simultaneously asking her to meet or reflect his own demand.[15]

---

[15]Jacqueline Rose, "Introduction II," in Jacques Lacan, *Feminine Sexuality: Jacques Lacan and the Ecole Freudienne,* ed. Jacqueline Rose and Juliet Mitchell, trans. Jacqueline Rose (New York: Norton, 1985), 35–36.

The male characters, the audience, even Monique all ask Véra to reflect their demands and their illusions of wholeness. Revealing the termination of analysis on stage exposes the countertransference of the characters as well as that of the audience.

A Prostitution Economy

The exchange model in which woman is the one commodity both supports and undermines the analytic project of the oedipal narrative. A translation of woman into commodity, according to Luce Irigaray, is symptomatic of representation as well as of an oedipal movement of narrative desire.[16] Revealing the emptiness of this exchange as a kind of crass titillation encouraged by constant deferral, however, reduces analysis and the desire it seeks to a mechanistic operation of a trade in equivalents. The commodification of Véra in the play's mimesis and in the structure of theater itself recasts the psychoanalytic quest for desire in economic terms. Making desire itself a commodity that is both the root of the problem and origin of a "cure" creates a narrative economy with exchangeable multiple products rather than the "truth." The presence of this second analogue dismantles the psychoanalytic model and resituates it at the heart of a theatrical project that has also lost its noble cause.

The money/desire economy represented within *Véra Baxter* begins with Jean Baxter, who exchanges money for renewed desire, sells his wife to regain his desire for her, and when he seeks to satisfy his desire elsewhere, pays for it by sending his wife money. Since Véra Baxter can "only be known through desire . . . outside of marriage" (29), the absent Jean Baxter tries to stage this desire to renew his satiated lust. Paying Michel Cayre to seduce his wife, Baxter hopes that selling her desire to another man will make her again desirable, for she will then be literally the object of desire of another. As the play only reveals Jean Baxter's desire/money economy through the telling of it, so Jean Baxter can only generate desire for his wife by means of the report of her staged infidelity—theatrically. To have desire he must imagine an identification with the desire of another. Véra is the price of her husband's desire, as was Dora, who, Freud says, "used to be overcome by the idea that she had been handed over to Herr K. as the price of his tolerating the relations between her father and his wife."[17]

---

[16]Luce Irigaray, "Commodities among Themselves," in *This Sex Which Is Not One*, 192–97.

[17]Freud, "Dora," *Standard Edition*, 7:34.

The infatuation of Cayre, the buyer, with Véra is a clear equation of money and desire; he becomes interested in a woman whose desire may be purchased at so high a price. In his narration to the Bar Customer, he reveals his uncertainty about his own role as a commodity purchased by Jean Baxter, but he also reveals that for him, too, money and desire are interchangeable. He admits that Véra "isn't even beautiful" (25) and attributes his attraction to her to the money. The combination of money and desire is too heady for Michel; knowing he has lost her from the first, he is seduced by her lack of desire for him and by the balance of the commodity value of two million francs owing in desire, in performance, in suffering. He says that he "tried to make up" for his exchange of money and desire, but he nearly admits that the attempt was probably an attempt to "get power" (25), an admission the Bar Customer actually makes for him by finishing his sentence and so taking his place in the economy.

Véra, however, is the one who completes the exchange. In the final scene, she tells the Stranger that Michel had "felt like meeting me because of the amount I was worth: two million francs" (36). The final cycle of Jean's plan is revealed in Véra's narration of his telephone call (parallel to the crucial call in scene 4) to her during her affair with Michel: "I asked him [Michel] if Jean Baxter knew what time it was supposed to happen. He said he didn't know. In the afternoon, at Michel Cayre's, there was a phone call. (*Pause*). I heard a scream ... The person on the phone, then they hung up ... a man" (36). Not only do the Stranger and the play's audience learn that Véra has been aware of her commodity status, but we hear the denouement, the final stab of Jean's desire narrated secondhand through Véra as she hears it through Michel's phone, which, like Michel, is merely an instrument of exchange. Véra becomes literally the vehicle of Jean's desire, conveying it and revealing it in the last scene of the play.

In this economy, desire, woman, and spectacle are interchangeable and ultimately evasive. They merely stand in for something else—the phallus, the something-to-be-seen. As stand-ins, they are displaced scenes—theaters—where the oedipal investment is expected to pay off in a reinforcement of a phallic identity on the part of the spectator. This phallic compensation brings into sharp focus Cixous's original complaint of alienation or complicity as it disentangles from the body of woman the surge of narrative desire which is preeminently phallic. Narrative desire is the search for a unified phallic certainty accomplished at the expense of the woman and driven by the desire to recognize that phallic wholeness reflected back from the woman. *Véra Baxter* denies this theatrical mirror of recognition by dismantling it, replacing it with a shifting set of lies that reveal the desire of the spectator on stage as well as in the theater. The mirror turns back on itself, dissecting and fragmenting the mechanism of desire and revealing the sexually differentiated roles of spectator and spectacle and the connection of those roles to a narrative model motivated by desire.

This desire is, as Lacan defines it, "the desire of the Other," and the gaze by which this desire is seen, operates in a "descent of desire" in which the "desire of the Other" becomes "desire *on the part of* the Other, at the end of which is the *showing (le donner à voir)*."[18] Theater, as the spectacle of telling, plays in the descent of desire, flirting with the showing of it. Seeking the desire of the other is seeing the truth of self as it is reflected back by the other, the subject created "within a split—a being that can only conceptualise itself when it is mirrored back to itself from the position of another's desire."[19] The characters in *Véra Baxter* who want to trick this desire and bring it to light seek to find their own desire as an analyst might inadvertently seek his own desire in a countertransference. But the desire of the other can never be seen since it "has no content as such. Desire functions as the zero unit in the numerical chain—its place is both constitutive *and* empty."[20] Thus, theater operates on the continual seduction by a desire to see or be the desire of the other, which cannot be seen. The search to be/see the desire of the other results in a circulating or shifting mirage that the other's desire, identity, satisfaction may be found somewhere other than where one is looking. The need to constantly look elsewhere forces a circulation; thus, Oedipus looks everywhere to solve his own riddle and the characters in *Véra Baxter* treat the desire of the other as a commodity, the trading of which veils with money and lies the loss that constitutes desire.

At the level of sexual division on which *Véra Baxter* is constructed, "the phallus—with its status as potentially absent—comes to stand in for the necessarily *missing* object of desire."[21] Money is the phallus that circulates as the men's answer to Freud's question "What does woman want?" While for Véra, her husband Jean's absence creates a literally missing phallus, all the characters and the audience are situated in relation to the missing object: the play "becomes a structure revolving around the question of where a person can be placed in relation to his or her desire. That 'where' is determined by the castration complex."[22]

[18]Jacques Lacan, *Four Fundamental Concepts of Psychoanalysis*, ed. Jacques-Alain Miller, trans. Alan Sheridan (New York: Norton, 1981), 115.
[19]Juliet Mitchell, "Introduction I," *Feminine Sexuality*, 5.
[20]Rose, *Feminine Sexuality*, 32.
[21]Mitchell, *Feminine Sexuality*, 24.
[22]Mitchell, *Feminine Sexuality*, 24.

Véra's ultimate destruction of this phallic economy is a kind of theatrical castration that dissolves the relation between narrative desire and spectacle dependent on the denial of castration. That Véra's final refusal to reflect takes place at the point of commerce called Les Colonnades is a reminder of the phallic nature of the exchange within a phallic environment.

Coming Back from Far Away

The exposed play of the phallus in the oedipal narrative of this outer play is no different from the critique of the metaphor of history in *India Song* except that it exposes itself in the very terms of its investment. The innovation of *Véra Baxter* is Duras's use of this oedipal narrative as a lure that enables another play—Véra's play—to evade spectacularization. By allowing the oedipal narrative to exist in its most symptomatic form, Duras effects not only an exposure of the relationship between spectacle and narrative but also a revelation of the relationship between the visibility of the oedipal and Véra's apparently unintelligible play of noise, which only emerges as coherent when the oedipal alliance to visibility is broken. The dissociation of the oedipal narrative and the spectacle occurs both as a result of its exposure and its unreliability (it is a false quest) and also because it is juxtaposed to and infected by another kind of theater—a theater of sound and body—which exists in defiance of the oedipal narrative but whose existence is enabled by the oedipal, since it plays in the gaps, slips, and destruction of it.

To interrupt this oedipal narrative, Duras appeals to psychoanalysis for another analogue—the Dora model—to suspend analysis at the point where it most implicates the countertransference of the spectator. Véra, like Dora, subverts this cycle of desire by terminating it while it circulates through the spectator; it is an interruption like that in a game of musical chairs which reveals that what has been seen as her desire is really the spectator's desire, a revelation that frees her for a moment from the equation of desire and commodity. Like Dora, whom Hélène Cixous sees as stealing "their little investments" and slamming "their door," Véra is "the name of a certain force, which makes the little circus not work any more."[23] Truncated, castrated in its course by Véra's refusal of the Stranger's offer of identification, the phallic lure of the analytic history collapses, revealing another theater playing audibly but invisibly in its gaps. This other play is a theater of hysterics "com-

---

[23]Cixous, *Newly Born Woman*, 99, 157.

ing back from far away,"[24] a theater of sound and body—voices, turbulence, ocean—a witches' theater not in resistance to but different from the analytical model, a theater of sound rather than sight, symbolized by Véra's relation to the "Outside Turbulence."

The breach in the oedipal veil retrospectively reveals this other kind of theater at the point where the Stranger attempts to see Véra's desire. In scene 5 he comes to the Colonnades and confesses that he has been audience to both Véra and Monique's conversation and the telephone call with Jean. Becoming the substitute analyst, as he did in scene 2, the Stranger is drawn to Véra, the apparent victim of the economy, but wants, under the guise of his sympathy, to be included in the exchange of desire as he has been included in the exchange of narrative. Claiming he was attracted by recognition of her name, a name he connects to one of Michelet's witches in another history, the Stranger attempts to provoke recognition from Véra. What she does see in the Stranger is that he might, like her, "at one point" have wanted to die (41), and with this identification she appears to begin a connection with him. When the Stranger responds, accepting the transference and admits, "That's one possible identity (*pause*) I might hold on to, for you" (41), Véra only responds: "The electricity's been turned off. (*No response from the Stranger*) We'll close up..." (41). Véra appears to have lured him by suggesting their mutual identification with death, and the Stranger is caught in his overeagerness to establish a link with her. The recognition of death frees Véra from the economy as it reiterates the fate of her marriage and of her lover, who has died in an accident; it is the recognition of the death of her desire. As she says, "I don't know how to want anything anymore" (40). The Stranger is entangled in his own trap of death and desire, having forgotten that Véra, like the witches to whom he compares her, occupies her own world and her own discourse. The exchange cannot be made. The audience/Stranger is caught; the character Véra is cured.

Véra's resistance, slight and enigmatic as it might be, is enough to bring the subversive second play to light, precisely as the lights on stage "go out" and illuminate a distant scenery house which has been the source of the Outside Turbulence in scenes 3 through 5. The hint of another play, a play of resistance, invites a retrospection that illuminates the role of the Outside Turbulence and Véra's barely mentioned infidelities and the significance of Véra's connection with the witches. Although a misleading countertransference can set "off the whole pro-

---

[24]Cixous, "Mer," 69.

cess again,"[25] in *Véra Baxter* the process restarts as a recognition of the "other scene," of the symbolic relation of difference as a structural fact in the play, replicated in the location of Véra's theater, which has played on within the lure of the oedipal search. Undoing spectacle, this other play is organic and subversive, quite literally speaking in the gaps and silences of the conversations, commenting on the circulation—the commercialization—of truth, generalizing desire, merely wanting. *Véra Baxter* is like the magic act that works by tricking the audience into focusing its attention on a disappearing coin while the magician prepares to pull a rabbit out of a hat; in the magic act we never hear the noise of the rabbit.

In *Véra Baxter* the noise is continually present in the Outside Turbulence; the struggle to escape becomes the real audible play that accompanies the magician's prestidigitation. Recalling Cixous's theory that theater should go "beyond the confines of the stage, lessening our dependency on the visual and stressing the auditory,"[26] the noise of the Outside Turbulence brings the unseen parts of the stage into play and simultaneously evokes foreground and background. An additional layer of witness which constantly interrupts and challenges the monolithic search for desire in the oedipal narrative, the "Outside Turbulence" is a kind of group noise (like that of an audience or the weather) which is not insensitive to the import of the characters' narrative revelations. Personified sound, the performance of the Outside Turbulence is orchestrated so that it, the witness behind the stage, is made to comment on the characters' claims to truth. When the Customer comments in scene 1, "They wouldn't have gone to so much trouble (*smile*) to lie if it weren't to protect ... something else ... for example ... some sort of ... truth ... some feeling" the "Outside Turbulence grows more audible, harsh, ironic. It is commenting ironically on the 'truth' in question" (23). Since it only materializes in sound and since its volume rises and falls, making it appear to enter and exit, it constantly undermines the spectacular nature of the theater on stage, diverting attention from the visual and drawing attention both to the absurdity of the characters' claims and to the act of watching. As a non-character and unattached sound, the Outside Turbulence appears to be random personified subversion until Véra refuses the advances of the Stranger in scene 5. At that point the connection between the turbulence and Véra is clarified: as Véra fails to respond to the Stranger's offer of identification, the Outside Turbulence wanes, becomes silent, as if its real function has

---

[25]Jacques Lacan, "Intervention on Transference," in *Feminine Sexuality*, 71.
[26]Cixous, "Mer," 547.

been to represent Véra. As audience, the Outside Turbulence has been set against the Stranger, against the voyeuristic consumption of desire throughout the play. In this way the Outside Turbulence becomes part of a competing play from Véra's side, which literally invades the other play as sound instead of participating as a distanced witness or voyeur. The Outside Turbulence sets up another audience that speaks to us through the space of the play and documents the sounds of the struggle of the escape from the economy.

Before he offers death as a basis for identification, the Stranger tries to exert control over Véra by linking her with medieval witches. His story of the witches on the Atlantic coast is a veiled threat and inadvertent wisdom; though he attributes their "talking to the trees, to the sea, to the animals in the forest" (40), to the absence of men, Véra's question, "Were they burned?" (40), is more to the point. As the Stranger admits it, he adds, "One of them was called Véra Baxter" (40), thus connecting her to the witches and to death. His allusion to witches is an exact description of the play, materialized in the Outside Turbulence, that has gone on while "the husbands were almost never there," were off fighting in the crusades as Jean and Michel fight their own economic crusade in an attempt to conquer and colonize Véra's desire. The Stranger's allusion to medieval witches is an allusion to women outside the circle of commodity, whose husbands have gone to the crusades and left them alone talking to and through the "Outside Turbulence." The obvious comparison of Véra to the witches is the Stranger's threat to keep her within the economy; yet he is also perilously close to understanding the "other" drama that has played. Véra's play, like that of the witches, has been with the trees and the noise, on an axis other than the visual, in an economy that shows only in the symptoms resulting from the clash of the two plays. Thus, the silences, the sounds of the oceans, the wind, and the trees talk back in the Outside Turbulence. In these sounds, Véra's past actions are read and predicted as one would read an archeological site after the death and burial of a civilization. Hers is a play in hysterical form manifested in the gaps but, like the unconscious, a force nonetheless. Véra, the witches, make things run, generate power that must always be examined and tested to be brought under control.

As an example of the "political gesture" urged by Cixous in "Aller à la mer," *Véra Baxter* proposes a way to put theoretical suggestions for a feminist theater into practice. While projecting how a feminist theater might work, Duras's metatheatrical dissection of the audience-stage relationship and the establishment of the subversive relationship between Véra and the Outside Turbulence actually creates a microcosmic vision of the relationship between a modern but Aristotelian and oedipal theater, in which woman is situated as spectacular object, and a feminist theater, which operates to subvert and alter the first model. Using the desire inherent in the oedipal model as a lure, the feminist theater coexists, operating in the gaps until in Véra's refusal it deprives the machine of the desire necessary for its operation and closure. In this oedipal environment, however, the feminist theater operates in the position of the unconscious, repressed but never eliminated or mastered by the other form.

Can woman speak, like the unconscious, only from the slips and gaps in an oedipal fabric that reclaims all to its own movement of desire? Is her representation to be only in terms of her unrepresentability—in the rebellious act of failing to provide something to be seen by the frustrated male gaze and in shifting from vision to sound, foreground to background, logos to a field of undifferentiated being? Like Cixous's question about the position of the spectator, the question of the performance is bound by oppositions that, as parts of representation, merge rather than produce difference. Only, it seems, in the moment of subversion does difference exist before the comprehension of its difference winds it back into the machine.

Exploiting the oedipal coincidence of theater and psychoanalysis provides another pretext for dismantling spectacle, but even this tactic relegates its critique to a dependent position. The exposure of the prostitution economy of theater and psychoanalysis indicts and reduces them, but it still plays within a realm of commerce as a kind of feminist consumer's advocate. Psychoanalysis embodies the problem, but the deconstruction of psychoanalysis cannot provide the solution, except insofar as it produces the gaps through which an other representation might slip. By providing in theater a spectacular decoy, however, Duras plays a psychoanalytic game that fools and misleads the gaze so that the unseeable might for a moment be seen.

The prognosis, then, may be dubious for a purely feminist theater but promising for theater itself, which benefits from the feminist psychoanalytic exposure and critique of its assumptions as it did from the critique made by Bertolt Brecht. It may seem that women's theater is doomed to its dependent and ambivalent relationship with the oedipal spectacle. "In the rustling darkness of a theater," says Cixous in 1984, after more experience, "even enemies make contact, savouring or suffering the same blindness, opponents recognize one another as being equally moved and threatened by the unknown; they huddle together,

Judith Roof

and before or during their battles, they also love one another."[27] Perhaps a feminist theater can move beyond this ambivalent sameness in the face of the spectacle. Though it may only exist in relation to tradition, through its decentering of the visual, its privileging of sound, and its trick of the decoy, the satisfying wholeness of the image in the theatrical mirror may be fragmented by the awareness coming back from the other side of difference.

[27]Quoted in Jeannette Savona, "French Feminism and Theatre: An Introduction," *Modern Drama* 27 (1985), 542.

Postscript: A Brooding Omnipresence

Judith Roof

> I don't mention the unmentionable, unimaginable, looming item which
> has dominated this conference at all.
>
> Carol Neely, 3 May 1986

This brief postscript examines selected comments, slips, and asides made during the oral presentation of the essays included in this volume and which arise on the margins of this printed text—on the vocal side of the opposition between voice and text. These verbal eruptions best illustrate and enact the problematic relationship between a "master discourse," such as psychoanalysis, and the less organized and systematic positions of feminist theory. As the texts were read and disturbed by the unpredictable voices of the speakers, that which was inside and unconscious was suddenly audible and overt, creating discord and inconsistency in the intended flow of logical argument, becoming a competing part of the text/context which both enabled and suppressed this other text. In danger of being omitted or silenced by the conventions of publication and academic communication, the remarks and slips originally ingrained in the live event are symptoms that reveal the truly unsettled nature of a superficially sedate and professional colloquy in which every effort was made to negotiate a cooperative and open-minded peace between disparate points of view. Carol Neely's deliberate omission of a key Lacanian term, as the only overt refusal to employ psychoanalytic terminology, suggested the entire realm of referents the term evokes and illustrated the impossibility of entirely escaping the suspiciously gendered vocabulary used to conceptualize sexual difference. Most participants accidentally mispronounced words during their presentations, but both Mary Ann Doane and Madelon Sprengnether misread crucial and suggestive words, re-

341

vealing some of the unresolved conflicts and anxieties masked by the smooth control of their discourse. Neely's reference to but determination *not* to mention the Lacanian signifier of difference, Doane's substitution of the word *castrated* for *constructed*, and Sprengnether's replacement of *expressions* with *repressions* reveal a resistance to and rebellion against the genderless gendered terminology of psychoanalysis as well as a reassertion of essentially feminist positions from the marginal areas where women are traditionally assumed to operate.

Carol Neely's refusal to name that theoretically insistent signifier is both a recognition and an avoidance of the terminology of Lacanian psychoanalysis. While its presence looms large in its absence, Neely's rejection of the term is a recognition of the persistent difficulty its nomenclature poses for feminists who suspect psychoanalysis of having a distinctly patriarchal bias. *Saying* it was to be omitted evoked laughter after two days of discussion because the term was an obstacle almost every paper had to surmount. On one level, playing with the phallus had become absurd; on another, it consistently and maddeningly reasserted itself as the transcendental signifier of the difference at issue. Inserted into every figure of sexuality, every binary opposition, the terminology had a tendency to reclaim the investigation of difference for itself, while the woman was always the "other" and beside the point. The deliberate omission of the terminology after centering it for a moment might be seen as a feminist gesture attempting to displace the central term in favor of the eccentric effects of the operation of difference as it plays out through history and literature. Neely's strategy of omitting it suggests that the term is finally not necessary, is arbitrary, and need not be considered except in its omission. If the signifier of difference is absent, then the nature of difference changes, is mediated and escapes from the binary structure that organizes the representation of difference. Hence, Neely's refusal ultimately has a leveling effect that shifts attention away from psychoanalysis per se to its application in a feminist, historical examination.

Neely's omission embodies the tendency toward mediation displayed by many of the papers, which supplant in some way the somewhat rigid and gendered oppositions that bear between them the mark of this transcendental phallic signifier, shifting it from inside to outside, from center to circumference. Theoretically, the phallic signifier continues to play despite our lack of recognition, despite any failure to name it; omnipresent, it performs openly in most of the essays in this collection as many base their arguments in part upon shifting sets of binary oppositions—inside/outside, voice/text, resistance/mastery, female/male, mother/father, body/language, absence/presence, fantasy/reality—and the simple but contradictory system of equivalents—female signifying mother, body, absence, voice, resistance, truth, virgin, whore, monster, witch; and male signifying father, language, presence, mastery, theory, authority, and text. The binary structure that characterizes the conceptualization and representation of sexual difference and constitutes and conditions both feminism and psychoanalysis collapses when the pairs are mediated, forcing the relocation of this formerly shifting, now fleeing, signifier. Paradoxically, of course, Neely herself marked the difference of her own presentation by evoking the phallic signifier in the outer, oral framework of her paper. Mentioning her failure to invoke it seemed to partition her paper into a nonpsychoanalytic (and therefore psychoanalyzable) category different from the rest of the papers. There is no escape from it. And such is the frustration of feminism in the context of psychoanalysis.

That this word is indeed a stumbling block of major proportion was also convincingly illustrated by Mary Ann Doane's slip in the final summarizing line in her discussion of the exchange of woman and phallus as figure of truth. When she states that "both Derrida and Lacan envy the woman they have *castrated,*" instead of "both Derrida and Lacan envy the woman they have *constructed,*" she revealingly characterizes the effects of Lacan's theorizing of the phallus on the philosophical conception of the woman as truth. Maintaining that while Nietzsche and Derrida position woman as the representation of the play of truth and falsehood (or "undecidability"), in which woman "enables the philosophical operation, becomes its support," Doane claims that Lacan replaces this woman behind the veil with the phallus, appropriating a previously feminized position for this inescapably masculine signifier. While Doane discusses the apparent feminization of the word as a result of its occupation of a previously feminine place in philosophy, she notes the confusion, the slippage, which occurs as the word occupies all places—masculine, feminine, and beyond to the notion of lack itself and the split in "the subject's relation to language and the unconscious." Though this all might seem reasonable in terms of Lacanian psychoanalysis, Doane says in the penultimate line of her discussion, as if preparing for the slip to come, "Whether or not the phallus is feminized, truth, in the Lacanian text, insofar as it concerns a question of veiling, is usurped for the phallus, no longer figured explicitly through the woman, who nevertheless comes to represent an absolute and unattainable state of *jouissance.*" The woman has been supplanted, been made again to lack, to fail to signify all but the unreachable, supplementary *jouissance.* In other words, in her figurative function, she has indeed been castrated, made to lack.

Judith Roof

Although the figure of the woman who operates in philosophy has never been confused with the category of woman as subject which drives feminist theory, the displacement of the woman by the phallus in the intersection of psychoanalysis and philosophy shifts the signifier "woman" from an incarnation of truth to the speechless *jouissance* of self-incarnation, in other words, to not incarnating anything at all. This eviction of woman from the affairs of philosophy might be viewed as a positive gesture, nullifying part of the insidious equation that has objectified woman; nevertheless, on this symbolic plane, it silences her, terminates her signification. Though woman is the object sought rather than the seeker of truth, her disappearance masculinizes philosophy and identifies the woman with the phallus as object of desire. Since feminism attempts to speak from the side of the woman, this symbolic mutation brings into question the possibility of speaking from a female perspective in a philosophical discourse without also assuming a phallic position or desiring the phallus of truth. Even if this phallic position is symbolic and not intended to be gendered, the assumption of a rigid feminist theoretical stance is often challenged as authoritarian, hierarchical, masculine, phallic—a contradiction in terms. Lacan's move might in fact extend to feminist positions insofar as they are the obverse of the figure of woman as truth, denying their ability to speak without simply being relative to the masculine, without being derivative and auxiliary—correctives rather than something else entirely. They, too, lack; their positions are impossible as language itself reassimilates them, returns them to the fold guided by the great phallic shepherd.

Doane's slip is, thus, predictable in the context of her own argument and would seem to reveal an annoyance, a dissatisfaction, a complaint based initially on the disenfranchising confusion inherent in the terminology of psychoanalysis. For though we are told not to take these tropes literally, as gendered actors in the field of theory, they still do the violence, still seem to be attached to the very same mayhem done to the figure of woman in the representation of sexual difference, in the privileging of the visible, in the unattributable, actorless limits of the system, which cannot comprehend "other" in terms outside of a presence/lack dichotomy. In this context, her slip is less a slip than a valid substitution, a characterization of the process she painstakingly describes expressed under the guise of accident and thus uttered in one of the only ways such rebellion can be registered.

The slips and mispronunciations made during reading may also be interpreted as evidence of some other scenario, of an irrepressible unconscious that makes itself visible in the slips and gaps represented in dreams and in the mistakes of everyday life. As Freud notes in "The

Psychopathology of Everyday Life," he rarely finds that slips of the tongue are phonetically created; rather, he "discover[s] a disturbing influence in addition which comes from something *outside* the intended utterance; and the disturbing element is either a single thought that has remained unconscious, which manifests itself in the slip of the tongue and which can often be brought to consciousness only by means of searching analysis, or it is a more general psychical motive force which is directed against the entire utterance."[1] While the words Doane confuses are certainly similar in length and sound, the "something outside the intended utterance" may well be an unconscious resentment, anger, or perception of the "disturbing influence" Lacan's use of phallic terminology might have on her own ability to speak as an authority and a woman. In the context of the paper, it is the woman who is both envied and castrated; the second term would seem to obliterate the first. In slipping, Doane questions Lacan's and Derrida's envy after asserting it, but a kind of reversal might also operate here: it is not the envied woman who has been castrated but rather the woman who envies Lacan and Derrida who is both castrated and wishes to castrate them. Even though castration is not exactly the opposite of construction, since castration is a construction of lack, and though the construction of castration is not to be taken literally as a kind of surgical excision even on this symbolic plane, the desired castration removes the symbolic phallus whose veiled mirage prohibits the woman from signifying anything but *jouissance.* What is revealed here is a kind of phallus envy which has to do with the ability to speak. Just as Neely wished to excise the word from her paper, Doane might also wish its removal, but the wishes can only exist in the margins, the subtexts, the accidents that escape scrutiny until the deed is done—whence, perhaps, comes the castrating bitch figure of feminism.

Like Doane, Madelon Sprengnether reveals the tension inherent in the sometimes troublesome conjunction of feminism and psychoanalysis in her mispronunciation of *expressions* as *repressions.* The presentation of her essay was a study in the expression of repression; it illustrated the revival of a repressed story of women's development as expressed in women's fiction, while partially repressing an explanation of Freud's repression of the preoedipal mother. Beginning, as Neely did, by defending the secondary nature of psychoanalytic theory in her paper and justifying its relative suppression, Sprengnether stressed the role of the preoedipal mother in female development. Her explanation of the

---

[1] Sigmund Freud, "The Psychopathology of Everyday Life," *The Standard Edition of the Complete Psychological Works* (London: Hogarth, 1953–74), 6:61.

importance of the preoedipal mother follows an examination of the repressive role of the castration complex in the son's suppression of the mother's death-dealing potential. As she suggested, "The castration complex functions theoretically in Freud's system to shield the son from a direct apprehension of the radical otherness of mother, who not only does not simply mirror her infant's infatuation but whose power to withhold love appears to threaten his annihilation." She decided not to present a short segment of her text which specifically links his theory of the female child's repression of her preoedipal maternal attachment to Freud's own *repression* of that attachment in the development of his theory, and her decision represses a central instance of Freud's repression, which is retrieved only later in her slip. She, in effect, replicates Freud's repression. While the theoretical introduction of her paper expresses the mechanism of this repression of the preoedipal mother as it occurs on the side of the son, it delays the story of the daughter—in fact places it second in relation to the theory she wishes to deemphasize. Thus, in the arrangement of her argument she first represses Freud's repression of the daughter's relationship to the mother, then places the story of the daughter chronologically second to theory. Whatever virtues this structure has as an argument, it sets the suggestive stage for her substitution of repression for expression in her theoretical analysis.

The fear of the repression of expression is connected to the importance of castration which, as Doane's slip illustrated, is a threat to one's capacity as subject, as one who can express verbally. Sprengnether's occupation with castration, her turning it back upon Freud as his defense against the unmanageable preoedipal mother, is a partial denial of its effects as they apply to the female and an assumption of the authority to speak in those places Freud ignored or repressed. Anxiety about the repression of theory, however (and her repression of his repression), returns in her later rupture of the text: "Freud's bad faith in regard to the preoedipal (m)other, however, betrays itself repeatedly in asides, footnotes, and occasional *repressions . . . expressions* (I hope I'm free now) of ignorance on the subject of femininity." The substitution of *repressions* for *expressions* in the context of this sentence, like Doane's slip, proposes a valid replacement of the intended word which describes Freud's attitude toward the preoedipal state Sprengnether wants to revive; it is precisely her point that Freud has repressed the independent development of the female individual. Sprengnether's misstatement suggests that she again wants to repress Freud's ignorance, his repressions, which omit the story she wants to tell. His expressions of ignorance "on the subject of femininity," while honest, nonetheless reflect lacunae in the theoretical understanding of woman, gaps that contribute to the ease with which women are assigned a position of lack, since lack of theorizing is their lot. Like Freud, however, Sprengnether seems to betray herself in asides and in her own occasional repressions. The repetition of the word *repressions* recalls the passage omitted in her reading, which returns uncannily in the sentence prefacing her discussion of Freud's essay on the uncanny. Its reinsertion as a mistake signals the conflation of both Freud's and Sprengnether's repression—his of the preoedipal mother, hers of him.

Although repression is a reversal of expression, this reversal is not innocent in an essay where the expression of this repressed material is at stake. Like Doane's, Sprengnether's slip might also refer to her own—to female—fear of repression in theory, where the figure of woman slides in favor of the phallus, and in literature, where the erection of an alternative story risks replicating the story already in place, where the feminine turns into the masculine and woman is still elusive and unreachable. This fear of theoretical elision is reflected also in Sprengnether's parenthetical expression of relief: "I hope I'm free now." The phrase literally refers to the rash of slips which plagued participants (slips are necessarily publicly suspect at a conference on feminism and psychoanalysis), but it could just as easily refer to a wish to be free of Freud or "to be free of ignorance on the subject of femininity" as she finishes out the sentence. The aside suggests also that Freud's expressions of ignorance were really repressions of ignorance "on the subject of femininity," an admission that could free her from an oblique dependence on his theory. The aside possibly reveals her wish to be free of that theory which represses the expression of a different female origin—an origin that might enable the female's escape from a repressive system. It also reveals a fear that theorizing this revision of the Fall might in some measure repress it, as theoretical analysis operates in the capture, if not extinction, of the elusive story of woman she wishes to bring to light.

These examples are not random or unmotivated choices, of course. I thought my principle of selection was to single out the most egregious, the richest, the most emphatic occurrences. I see now that I, too, was preoccupied with castration and repression as they emanate from the phallus, from psychoanalytic theories, which do seem always to supplant the feminist as the phallus supplants the figure of woman as truth. Why do the slips slide around the phallus? Certainly, an anxiety over repressing theory and a repression of anxiety about theory are inherent in the conjunction of feminism and psychoanalysis; the tension of this union of theories motivates the slips, which return unerringly to the phallus as the displaced generator of anxiety. The ultimate trap of

feminist psychoanalytic criticism is this phallus fixation, equally evident in acknowledgment and denial.

The anxieties revealed by the slips and asides were also rebellions,
refusals in response to the tangible effect of the irrepressible mastery of
psychoanalysis. Even in the title of the conference, where feminism
was deliberately placed first, feminism was consistently displaced by
participants who reinserted psychoanalysis as the first term. When Paul
Smith asks why no one has questioned the role of men as presenters at
this conference—questions, in effect, the role of men in feminism—it
seems in some way the feminist psychoanalytic critics, male and female, are almost all men in feminism who simultaneously resist the
contradictions inherent in that role. As always the question is not one
of biology but of position in the nagging dialectic of the conception and
representation of sexual difference.

As I write about the margins, I reproduce these contradictions again.
My attempts to recover and preserve the discourse of the margins places
those margins in the center, at least for a moment. My recapture of
them, however, is accomplished in distinctly psychoanalytic terms; I
have objectified, reduced, and tamed those instances of rebellion while
bringing the unmentionable looming object again to the fore. Thus, the
process of discussing the slips and asides makes them again beside the
point. Once again, feminism is beside the point. This postscript, as
separate, apart, playing in the margins, has also, to quote Carol Neely
who quoted Andrew Ross who cites Henri Lefebvre, "always already
been beside the point." And that is the point.

Contributors

CYNTHIA CHASE is Associate Professor of English at Cornell University. She is the author of *Decomposing Figures: Rhetorical Readings in the Romantic Tradition* and coeditor of *Wordsworth and the Production of Poetry, Diacritics* 17 (Winter 1987). She is working on a book on romanticism and literary theory.

MARY ANN DOANE is Associate Professor of Modern Culture and Media at Brown University. She is the author of *The Desire to Desire: The Woman's Film of the 1940s* and coeditor of *Re-vision: Essays in Feminist Film Criticism.* Her current research is on technology, representation, and sexual difference.

RICHARD FELDSTEIN teaches English at Rhode Island College and is coeditor of the journal *Literature and Psychology.* He has published essays on twentieth-century literature and film and coedited *Discontented Discourses: Feminism/Textual Intervention/Psychoanalysis,* as well as the forthcoming collections *Lacan, Language, and Literature* and *Psychoanalysis and . . .*

JERRY ALINE FLIEGER teaches French, critical theory, and women's studies at Rutgers University. She has published extensively on psychoanalysis and modern criticism in such journals as *Diacritics, SubStance, MLN,* and *French Forum,* and is the author of a book on the comic mode in twentieth-century French literature, *The Purloined Punch Line: Freud's Comic Theory and the Postmodern Text.*

JANE GALLOP is Herbert S. Autrey Professor of Humanities at Rice University, where she teaches women's studies. Her books include *The Daughter's Seduction: Feminism and Psychoanalysis; Reading Lacan;* and *Thinking Through the Body.*

SHIRLEY NELSON GARNER, Professor of English at the University of

Minnesota, Twin Cities, is a coeditor (with Claire Kahane and Madelon Sprengnether) of *The (M)other Tongue: Essays in Feminist Psychoanalytic Interpretation* and (with the Personal Narratives Collective) of *Interpreting Women's Lives: Theories of Personal Narratives.* She has published articles on Shakespeare and various women writers. She is a founder and on the editorial board of *Hurricane Alice,* a feminist review.

BARBARA JOHNSON is Professor of Romance Languages and Literatures at Harvard University. She is the translator of Jacques Derrida's *Disseminations,* editor of *The Pedagogical Imperative: Teaching as a Literary Genre,* and author of *The Critical Difference: Essays in the Contemporary Rhetoric of Reading* and *A World of Difference.*

CLAIRE KAHANE is Associate Professor of English and director of the Center for the Psychological Study of the Arts at the State University of New York at Buffalo. She is a coeditor of *In Dora's Case: Psychoanalysis, Hysteria, Feminism,* and *The (M)other Tongue,* and has written various articles exploring the problematics of feminine identity in the work of Flannery O'Connor and Virginia Woolf. She is working on a book on hysteria, feminism, and modernism.

CAROL THOMAS NEELY, who teaches at Illinois State University, is the author of *Broken Nuptials in Shakespeare's Plays* and coeditor (with Carolyn Ruth Swift Lenz and Gayle Green) of *The Woman's Part: Feminist Criticism of Shakespeare.* She has published articles on Shakespeare's plays, Renaissance sonnet sequences, and feminist theory and is working on a series of essays on discourses of gender in Renaissance culture.

MARY POOVEY teaches at Johns Hopkins University and is the author of *The Proper Lady and the Woman Writer: Ideology and Style in the Works of Mary Wollstonecraft, Mary Shelley, and Jane Austen.* The essay included in this volume is part of a forthcoming book to be titled *Uneven Developments: The Ideological Work of Gender in Mid-Victorian England.*

ELLIE RAGLAND-SULLIVAN teaches in the department of English at the University of Florida, Gainesville. Her books include *Rabelais and Panurge: A Psychological Approach to Literary Character* and *Jacques Lacan and the Philosophy of Psychoanalysis.* She has also published essays in the *Literary Review, SubStance, Modern Language Journal, Ornicar?* and is completing a book, *From Freud to Lacan.*

JUDITH ROOF is Assistant Professor of English at the University of Delaware. She has published essays on Beckett, Pinter, Woolf, and Duras. She is completing a book, *Metaphors of Seeing in Modern*

Drama, and is at work on a study of the representation of lesbian sexuality.

JACQUELINE ROSE teaches at the University of Sussex, England. She is the editor (with Juliet Mitchell) and translator of *Feminine Sexuality: Jacques Lacan and the Ecole Freudienne* and the author of *The Case of Peter Pan; or, The Impossibility of Children's Fiction* and of *Sexuality in the Field of Vision.*

ANDREW ROSS teaches English at Princeton University and has published widely on cultural theory and sexual politics. He is the editor of *Universal Abandon? The Politics of Postmodernism,* and the author of *The Failure of Modernism: Symptoms of American Poetry,* and *No Respect: Intellectuals and Popular Culture.*

PAUL SMITH teaches literary and cultural studies at Carnegie Mellon University. He is author of *Pound Revised* and *Discerning the Subject* and coeditor (with Alice Jardine) of *Men in Feminism.*

MADELON SPRENGNETHER is Professor of English at the University of Minnesota. She has published articles on Lyly, Spenser, Nashe, and Shakespeare and is a coeditor of *The (M)other Tongue: Essays in Feminist Psychoanalytic Interpretation.* She is completing a book titled *The Spectral Mother: Freud, Feminism, and Psychoanalysis.*

Index

Index

Index

Index

Library of Congress Cataloging-in-Publication Data

Feminism and psychoanalysis.

"Papers delivered at the 'Conference on Feminism & Psychoanalysis' held
at Normal, Illinois, in May 1986"—Pref.
Includes index.
1. Women and psychoanalysis—Congresses. 2. Feminism—Con-
gresses. 3. Psychoanalysis and literature—Congresses. 4. Feminism and
literature—Congresses. I. Feldstein, Richard. II. Roof, Judith, 1951–   .
III. Conference on Feminism & Psychoanalysis (1986 : Normal, Ill.)
BF175.4.F45F46   1989   150.19'5'088042   88–43235
ISBN 0–8014–2298–1 (alk. paper)
ISBN 0–8014–9558–X (pbk. : alk. paper)